ENVIRONMENTAL REGULATIONS

handbook

Kenneth M. Mackenthun

Jacob I. Bregman

LEWIS PUBLISHERS
Boca Raton   Ann Arbor   London

Library of Congress Cataloging-in-Publication Data

Environmental regulations handbook / edited by Kenneth M. Mackenthun
and J. I. Bregman.
    p.   cm.
  Includes bibliographical references and index.
  ISBN 0-87371-494-6
  1. Environmental law—United States. 2. Environmental policy—United
  States.   I. Mackenthun, Kenneth Marsh, 1919– .
  II. Bregman, Jacob I.
KF3775.E545   1991
344.73'046—dc20
[347.30446]   91–26640
                                               CIP

LEWIS PUBLISHERS, INC.
121 South Main Street, Chelsea, MI 48118

PRINTED IN THE UNITED STATES OF AMERICA 0 1 2 3 4 5 6 7 8 9

Dedicated to all who actively support an environmental ethic

Kenneth M. Mackenthun, in a 44-year career in water pollution investigation and control, water resources management, and regulation development, has produced over 90 technical publications including 10 books. He graduated cum laude with a degree in Biology from Emporia (Kansas) College and he obtained an M.A. in Zoology from the University of Illinois in 1946.

Mr. Mackenthun spent 18 years with the U.S. Environmental Protection Agency (EPA) and its predecessor, the U.S. Public Health Service. He rose to the position of Acting Deputy Administrator for Water Planning and Standards with the EPA, where he supervised 220 employees in four Divisions: Effluent Guidelines Division, which developed effluent limitations for industrial effluents; Water Planning Division, which developed and administered water pollution control management plans; Monitoring and Data Support Division, which provided water quality reports to the Congress and maintained water quality data storage and retrieval systems; and the Criteria and Standards Division, which managed water quality standards and developed water quality criteria. Mr. Mackenthun was responsible for EPA compliance with the following sections of the Clean Water Act: Estuarine Report to Congress; In-Place Pollutant Removal; National Water Quality Standards; Water Quality Criteria Developments; Report on Methods & Procedures to Restore Lakes; Maintaining the Toxic Pollutants List; Hazardous Substances Discharges; Vessel Sewage Discharge Regulations; Clean Lakes Restoration Program; Dredge or Fill Materials Discharge Program.

Mr. Mackenthun also worked for the Wisconsin Department of Conservation and Board of Health for 16 years and served as Vice President of Enwright Laboratories in South Carolina for 3 years. At Bregman & Company, Inc., he manages a number of Environmental Impact Statement (EIS) projects in areas such as national cemeteries, the production of explosives, and agricultural services.

Dr. Jacob I. Bregman holds a B.S. in Chemistry from Providence College and M.S. and Ph.D. degrees (1951) in Physical Chemistry from the Polytechnic Institute of Brooklyn. In his 40 years of professional experience, he has published 60 papers, written 6 books and holds 6 patents. He is a member of several scientific societies including the honor societies of Phi Lambda Upsilon and Sigma Xi.

Dr. Bregman served as head of Nalco Chemical Company's Physical Chemistry Laboratory from 1950 to 1959. From 1959 to 1967, he was the Director of Chemical Sciences at the IIT Research Institute. He then served as Deputy Assistant Secretary for Water Quality, U.S. Dept. of Interior from 1967 to 1969. During that period, the Federal Water Pollution Control Administration (the forerunner of the water and hazardous waste portions of the present U.S. EPA), the Office of Saline Water and the Office of Water Resources Research reported to his office. He also served concurrently as a Federal Commissioner to the Ohio River Sanitary Commission.

After leaving the Federal Government, Dr. Bregman founded and became the first President of WAPORA, Inc., an environmental consulting firm that he built up to over 200 scientists with an international reputation. In 1984, he started Bregman & Company, Inc., also an environmental consulting firm, that has attained a prestigious position in environmental policy, regulations, and impact statements. Dr. Bregman also serves as a Professorial Lecturer in the Graduate School of Engineering and Applied Science, George Washington University, teaching courses in environmental impact statements and other environmental topics.

Dr. Bregman has overseen the preparation of over 200 environmental impact statements and assessments during his career. Clients have included each of the ten U.S. EPA regions, several district offices of the Corps of Engineers, most Federal government agencies and several state and local groups. Topics of EIS work have run the gamut from highways to refineries, with almost every conceivable type of construction activity being covered. At Bregman & Company, he has overseen the preparation of 10 such documents during the past 2 years.

AN ENVIRONMENTAL ETHIC

Born from a mountain topped with snow, a stream
    Searches endlessly, relentlessly for a place to rest.
Cold, sparkling clear, meandering, or so it would seem,
    Its downhill thrust makes it compete with the best.

Like deep thoughts nurtured by reason, experience and time's span,
    A river, complex, intriguing, sometimes placid, sometimes harsh,
Is born of streams, fertilized by lands, used and defiled by man,
    And searches onward for nature's rest; or to coexist with a marsh.

A pause in river's flow — a lake — the placid, picturesque eye
    Through which one beholds the Earth's symmetric depth and beauty,
Surface reflections of trees and sky; finny friends beneath pass by
    Living for the hour, unaware of predator and prey that is Nature's duty.

Near shores, marshes, bogs, wetlands often may be found.
    Nursery areas, nutrient traps, protectors of waters they are;
Home of ducks, fish, plants, invertebrates — much life abound,
    Breadbaskets of the water environment for near and far.

Into these, the land gives of that which people cast down,
    The air deposits pollutants far from source to blight,
People need consider not the easy to do; and hope must abound,
    That instead they consider that which is environmentally right.

Preserve the ecosystem! Enhance existing quality! These calls go forth.
    For success such seeds for progress must be implanted in fertile minds
With searching environmental conscience, from which to cement their worth
    Into a unified ethic, and preserve the universe for all times.

Kenneth M. Mackenthun

ACKNOWLEDGMENTS

Acknowledgment and appreciation for invaluable assistance are given those who contributed directly or indirectly, currently or in the past, to this book's development. Special thanks and appreciation are given to Mrs. Dorothy Mackenthun and Mrs. Mona Bregman for their support, encouragement, and tolerance of evenings and weekends devoted to its development. Special thanks and appreciation, also, to Ms. Lori A. Thompson for her diligence and perseverance in the demanding tasks of typing, arranging, and proofing copy.

CONTENTS

Dedication
Authors
"An Environmental Ethic"
Acknowledgments
Contents

LIST OF TABLES AND FIGURES

1 INTRODUCTION

THIS BOOK

This book is intended to provide

- An insight into major programs, laws, regulation, and activities that protect our environment
- An information source for those seeking to learn about environmental programs, and the functions and actions of government
- An understanding of environmental investigations, damage assessment, sampling and analyses, quality assurance, and environmental impacts
- A history of events that caused some laws to come into being and a chronology of how some achieved passage in the Congress

The chapters of this book address a wide array of environmental programs designed to protect the air, water, land, and worker environments. The environment contains many variables and interacting forces. It cannot be defined with quantitative precision for all of its components. Some laws were written beyond the scope of regulations to define their effect, and thus to implement their intent. They had to be changed before they could serve the purposes of their makers.

This book has been written from the viewpoint of participants and observers in environmental programs for the past four and a half decades. This time spans from the days when the black liquor of sulfite pulp and paper mills flowed to receiving streams, garbage was collected and barged to the center of the Mississippi River for disposal, and truckloads of barnyard manure were dumped in already fertile ice-covered lakes in an effort to increase productivity. Our concerns now focus on pollutants contained in runoff from the land, septic tank leachates, and lawn fertilizers.

Throughout the past 45 years, history has been formed on the environmental experiences of society, and programs were born from those experiences. Some of that history is presented in this book. A student of history is a teacher of the future. From that history, we learn why things are the way they are in a nation of laws and regulations.

THE CURRENT STATUS

The development of environmental laws and regulation has accelerated during the last 30 years to the point that they have become an accepted critical factor in the growth and quality of life in this country. By contrast, in the earlier part of the 20th century relatively little attention was paid to the state of the environment. To illustrate this dramatic change in the American way of doing business, the material that follows will describe how clean water has become an essential ingredient of our activities.

The U.S. concern with water and water quality dates back at least to the River and Harbor Act of 1899. Many states had water pollution control legislation in the 1930s and 1940s. The water program has the longest history of any environmental control program. It therefore is fitting to review the present status of water quality. This can be done because states are required by Section 305(b) of the Clean Water Act to submit a biennial report to the Environmental Protection Agency (EPA) that describes the water quality of the state. EPA, in turn, prepares a National Water Quality Inventory, which is submitted to the Congress biennially. The latest report summarizes the 1988 state reports.

The states designate their waters for beneficial uses, such as drinking water supply, contact recreation, and warm- and cold-water fisheries. Among the states that reported on support of these beneficial uses, a combined total of about 300,000 river miles were found to support beneficial uses, or about 70% of the river miles assessed in these states. For those river miles not supporting the designated uses, the states reported that siltation, nutrients, fecal coliform bacteria, and organic enrichment with accompanying low dissolved oxygen were the principal causes of impairment; there were additional but relatively lower impacting causes.

States reporting on the support of designated beneficial uses in lakes showed a combined total of about 12 million lake acres supporting those uses, or 74% of the assessed lake acres in those states. The most extensive causes of use impairment in lakes are nutrients, siltation, and organic enrichment, along with low dissolved oxygen. Nutrients such as phosphorus and nitrogen are the principal causes of cultural eutrophication, which is a major alteration of lake ecology, characterized by the excessive growth of aquatic algae and other vegetation. The most extensive sources of pollution of lakes, as reported by the states, are agriculture, hydrologic and habitat modification, storm sewers and runoff, land disposal, and municipal discharges.

The states reported that a combined total of about 19,000 square miles of estuaries were found to support beneficial uses as designated in water quality standards, or about 72% of the estuarine square miles assessed in those states. The most extensive causes of use impairment in estuaries are nutrients, pathogens, and organic enrichment with low dissolved oxygen. The most extensive sources of pollution in estuaries are municipal discharges, resource extraction, and storm sewer discharges.

Nearly 3800 coastal shoreline miles were assessed by 12 states and territories in 1988. Eighty-nine percent of the coastline miles assessed were determined to support designated beneficial uses.

By far the most often cited cause of wetland loss reported by the states is land development for residential or commercial purposes. Second-home development and urban encroachment are commonly cited. Other reported causes include agricultural and resource extraction activities. Agriculture was considered as a major historical cause of wetland loss but appears to be a lesser current threat because of strict wetlands loss regulations.

Twenty-eight states reported that they monitored for toxic substances in about 67,500 mi of rivers, 23 states monitored for toxic pollutants in about 4,081,600 lake acres, 13 states monitored 5,980 square mi of estuaries, and 4 states reported that they monitored 560 coastal shoreline mi. For each ecosystem, 25 to 30% of the respective areas were affected by elevated levels of toxic substances.

Many chemicals in water, even in low concentrations, may be absorbed or ingested by aquatic organisms that are, in turn, consumed by larger predators such as fish. Toxic pollutants can bioaccumulate in the tissues of fish, which pose a potential health hazard to people, as well as birds and other animals who eat fish. In 1988, 29 states reported finding concentrations of toxic contaminants in fish tissue exceeding FDA action levels or other levels of concern in localized areas. Many states respond to the finding of elevated levels of toxic substances by imposing fishing bans or fish consumption advisories. In 1988, 47 states, jurisdictions, and interstate commissions provided information on fishing advisories and bans in their waters. Of these, eight states reported that no fishing restrictions were in place. Thirty-nine states reported a total of 586 advisories, and 21 states reported 135 fishing bans. The pollutants most commonly identified as causing advisories or bans include PCBs, chlordane, mercury, dioxin, and DDT. General categories of sources contributing these contaminants include industrial discharges, land disposal operations, nonpoint sources, spills, in-place contaminants, atmospheric deposition, and agricultural activities. Twenty-one states reported that 4487 stream miles were affected, 4 states reported that 334 estuarine square miles were affected, and 12 states reported that 2,835,984 lake acres were affected.

States were asked to provide their needs and recommendations for emphasis in a national water-pollution control program. The states responded with nine principal concerns:

1. The identification, prevention, and control of nonpoint sources of pollution
2. The enhancement of water quality monitoring with increased emphasis on biological monitoring
3. Continued funding for the maintenance, upgrade, and construction of municipal sewage treatment facilities
4. The identification and control of toxic substances
5. The continued refinement of water quality criteria and standards
6. The identification and mapping of groundwater resources and providing an effective groundwater protection program
7. The appropriation of funds to support the Clean Lakes Program
8. The integration and enhancement of computerized data management systems
9. Increasing efforts to protect valuable wetland resources

How would the above list have changed if it had been prepared one or two decades ago? Certainly, the control of point-source pollutants would have been high on the list, and this concern did not make the present list of nine. The control of nonpoint sources of pollution probably would not have made the list a decade or two ago. The other concerns would have been the concerns of many.

AN ENVIRONMENTAL ETHIC

In the mid-1800s, Henry David Thoreau was the beacon who extolled the virtues of nature and conservation. He wrote, "A lake is the landscape's most beautiful and expressive feature. It is earth's eye; looking into which the beholder measures the depth of his own nature." (Thoreau, 1954). A century and half later, Aldo Leopold, just prior to his untimely death on the sandy soils of Prairie de Sac, Wisconsin, attempted to establish an ecological conscience in his contemporaries. A land ethic, he said, reflects the existence of an ecological conscience, and this in turn reflects a conviction of individual responsibility for the health of the land. Health is the capability of the land for self-renewal. Conservation, he said, is our effort to understand and preserve this capacity (Mackenthun, 1982).

In *A Sand County Almanac*, Leopold said that a system of conservation based solely on economic self-interest was hopelessly lopsided. Each question should be examined in terms of what is ethically and aesthetically right, as well as what is economically expedient. A thing is right when it tends to preserve the integrity, stability, and beauty of the biotic community. It is wrong when it tends otherwise.

In the same era, but a decade later during the later 1950s, Ernie Swift, who rose from conservation warden to Director of the Wisconsin Department of Conservation, to Executive Director of the National Wildlife Federation, compiled some of his later-in-life writings into *The Glory Trail*, (Swift, 1958) and *By Which We Live* (Swift, *1957*). We should all be reminded, he said, that livestock can overgraze a pasture, that deer can overgraze a forest, and that people can overgraze a continent. In *The Glory Trail*, he wrote, "No one can outrage nature and prosper; nature has means of cruel and bitter retaliation."

Herb Stokinger, of the U.S. Public Health Service, writing in *Science* in 1971, stated that

- "Standards must be based on scientific facts, realistically derived, and not on political feasibility, expediency, emotion of the moment, or unsupported information;
- All standards, guides, limits, and so on, as well as the criteria on which they are based, must be completely documented;
- The establishment of unnecessarily severe standards must be avoided; and
- Realistic levels must be determined. However, these fine concepts are not transformed easily into regulatory language." (Mackenthun, 1982).

From a review of the regulatory arena, certain principles seem important:

- The purpose of an environmental regulation is to adequately protect, in a broad sense, the environment for humans.
- Because of the infinite variation in biological and chemical reactions to environmental change and perturbations, regulations must allow flexibility for adjustment to a particular station. The burden of proof for a more restrictive regulation logically rests with government; the burden of proof through appropriate investigation and assessment for justifying relaxation rests with the discharger.
- Political and legislative deadlines often have fostered benign cynicism because of their unrealistic nature in a regulatory world of abundant checks and balances.
- Determining current state-of-the-art knowledge related to any particular subject is a time-consuming endeavor. The search for an answer in the realm of the unknown is research operating through undeterminable time.

In its 20 years of existence, the EPA has issued a volume of new regulations every couple of years. There is no reason to expect this regulation rate to decrease substantially. Regulation is a necessary means of bringing order to society.

Corporations have employees whose job it is to keep current with the environmental regulations, and probably as much effort is spent in determining where the regulatory language does not apply as where it does. Thus, it is difficult to determine how well an environmental ethic is progressing in the nation. It is overwhelmed by regulations and efforts to comply with these requirements. Certainly, an environmental ethic is alive in the minds of many. It is important that it be cultivated and extended to many more. Knowledge of the environment, its fragility in many areas, and its tenacity to survive abuse and recover in other areas is paramount to the development of an ecological conscience. Knowledge of the regulatory structure is equally important and helpful.

REFERENCES CITED AND SELECTED READING

Leopold, A. 1949. *A Sand County Almanac*. Oxford University Press, New York.

Mackenthun, K. M. 1982. Environmental Controls: Are They Swords of Damocles? *J. Water Poll. Contr. Fed.* Vol. 54, pp. 1061–1066.

Thoreau, Henry David. 1954. *Walden; or Life in the Woods*, Ticknor and Fields, Boston, MA.

Swift, E. 1957. *By Which We Live*. The National Wildlife Federation, Washington, D.C.

Swift, E. 1958. The Glory Trail (The Great American Migration and Its Impact on Natural Resources). The National Wildlife Federation, Washington, D.C.

U.S. EPA. 1990. "National Water Quality Inventory 1988 Report to Congress." U.S. Environmental Protection Agency, Washington, D.C. (EPA-440-4-90-003).

2 THE CONCEPTION OF ENVIRONMENTAL LAWS

The following key environmental laws will be discussed in this chapter in detail, along with abbreviated discussions of the Occupational Safety and Health Act and the Endangered Species Act. There are at least as many additional acts that affect the environment to lesser degrees. The discussion focuses on how the acts were conceived and their meanings.

- **NATIONAL ENVIRONMENTAL POLICY ACT of 1969** (P.L. 91-190) established a national policy for the environment and provided for environmental impact statements and environmental consideration in all federal actions.
- **CLEAN WATER ACT** 1977 (P.L. 95-217) provides for uniform, enforceable national standards and permit programs for clean water.
- **SAFE DRINKING WATER ACT of 1974** (P.L. 93-523) requires standards and regulations to be established for drinking water applicable to public water systems.
- **CLEAN AIR ACT of 1970** 1977 (P.L. 95-95) provide for the protection and enhancement of air quality through the regulation of pollutant emissions and establishment of air quality standards.
- **TOXIC SUBSTANCES CONTROL ACT of 1976** (P.L. 94-469) controls hazardous chemical substances, excluding pesticides, in the marketplace and provides for authority to require the testing of a chemical's toxicity.
- **FEDERAL INSECTICIDE, FUNGICIDE, AND RODENTICIDE ACT of 1972** (P.L. 92-516) requires that all pesticides used in the U.S. must be registered with and classified by EPA for general or restricted use.
- **MARINE PROTECTION, RESEARCH, AND SANCTUARIES ACT of 1972** (P.L. 92-532) regulates the dumping of materials into the ocean waters.
- **RESOURCE CONSERVATION AND RECOVERY ACT of 1976** (P.L. 94-580) requires a regulatory system for the generation, treatment, storage, and disposal of hazardous wastes.

⊙ **COMPREHENSIVE ENVIRONMENTAL RESPONSE, COMPENSA-
TION, AND LIABILITY ACT of 1980** (P.L. 96-510), as amended in 1986, by
the Superfund Amendments and Reauthorization Act, establishes a program to
mitigate releases of hazardous waste from inactive hazardous waste sites that
endanger public health and the environment.

The decade of the 1970s brought forth a framework of federal laws providing
environmental protection. As a group, they were designed to protect the air, the land,
and the water above and within the land. They were designed to protect human health,
the air we breathe, the water we drink, the fish we consume. They were designed to
protect aquatic life and to provide a quality suitable for recreation in and on the water.
They are interrelated in that they are designed to function in concert, one with the other,
in providing an umbrella of protection. Most have been amended since initially enacted
in order to extend and solidify their initial requirements. A discussion of each law
follows.

NATIONAL ENVIRONMENTAL POLICY ACT OF 1969

Launching the environmental movement of the 1970s, the National Environmental
Policy Act of 1969 was signed into law on January 1, 1970. With its signing, President
Nixon declared, "The 1970s absolutely must be the years when America pays its debt
to the past by reclaiming the purity of its air, its waters and our living environment. It
is literally now or never."

This law did four things. It established national environmental policy, defined
national goals, created the Council on Environmental Quality in the Executive Office
of the President, and mandated the development and filing of an Environmental Impact
Statement (EIS) for any federal action significantly affecting the quality of the human
environment.

The National Environmental Policy Act, or NEPA as it is most often called, is remembered most frequently for its requirement of an EIS for major federal actions
affecting the environment. The NEPA process forces a consideration and understanding of potential environmental impacts resulting from a given action. NEPA requires
that the EIS shall detail the impacts on the human environment of the proposed action,
list any adverse environmental effects that cannot be avoided should the proposal be
implemented, name alternatives to the proposed action, present the relationship
between local, short-term uses of the human environment and the maintenance and enhancement of long-term productivity, and describe any irreversible and irretrievable
commitments of resources that would be involved in the proposed action should it be
implemented. An EIS is available for public comment during its draft stage.

The EIS process often is preceded by an Environmental Assessment (EA), which
is a short version of an EIS and is based mainly on available information. As a result
of the EA, the agency makes the decision on whether to go to a full-blown EIS or to
write a Finding of No Significant Impact (FONSI), which ends the NEPA process.

The U.S. Environmental Protection Agency (EPA) has been delegated the management of the official reviewing and filing system for all federal EISs and EAs. About 10,000 environmental assessments for projects with minimal environmental impacts are prepared annually by federal agencies. About 450 EISs are prepared annually for projects that the proposing agency views as having significant potential for environmental impacts. EPA reviews all of the EISs and about 20% of the EAs.

CLEAN WATER ACT

The most recent major rewrite of water pollution control legislation occurred in 1972 with the Federal Water Pollution Control Act Amendments. Some sections of this legislative package were in development for years, and several sections have an interesting and informative history. For the present, however, let us consider the legislative actions centered around passage of this law.

Although many were involved, the strong will of Senator Edmund Muskie of Maine and the writings of Leon Billings, his administrative assistant at the time, are apparent throughout. Muskie was a key member of the Senate Committee on Environment and Public Works, which developed and passed Senate Bill, S-2770. The House Committee on Public Works and Transportation, under the leadership of Representative Robert E. Jones of Alabama, developed and passed House Bill, HR-9560. In developing its bill, the Senate employed two able environmentalists, Tom Jorling, then a professor at Williams College in Williamstown, Massachusetts and George Woodwell of the Brookhaven National Laboratories in Upton, New York, to consult and draft certain passages of legislation.

Environmental lobbyists, such as the Natural Resources Defense Council, Environmental Defense Fund, Citizens for a Better Environment, et al., were in constant communication with staffs of both the House and Senate committees throughout the process, as were industrial groups, such as the Chemical Manufacturers Association and others. Program directors of the EPA were called before the Senate and House committee staffs and questioned on their program accomplishments or lack of such, as well as program implementation problems. The EPA comments on draft legislation were officially submitted by its Administrator to both houses of Congress. S-2770 and HR-9560 had major differences. As one example, the Senate believed that the concept of water quality standards was not working and S-2770 contained no provisions for their reauthorization. HR-9560, however, contained provisions for their continuation and legislative expansion. The House won in conference. Both Bills went to a joint Senate-House Conference Committee for resolution of the differences. Following revised language and passage by the Conference Committee, the revised bill went back to the full Senate and House, where Public Law 92-500 was passed. President Nixon vetoed the bill, but it was passed over his veto by the Senate and House.

The substantial body of information, including statements by members of the House and Senate, committee hearings, the EPA Administrator's comments, comments from other department heads, and all changes to bills are published verbatim. A committee report is published by the House Committee, the Senate Committee, and the Conference Committee. This body of information later is combined into one or more volumes of legislative history for a particular law. By reading the legislative history, one can determine the thought and rationale behind the development of a legislative section.

Beginnings

The dynamic federal philosophy of legal constraints against water pollution had its genesis in the River and Harbor Act of 1899. This act constituted the first specific federal water pollution control legislation. Section 13 of the act made it unlawful to throw, discharge, or deposit any refuse matter of any kind or description, other than that flowing from streets and sewers and passing therefrom, in a liquid state into any navigable waters. This section made it equally unlawful to deposit material of any kind on the bank of any navigable water or its tributary where it was liable to be washed into the navigable water. The U.S. Army Corps of Engineers could grant permission for the deposit of any material that might otherwise violate the language of Section 13. The Department of Justice was given authority to enforce the provisions of the River and Harbor Act of 1899 as they pertain to water pollution. A statement within the penalty provisions provided that one half of any fine collected for violation of this act shall be paid to the person or persons giving information that shall lead to conviction.

The provisions of this law lay dormant for many years. In the very late 1960s, however, the law was tested and found to be sound by citizens who collected samples and other information from waste discharge points along the nation's waterways. On December 23, 1970, Executive Order 11574 was issued proclaiming that the executive branch of the federal government would implement a permit program under Section 13 to regulate the discharge of pollutants and other refuse matter into the navigable waters and that the U.S. Army Corps of Engineers was to be the permitting authority. The Corps of Engineers was flooded with permit requests and soon became overwhelmed by this new environmental program of considerable magnitude. It was not until mid-October 1972 that this matter was transferred to the U.S. EPA by authority of Section 402 of the Federal Water Pollution Control Act Amendments, which established the National Pollutant Discharge Elimination System (NPDES).

The Public Health Service Act of 1912 contained provisions authorizing investigation of water pollution relating to the diseases and impairment of humans. In 1924, the Oil Pollution Act was enacted to control oil discharges in coastal waters that might be damaging to aquatic life, harbors and docks, and recreational facilities. In 1948, Public Law 845, enacted by the 80th Congress, provided pollution control activities in the Public Health Service of the then Federal Security Agency and in the Federal Works Agency. This law provided the consent of the Congress for two or more states to enter into agreements or compacts for pollution abatement; it provided for loans to any state, municipality, or interstate agency for the construction of necessary treatment works; and it established the framework for federal action to control interstate water pollution. At that time, however, the Surgeon General was to give "formal notification" of pollution violation of interstate waters. The interstate conference and other enforcement measures were to follow in Section 8 of Public Law 660, the Water Pollution Control Act Amendments of 1956. In addition, P.L. 660 provided grants for state water-pollution control programs and authorized the granting of federal funds to any state, municipality, or intermunicipal or interstate agency for the construction of necessary treatment works to prevent the discharge of untreated or inadequately treated sewage or other wastes into any waters, and for the purpose of reports, plans, and specifications in connection therewith. Currently, the sewage treatment-plant construction grants program, after 35 years of operation, is beginning to be phased out through legislative action.

Amendments in 1961 extended federal authority to enforce the abatement of pollution in interstate, as well as navigable, waters. They provided that in the planning for any reservoir, consideration shall be given to inclusion of storage for regulation of stream flow for the purpose of water quality control, except that any storage and water releases were not to be provided as a substitute for adequate treatment or other methods of controlling wastes at the source.

Development

The Water Quality Act of 1965 established the Federal Water Pollution Control Administration within the Department of Health, Education, and Welfare. It provided for the creation of water quality standards to enhance the quality of the nation's interstate and coastal waters. In setting water quality standards, the states were mandated to determine, after public hearings, the uses to be made of particular reaches of interstate water. Following this determination, criteria were to be adopted that were applicable to interstate waters, and a plan for the implementation and enforcement of the water quality criteria was to be adopted. Reorganization Plan No. 2 of 1966, effective May 10, 1966, transferred the Federal Water Pollution Control Administration to the Department of the Interior. The state standards had to be approved by the Secretary of the Interior, (now transferred to the EPA Administrator), who frequently insisted on tougher standards for temperature and dissolved oxygen, as well as requiring nondegradation of pristine waters. This latter item, nondegradation, is worthy of further mention. The junior author of this book, while Deputy Assistant Secretary of the Interior, was one of the authors of the requirement that all state water quality standards must require that waters now substantially above the required standards for contaminants must not be allowed to be degraded to the level of the standards without a substantial showing by the state, including presentation at public hearings, that the allowed amount of degradation is essential and will not change the designated uses of that water. The purpose of this requirement was to ensure that pristine streams, such as those in mountains that, for example, presently have dissolved oxygen values of 7 or 8 ppm are not to be degraded to the 5 ppm standard usually required for best uses, without an overwhelming show of need. The same conditions would apply to other standards, such as those for temperature and bacterial content.

The Water Quality Improvement Act of 1970 changed the name of the Federal Water Pollution Control Administration to the Federal Water Quality Administration.

New and comprehensive sections were added on the control of pollution by oil, control of hazardous polluting substances, principally hazardous substances spills, and the control of sewage from vessels. Although all of these programs made some progress toward controls at this time, substantial control programs did not develop until after the passage of the Federal Water Pollution Control Act Amendments of 1972. Reorganization Plan No. 3 was forthcoming in 1970, which transferred all federal water pollution control programs to the Administrator of the EPA. This independent agency, reporting to the president, was granted jurisdiction over water-pollution control programs, air-pollution control programs, solid-waste abatement programs, radiological and pesticidal programs, and noise abatement.

The Present Legislation

Although borrowing heavily from past legislative experience and laws, the major overhaul of water pollution control legislation occurred with the Federal Water Pollution Control Act Amendments of 1972. It has since been amended 17 times. With the amendments in 1977, it became known as the Clean Water Act and established national goals and policy. Two are noteworthy. Congress declared it to be a national goal that, wherever attainable, a water quality that provides for the protection and propagation of fish, shellfish, and wildlife and provides for recreation in and on the water be achieved. Further, Congress declared it to be the national goal that the discharge of toxic pollutants in toxic amounts be prohibited. The Act has a great many provisions, including state water-pollution control program grants, grants for treatment works, reports, studies, and research. Also, it provides for standards and enforcement, and permits and licenses.

Among the standards are effluent limitations, water quality standards, pretreatment effluent standards, and standards to control sewage discharges from vessels. Water quality standards, adopted by states and approved by the EPA, identify water uses, provide water quality criteria to support such designated uses, and include the antidegradation policy discussed earlier. The EPA has published recommended water quality criteria for various water chemical and physical items to meet specific uses. The EPA may promulgate water quality standards when states or Indian tribes have adopted standards that do not meet the requirements of the Clean Water Act. These standards protect ambient waters and their uses and are reviewed for possible revision every 3 years. States hold public hearings in the review process. At least 30 states now have more than 20 toxic-pollutant water quality criteria in their water quality standards. Water quality criteria provided the linchpin for water quality standards. Criteria are based upon the latest scientific evidence and provide concentrations for individual pollutants to protect human health in water ingestion, and in the consumption of fish and shellfish, and to protect aquatic life and recreational and agricultural uses. A major thrust is the development of sediment criteria for toxic pollutants.

Effluent limitations are based not on water quality requirements but on the available treatment technology to control pollution for a particular industrial waste. Effluent limits may be expressed in concentrations or in quantities such as pounds per day of a particular constituent of the wastewater. These serve as guides to permit writers when developing discharge permits under the National Pollutant Discharge Elimination System of Section 402 of the Act. Discharge permits must meet water quality standards that are established in the receiving waters. The language of the law is not direct in this requirement. Section 402 states that a discharge must meet all applicable requirements under Sections 301, 302, 306, 307, 308, and 403 of this Act. Water quality standards are found in Section 303, but Section 301(b)(1)(c) provides the requirement that water quality standards be met. This is best done by using water quality modeling to determine effluent discharge concentrations of contaminants that will not cause the water body to violate the standards.

Pursuant to Section 307, a list of 65 toxic pollutants was published near the end of January, 1978. The development of this list has been well documented by Hall (1977). The rationale behind some of the pollutants and their selection for this list provides an informative historic perspective, however. In the early 1960s, under the technical support provisions of existing water pollution control law, the governor of Louisiana requested federal assistance in determining the cause of periodic fish mortalities in the lower Mississippi River. Fish would die in the winter time and the thought was that endrin applied to sugar cane fields adjacent to the river might be washing into the river in sufficient quantities to kill fish. An intensive 2-year investigation ensued. Endrin was found to be the cause, but it was found most concentrated in a discharge sewer in Memphis, Tennessee. The fish would bioaccumulate the endrin in their fatty tissues as a sublethal dose. However, during cold water temperature the metabolism of the fish diminished, they ate less, and they absorbed the fatty tissues from which the endrin entered their bloodstream in a sufficient concentration to be lethal to the more sensitive individuals of the species. As this study ended, the governor made a second request for a determination of the cause of off-flavor in the New Orleans water supply. Following a study, the cause was found to be low concentrations of certain petrochemicals. As these petrochemicals were subjected to the chlorination process in a public water supply, they formed chlorinated hydrocarbons and became of cancer-causing concern. One of the individuals on the committee that initially prepared the list of 65 toxic pollutants had published some of the data from the New Orleans study and was familiar with it. Several of the classes of compounds from this study were subject to the criteria developed for selecting the 65 toxic pollutants, and they passed the test for selection.

Section 404 is the mechanism for issuing permits for the discharged of dredged or fill material. It is the principal means within the Clean Water Act to prevent the unnecessary destruction of wetlands. Throughout its implementation, it has been a controversial part of the Act because the issues surrounding the granting or nongranting of a permit usually involve land development. Section 404 begins with four significant provisions; it states that (1) The U.S. Corps of Engineers may issue a permit, after notice and opportunity for public hearings, for the discharge of dredged or fill material into the navigable waters "at specified disposal sites"; (2) in specifying disposal sites, the Corps of Engineers must use guidelines developed by the EPA in conjunction with the corps; (3) where the guidelines would prohibit the specification of a site, the Corps could issue a permit regardless, based upon the economic impact on navigation and anchorage; and (4) the EPA is authorized to veto permitting a site based upon environmental considerations. Regulations have been promulgated specifying how each of these actions will be managed.

Section 401 is a significant section, also, because it requires any applicant for a federal license or permit to obtain a certification from the state that any discharge connected with the action will not violate certain sections of the Clean Water Act, including existing water quality standards. No license or permit shall be granted if certification has been denied by the state, interstate agency, or the administrator of the EPA, as the case may be.

The 1987 amendments to the Clean Water Act greatly strengthened the requirement for the development of water quality-based discharge permits. States must identify segments of waterways where technology-based controls on industrial discharges and existing water quality-based controls are inadequate to meet water quality standards for toxic pollutants or to protect public health, public water supplies, agricultural and industrial uses, and the protection and propagation of a balanced population of wildlife, fish, and shellfish, and to allow recreation in or on the water. As a second step, individual control strategies are to be developed for each segment of waterway identified. The state must determine that the individual control strategies will result in achieving water quality standards not later than 3 years after the date of the establishment of the strategy.

SAFE DRINKING WATER ACT

Known as Title XIV, Safety of Public Water Systems, laws to protect the quality of drinking water have been around a long time. Since their inception, they have required the issuance and enforcement of drinking water standards to protect the health of the consumer. First adopted in 1914, Public Health Service Drinking Water Standards were designed only to protect the health of the traveling public. Drinking Water Standards were revised in 1942 and 1962, but they remained applicable only to interstate carriers, such as buses, trains, and airplanes. Finally, P.L. 93-523, enacted on December 16, 1974, made drinking water standards applicable to all public water systems with at least 15 service connections and serving at least 25 individuals. National Interim Primary Drinking Water Regulations were promulgated in 1975.

The Safe Drinking Water Act requires the promulgation of primary drinking water regulations that specify maximum contaminant levels for constituents that may have any adverse effect on the health of persons, and of secondary drinking water regulations that specify maximum contaminant levels requisite to protect the public welfare. No national primary drinking water regulation may require the addition of any substance for preventive health care purposes unrelated to the contamination of drinking water. States have primary enforcement responsibility for the provisions of the act.

The Safe Drinking Water Act contains a prohibition on the uses of lead pipes, solder, and flux in public water systems. It provides for the protection of underground sources of drinking water through the issuance of regulations for state underground injection programs, the provision of petitions by citizens for no new underground injection programs, and sole-source aquifer protection where the vulnerability of an aquifer is due to hydrogeologic characteristics. Recent amendments to the Act provide for a wellhead protection program and the identification of anthropogenic sources of contaminants to wells.

Laws provide requirements for action on a particular issue by a federal agency. Requirements may be couched in general language with latitude reserved for agency judgement. The action may be a study, regulation, or guidance. Dates are established for deliverables. Regulations by a federal agency define the laws, specify the conditions to be met, provide a time frame for action, and provide enforcement procedures for compliance.

CLEAN AIR ACT

In developing the Clean Air Act, the Congress found that the growth in the amount and complexity of air pollution brought about by urbanization, industrial development, and the increase of motor vehicles has resulted in mounting dangers to the public health and welfare, including injury to agricultural crops and livestock, damage to and the deterioration of property, and hazards to air and ground transportation. Its declared purpose is to protect and enhance the quality of the nation's air resources so as to promote the public health and welfare, and the productive capacity of its population.

The Clean Air Act provides for research, investigation, and training. It provides for regulatory controls on stationary sources for air pollution, as well as mobile sources of air pollution. It requires the development and issuance of air quality criteria for those pollutants that may endanger public health or welfare. National primary ambient air quality standards to protect the public health and national secondary ambient air quality standards to protect the public welfare are to be issued for each pollutant for which criteria have been developed. Each state has the primary responsibility for assuring air quality within the entire geographical area comprising the state by submitting an implementation plan that will specify the manner in which primary and secondary ambient air quality standards will be achieved and maintained within each air quality control region in the state.

National emission standards for hazardous air pollutants are required to be developed. A hazardous air pollutant is defined in the law as one where no ambient standard is applicable and where the pollutant may cause or contribute to air pollution that may result in increased mortality, or serious irreversible or incapacitating reversible illness.

Standards of performance for new stationary sources with the establishment of allowable emission limitations are mandated. No major emitting facility may be constructed without a permit with emission limitations. It must be demonstrated that emissions will not cause or contribute to air pollution in excess of any allowable increase or maximum allowable concentration for any national ambient air quality standard in any air quality control region, or any other applicable emission standard. The proposed facility must be installed with the best available control technology for each pollutant subject to regulation under the act.

The Clean Air Act has an antidegradation provision in requirements for prevention of significant deterioration of air quality in order to preserve, protect, and enhance wilderness areas, and national or regional natural recreational, scenic, or historic areas. A state must develop plans to implement this provision.

Further, plans must be developed to bring those areas into attainment where the national ambient air quality standards now are violated. One means of achieving attainment is mandatory inspection of vehicular emissions in such nonattainment areas. The Clean Air Act addresses motor vehicles, the development of emission and fuel standards, the testing of fuels and fuel additives, and fuel economy improvement for new motor vehicles.

Section 309 is especially encompassing and provides broad powers to the Administrator of the U.S. EPA. Section 309 states that the Administrator shall review and comment in writing on the environmental impact of any matter relating to duties and responsibilities granted to the EPA contained in any legislation proposed by any Federal department or agency, newly authorized federal projects for construction, and any major federal agency action; and proposed regulations published by any department or agency. Any written comments shall be made public at the conclusion of any review. In the event the EPA determines that any such legislation, action, or regulation is unsatisfactory from the standpoint of public health or welfare or environmental quality, the Administrator's determination shall be published and the matter shall be referred to the Council on Environmental Quality. This section, in conjunction with Section 404 of the Clean Water Act, provides broad powers in environmental controls.

TOXIC SUBSTANCES CONTROL ACT

The Toxic Substances Control Act (TSCA) provides authority to regulate the manufacture, distribution, and use of chemical substances. In developing this legislative package in 1976, the Congress found that, among the many chemical substances and mixtures that are constantly being developed and produced, there are some whose manufacture, processing, distribution in commerce, use, or disposal may present an unreasonable risk of injury to health or the environment.

The TSCA provides the EPA with the authority to gather certain kinds of basic information on chemical risks from those who manufacture and process chemicals. It requires companies to test selected existing chemicals for toxic effects and requires the EPA to review new chemicals before they are manufactured. To prevent unreasonable environmental risk, the EPA may select from a broad range of regulatory controls, ranging from requiring hazard-warning labels to outright ban on the manufacture or use of especially hazardous chemicals. The EPA may regulate a chemical's unreasonable risks at any stage in its life cycle, including the manufacturing, processing, distribution in commerce, use, or disposal.

Eight product categories are exempt from regulatory action under this law. These are pesticides, tobacco, nuclear material, firearms and ammunition, food, food additives, drugs, and cosmetics.

If there is a finding that an existing chemical may present an unreasonable risk of injury to health or the environment, the EPA can require the manufacturers or processors of the chemical to test its health and environmental effects. Testing protocols and requirements have been developed. Testing requirements are imposed only after a rulemaking proceeding, which includes opportunities for both public comments and an oral presentation at a hearing. Manufacturers or importers of a new chemical or of an existing chemical with an intended significant new use must give the EPA a 90-day advance notification of their intent to manufacture or import such a chemical.

The premanufacture notice is to include the identity of the chemical; its molecular structure; proposed categories of use; an estimate of the amount to be manufactured, imported, or processed; the byproducts resulting from the manufacture, processing use, and disposal of the chemical; estimates of exposure; and any test data related to the health and environmental effects of the chemical. If a rule requiring testing of the chemical or its chemical class has been issued, the notice must include test data developed from that testing along with the other information.

Under the TSCA, the EPA has the authority to prohibit or limit the manufacture, import, processing, distribution in commerce, use, or disposal of a chemical when any activity is found to pose an unreasonable risk of injury to human health or the environment. A manufacturer or processor may be required to make and keep records of the processes used in manufacturing a chemical and to conduct tests to ensure compliance with any regulatory requirements. Notice of any unreasonable risk of injury presented by a chemical may be required to be provided to a purchaser. A manufacturer or processor may be required to recall a substance that presents an unreasonable risk.

A rule limiting, but not banning, a chemical may be made immediately effective when initially proposed in the *Federal Register* if the EPA determines that the chemical is likely to present an unreasonable risk of serious or widespread injury to health or the environment before normal rulemaking procedures could be completed. For a rule prohibiting the manufacture of a chemical, the EPA must obtain a court injunction before the rule can be made immediately effective.

FEDERAL INSECTICIDE, FUNGICIDE, AND RODENTICIDE ACT

Under the Federal Insecticide, Fungicide, and Rodenticide Act (FIFRA), all pesticides must be registered with the EPA before they may be sold or distributed in commerce. FIFRA sets an overall risk-benefit standard for pesticide registration, requiring that pesticides perform their intended function, when used according to labeling directions, without posing unreasonable risks of adverse effects on human health or the environment. In making pesticide registration decisions, the EPA is required by law to take into account the economic, social, and environmental costs and benefits or pesticide uses. Pesticide registrants, i.e., those who wish to register a pesticide, are responsible for providing all test data necessary to meet the EPA's registration requirements.

Each applicant for registration of a pesticide shall file a statement that includes the name and address of the applicant, the name of the pesticide, a complete copy of the labeling with a statement of all claims to be made and any directions for the use of the pesticide, a full description of the tests made and the results of testing upon which claims are based, the complete formula of the pesticide, and a request that the pesticide be classified for general use, for restricted use, or both. Except for the protection of trade secrets, the data called for in the registration statement becomes public information. *General use* of a pesticide means that with a widespread and commonly recognized practice, the pesticide will not generally cause unreasonable adverse effects on the environment. *Restricted use* means that with a widespread and commonly recognized practice and without additional regulatory restrictions, the pesticide may generally cause unreasonable adverse effects on the environment, including injury to the applicator.

The 1988 amendments to FIFRA require the reregistration of all pesticides that have been registered in the past. This substantial program requires the EPA to publish lists of pesticide active ingredients subject to reregistration and to ask registrants of pesticide products containing those active ingredients whether they intend to seek reregistration. There are approximately 600 pesticide active ingredients that require reregistration under FIFRA. If reregistration is not sought, the registration will be canceled.

As a second phase, registrants are required to respond to the EPA concerning their intention to seek reregistration and to identify missing and inadequate scientific studies required to satisfy the EPA's current data requirements. Subsequently, registrants are required to summarize and reformat key existing studies to facilitate EPA review, to certify that they possess or have access to data from studies, to identify any studies that indicate adverse effects, and to make a commitment to generate new test data or to share the cost of obtaining such new data.

The EPA is required to complete its review of submissions made by registrants to independently identify data gaps and to issue requirements for registrants to fill those gaps. The EPA is to conduct a thorough, comprehensive examination of all data submitted in support of pesticide reregistration. Based upon this review, the agency either will reregister a pesticide or take other appropriate regulatory action.

Other provisions of FIFRA include the requirement for federally approved state programs for the certification of applicators in the use of restricted-use pesticides. An experimental use permit may be issued if it is determined that an applicant for such a permit needs to accumulate information necessary to register a pesticide. If it is determined that a pesticide, or its labeling, or other material required to be submitted does not comply with the provisions of FIFRA, or when used in accordance with widespread and commonly recognized practice generally causes unreasonable adverse effects on the environment, the EPA can issue a notice to cancel a registration or to hold a hearing to determine whether or not to cancel a registration. In the event of a finding of imminent hazard, action may be taken to suspend the registration of a pesticide immediately. *Imminent hazard* is defined as when the continued use of a pesticide during the time required for cancellation proceedings would be likely to result in unreasonable adverse effects on the environment or will involve unreasonable hazard to the survival of a species declared endangered by the Secretary of the Interior.

MARINE PROTECTION, RESEARCH, AND SANCTUARIES ACT

Although other laws become involved, there are two basic authorities designed to protect the quality of oceanic waters under the Marine Protection, Research and Sanctuaries Act of 1972 as amended and the Convention on the Prevention of Marine Pollution by Dumping of Wastes and Other Matter. The convention is an international agreement binding the United States and other signatories to adopt regulatory programs to control the ocean dumping of waste materials; it was ratified by the president on September 25, 1973 and became effective August 30, 1975.

The Act

In enacting the Marine Protection Research and Sanctuaries Act of 1972, the Congress found that unregulated dumping of material into ocean waters endangers human health, welfare, and amenities; the marine environment; ecological systems, and economic potentialities. The Congress declared that it is the policy of the United States to regulate the dumping of all types of materials into ocean waters and to prevent or strictly limit the dumping into ocean waters of any material that would affect adversely those environmental qualities delineated above.

Section 102 of the act established the issuance of permits by the EPA as the only legal means of transporting any material for the purpose of dumping it into ocean waters, except for dredged material. The Act prohibits the dumping of radiological, chemical, and biological warfare agents and high-level radioactive wastes. For other wastes, the EPA must determine through applicable criteria that their permitting for dumping will not unreasonably degrade or endanger human health, welfare, or amenities, or the marine environment, ecological systems, or economic potentialities.

In establishing criteria to regulate ocean dumping, the Act requires that consideration be given to the need for the proposed dumping; the effect on human health and welfare, including economic, aesthetic, and recreational values; the effect on marine resources and ecosystems; the persistence and permanence of the effects of the dumping; recycling and land-based alternatives; and other factors.

With respect to dredged material, the Act provides that the Secretary of the Army shall apply the criteria established by the EPA and make an independent determination of need for dumping. Prior to issuing a permit for dumping of dredged material, the secretary is directed by the Act to notify the EPA of an intent to do so. If the administrator of the EPA disagrees with the determination of the secretary as to compliance with the criteria established pursuant to the act, or with restrictions relating to critical areas, the dredged material permit shall not be issued unless the EPA grants a waiver of requirements. In order to obtain a waiver, the Secretary of the Army must certify that there is no economically feasible method or site available other than a dumping site that would result in noncompliance of the criteria. He must request a waiver from the administrator of the specific requirements involved.

The Act was amended in 1988 by the Ocean Dumping Ban Act. These amendments prohibit the dumping of sewage sludge and industrial wastes in the oceans within 6 months of enactment unless the dumper has entered into a compliance or enforcement agreement with the EPA to end ocean dumping, and prohibits the dumping of municipal sewage sludge and industrial wastes in the oceans after December 31, 1991. The definitions for both sewage sludge and industrial wastes contain the terminology, "which may unreasonably degrade or endanger human health, welfare, or amenities, or the marine environment, ecological systems, and economic potentialities." The amendments prohibit, within 6 months of enactment, the dumping of medical waste in the oceans, and impose civil and criminal penalties.

The Convention

The Convention prohibits the dumping of organohalogen compounds, mercury and mercury compounds, cadmium and cadmium compounds, persistent plastics and other persistent synthetic materials, crude oil, and other specified oils, all except trace contaminants. High-level radioactive wastes or other high-level radioactive matter and materials, in whatever form, produced for biological and chemical warfare, are prohibited without exception. A number of listed compounds require a special permit for ocean dumping.

The convention delineates provisions to be considered in establishing criteria governing the issuance of permits for the dumping of matter at sea. There is a close similarity between the requirements of the Act and the Convention.

Relationship of the Act to the Clean Water Act

As noted earlier, Section 404 of the Clean Water Act provides that the Secretary of the Army may issue permits after notice and opportunity for public hearings for the discharge of dredged or fill material into the navigable waters of the United States at specified disposal sites. In defining the applicability of guidelines for specification of disposal sites for dredged or fill material pursuant to the Clean Water Act, the EPA has made it clear that such guidelines will be applied in the review of both proposed discharges of dredged or fill material into navigable waters that lie inside the baseline from which the territorial sea is measured, and the discharge of fill material into the territorial sea. The discharge of dredged material into the territorial sea is governed by the Marine Protection, Research, and Sanctuaries Act and the regulations and criteria issued pursuant thereto. The Convention on the Territorial Sea and the Contiguous Zone was signed by the United States and other nations on April 29, 1958. It provides definitions and means of measuring the territorial sea. The normal baseline for measuring the breadth of the territorial sea is the low-water line along the coast and in localities where the coastline is deeply indented. If there is a fringe of islands along the coast, the method of straight baselines joining appropriate points may be employed in drawing the baseline from which the breadth of the territorial sea is measured. No permit shall be issued for a dumping of material that will violate applicable water quality standards.

Other Associated Laws

The Marine Plastic Pollution Research and Control Act of 1987 requires a study by the EPA on methods to reduce plastic pollution, including a list of improper disposal practices, a list of specific plastic materials that may injure fish and wildlife or degrade the economic value of coastal waterfront area, a description of existing activities aimed at reducing plastic in marine environments, an evaluation of potential substitutes for some plastic materials, recommendations for recycling incentives, and commentary on the potential development of degradable materials. The Medical Waste Tracking Act of 1988 requires 24-month demonstration programs for the tracking of medical wastes in New York, New Jersey, Connecticut, and the Great Lake States unless a governor notifies the EPA that the state will not participate. The Degradable Plastic Ring Carrier Act of 1988 directs the EPA to require by regulation within 2 years that plastic ring carriers be made of degradable materials, unless EPA determines that the byproducts from degradable ring carriers create a greater threat to the environment than do nondegradable ring carriers. The Organotin Antifouling Paint Control Act of 1988 requires a 10-year monitoring program jointly conducted by the EPA and the National Oceanographic and Atmospheric Administration to monitor the water column, sediments, and aquatic organisms in representative estuaries and prohibits the use of certain antifouling paints. It continues Navy research programs on toxicity and environmental risk assessment associated with the use of paints containing organotin compounds, focuses Navy and EPA research on alternative antifoulant paints, and provides a phase-out schedule for sale and application of existing stocks. The River and Harbor Act of 1989 prohibits the deposit of refuse in navigable waters generally.

RESOURCE CONSERVATION AND RECOVERY ACT

With respect to the Resource Conservation and Recovery Act (RCRA), the Congress made a number of findings. Generally, it found that millions of tons of recoverable material that could be used are needlessly buried each year; that land is too valuable a national resource to be needlessly polluted by discarded materials; and that open dumping is particularly harmful to health, contaminates drinking water from underground and surface supplies, and pollutes the air and the land. The Congress declared it to be the national policy that, wherever feasible, the generation of hazardous waste is to be reduced or eliminated as expeditiously as possible. Waste that is nevertheless generated should be treated, stored, or disposed of so as to minimize the present and future threat to human health and the environment.

The RCRA requires a cradle to grave management and control system for hazardous wastes. It requires the listing of particular hazardous wastes and the development of criteria for their identification and listing. RCRA requires the EPA to develop standards applicable to generators of hazardous waste, as well as to the transporters of hazardous wastes and to the owners and operators of hazardous waste treatment, storage, and disposal facilities. It provides for the issuance of permits for hazardous waste treatment, storage, or disposal facilities. It authorizes state hazardous waste programs for the purposes of management and enforcement. It requires recordkeeping and a paper trail that accompanies the movement of hazardous waste.

The RCRA was amended by the Hazardous and Solid Waste Amendments of 1984. These amendments established a national policy that the generation of hazardous wastes be reduced or eliminated as expeditiously as possible and provided a presumption that land disposal should be a method of last resort for the disposal of hazardous waste. The placement of the bulk or noncontainerized liquid hazardous waste or free liquids contained in hazardous waste in any landfill was prohibited. Regulations were to be developed by the EPA to minimize the disposal of containerized liquid hazardous waste in landfills. Further restrictions were placed on the disposal of solvents and other liquids containing specific and listed concentrations of certain metals.

In further requirements, the amendments mandated EPA to submit a schedule to Congress reviewing all hazardous wastes listed and to promulgate regulations prohibiting one or more methods of land disposal for the hazardous wastes listed on the schedule, except for such methods as the administrator of the EPA may determine will be protective of human health and the environment for as long as the waste remains hazardous. Stringent restrictions were placed on surface impoundments receiving hazardous wastes. Additional requirements were placed on the petitioning for delisting a listed hazardous waste at a particular facility.

Owners and operators of underground storage tanks that are used to contain an accumulation of a regulated substance were to report such use within 12 months to the EPA. Within 30 months, regulations on leak detection, prevention, and correction for underground storage tanks were to be promulgated. Petroleum or any fraction thereof that is a liquid was identified as an additional regulated substance.

Small-quantity generators of hazardous waste, defined as those generating between 100 and 1000 kg/month, were brought into the RCRA regulation by the amendments. Small-quantity generator hazardous wastes must be disposed of at a permitted, licensed, or registered facility. These generators may store such wastes up to 180 days. Prior to the 1984 amendments, they were excluded from regulation.

The chronology of this law, as it was introduced, debated, and passed by the Congress, is shown below. It was signed by the president on November 9, 1984.

May 3, 1983:	H.R. 2867 was introduced to House of Representatives and referred to the Committee on Energy and Commerce.
May 17, 1983:	Reported out of the Committee on Energy and Commerce with committee debate and views, 119 pages.
June 9, 1983:	Committee on Energy and Commerce submitted a Supplemental Report with additional views and correcting errors in initial report, 26 pages.
June 17, 1983:	Reported from the Committee on the Judiciary with views, and ordered to be printed, 59 pages.
	Committee on the Judiciary printed supplemental views and committed to the Committee of the Whole House, 21 pages.

November 3, 1983:	House debate, Congressional Record — House, H. 9133, 51 pages. House passed H.R. 2867, now 106 pages, and referred it to Committee on Environment and Public Works.
March 7, 1983:	S. 757 introduced to the Senate and referred to the Committee on Environment and Public Works.
October 28, 1983:	Reported from committee and printed, 93 pages. Committee on Environment and Public Works issued its report on S. 757 with views, 110 pages.
July 24, 1984:	Action postponed indefinitely.
August 9, 1984:	Previous action vitiated; ordered placed on calendar; passed Senate.
August 10, 1984:	Conferees appointed to Conference Committee for H.R. 2867.
October 3, 1984:	Conference Report, H.R. 98-113, to accompany compromise Bill, H.R. 2867, ordered to be printed.
October 3, 1984:	H.R. 2867 passed House.
October 3, 1984:	H.R. 2867 passed Senate.

COMPREHENSIVE ENVIRONMENTAL RESPONSE, COMPENSATION, AND LIABILITY ACT

Superfund, or CERCLA, as the Comprehensive Environmental Response, Compensation, and Liability Act is called, was passed in 1980 and signed on December 11 of that year. Its purpose was to provide authorities the ability to respond to the release of hazardous waste from inactive hazardous waste sites that endanger public health and the environment, to establish prohibitions and requirements concerning inactive hazardous waste sites, and to provide for the liability of persons responsible for releases of hazardous waste from inactive hazardous waste sites. Superfund authorizes the EPA to order legally responsible parties to clean up hazardous substances at a site or vessel from which there is an actual or threatened release. If they decline, the government can use the federal "Superfund" money to do it and collect from the responsible parties in a cost recovery action. Responsible parties include present and past owners and operators of a site, generators of hazardous substances that were sent to the site, and transporters of hazardous substances who selected the site as a disposal area.

Case law has held that these potentially responsible parties are strictly, jointly, and severally liable for the cleanup response costs. These costs include not only all costs of removal and remedial action by the federal or state government, but costs of investigation, litigation, and oversight. *Hazardous substance* is broadly defined as any such substance designated under this act, the Clean Water Act, the Solid Waste Disposal Act, the Clean Air Act, and the Toxic Substances Control Act.

CERCLA provided for notification to the EPA of the existence of hazardous waste facilities by any person who owns or operates, or who at the time of the disposal owned or operated a hazardous waste facility, or who accepted hazardous substances, or who transported, stored, treated, or disposed of such substances. A substantial penalty was provided for those who knowingly failed to notify the EPA. CERCLA provided for the revision and republishing of the National Contingency Plan that provides the operating details of managing the program and the cleanup operations. The National Contingency Plan also provides for the National Priority List of hazardous waste sites for remedial action.

CERCLA has been amended by the Superfund Amendments and Reauthorization Act (SARA) of 1986. In these amendments, the Congress expanded the EPA's response authority, provided deadlines for response action and gave the EPA the authority to condemn property, changed liability and enforcement provisions, added a citizen suit provision, and broadened the application of the law to include federal facilities. New provisions were added dealing with emergency planning and community right to know. Liability always has been of concern regarding hazardous waste, especially in a change of ownership of property. Related to the possibility of hazardous waste presence on a parcel of property, a new owner must demonstrate that, at the time of acquisition, he or she undertook all appropriate inquiries into the previous ownership and uses of the property consistent with good commercial or customary practice in an effort to minimize liability.

Title III of SARA is the Emergency Planning and Community Right-To-Know Act of 1986. This act establishes requirements for federal, state and local governments and industry regarding emergency planning and reporting on hazardous and toxic chemicals. It has four major sections, including emergency planning, emergency release notification, community right-to-know reporting requirements, and toxic-chemical release inventory reporting. In regard to emergency planning, the governor of each state must designate a State Emergency Response Commission, which, in turn, is required to designate emergency planning districts and local emergency planning committees. The local emergency planning committee must include elected state and local officials; police, fire, civil defense, and public health professionals; environmental, hospital, and transportation officials; broadcast and print media; and owners and operators of facilities subject to the emergency planning and notification requirements. An emergency response plan must be developed. Facilities must immediately notify the commission and committee if there is a release into the environment of a listed hazardous substance that exceeds the reportable quantity for that substance.

Under the community right-to-know reporting requirements, the facilities that must prepare material safety data sheets (MSDS) under the Occupational Safety and Health Administration regulation must submit either copies of the MSDSs or a list of MSDS chemicals to the State Emergency Response Commission and the local emergency planning committees, as well as the local fire department with jurisdiction over the facility. Currently, OSHA regulations require all employers to have or prepare MSDSs for the chemicals they use. Further, a facility must submit an emergency and hazardous chemical inventory form to the same entities receiving the MSDSs or a list of them. The emergency and hazardous chemical inventory form provides an estimate of the maximum amount of chemicals for each category present at the facility at any time during the preceding calendar year, an estimate of the average daily amount of chemicals in each category, and the general location of hazardous chemicals in each category. Lastly, a Toxic Chemical Release Inventory Form, submitted annually, informs the public and government officials about routine releases of toxic chemicals to the air, land, or water environment as a result of normal business operations.

OCCUPATIONAL SAFETY AND HEALTH ACT

As the name implies, this 1970 act provides for safety and health protection in the workplace. The National Institute of Occupational Safety and Health (NIOSH) is responsible for undertaking research and developing recommended health and safety standards, including limits of exposure to potentially hazardous substances or conditions in the workplace. Appropriate preventive measures designed to reduce or eliminate adverse health effects or hazardous substances are also recommended. The NIOSH recommends and the Occupational Safety and Health Administration promulgates the health and safety standards.

ENDANGERED SPECIES ACT

The Endangered Species Act provides the authority for the Secretary of the Interior to preserve species of animals and plants that are in danger of extinction and to conserve the ecosystems upon which they depend. The Secretary may acquire habitats and conduct investigations. The act provides for cooperative agreements between the federal and state governments that contain a list of federally endangered or threatened and state endangered or threatened species. It provides for the development of a state conservation plan with objectives, the problems that a species is facing, and the strategy for a corrective program. The federal fund share in support of cooperative agreements with states shall not exceed 75%, except that under certain specified conditions this share may be increased to 90%. The Endangered Species Act becomes of particular importance in the development of EISs, as discussed in Chapter 20. It was signed into law on December 28, 1973, as Public Law 93-205.

IMPACTING FEDERAL LEGISLATION

Federal laws are shaped and molded principally by events and time, and are dramatically influenced by the philosophies of the persons in power in the House and in the Senate, particularly in the appropriate committees in which a bill is developed. There are several means whereby the average citizen can influence environmental legislation. Probably the most effective is through communication directly with Senators or Representatives responsible for the legislation. Ask to be informed of congressional hearings on a particular bill or to present a statement at such a hearing if you have information pertinent to committee deliberations. One may write to the President of the United States with thoughts on a particular bill. Upon arrival, these letters are dispatched to the appropriate authority within the federal government. One may contact an employee of an agency that would be involved directly with implementing the legislation being developed; however, it must be remembered that such an employee must forward such information through an administrative chain of command that eventually would reach the agency's office whose responsibility it would be to prepare agency comments on the proposed legislation. In this process, it goes without saying that a group has more political weight than an individual, and a national organization has more weight than a local group.

REFERENCE CITED AND SELECTED READING

Hall, R.M., Jr. 1977. The Evolution and Implementation of EPA's Regulatory Program to Control the Discharge of Toxic Pollutants to the Nation's Waters. In: "Hearings before the Subcommittee on Investigations and Review of the Committee on Public Works and Transportation," U.S. House of Representatives, House Document 95-32, pp. 649–662.

3

REGULATIONS, THE *FEDERAL REGISTER*, AND CODIFICATION

NEED

Laws enacted by the Congress in the environmental area frequently require that the EPA or another specified federal agency develop regulations to enforce provisions of the law. The regulations thus interpret the law in specific language. This interpretation may be challenged in court in terms of whether or not the regulations carry out the Congressional intent after they are promulgated.

Regulations define the regulated community. They specify conditions and requirements to be met. They provide a schedule for compliance, and they record any exceptions to the regulated community.

Generally, a law will require one or more particular regulations. Often a law will state that the secretary of a department, or the Administrator of the EPA "shall by regulation" implement some specific action. Occasionally, a law will provide discretionary power and will state that some action "may by regulation" be implemented. Regulations are needed to explain how a section of a law will be managed by the responsible government authority.

REGULATION DEVELOPMENT

In the Environmental Protection Agency (EPA), the development of regulations follows an established procedure. The program office assigned responsibility for the development of a regulation prepares an Action Memorandum to the Administrator outlining the authority, need, provisional economic considerations, EPA resource requirements, and requesting permission to begin work on the regulation. With the Action Memorandum, there is submitted a Development Plan that details required interagency coordination, public and state government involvement, interaction with other government programs and agencies, development schedule, and specific EPA interdepartmental personnel who will be asked to serve on a Work Group. When the Administrator's permission is granted, the program office assembles pertinent information and prepares a draft regulatory document. A Work Group meeting is convened and the issues related to a particular regulation are debated. Contractors may be used to prepare a supporting development document and to assist with estimating the economic impacts of regulatory alternatives. There may be many Work Group meetings before there is general agreement on most aspects of the developing regulation.

When the Work Group can no longer enhance the developing regulation, it goes to a policy group called a Steering Committee, which has representation from all agency Assistant Administrators. The developing regulation is presented to this group by the program office along with a memorandum detailing issues and their resolution or nonresolution by the Work Group, a thorough discussion of economic impacts of the potential regulation, and reporting and paperwork impacts that would be caused by the proposed regulation. If the Steering Committee concurs, the developing regulation moves forward. If there is nonconcurrence on the part of the Steering Committee, the developing regulation goes back to the Work Group for additional consideration and development.

Following its eventual release by the Steering Committee, the regulatory package goes through a sign-off process called the Red Border Review because of the distinguishing red border on the concurrence sheet on the outside of the package. Here, each assistant administrator must concur or nonconcur with comments. Only after this recommending process, does the Administrator receive the regulatory package and sign the submitted language for publication as a proposed rule in the *Federal Register,* or reject the effort and return it for further staff work.

A proposed rule has no regulatory authority. It contains a preamble, which provides agency rationale for each section of the proposed regulation, the authority for the regulation, the calendar window for the public comment period, a summary of the proposed action, a contact person with a phone number, and regulatory language. Each public comment on the proposed regulation must be considered by an agency and rationale must be presented in the preamble to the final regulation for acceptance or rejection of such comments. Concurrent with the public comment period, an agency may hold a number of administrative hearings on the proposed regulation to further solicit public involvement. Following public comments, the entire process of regulation development is begun anew as the program office assesses comments received, prepares to modify or support the regulatory language, and proceeds to develop a final rule. The final rule is developed in the same fashion as the proposed rule with Work Group meetings, a Steering Committee meeting or meetings, and Red Border concurrence or nonconcurrence by the assistant administrators. When a final rule is promulgated, action to change it must be through the courts. A regulation has the force and effect of law.

As an example, pretreatment standards for existing sources were published for the electroplating industry on September 7, 1979, challenged in the Court of Appeals, sections were remanded to the agency, amendments were proposed on July 3, 1980, and the regulation was promulgated on January 28, 1981. On August 31, 1982, proposed regulations with a 60-day public comment period defined *best practicable treatment* technology and *best available treatment* technology. They established new source performance standards and pretreatment standards for the industry. Applicable effluent limitations were set in accordance with sections 301, 304, 306, 307, 308, and 501 of the Clean Water Act (47 *Federal Register* 38462, August 31, 1982).

These proposed regulations became final regulations on July 15, 1983 (48 *Federal Register* 32462, July 15, 1983). In June, 1983, a 730-page Development Document was published by the EPA in support of the rule (EPA-440/1-83/091). The Development Document provides data on the EPA and industrial testing to characterize waste streams, information on control and treatment technologies, and the rationale for the standards and effluent limitations derived.

THE *FEDERAL REGISTER*

The *Federal Register* is a weekday, daily, official newspaper of the regulatory side of the federal government, published by the U.S. Government Printing Office.

Each issue contains a contents section arranged according to the agencies responsible. The agencies, in turn, are arranged in alphabetical order. The format is virtually the same in each issue. First come presidential documents, such as proclamations and executive orders. These are followed by rules and regulations, which include final rules, interim rules, and interim final rules; proposed rules, which include notices of proposed rulemaking and proposed rules; and notices. Each issue contains two very helpful lists. Near the front of each issue is a cumulative list of CFR parts affected in the issue, and near the rear of each issue is a listing of CFR parts affected during the month of issue.

FR is the standard abbreviation for *Federal Register,* and CFR means the Code of Federal Regulations. Each federal agency is assigned a title for codification of regulations; for example, Title 40 is for protection of environment, under which the EPA publishes its rules and other official information. Title 50 belongs to wildlife and fisheries, and Title 32 to national defense. Thus, "40 CFR" designates an official published action by the EPA. Regulatory actions are codified in numbered parts and sections. These parts designate general subject areas, and the sections within each part are numbered consecutively. Thus 40 CFR 141.11 may be interpreted as an EPA regulation wherein 141 identifies the regulation as National Primary Drinking Water Regulations, and the 11th section within the regulation specifies maximum contaminate levels for inorganic chemicals in drinking water supplies. With the aid of the lists for CFR parts affected in each FR, an investigator can determine by examining only one page whether or not a particular subject of interest has been addressed; how it may have been addressed as a presidential proclamation, executive order, proposed rule, rule, or notice; and the page number with the month where it is addressed.

The *Federal Register* usually is cited by using the volume number and page number. Often the date of the issue containing the citation is added as a quick reference to the citation, so that 55 FR 35420, becomes 55 FR 35420, September 10, 1990.

Environmental regulations are codified on July 1 of each year and published in several volumes of Title 40, Code of Federal Regulations. The code contains only the regulatory language. It does not contain the preamble to the regulation, which was part of the regulation when it was promulgated in the *Federal Register*. As new regulations are promulgated or as existing regulations are modified or changed in any way, they are published in the code as new issues are developed. The code is a handy reference manual to regulations. As a matter may come into litigation, however, it is the complete regulation with its preamble, as it was published initially in the *Federal Register*, that becomes the point of focus.

TYPES OF ACTIONS

The notices published by federal agencies address a variety of subjects. They may announce the availability of a Draft Environmental Impact Statement for public comment, the availability of a resource document relating to a particular regulation, an environmental assessment and findings of no significant impact, or provide the details of a meeting that is open to the public. Generally, notices provide information or seek public involvement and comments.

An advanced notice of proposed rulemaking or a notice of proposed rulemaking is, as the title implies, an early warning of agency thoughts regarding a regulation. Generally it means that an agency presently is not committed to a course of action, but is considering it. The reaction, involvement, and comments of the public are sought at an early stage in rule development. Additional information may be required to support some aspect of rule development. The reaction an agency receives as a result of this action may influence, to a considerable degree, the course of action the agency will pursue. A notice of proposed rulemaking is written informally and usually is not lengthy. It contains the proposed action; name of the agency; type of action, i.e., notice of proposed rulemaking; a summary of the proposed action; date that comments must be received; address where comments should be sent; name, address, and telephone number of a contact person for the notice; and an invitation for comments, along with any explanatory information regarding the particular nature of comments or information desired.

Developing regulations may take the form of a proposed rule, temporary rule, interim rule, interim final rule, and final rule. A proposed rule leading eventually to a final rule is the general regulatory course of action. A proposed rule may be the first opportunity that the public has to examine the considered thoughts of an agency on a particular issue. A proposed rule is open for public comment for a period of 45 to 60 days. Often there is a series of hearings throughout the United States to explain the proposed rule and to provide the public an opportunity for oral or written comments following a hearing. A proposed rule does not have regulatory standing; it is not binding, nor does it require regulatory action.

Occasionally, it is necessary for an agency to implement an action before it otherwise would be implemented through the normal course of action. An interim final rule may be the result. In this event, the rule is in effect upon the date published or specified in the rule, but the rule is open for a period of time for public comment. When the comment period has closed, and the comments reviewed, certain aspects of the rule may be amended. A final rule has the force and effect of law upon its effective date, which is specified in the rule.

ANATOMY OF PROPOSED RULE

A proposed regulation provides the agency name, the parts of 40 CFR that are addressed, the name of the regulation, the agency sponsoring the proposed rule, and the action, i.e., proposed rule. This information is followed by a summary of the action, the date when comments must be received, information on times and locations of any public meetings to be held pursuant to the proposed regulation, the address where comments are to be sent, the name and address of an official contact for the proposed regulation with a telephone number, and a listing of the information and subjects addressed in the preamble to the proposed rule. The preamble follows this preliminary material.

The preamble provides the background, authorization, and rationale for the proposed rule. It may discuss the relationship of the regulation to the law, past court decisions pursuant to the regulation, and any historical perspective that may bear on the regulation. Generally, the preamble will individually consider each of the separate sections of a regulation, identify issues associated with any section, and provide a rationale for agency resolution of issues, options considered, and decisions reached. The purpose of a preamble is to explain why a course of action was taken in a regulation in such a way that the public may understand the agency's position. It should explain, in a nonregulatory language, what a section of a regulation is intended to accomplish. The preamble discusses the economic impact of a regulation and how the regulation meets the requirements of the Paperwork Reduction Act and the Regulatory Flexibility Act. Again, this very important part of a regulation will not be printed in the CFR. No part of a proposed regulation appears in the CFR. The preamble remains available only if there is access to the initial *Federal Register* publication of the proposed rule; it is not reprinted when the rule is promulgated.

The preamble may be lengthy. In the proposed rule for Standards for the Disposal of Sewage Sludge, for example, the preamble occupied 130 pages of triple-column *Federal Register* print; the proposed regulation that followed occupied 21 pages only. Following the preamble, there is the proposed regulatory language, which may in turn include appendix material, such as application forms or other matter associated with the regulation.

ANATOMY OF FINAL RULE

A great many comments may be received as a result of proposing a regulation. When this occurs, each comment is assessed and placed into a broader grouping of comments, such as those that may relate to issues of sampling, temperature effects, economic considerations, and other matters. In this manner, an agency is able to address all comments received by addressing in depth the 10 to 20 broader issues, rather than addressing individually each of 6000 or so comments, and creating repetition among both the stating of comments and the responses to comments. The preamble to a final regulation includes an agency's response to comments from the public as a result of a proposed regulation. This preamble is not printed in the Code of Federal Regulations.

The final rule, as did the proposed rule, begins with an identification of the federal agency, the parts of 40 CFR affected, the title of the regulation, and the action, i.e., the final rule. This is followed by a concise summary, a statement of the effective date, an agency contact with telephone number to obtain further information, and the date and location where the public record for the rulemaking will be available for review.

The preamble may contain a description of the legal authority for the rule, the scope of the rulemaking, other background information, the development of the final rule, and a summary of the significant changes between the proposed and final rule. The agency's responses to public comments received as a result of the proposed rule are provided. The cost and economic impact of the rule are discussed. Other information that would contribute to the public's understanding of the rule or the resolution of issues associated with the rule may be included.

Following the preamble, the rule is printed. As discussed earlier, the rule is contained in the next edition of the CFR, which in the case of EPA regulations is July 1 of each year.

4 WATER QUALITY CRITERIA AND STANDARDS

HISTORY OF THE PROCESS

The Water Quality Act of 1965 authorized the establishment and enforcement of water quality standards for interstate waters, including coastal waters. In developing water quality standards, the states initially held public hearings to define particular water uses for the states' interstate streams. Such water uses included domestic water supply, recreation, fish and other wildlife, agricultural, and industrial. Following the designation of water uses for particular stream reaches, water quality criteria were to be established by the states to ensure that the water would be of a quality to support the designated use. In addition, an implementation program was established that outlined the pollution-abatement measures that would be required to meet the designated criteria. An antidegradation policy was required to be adopted by the states. As a minimum, the antidegradation policy ensures the maintenance and protection of existing uses and water quality necessary to protect those uses, provides for the protection of high quality waters, and maintains water quality in waters that are outstanding national resources. The states then submitted the individual water quality standards to the EPA and, upon approval, the standards became federal-state water quality standards. The first responsibility for implementing and enforcing the water quality standards rests with the state. If the state does not act on a violation, however, federal enforcement action can ensue.

The criteria that were adopted to protect interstate and coastal waters varied to some extent among the several states. In general, the criteria specified a minimum water quality applicable in all places at all times. Minimal water quality criteria would prevent the discharge of materials attributable to pollutional discharges that would float as unsightly objects, settle to form putrescent sludge deposits, impart tastes or odors to water or fish or other organisms, result in a toxic action to fish or other water users, or serve to stimulate the growth of undesirable biota. Generally, specific numerical criteria were recorded for the water temperature, dissolved oxygen, pH, and often other water quality constituents. Specific criteria for nitrogen and phosphorus were designated for some of the major lake water resources.

The 1972 amendments to the Federal Water Pollution Control Act provide, in Section 303, that water quality standards shall be developed and apply to all waters of the United States. In addition to setting water quality standards, where effluent limitations will not be stringent enough to meet water quality standards, the states are required to establish maximum daily loads of pollutants permitted in the waters that will allow the propagation of fish and wildlife. A similar assessment must be made for thermal discharges. States are required to develop a continuing planning process that is able to deal with the changing patterns of water pollution within the state. Beginning in 1975, the states were required to submit to the EPA biennial reports with an inventory of all point sources of discharge, an assessment of existing water quality and projected goals, and proposals of programs for nonpoint source control.

The EPA reviews and combines these reports into a biennial National Water Quality Inventory Report to the Congress. The 1987 amendments to the Clean Water Act added Section 518. This section authorizes the EPA to treat federally recognized Indian tribes as states for certain provisions of the act, including the water quality standards program.

THE PROGRAM

The water quality standards program operates under Section 303 of the Clean Water Act. The current regulations implementing this section were published on November 8, 1983 and are codified at 40 CFR 131. As stated in these regulations, the purpose of a water quality standard is to define the water quality goals of a water body by designating the use or uses to be made of the water and by setting criteria necessary to protect the uses. States adopt water quality standards to protect public health or welfare, to enhance the quality of water, and to serve the purposes of the Clean Water Act. To serve that purpose, the standards should, wherever attainable, provide water quality for the protection and propagation of fish, shellfish, and wildlife and for recreation in and on the water; and take into consideration the use and value of public water supplies; propagation of fish, shellfish, and wildlife; recreation in and on the water; and agricultural, industrial, and other purposes, including navigation.

Such standards serve the dual purposes of establishing the water quality goals for a specific water body and as the regulatory basis for the establishment of water-quality-based treatment controls and strategies beyond the technology-based levels of treatment required by Sections 301(b) and 306 of the Act.

The 1987 amendments to the Clean Water Act affect the water quality standards program in two ways. They require states to adopt numeric criteria for toxic pollutants on the Section 307(a) toxic pollutant list when the EPA criteria recommendations are available and where the discharge or presence of those toxic pollutants could reasonably be expected to interfere with designated water uses. In addition, Section 518 of the amendments authorizes the EPA to treat federally recognized Indian tribes as states for the purposes of establishing water quality standards.

At least every 3 years, a state holds public hearings for the purpose of reviewing applicable water quality standards and, as appropriate, modifying and adopting standards. Following this review, the state-adopted standards are submitted to the EPA for approval. If the EPA determines that a state's water quality standards do not meet the requirements of the Clean Water Act, the state is informed of the changes that are needed to bring the standards up to the required level. If the state does not make the required changes, the EPA begins the process of promulgating a federal regulation setting forth a new or revised water quality standard for the waters affected. The EPA has the authority to promulgate federal regulations when a determination is made that a new or revised standard is necessary to meet the requirements of the Clean Water Act, even if the state has not submitted water quality standards to the EPA.

Each state must specify appropriate water uses to be achieved and protected for all waters. Such a use may or may not presently be attained. However, in no case shall a state adopt waste transport or waste assimilation as a designated use for any waters of the United States. A state must ensure that its water quality standards provide for the attainment and maintenance of the water quality standards of downstream waters in another state. States may adopt seasonal uses, and states may remove a designated use that is not an existing use under certain conditions. States may not remove an existing use designation, which is defined as a use actually attained in a water body on or after November 28, 1975, the date of promulgation of the original water quality standards regulation. A nonexisting designated use may be removed where there is a demonstration that attainment is not feasible because of naturally occurring pollutant concentrations; natural, ephemeral, intermittent, or low-flow conditions or water levels; human-caused conditions or sources of pollution that cannot be remedied or would cause more environmental damage to correct than to leave in place; dams, diversions, or other types of hydrologic modifications; and physical conditions, such as lack of proper substrate, cover, flow, depth, pools, and riffles. To develop a successful demonstration for removing a designated use, a use attainability analysis may be performed. This is an assessment of the physical, chemical, and biological factors that affect the attainment of a use.

States must adopt water quality criteria that protect the designated use or uses of a water body. Such criteria must be based on sound scientific rationale and must contain sufficient parameters or constituents to protect the designated use. For waters with multiple use designations, the criteria shall support the most sensitive use. States must review water quality data and information on discharges to identify specific water bodies where toxic pollutants may be adversely affecting water quality or the attainment of the designated water use or where the concentrations of toxic pollutants are at a level to warrant concern. They must adopt criteria for such toxic pollutants applicable to the water body sufficient to protect the designated use. Criteria may be expressed in either numeric or narrative form.

An antidegradation policy and methods for implementing such a policy are a part of water quality standards. The EPA regulations at 40 CFR 131 specify that existing in-stream uses and the level of water quality necessary to protect the existing uses shall be maintained and protected. Where the quality of the waters exceeds levels necessary to support the propagation of fish, shellfish, and wildlife, and recreation in and on the water, that quality shall be maintained and protected unless the state finds, after full satisfaction of the public participation provisions of the state's continuing planning process, that allowing lower water quality is necessary to accommodate important economic or social development in the area in which the waters are located. In allowing lower water quality, the state shall ensure water quality adequate to protect existing uses fully. Further, the state must assure that there will be achieved the highest statutory and regulatory requirements for all new and existing point sources and all cost-effective and reasonable best management practices for nonpoint source control.

Where high quality waters constitute an outstanding national resource, such as waters of national and state parks and wildlife refuges, and waters of exceptional recreational or ecological significance, that water quality shall be maintained and protected. States are not specifically required to incorporate antidegradation policies in the water quality standards, but the policy must be formally adopted and be specifically referenced in the water quality standard.

CRITERIA FOR AQUATIC LIFE

The concept of water quality criteria began with an assessment of concentration-response reactions for aquatic life. The type of response noted generally was death of the test organism. The literature on water quality criteria can be traced to the early 1900s. The effects of industrial wastes on fish were published as early as 1907 (Marsh, 1907). Shelford (1917) published effect data on fish for a large number of gas-plant waste constituents where experiments were performed using fish as test organisms in test chambers. In this early publication, Shelford reiterated that the toxicity of waste differs for different species of fish and generally is greater for the small and younger fish. Powers (1917), working with Shelford, experimented with goldfish as a test animal for aquatic toxicity studies.

A monumental early effort to describe and record the effects of various concentrations of a great number of substances on aquatic life was made by Ellis (1937). He reviewed the existing literature for 114 substances in a 72-page document and listed the lethal concentrations found by various authors. Ellis provided a rationale for the use of standard test animals in aquatic bioassay procedures and used the goldfish, *Carassius auratus,* and the entomostracan, *Daphnia magna,* as test species on which experiments were made in constant-temperature cabinets. Early efforts to summarize knowledge concerning water quality criteria took the form of a listing of the concentration, the test organism, the results of the test within a time period, and the reference for a cause-effect relationship for a particular water contaminant. In early bioassay efforts, insufficient attention was given to the quality of the dilution water used for the experiment and to the effects of such dilution water on the relative toxicity of the tested contaminant. As a result, conclusions from the citations of the various references were left to the discretion of the reader.

A 512-page book entitled *Water Quality Criteria,* was published by the state of California in 1952. It was an effort to review the existing literature and was documented with 1369 references. In March of the same year, the senior author compiled a "Selected Review of the Literature on Toxic Materials Affecting Biological Life in Streams and Sewage Treatment Processes", which was reproduced and distributed by the U.S. Department of Health, Education, and Welfare, Public Health Service. The state of California's 1952 book was expanded into a second edition edited by McKee and Wolf, and published in 1963 by the Resources Agency of California, State Water Quality Control Board. This edition was an effort to bring together, under one cover, the world's literature on water quality criteria. It contained 3827 references. Specific concentrations were arranged in ascending order, indicating the degree of damage to fish in the indicated time and under the conditions of exposure. The results of such a tabulation presented a range of values and, as would be expected by those investigating such conditions, there often was an overlap in values among those concentrations that had been reported as harmful by some and nonharmful by others.

In 1966, the Secretary of the Interior appointed a number of nationally recognized scientists to a National Technical Advisory Committee to develop water quality criteria for five specified uses of water: agricultural, industrial, recreational, fish and wildlife, and domestic water supply. In 1968, the "Report of the Committee on Water Quality Criteria" was published. The book was intended to be used as a basic reference by personnel in state water-pollution control agencies engaged in water quality studies and water-quality standards-setting activities. In some respects, this volume represented a marriage between the best available experimental or investigative concentration-response information recorded in the literature and the judgments of recognized water quality experts with long experience in associated management practices. Its publication marked a change in the concept of water quality criteria from one that listed a series of concentration-effect levels to another that recommended concentrations that would ensure the protection of the quality of the aquatic environment for a specified use. When a specific aquatic life recommendation for a particular water pollutant could not be made because of either a lack of information or conflicting information, a recommendation was made to substitute a designated application factor based upon data obtained from a 96-hour bioassay using a sensitive aquatic test organism and receiving water as a diluent for the toxicity test. This book also marked a change in criteria document identification. Because of the color of the book's cover, it became known as the "green book".

The U.S. EPA contracted with the National Academy of Sciences and the National Academy of Engineering to expand the concept of the 1966 National Technical Advisory Committee's "Water Quality Criteria" and to develop a water quality criteria document that would include current knowledge of the time. The result was "Water Quality Criteria, 1972" (1974). The book's cover was blue and it is known as the "blue book".

The Federal Water Pollution Control Act Amendments of 1972 mandated that the EPA publish water quality criteria accurately reflecting the latest scientific knowledge on the kind and extent of all identifiable effects on health and welfare that may be expected from the presence of pollutants in any body of water. The result was "Quality Criteria for Water", the "red book" (1976). As stated in the foreword to this book, proposed water quality criteria were developed and a notice of their availability was published on October 26, 1973 (38 FR 29646). This volume represented a revision of the proposed water quality criteria based upon a consideration of comments received from other federal agencies, state agencies, special interest groups, and individual scientists. The thrust of the volume was to recommend criteria levels for a water quality that will provide for the protection and propagation of fish and other aquatic life and for recreation in and on the water in accord with the goals of the Clean Water Act. Criteria also were presented for domestic water supply use of ambient water.

Soon after publication of the red book, the Water Quality Section of the American Fisheries Society undertook a review and critique of it (Thurston et al., 1979). The American Fisheries Society effort provided its criticism for each of the criteria presented in the red book, including a substantial number of more recent literature citations to substantiate the critique and recommendations for improvement of EPA's publication.

The next water quality criteria effort was in 1980. The EPA published individual ambient water quality criteria documents for each of the 65 toxic pollutants listed under Section 307(a)(1) of the Clean Water Act. These comprehensive documents provide a criteria summary for aquatic life and for human health resulting from consumption of 2 l of water and 6.5 g of fish or shellfish per day that contain or were exposed to a particular concentration of a pollutant. The documents also provide a discussion of aquatic life toxicology, mammalian toxicology, and human health effects, the basis for the formulation of the criteria, and references to support the literature reviewed. Some of these documents for individual pollutants have been revised since the 1980 publication; some in 1984, and some in more recent years.

In 1986, the EPA published "Quality Criteria for Water 1986", the "gold book". This was an effort to bring under one cover all of the officially recognized criteria and the statements associated with the criteria presentation. The rationale and background information and data supporting the criteria are not presented in this document. Thus, the gold book includes some of the criteria material from the red book where such material has not been updated by more recent EPA publications, as well as the criteria summaries from the 1980 publications related to the 65 toxic pollutants and more recent criteria publications. This was an effort to keep all interested parties current with the latest official water quality criteria, because there was provision for issuing updates to this publication as criteria, for additional water constituents are developed, or as existing criteria may be revised. Updates to the initial publication have been issued.

Thus, through the years, there has been an evolution in water quality criteria development as testing and data reporting have become more sophisticated. Likewise, there has been a change in presenting the information. Beginning with the green book in 1968, criteria have been presented as numeric concentrations that, in the judgment of the issuing authority, will protect a particular use of the aquatic resource.

It should be mentioned that the 1968 green book presented general water quality requirements that continue in water quality standards use today in most state standards. These are the so-called "free froms". The 1968 recommendations were that surface waters should be free from substances attributable to discharges or wastes, such as

1. Materials that will settle to form objectionable deposits
2. Floating debris, oil, scum, and other matter
3. Substances producing objectionable color, odor, taste, or turbidity
4. Materials, including radionuclides, in concentrations or combinations that are toxic or that produce undesirable physiological responses in human, fish, and other animal life and plants
5. Substances and conditions or combinations thereof in concentrations that produce undesirable aquatic life

Water quality criteria represent a nonregulatory, scientific assessment of ecological effects. Presented as criteria, they are not enforceable. However, when water quality criteria associated with specific stream uses are adopted as state water quality standards, they become enforceable maximum levels of a pollutant in ambient waters. Thus, water quality criteria become regulatory when adopted in a standard, permit, or regulation.

The EPA protocol for criteria derivation is complex. Guidelines for deriving numerical national water quality criteria for the protection of aquatic organisms and their uses are 98 pages in length (Stephan et al., 1985). These guidelines also are presented as Appendix A of the gold book. For example, the required data to derive a criterion for freshwater aquatic organisms only and their uses include:

1. Results of acceptable acute tests with at least one species of freshwater animal in at least eight different families such that all of the following are included:
    a. the family Salmonidae in the class Osteichthyes
    b. a second family in the class Osteichthyes, preferably a commercially or recreationally important warm-water species (e.g., bluegill, channel catfish, etc.)
    c. a third family in the phylum Chordata (may be in the class Osteichthyes or may be an amphibian, etc.)
    d. a planktonic crustacean (e.g., cladoceran, copecod, etc.)
    e. a benthic crustacean (e.g., ostracod, isopod, amphipod, crayfish, etc.)
    f. an insect (e.g., mayfly, dragonfly, damselfly, stonefly, caddisfly, mosquito, midge, etc.)
    g. a family in a phylum other than Arthropoda or Chordata (e.g., Rotifera, Annelida, Mollusca, etc.)
    h. a family in any order of insect or any phylum not already represented.
2. Acute-chronic ratios with species of aquatic animal in at least three different families provided that of the three species:
    a. at least one is a fish
    b. at least one is an invertebrate
    c. at least one is an acutely sensitive freshwater species (the other two may be saltwater species).
3. Results of at least one acceptable test with a freshwater alga or vascular plant. If plants are among the aquatic organisms that are most sensitive to the

materials, results of a test with a plant in another phylum should also be available.

4. At least one acceptable bioconcentration factor determined with an appropriate freshwater species, if a maximum permissible tissue concentration is available.

CRITERIA FOR HUMAN HEALTH

Mammalian toxicology and human health effects data and discussion were a substantial part of the 1980 EPA individual criteria documents for each of the 65 toxic pollutants. This presentation reviewed the literature and data on animal studies and any human data that may be available. Exposure was discussed, including ingestion from water, ingestion from food, inhalation, and skin absorption. The pharmacokinetics within the system were considered including absorption, distribution, metabolism, and excretion. With this background, the acute, subacute, and chronic toxicity were considered, as well as synergism and antagonism, teratogenicity, mutagenicity, and carcinogenicity. Then, the existing guidelines and standards for the particular substance were discussed, the current levels of exposure were considered, and the special groups at risk were identified. For example, for a compound like polychlorinated biphenyls, the special groups at risk include industrial workers exposed in the workplace, individuals consuming large amounts of contaminated fish, such as sport fishermen, because of the compound's high bioconcentration factor of 31,200, and nursing infants who, per kilogram of body weight, may accumulate significant body burdens from the levels in human breast milk. The weight of evidence indicates that polychlorinated biphenyls are carcinogenic in rodents. Based upon the results of these animal feeding experiments and the assumptions that a person weighing 70 kg or about 150 pounds will, throughout a 70-year lifetime, drink 2 l of contaminated water per day and consume 6.5 g of contaminated fish and shellfish per day, a water criterion of 0.79 ng/l (parts per trillion) for a risk level of 10^{-5} was developed. A risk level of 10^{-6} would have a criterion of 0.079 ng/l, and a risk level of 10^{-7} would have a criterion of 0.0079 ng/l. A risk of 10^{-5}, for example, indicates a probability of one additional case of cancer for every 100,000 people exposed, and a risk of 10^{-6} indicates one additional case of cancer for every million people exposed.

Another source of applicable human health information is that of health advisories prepared for individual compounds by the Criteria and Standards Division of EPA's Office of Drinking Water. As declared in the preface of each document, health advisories provide specific advice on the levels of contaminants in drinking water at which adverse health effects would not be anticipated and that include a margin of safety so as to protect the most sensitive members of the population at risk. A health advisory provides health effects guidelines and analytical methods, and recommends treatment techniques on a case-by-case basis. The advisories are normally prepared for 1-day, 10-day, longer term, and lifetime exposure periods where available toxicological data permit.

The normal format for the health advisory document is similar to that described for the human health portion of the 1980 water-quality criteria documents. The document discusses sources of exposure, environmental fate, and pharmacokinetics, including absorption, distribution, excretion, and metabolism. Human exposure effects and animal experiments are considered with short-term and longer term exposure effects, reproductive effects, developmental toxicity, carcinogenicity, and genotoxicity. The health advisories then are developed both for a 10-kg child and a 70-kg adult. Other criteria, guidance, and standards are discussed; analytical methods for the contaminant are presented and treatment technologies are reviewed.

THE INTEGRITY OF WATER

The Federal Water Pollution Control Act Amendments of 1972 associated the word *integrity* with water quality when in Section 304(a)(2)(A), there was a requirement for the EPA to develop information on the chemical, physical, and biological integrity of all navigable waters, groundwaters, waters of the contiguous zone, and the oceans. In March, 1975, the EPA held an invitational symposium with 22 speakers that resulted in formal papers and comments by recognized water experts representing a variety of disciplines and societal interests (U.S. EPA, 1977). The focus of the symposium was on the definition and interpretation of water quality integrity as viewed and discussed by representatives of state governments, industry, academia, conservation and environmental groups, and members of the general public. The symposium was structured to address quantitative and qualitative characteristics of the physical, chemical, and biological properties of surface and groundwaters. The reading of the proceedings of this symposium is recommended.

ENFORCEABILITY

Water quality standards are enforceable principally through permits, actions by a state or the EPA as a standard issuing authority, and by citizen suits.

Section 402 of the Clean Water Act provides for the issuing of National Pollutant Discharge Elimination System permits upon condition that such discharges will meet all applicable requirements of Section 301. Section 301(b)(1)(C) requires effluent limitations necessary to meet water quality standards.

Section 401 of the Clean Water Act provides that any applicant for a federal license or permit to conduct any activity that may result in any discharge into the waters of the United States shall obtain a certification from the state in which the discharge originates or will originate that the discharge will comply with the applicable provisions of Section 301, as discussed in the above paragraph, and Section 303, the water quality standards implementing section.

Section 505 of the Clean Water Act provides for citizen suits. Under this section, any citizen may commence a civil action against any person who is alleged to be in violation of an effluent standard or limitation under this chapter. For purposes of this section, the phrase *effluent standard or limitation under this chapter* means an unlawful act under Section 301 or Section 402 of the Clean Water Act. Both of these sections require compliance with applicable water quality standards.

Section 303 of the Clean Water Act provides the Administrator of the EPA with the authority to review any water quality standard adopted by a state. When it is determined that a standard is not consistent with the requirements of the Clean Water Act, the EPA is to promulgate a new or revised water quality standard for the waters involved.

Adherence to water quality standards is not restricted to Clean Water Act activities. Section 102 of the Marine Protection, Research, and Sanctuaries Act provides for the EPA to issue permits for the transportation of material for the purpose of dumping it into ocean waters. Section 102(a) states that no permit shall be issued for a dumping of material that will violate applicable water quality standards.

CURRENT STATUS

The EPA has stated that it believes that an effective state water quality standards program should include both the chemical specific ambient water criteria and the narrative "free froms" approach described earlier in this chapter under Criteria for Aquatic Life (U.S. EPA, 1988). Numeric criteria for specific chemicals are important where the cause of toxicity is known, or for protection against potential human health impacts. Numeric water quality criteria may also be the best way to address certain nonpoint source pollution problems. The narrative standard can be the basis for limiting toxicity where a specific toxic pollutant can be identified as causing the toxicity, but there is no numeric criterion in state standards. The narrative standard can also be used to limit whole effluent toxicity where it is not known which chemical or chemicals are causing the toxicity.

The 1987 amendments to the Clean Water Act in Section 303(c)(2)(B) required that whenever a state reviews or adopts new water quality standards, such state shall adopt criteria for all toxic pollutants listed pursuant to Section 307(a)(1) for which criteria have been published, the discharge or presence of which in the affected waters could reasonably be expected to interfere with the designated uses adopted by the state. Such criteria shall be specific numerical criteria for such toxic pollutants.

To comply with this significant modification of the law, a state needs to adopt aquatic life and human health criteria, where necessary, to support the appropriate use. Criteria for the protection of human health are needed for water bodies designated for public water supply. For those pollutants designated as carcinogens, the recommendation for a human health criterion generally is more stringent than the aquatic life criterion for the same pollutant. In contrast, the aquatic life criteria recommendations for noncarcinogens generally are more stringent than the human health recommendations. Earlier in this chapter, under Criteria for Human Health, the very low recom-

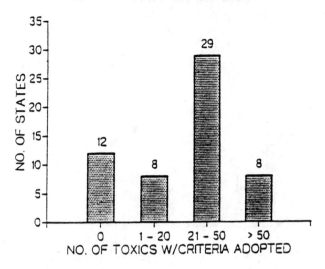

FRESHWATER AQUATIC LIFE USES

Figure 4-1.   States and territories with numeric criteria for toxic pollutants for freshwater aquatic life.

mended concentrations for polychlorinated biphenyls were discussed. These low concentrations were due, in part, to the compound's high bioconcentration factor. Another example is that of dioxin, 2,3,7,8,-TCDD. Twenty-seven states and territories have adopted numeric criteria for dioxin for the purpose of protecting human health. The EPA has approved 15 of the 27 standards. The state-adopted criteria for dioxin range from 0.005 to 1.2 parts per quadrillion, but the majority are at 0.013 part per quadrillion (U.S. EPA, 1990). These very low criteria values, now legally adopted into enforceable water quality standards, will be expected to have a significant impact on the NPDES program that is discussed in the next chapter and the facilities regulated by it.

All states and territories have water quality standards. Of significance is that 45 of 57 states and territories have adopted numerical criteria for toxic pollutants for freshwater aquatic life uses (Figure 4-1). Of the 45 states, 8 have adopted criteria covering 1–20 pollutants, 29 have adopted criteria covering 21–50 pollutants, and 8 have adopted criteria covering more than 50 pollutants (U.S. EPA, 1990a). For the protection of human health, 39 of 57 states and territories have adopted numerical

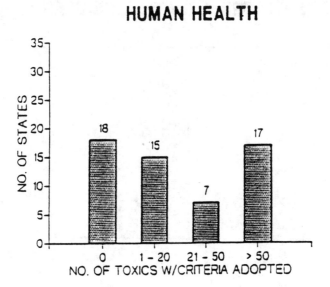

Figure 4-2.   States and territories with numeric criteria for toxic pollutants for human health protection.

criteria for toxic pollutants (Figure 4-2). Of the 39 states, 15 have adopted criteria covering 1–29 pollutants, 7 have adopted criteria covering 21–50 pollutants, and 17 have adopted criteria covering more than 50 pollutants (U.S. EPA, 1990a).

REFERENCES CITED AND SELECTED READING

California. 1952. "Water Quality Criteria." State Water Pollution Control Board, Sacramento, California.

Ellis, M. M. 1937. Detection and Measurement of Stream Pollution. *Bull. U.S. Bur. Fish.* 48:365–437.

Mackenthun, K. M. 1952. "Selected Review of the Literature on Toxic Materials Affecting Biological Life in Streams and Sewage Treatment Processes." Committee on Water Pollution, Madison, WI (mimeo).

Marsh, M. C. 1907. "The Effect of Some Industrial Wastes on Fishes." Water Supply and Irrigation Paper No. 192, U.S. Geological Survey, pp. 337–348.

McKee J. E. and H. W. Wolf.1963. "Water Quality Criteria." State Water Quality Control Board, Sacramento, CA, Pub. 3-A.

NAS. 1974. "Water Quality Criteria, 1972." National Academy of Sciences, National Academy of Engineering, U.S. Government Printing Office, Washington, D.C.

Powers, E.B. 1917. The Goldfish (*Carassius carassius*) as a Test Animal in the Study of Toxicity. *Ill. Biol. Mon.* 4:127–193.

Shelford, V.E. 1917. An Experimental Study of the Effects of Gas Wastes upon Fishes, with Especial Reference to Stream Pollution. *Bull. Ill. State Lab. Nat. Hist.* 11:381–412.

Stephan, D.E., D. I. Mount, et al. 1985. "Guidelines for Deriving Numerical National Water Quality Criteria for the Protection of Aquatic Organisms and their Uses." U.S. Environmental Protection Agency, Office of Research and Development, Duluth, MN, Narrangansett, RI, and Covallis, OR.

Thurston, R.V., R. C. Russo, et al. 1979. "A Review of the EPA Red Book: Quality Criteria for Water." Water Quality Section, American Fisheries Society, Bethesda, MD.

U.S. EPA. 1976. "Quality Criteria for Water." U.S. Environmental Protection Agency, Washington, D.C. (EPA 440/0-76-023).

U.S. EPA. 1977. "The Integrity of Water, Proceedings of a 1975 Symposium." U.S. Government Printing Office, Washington, D.C.

U.S. EPA. 1980. "Individual Ambient Water Quality Criteria Documents for 65 Toxic Pollutants." U.S. Environmental Protection Agency, Office of Water Regulations and Standards, Criteria for Standards Division, Washington, D.C.

U.S. EPA. 1986. "Quality Criteria for Water 1986." U.S. Environmental Protection Agency, Washington, D.C. (EPA 440/5-86-001).

U.S. EPA. 1988. "State Water Quality Standards Summaries." U.S. Environmental Protection Agency, Washington, D.C. (EPA 440/5-88-031).

U.S. EPA. 1988. "Guidance for State Implementation of Water Quality Standards for CWA Section 303(c)(2)(B)." U.S. Environmental Protection Agency, Office of Water Regulations and Standards, Criteria and Standards Division, Washington, D.C.

U.S. EPA. 1990. "Tracking Report: State Water Quality Criteria for Dioxin (2,3,7,8-TCDD)." U.S. Environmental Protection Agency, Office of Water Regulations and Standards, Criteria and Standards Division, Washington, D.C.

U.S. EPA. 1990a. "Status Report: State Compliance with CWA Section 303(c)(2)(B) as of February 4, 1990." U.S. Environmental Protection Agency, Office of Water Regulations and Standards, Criteria and Standards Division, Washington, D.C.

5   WATER DISCHARGE PERMITS

BASIS IN LAW

Section 301(a) of the Clean Water Act provides that "Except as in compliance with this section and Sections 302, 306, 307, 318, 402, 404 of this Act, the discharge of any pollutant by any person shall be unlawful." Section 302 provides for effluent limitations more stringent than best available treatment when found necessary to assure protection of public health; public water supplies; agricultural and industrial uses; the protection and propagation of a balanced population of shellfish, fish, and wildlife; and to allow recreational activities in and on the water. Section 306 provides for the development of national effluent standards of performance and will be discussed later in this chapter. Section 307 provides for toxic and pretreatment standards. Section 318 provides that "The Administrator is authorized, after public hearings, to permit the discharge of a specific pollutant or pollutants under controlled conditions associated with an approved aquaculture project under Federal or State supervision pursuant to Section 402 of this Act." Section 402 is the topic of this chapter. Section 404 authorizes the permitting of discharges of dredged or fill material into the waters of the United States.

Section 402(a) provides that in part that "The Administrator may, after opportunity for public hearing, issue a permit for the discharge of any pollutant, or combination of pollutants, ... upon condition that such discharge will meet either all applicable requirements under Sections 301, 302, 306, 307, 308, and 403 of this Act, or prior to the taking of necessary implementing actions relating to all such requirements, such conditions as the Administrator determines are necessary to carry out the provisions of this Act." Section 301(b)(1)(C) mandates compliance with water quality standards.

Section 502(a) provides that "The Administrator is authorized to prescribe such regulations as are necessary to carry out his functions under this Act."

Section 101(e) mandates that "Public participation in the development, revisions, and enforcement of any regulation, standard, effluent limitation, plan, or program established by the Administrator or any State under this act shall be provided for, encouraged, and assisted by the Administrator and the States. The Administrator, in

47

cooperation with the States, shall develop and publish regulations specifying minimum guidelines for public participation in such processes."

The River and Harbor Act of 1899, as it related to permitting discharges to navigable waters, was discussed earlier in Chapter 2. Section 402(a) of the Clean Water Act specifies that no permit for a discharge into the navigable waters shall be issued under Section 13 of the Act of March 3, 1899 after the Federal Water Pollution Control Act Amendments were enacted on October 18, 1972. Section 402 specifies further that any permits issued under the earlier act shall be deemed to be permits under this title. Actually, the 1899 act permit program was struck down in December, 1971, by a decision of the Federal District Court in Ohio (*Kalur vs. Resor*), which held that the issuance of permits constituted a "major environment act" requiring the preparation of an environmental impact statement for each permitted facility under the National Environmental Policy Act of 1969.

THE NPDES PROGRAM

The National Pollutant Discharge Elimination System (NPDES) program was mandated by Section 402 of the Federal Water Pollution Control Act Amendments of 1972. With those amendments, the Congress shifted national efforts for the control of water pollution from water quality standards to a permit system with effluent or "end-of-pipe" standards based primarily on increasingly stringent levels of treatment technology. An NPDES permit is required for the discharge of pollutants from any point source into waters of the United States. A national goal, as stated in the Clean Water Act, is that the discharge of toxic pollutants in toxic amounts be prohibited. States have been encouraged to assume leadership in the permitting process through EPA delegation of authority to operate state NPDES programs. Thirty-nine states have been delegated authority to issue discharge permits; EPA issues permits for states without NPDES authority. EPA also reviews major state-issued permits where states have NPDES-delegated authority.

Although they contain a reopener clause in which an existing permit can be modified under certain conditions, NPDES permits are valid for 5 years, after which the permittees must reapply. The first round of NPDES permits issued between 1972 and 1976 provided for control of traditional pollutants and focused on biochemical oxygen demand, total suspended solids, pH, oil and grease, and some metals based principally on the best professional judgment of the responsible permit writer. As effluent guidelines were developed and promulgated, those applicable guidelines were placed into permits by the permit writers as the permits expired and were renewed. Presently, because industry has installed best available treatment technologies to control pollution in response to permit requirements through the years, water-quality-based permits are written to control the discharge of toxic pollutants.

In its evolution and development, the NPDES permit program has been influenced by a number of factors:

1. **The 1976 settlement agreement**. In the mid-1970s, public interest groups sued the EPA for failure to implement control of toxic pollutants under Section 307 of the 1972 Federal Water Pollution Control Act Amendments. As a result of this lawsuit, a settlement agreement was negotiated and signed by the EPA, the Natural Resources Defense Council, and other litigants. This agreement specified 65 priority pollutants and required the development of effluent guidelines and water quality criteria under detailed and stringent time frames for these pollutants.

2. **The 1977 Clean Water Act Amendments**. The 1976 settlement agreement virtually was codified into the statutes by the 1977 Clean Water Act Amendments. The settlement agreement priority pollutants were defined as toxic pollutants by these amendments, and their promulgation as toxic pollutants was required within 30 days.

3. **EPA's 1984 toxics pollutant policy**. The national policy for water quality-based permits recognized that in some cases technology-based controls of toxic pollutants would be insufficient to prevent adverse water quality impacts. The policy, therefore, provided for an integrated strategy consisting of both biological and chemical methods to address toxic and nonconventional pollutants from industrial and municipal sources.

4. The continuing development of **water quality-based toxics control**, including the use of toxicity reduction evaluations to identify, isolate, control, and eliminate the discharge of toxic pollutants in toxic amounts.

5. **Stormwater control**. The 1987 Clean Water Act amendments added Section 402(p), which requires the EPA to establish a stormwater permit program. Cities with a population greater than 250,000 must file permit applications by February 1990, and cities with a population greater than 100,000 but less than 250,000, must file permit applications by February 1991. Industries with stormwater discharges must file permit applications by February 1990. The permits issued must reduce pollutants to the maximum extent practicable for municipalities or to technology-based requirements for industry.

The NPDES permit is a specific document that provides the reference point for enforcing federal and state effluent limitations for any point source discharge. Indirect discharges through publicly owned treatment works are regulated by the NPDES permit for the discharge from the treatment works and by pretreatment standards placed on discharges to the treatment works. The elements of an NPDES permit include:

1. Identification and description, with a unique number for each discharge addressed by a permit for an identified facility.

2. Effluent limits for each discharge based upon effluent guidelines, new source performance standards, toxic effluent standards, applicable water quality standards, and the best professional judgment of the permit writer. Limits may be expressed in terms of average monthly and maximum daily amounts, such

as weight per unit of product, or concentrations, such as weight per volume of wastewater.

3. Requirements on monitoring, including the constituent to be monitored, periodicity of monitoring, and method of sampling and analysis.
4. Reporting requirements.
5. Special conditions to be met by a permittee, which may include biological toxicity testing or biological assessment of the effluent receiving water.
6. A compliance schedule if applicable standards cannot be met at time of permit issuance.
7. Other conditions or requirements. In 1979 and 1980, the permit program was revised to include the use of best management practices (BMPs) on a case-by-case basis to minimize the introduction of toxic and hazardous substances into surface waters. Such BMPs are industry practices used to reduce secondary pollution, such as the covering of raw materials storage piles to protect against storm events and resultant runoff. BMPs do not have numerical limits and generally are "common-sense" pollution prevention measures.

The process of issuing a NPDES permit includes:

1. The filing of an application by the potential permittee. The application requires a considerable amount of detailed information on the wastewater to be discharged and the manufacturing or other processes that contribute to the constituents of a wastewater. The results of sampling and analysis of the wastewater are required.
2. The production of a draft permit by the regulator's permit writer.
3. The issuance of a public notice describing in general terms the draft permit and its availability, and a request for comments within a specified period.
4. The consideration of the public comments received and the issuance of a final permit.

With the issuance of a discharge permit, a permittee has certain responsibilities related to effluent monitoring. The results of effluent monitoring are reported on discharge monitoring reports, which are submitted on a monthly or quarterly basis. EPA's Permit Compliance System serves as a computerized storage and retrieval system for the permit program. It also serves as a tracking and report preparation system for individual NPDES permit requirements and other information, compliance schedules and compliance, and discharge monitoring report data.

A permittee currently is supplied performance evaluation samples, furnished by the EPA, Cincinnati, Ohio laboratory, for the constituents that the permittee must monitor in wastewater to meet permit conditions. If analytical data from the performance evaluation samples are of inferior quality, an inspection is made by the applicable EPA region or state to determine the cause. Routine performance audit inspections are also made of permittees and may include permit compliance evaluation or biological toxicity testing. Enforcement action has been taken against permittees for violating quality assurance procedures.

THE 65 TOXIC POLLUTANTS

In the early 1970s, following the statutory deadlines imposed on the EPA for implementing Section 307 of the 1972 Federal Water Pollution Control Act Amendments, four suits were brought against the EPA by the Natural Resources Defense Council, the Environmental Defense Fund, the National Audubon Society, Businessmen in the Public Interest, and Citizens for a Better Environment (House 95-32). These suits, later consolidated, charged the EPA with failure to adequately implement Section 307 of the Act. They sought broad relief to control the discharge of harmful pollutants both directly to the navigable waters and indirectly through publicly owned treatment works. It soon became clear to the agency that it likely would not win these suits and that an identification of pollutants of concern and a strategy for their control were necessary. In October 1975, the agency established a work group to develop a prioritized list of pollutants of concern. The work group began by examining lists of pollutants prepared by six organizations, including a combined list from the Environmental Defense Fund and the Natural Resources Defense Council, the Stanford Research Institute, and EPA's Office of Toxic Substances, Office of Water Supply, Office of Water Planning and Standards' Effluent Guidelines Division, and Criteria and Standards Division. A large body of pollutants resulted, and it was necessary to place these in priority and reduce the number of pollutants to a manageable quantity.

The work group subjected the pollutants to selection criteria arranged in two tiers. Tier I criteria consisted of a review of

1. Toxicity to humans including evidence of acute effects on humans or test animals and evidence of chronic effects in the areas of carcinogenicity, mutagenicity, teratogenicity, reproduction effects, organ system and system effects, and behavioral effects
2. Toxicity to fish and wildlife
3. Persistence, including mobility and environmental degradability
4. Bioaccumulation factors
5. Toxicity, persistence, and bioaccumulation of degradation products and metabolites of parent compound
6. Synergistic propensities and effects

Tier II criteria consisted of a review of

1. Extent of point source discharges into water, including qualitative presence and quantitative levels found in effluents
2. Potential exposure to humans, aquatic organisms, and other wildlife
3. Quantity of production in the United States
4. Use patterns
5. Analytical methodology capabilities

To further reduce the list, the pollutants were screened for evidence of actual presence in effluent, as well as surface water, drinking water, or fish, and evidence of carcinogenic, mutagenic, or teratogenic effects in laboratory test systems, or human epidemiological studies, or for which a high degree of toxicity to aquatic systems had been demonstrated. Eventually, three priority lists of pollutants were established. Priority pollutants on all three priority lists have a known occurrence in point source effluents, in aquatic environments, and in fish or drinking water.

Priority list I consists of 29 substances or generic categories wherein there is substantial evidence of carcinogenicity, mutagenicity, or teratogenicity in human epidemiological studies or in animal bioassay systems and a likelihood that point source effluents contribute substantially to human hazards, at least locally. Priority list II contains 18 compounds or generic categories wherein the hazard risk is less than for the list I pollutants. Priority list III also contains 18 compounds or generic categories wherein toxic effects are produced at higher concentrations than for the pollutants in List II and there is no substantial evidence that these compounds have primary carcinogenic, mutagenic, or teratogenic effects.

The list of 65 priority pollutants contained such items as "arsenic and compounds", "beryllium and compounds", "cadmium and compounds", "copper and compounds", and "polychlorinated biphenyls." For those confronted with developing regulatory effluent guidelines from such a list, it became necessary to identify those particular pollutants that can be regulated and measured in a permit program. In some cases, analytical methods had to be developed. For the purpose of regulation, 129 particular pollutants were developed from the initial list of 65 priority pollutants. These are listed in Tables II and III of Appendix D to 40 CFR 122.21.

THE 1976 SETTLEMENT AGREEMENT

The Settlement Agreement was signed on June 7, 1976 by representatives of the Natural Resources Defense Council, Citizens for a Better Environment, the EPA, and the National Coal Association and Member Companies. The agreement specified that for 21 identified industrial point source categories and 65 priority pollutants, regulations shall be developed and promulgated that shall establish and require achievement at the earliest possible time of effluent limitations and guidelines that shall require application of the best available technology economically achievable and result in reasonable further progress toward the national goal of eliminating the discharges of all pollutants, including toxic pollutants. Effluent limitations and guidelines, new source performance standards, and pretreatment standards for pollutants introduced into publicly owned treatment works were to be promulgated under the agreement.

Stringent promulgation dates were assigned to effluent guidelines development. As it turned out, these dates could not be met. The settlement agreement was amended in court on one or two occasions, and the guidelines were promulgated substantially later.

The agreement further stipulated that not later than June 30, 1978, after opportunity for public comment, the Administrator shall publish, under Section 304(a) of the act, water quality criteria accurately reflecting the latest scientific knowledge on the kind and extent of all identifiable effects on aquatic organisms and human health of each of the 65 listed pollutants. These were the EPA 1980 water quality criteria discussed in Chapter 4.

Paragraph 9 of the agreement provided for quarterly oral briefings to inform the parties to the litigation of the agency's progress in implementing the agreement.

In his order of June 9, 1976, Judge Flannery found that the agreement represented a "just, fair, and equitable resolution of the issues raised" in the lawsuits and incorporated it by reference. He consolidated the four cases and directed the agency to comply with the agreement. Jurisdiction was retained to effectuate such compliance. Judge Flannery further noted in the order that his action in no way precluded anyone from challenging in any way any regulations that might be issued under the agreement and decree and that the decree expressed no opinion on the validity of such future regulations (Hall, 1977).

EFFLUENT GUIDELINES DEVELOPMENT

Effluent guidelines establish national technology-based limitations and standards to control or eliminate the discharge of toxic pollutants from industrial sources into waterways and publicly owned treatment works. They are based on the highest level of technology economically achievable and technically feasible. They address an industrial category with its applicable subcategories, e.g., the iron and steel manufacturing point source category with the subcategories ironmaking and steelmaking. Effluent guidelines are easily adapted to permits to regulate a point- source pollutant discharge.

Effluent guidelines involve engineering and economic studies, wastewater characteristics, treatment options, and economic effects of potential regulations upon the affected parties. This process includes examining industrial processes, products, raw materials, byproducts, effects on other environmental media, age of equipment, size of the industrial group, performance, costs, and economic and environmental effects. Proposed regulations, published for public comment, include the selection of viable treatment options. Often there is litigation following the promulgation of final guidelines. Technical information for the development of litigation responses and legal briefs must be developed, administrative and court records maintained, and affidavits prepared.

The phases of an effluent guideline include:

1. Data collection phase, including sampling and analyses of wastewaters and site visitations of particular industrial facilities to observe industrial processes and treatment controls
2. Development and sending of Section 308 letters to require submission from industrial facilities of additional information on treatment technologies
3. Economic impact studies of alternative effluent limitations
4. Development, proposal, and promulgation of technology-based effluent limitations guidelines and pretreatment standards

Section 308 of the Clean Water Act provides that whenever needed in developing or assisting in the development of any effluent limitations, the Administrator shall require the owner or operator of any point source to sample effluents in accordance with methods, locations, intervals, and in such manner as the Administrator shall prescribe and provide such other information as he may reasonably require. A Section 308 letter is a powerful tool in effluent guidelines development. Through it, the EPA may obtain any reasonable existing information or require a letter's recipient to conduct sampling and analysis to obtain the desired information. Generally, many such letters to obtain information may be sent during the development of a guideline. Before the EPA can send such a letter, however, the president's Office of Management and Budget must approve its contents.

An essential element in the effluent guidelines program is the ability to analyze for hundreds of toxic and nonconventional pollutants in a wide variety of complex waste streams. This analysis is necessary to provide regulators and control authorities with reliable and accessible data. To accomplish this task, the EPA operates a sample control center that provides essential functions for a database, including quality assurance and quality control for thousands of samples analyzed annually. It compiles and updates a compendium of all agency methods for over 1700 compounds, which is called the list of lists. This compendium of substances of environmental concern provides identifying features and appropriate analytical methods for each listed chemical. In addition, an annual symposium is sponsored by the EPA for regulators where the most current analytical methods developed through EPA research are discussed by experts.

Amendments to the Clean Water Act in 1987 require the EPA to publish its plans to review and revise existing effluent guidelines and to promulgate new guidelines for dischargers of toxic and nonconventional pollutants. In addition, the act required the EPA to identify categories of industrial sources discharging toxic or nonconventional pollutants for which guidelines have not been published previously and to establish a schedule for their issuance. Treatment technologies have advanced since some guidelines initially were published, and they need to be brought up to date.

The agency published a notice that new or revised guidelines are anticipated for 5 industrial categories, and that 15 industrial categories are potential candidates for revised or new effluent limitations and guidelines. The 5 industrial categories where effluent guidelines development is underway include pesticide manufacturers, packagers, and formulators; offshore oil and gas extraction; nonferrous metals forming; nonferrous metals manufacturing; and pulp, paper, and paperboard manufacturing.

NATIONAL POLICY FOR WATER QUALITY-BASED PERMITS

In its national policy, the EPA stated that as the water pollution control effort in the United States progresses and the traditional pollutants become sufficiently treated to protect water quality, attention is shifting toward pollutants that impact water quality through toxic effects. Compared with the traditional pollutants, regulation of toxic pollutants is considerably more difficult. The difficulties include (1) the great number of toxic chemicals that may potentially be discharged to receiving waters and the difficulties in their analysis; (2) the changes in the toxic effects of a chemical resulting from reactions with the matrix of constituents in which it exists; and (3) the inability to predict the effects of exposures to combinations of chemicals (49 FR 9016, March 9, 1984).

EPA's stated policy is "To control pollutants beyond Best Available Technology Economically Achievable (BAT), secondary treatment, and other Clean Water Act technology-based requirements in order to meet water quality standards, the Environmental Protection Agency (EPA) will use an integrated strategy consisting of both biological and chemical methods to address toxic and nonconventional pollutants from industrial and municipal sources. Where State standards contain numerical criteria for toxic pollutants, National Pollutant Discharge Elimination System (NPDES) permits will contain limits as necessary to assure compliance with these standards. In addition to enforcing specific numerical criteria, EPA and the States will use biological techniques and available data or chemical effects to assess toxicity impacts and human health hazards based on the general standard of 'no toxic materials in toxic amounts'."

The above policy applies to the EPA and the states. Chemical, physical, and biological data will be used to determine whether, after compliance with Best Conventional Technology/Best Available Technology (BCT/BAT) requirements, there will be violations of state water quality standards resulting from a discharge. The narrative prohibition of toxic materials in toxic amounts contained in all state standards is the basis for this determination, taking into account the designated use for the receiving water. For example, discharges to waters classified for propagation of cold-water fish should be evaluated in relation to acute and chronic effects on cold- water organisms, potential spawning areas, and effluent dispersion.

The principal advantages of chemical-specific techniques are that (1) chemical analyses usually are less expensive than biological measurements in simple cases; (2) treatment systems are more easily designed to meet chemical requirements than toxicity requirements; and (3) human health hazards and bioaccumulative pollutants can be best addressed at this time by chemical-specific analysis.

The principal advantages of biological techniques are that (1) the effects of complex discharges of many known and unknown constituents can be measured only by biological analyses; (2) the bioavailability of pollutants after discharge is best measured by toxicity testing; and (3) pollutants for which there are inadequate chemical analytical methods or criteria can be addressed.

Biological testing of effluents is an important aspect of the water-quality-based approach for controlling toxic pollutants (49 FR 9017). Effluent toxicity data in conjunction with other data can be used to establish control priorities, to assess compliance with state water quality standards, and to set permit limitations to achieve those standards.

The EPA policy goes on to state that under Section 308 and Section 402 of the Clean Water Act, the EPA or the state may require NPDES permit applicants to provide chemical, toxicity, and in-stream biological data necessary to assure compliance with standards. Where violations of water quality standards are identified or projected, the state will be expected to develop water-quality-based effluent limits for inclusion in any issued permit. Where there is a significant likelihood of toxic effects to biota in the receiving water, the EPA and the states may impose permit limits on effluent toxicity and may require an NPDES permittee to conduct a toxicity reduction evaluation.

BIOLOGICAL TOXICITY TESTING

Whole-effluent toxicity testing involves performing bioassays using two or more aquatic species as test organisms to determine any acute or chronic toxicity, as defined by test results. A bioassay is the exposure of test organisms to a concentration of an effluent or toxicant within a predefined time under controlled conditions to determine an identifiable effect, which may include test organism death. The EPA has published methods for measuring the acute and chronic toxicity of effluents and receiving waters to freshwater, marine, and estuarine organisms (U.S. EPA, 1985, 1988, and 1989).

An informal telephone survey of NPDES state and the EPA regional personnel was conducted in mid-1987 to determine the current use of effluent biological testing (U.S. EPA, 1987). EPA regions and NPDES-delegated states were asked the number of NPDES permits they administered, the number of permits with a biological toxicity testing requirement, the number of permits with expressed toxicity limits, and those with requirements for toxicity reduction evaluations. Other aspects of state water pollution control programs were also discussed.

Methods employed by states in their water pollution control programs include studies and assessments related to macroinvertebrates, fishes, algae, periphyton, protozoa, primary productivity, sediment toxicity tests, fish flesh tainting, fish and mussel flesh analyses for bioaccumulated substances, caged organism toxicity, fish and invertebrate chronic toxicity tests, sediment analyses, and fish avoidance reactions.

The results of the 1987 telephone survey showed that

- 38 states require industries to conduct toxicity testing.
- 27 states required municipalities to conduct toxicity testing.
- 1343 industrial NPDES permits require toxicity testing.
- 597 municipal NPDES permits require toxicity testing.
- The midwestern and western states have the fewest, if any, requirements for biological toxicity testing.
- Effluent toxicity limits are in industrial permits in 14 states and are found in 39% of the industrial permits that require biological testing.
- Effluent toxicity limits are in municipal permits in 10 states and are found in 78% of the municipal permits that require biological testing.
- 16 states have a toxicity testing requirement in industrial permits only.
- 8 states do not require effluent biological testing.
- 19 states project that as new permits are issued, or as existing permits are reissued, all major and significant minor permits will contain biological testing requirements.
- Using major permits as a means of comparison, 15 states require biological

toxicity testing in 50% or more of their industrial permits. California, Virginia, and West Virginia require biological testing in all of their major industrial permits and some minor permits.

- Using major permits as a means of comparison, 6 states require biological toxicity testing in 50% or more of their municipal permits. New Jersey requires biological testing in all of their municipal major permits and some minor permits.
- 10 states have toxicity reduction evaluation programs underway, and 13 additional states are beginning such programs.
- 5 states have, or will have within 1 year, biological laboratory certification programs.
- 16 states operate mobile biological laboratories for flow-through or chronic biological toxicity testing to generate new data or for compliance monitoring activities.
- 9 states have the capability for conducting definitive acute or chronic toxicity tests.
- 33 states conduct receiving water macroinvertebrate or fish assessments, related either to special study pollution investigations or to provide trend-monitoring determinations.

TOXICITY REDUCTION EVALUATIONS

A toxicity-reduction evaluation (TRE) is a planned effort to identify the cause of effluent toxicity and to determine measures and a schedule to correct the cause in order to meet applicable standards (Figure 5-1). A TRE is a step-wise process that combines toxicity testing and analysis of the physical and chemical characteristics of causative toxicants to identify the toxicants causing effluent toxicity, including treatment methods that will reduce the effluent toxicity (U.S. EPA, 1987). Determining the source of toxicity may require toxicity testing and following a waste stream within a facility until the source is isolated. Once a toxicity causative agent is identified, production processes may be modified to keep the agent out of the waste stream, or there may be a substitute for the implicated raw material, solvent, intermediate, or other chemical that is suspected of significantly contributing to effluent toxicity.

Another approach is to determine toxicity treatability measures through bench-scale treatability tests. When an effluent sample exhibits toxicity, another effluent sample is split into a number of smaller volumes. One volume is used as a control and a separate treatment is applied to the other volumes. Effluent treatments may include filtration; air stripping, under acidic, basic, and neutral conditions; addition of a reducing agent to bind chlorine and similar electrophiles; addition of a chelating agent to bind cations; and passing the effluent through a column that extracts organics under acidic, basic, and neutral conditions. The toxicity of the effluent after each of these treatments can then be tested and compared to the toxicity of the control samples.

Generally, the most effective approach to reducing effluent toxicity is to make every effort to identify the toxicants that are causing toxicity and to remove them from the

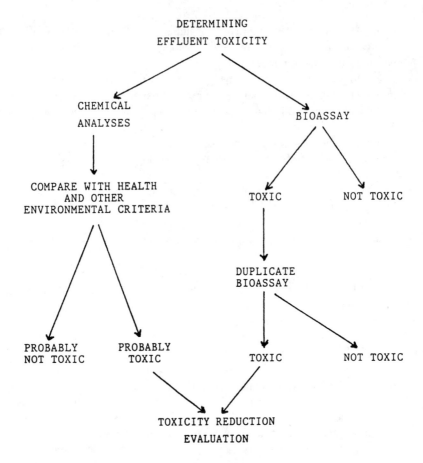

Figure 5-1.   Determining the need for a toxicity reduction evaluation.

waste stream. In some cases, the first step is chemical testing of the wastewater, because this may provide a viable clue to effluent toxicity.

Effluent toxicity should be confirmed with a follow-up toxicity test using the same type of test organism as in the initial toxicity test that showed effluent toxicity before a TRE is initiated. The language in most permits provides for this safeguard before an expensive TRE is instituted.

COMBINED SEWER OVERFLOWS

Combined sewer overflows (CSOs) are flows from a sewer that carry both domestic sewage and stormwater. They occur in many older portions of cities. When a storm event surcharges the sewer, a combined sewer overflows and discharges untreated sewage into the receiving water. The discharge occurs prior to reaching the headworks of a sewage treatment facility. EPA estimates that there are between 15,000 and 20,000 CSO discharge points currently in operation.

On August 10, 1989, the EPA issued its final National Combined Sewer Overflow Control Strategy (U.S. EPA, 1989a). The strategy sets forth three objectives:

1. To ensure that if CSO discharges occur, they are only as a result of wet weather
2. To bring all wet-weather CSO discharge points into compliance with the technology-based requirements of the Clean Water Act and applicable state water quality standards
3. To minimize water quality, aquatic biota, and human health impacts from wet-weather overflows

The strategy states further that CSOs are point sources subject to NPDES permit requirements, including both technology-based and water-quality-based requirements, except they are not subject to secondary treatment regulations applicable to publicly owned treatment works. All CSO discharges must be brought into compliance with technology-based requirements and state water-quality-based requirements, including compliance with water quality standards. The agency expects that this can be achieved using a combination of CSO control measures.

State-wide permitting strategies are being developed by the states to ensure implementation and consistency with EPA's CSO strategy (Whitescarver and Mackenthun, 1990a). The states must identify the communities with combined sewer systems and each particular CSO discharge point within these communities. The states are expected to set priorities in permitting and controlling the unpermitted and insufficiently permitted discharges. All CSOs without permits or not in compliance with technology-based or water-quality-based conditions are in violation of the Clean Water Act and are subject to enforcement action or citizen suits. The population served by CSOs is estimated at 43 million. Data submitted by the states as part of the 1984 Needs Survey indicate that 141 of the 366 U.S. urbanized areas are served in part by combined sewer systems.

The average pollutant concentration for combined sewer overflows has been compared to that of sanitary sewage. The CSOs were found to be higher in total suspended solids than sanitary sewage, about one half as great in concentration of biochemical oxygen demand, one fourth as great in total nitrogen, and about one fifth as great in total phosphorus (U.S. EPA, 1984). However, depending on the amount of rainfall, the mass loading to a receiving water resulting from CSO is great because of the volume of water discharged in a storm event. Forty-six priority toxic pollutants were detected in CSOs at least once during the 3-year study; 11 pollutants were detected greater than 50% of the time; and one pollutant, zinc, was detected in 100 % of the CSO samples. Thirteen of the toxic pollutants were detected between 10% and 50% of the time and 21 of the 46 pollutants were present less than 10% of the time. In addition to pollutant concentrations normally associated with sewage, CSOs transport litter, debris, and solids to the receiving waterway. These include the aesthetically displeasing floatable materials that may be deposited on beaches and in recreational and other water use areas. The nature of this material includes that which is cast into street gutters, abandoned on floodways or in storm drains, or flushed into sewers.

Four methods to achieve compliance with technology-based requirements for CSOs have been investigated. These include various screen technologies, swirl concentrators, the flow-balancing system being demonstrated in New York City, and end-of-pipe netting. Screen technologies include bar screens, fine stationary screens, horizontal rotary drum screens and microstrainers, and vertical shaft rotary screens. Each method has inherent advantages and disadvantages for a specific application.

The swirl concentrator uses a swirl action to separate solid particles from liquids. The principle is somewhat similar to the condition in a rotating teacup when tea leaves are present. When the cup is rotated and the tea leaves are allowed to settle, they concentrate in the center of the cup, not along the outside edge. The unit is operated without moving parts and requires no outside source of power. The device consists of a circular channel in which rotary motion of the inflowing liquid is induced by the kinetic energy of the inflow (Figure 5-2). Flow from a combined sewer enters a diversion chamber and bar screen before entering the swirl. The bar screen protects downstream facility components from large debris. The diversion chamber has an emergency bypass to prevent the swirl facility from being flooded.

The swirl facility is automatically activated when storm flows enter the swirl. Flow enters the lower portion of the circular chamber. The rotary motion causes the liquid to follow a long spiral path to be discharged from near the chamber's top through a downshaft. This overflow water may be disinfected and discharged or, in some cases, stored for later treatment. Because a flow detector prevents the flow in the chamber from completing its first revolution and merging with continuing inlet flow, there is rotational movement, but in the form of a gentle swirl.

The settleable solids entering the chamber spread over the full cross section of the channel and settle rapidly. Solids are entrained along the bottom, around the chamber, and are concentrated at the foul sewer outlet, where they then are transported to a treatment plant.

The scum ring acts as a baffle, keeping the floatables outside the clear overflow weir and preventing them from overflowing with the clean effluent. Floatables are directed by a floatables deflector to a floatables trap. The floatables trap is connected to a floatable storage area under the clear overflow weir plate. Floating material is drawn down beneath the weir plate by the vortex and dispersed under the weir plate around the downshaft. Floating solids are retained here until the water level recedes in the swirl chamber after a storm event. As this occurs, the trapped floatables are dropped and enter the foul sewer outlet, where they are transported to a sewage treatment plant.

There are 18 swirl concentrators in the planning, design, construction, or operations phase in the United States. The District of Columbia has just completed a 400-mgd treatment facility to treat overflows from the large Northeast Boundary Sewer. The $30 million facility features three 57-ft diameter swirl concentrators. These are the largest of any units in the United States.

The flow balancing system consists of a series of cells in a water body constructed by suspended reinforced plastic curtains from floating pontoons. The tank bottom is the receiving water bottom. When there is a CSO discharge, the CSO water will push the receiving water from one cell to another. The compartments are always full, either with

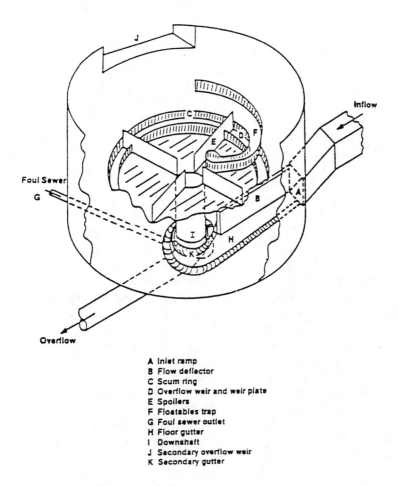

Figure 5-2.   An isometric view of a swirl regulator-concentrator.

receiving water or CSO water. The compartment walls are of flexible PVC fiberglass cloth, which are held down with concrete weights, but can expand outward when CSO flows exceed design flow.

Pumps in the CSO-entering cell transport the polluted water to a treatment system. As the CSO flow diminishes after a storm event, the receiving water flows back to the entrance cell, where eventually most or all of the polluted CSO flow can be pumped to a treatment system. It is a controlled but open system to the receiving water. The receiving water is used as a flow-balancing medium. The system is being demonstrated at Fresh Creek, New York City. The demonstration unit is about 300 ft long and 70 ft wide. It is effective in collecting floatables (Whitescarver and Mackenthun, 1990a).

STORMWATER PERMITS

Section 402(p) was established pursuant to the 1987 Clean Water Act Amendments. This section requires the filing of an application for a stormwater permit by February 4, 1990 for any stormwater discharge associated with industrial activities and for a stormwater discharge from a separate storm sewer system serving a population of 250,000 or more. Applications for a permit for a discharge from a municipal separate storm sewer system serving a population of 100,000 or more, but less than 250,000, must be filed by February 4, 1991.

An interesting example of this permit requirement is that many airports will need to file an application for stormwater-related industrial activities. There is concern about the environmental impacts that have been documented and attributed to deicer fluid concentrations in stormwater runoff. Like organic wastes and wastes high in nutrients, the receiving water effects depend in large measure on the amount of dilution they afford. Ethylene glycol is toxic to aquatic life, but not until substantial concentrations are present in receiving waters. Ethylene and propylene glycol both have high biochemical oxygen demands. Urea is high in nitrogen content and with biological degradation could result in ammonia concentrations toxic to aquatic life. Ethylene and propylene glycol are used in airplane deicer fluids; urea is used with other materials, principally in runway and taxiway deicing materials. Receiving-water environmental impacts that have been documented include fish kills, diminished dissolved oxygen, impaired fish food organism communities, glycol odors, algal nuisances, and glycol-contaminated surface water and groundwater drinking water systems.

A fish kill occurred downstream from the stormwater discharge at Lambert Field, St. Louis that was linked to ethylene glycol. A drinking water supply 1 mile downstream from the Albany, New York airport was temporarily shut down when total glycol at the drinking water intake exceeded the New York drinking water standards, which prohibit unspecified organic compounds in concentrations greater than 100 μg/l. The NPDES permit was rewritten to allow the use of propylene glycol only because it appears to be less toxic than ethylene glycol. Fish kills, low dissolved oxygen, and high ammonia nitrogen concentrations have occurred in the receiving water from Chicago's O'Hare airport. The waste deicing fluid was discharged to a lake from Eppley Airfield in Omaha, Nebraska, which caused winter dissolved oxygen reduction in the lake. Complaints of glycol odors from and color in the receiving stream of the Manchester, New Hampshire airport have been received. Ethylene glycol was reported to have eliminated aquatic life and impaired the operation of a sewage treatment plant in connection with stormwater discharges from the Pittsburgh airport.

The streams near Nashville airport in Tennessee are very small; increased biochemical oxygen demand, decreased dissolved oxygen, and depressed fish food organism communities have been observed. A substantial portion of the airport at Anchorage, Alaska drains to Lake Hood, which is the world's largest float plane basin and a part of the 7-square-mi airport. Complaints of odors, corrosion of plane floats, and algae have been received (Whitescarver and Mackenthun, 1990b).

REFERENCES CITED AND SELECTED READING

Hall, R.M., Jr. 1977. The Evolution and Implementation of EPA's Regulatory Program to Control the Discharge of Toxic Pollutants to the Nation's Waters. In: "Hearings before the Subcommittee on Investigations and Review of the Committee on Public Works and Transportation," U.S. House of Representatives, House Document 95-32, pp. 649–662.

House 95-32. 1977. "Hearings before the Subcommittee on Investigations and Review of the Committee on Public Works and Transportation," U.S. House of Representatives, House Document 95-32.

U.S. EPA. 1979. "NPDES Best Management Practices Guidance Document." U.S. Environmental Protection Agency, Cincinnati, OH (EPA-600/9-79-045).

U.S. EPA. 1985. "Methods for Measuring the Acute Toxicity of Effluents to Freshwater and Marine Organisms." U.S. Environmental Protection Agency, Cincinnati, OH (EPA/600/4-85/013, third edition).

U.S. EPA. 1985a. "Technical Support Document for Water Quality-Based Toxics Control." U.S. Environmental Protection Agency, Washington, D.C. (EPA-440/4-85-032).

U.S. EPA. 1987. "Program Survey — Biological Toxicity Testing in the NPDES Permits Program." U.S. Environmental Protection Agency, Permits Division, Washington, D.C.

U.S. EPA. 1987a. "Permit Writer's Guide to Water Quality-Based Permitting for Toxic Pollutants." U.S. Environmental Protection Agency, Washington, D.C. (EPA-440/4-87-005).

U.S. EPA. 1987b. "Biomonitoring to Achieve Control of Toxic Effluents." U.S. Environmental Protection Agency, Washington, D.C. (EPA/625-8-87/013).

U.S. EPA. 1987c. "Surface Water Monitoring: A Framework for Change." U.S. Environmental Protection Agency, Office of Water, Office of Policy, Planning and Evaluation, Washington, D.C.

U.S. EPA. 1988. "Short-Term Methods for Estimating the Chronic Toxicity of Effluents and Receiving Waters to Marine and Estuarine Organisms." U.S. Environmental Protection Agency, Cincinnati, OH (EPA/600/4-87/028).

U.S. EPA. 1988a. "NPDES Compliance Inspection Manual." U.S. Environmental Protection Agency, Office of Water Enforcement and Permits, Washington, D.C.

U.S. EPA. 1989. "Short-Term Methods for Estimating the Chronic Toxicity of Effluents and Receiving Waters to Freshwater Organisms" (Second Edition), U.S. Environmental Protection Agency, Cincinnati, OH (EPA/600/4-89-001).

U.S. EPA. 1989a. "National Combined Sewer Overflow Control Strategy." U.S. Environmental Protection Agency, Office of Water, Washington, D.C.

U.S. EPA. 1989b. "Generalized Methodology for Conducting Industrial Toxicity Reduction Evaluations (TREs)." U.S. Environmental Protection Agency, Cincinnati, OH (EPA/600-2-88-070).

U.S. EPA. 1990. "Biological Criteria, National Program Guidance for Surface Waters." U.S. Environmental Protection Agency, Washington, D.C. (EPA-440/5-90-004).

Whitescarver, J. P. and K. M. Mackenthun. 1990a. "Low Cost Methods for Solids Removal from Combined Sewer Overflows." Presented at the 1990 Annual Meeting of the Virginia Water Control Association. ERC Environmental and Energy Services Company, Reston, VA.

Whitescarver, J. P. and K. M. Mackenthun. 1990b. "EPA Stormwater Regulations and How They Apply to Airport Operators." Presented to the 1990 Annual Conference of the Airport Operators Council International. ERC Environmental and Energy Services Company, Reston, VA.

6   RECEIVING WATER STUDIES

THE REASONS FOR THE STUDIES

This chapter and Chapter 7 are devoted to water quality investigations and assessments of the flowing water and the standing water environments. Why are they presented in this book on environmental regulations?

The decade of the 1960s could be called the water quality investigative era. Water quality investigations were designed to determine the nature and extent, as well as the causes, of pollution in a waterway. The federal government and the states were involved with water quality investigations of lakes and river segments, including chemical, microbiological, and macrobiological testing and examination. The decade of the 1970s was the discharge permit era, with emphasis on industrial waste treatment technology to control pollution. The decade of the 1980s was the toxicity identification decade, with an increase in the use of bioassays to identify waste streams with constituents toxic to aquatic life. The decade of the 1990s may be the decade of the water quality assessment. Technically, there is little difference between a water quality investigation and a water quality assessment. The objective of the former is to determine the cause and degree of water quality impairment. The objective of the latter is to determine the quality of the ecosystem following emplacement of best available treatment technology and efforts to reduce or eliminate effluent toxicity in industrial discharges, as well as the construction of municipal treatment works, pretreatment programs, and sewage treatment plant operator's training programs. With the investment that society has made in waste treatment over the past two decades, there is a need to assess the aquatic ecosystem integrity that has developed as a result of these efforts.

Assessments of the quality of receiving waters have become a common requirement of discharge permits in many states. Such assessments have been a basis for permit negotiations between the permittee and the regulatory authority. This is a part of the requirement for adherence to established water quality standards for a specific part of a water body. They have been a focal point in water quality litigation. The EPA is implementing a program to introduce biological criteria, which actually are ecosystem criteria, into water quality standards. This would require some form of assessment as a routine monitoring tool. For those reasons, these chapters have been included.

THE PROBLEM AND ITS EFFECTS

The quality of flowing water is influenced by the physical conditions and the types and quantities of chemical constituents to which a reach of water is exposed. A change in water quality can be abrupt but devastating, gradual but extensive, or slight but insidious. Life within the water responds to these quality changes in a positive or negative way. Some organisms increase in abundance dramatically when organic matter or nutrients are plentiful. Other organisms diminish to amounts only sufficient to reproduce the species, or become replaced by those that are more tolerant of and adaptive to the changed condition.

The effects of pollution upon the water environment assume many characteristics, as well as an infinite variation in degree. The specific environmental and ecological responses to a given pollutant depend largely on its volume, combined with the characteristics of the wastewater and the volume and characteristics of the receiving water into which it flows. Pollutants may provide an aesthetic insult, a toxic action, a blanketing effect that destroys the stream or lake bed, a biodegradable, organically decomposable material that removes the dissolved oxygen from the water, a hazard to the health of humans and other animals that use the water, a substance that magnifies in concentration as it becomes escalated through the aquatic food web, an alterant of water temperature that is the prime regulator of natural processes within the water environment, and a supplier of fertilizing nutrients that stimulate excessive production among some aquatic species.

A general axiom of water pollution biology is that water pollution is associated with a reduction in the numbers of species of organisms that otherwise would be present in a particular aquatic situation. In a field examination, this species reduction can be demonstrated by comparing samples taken from a polluted area with those samples taken from a similar aquatic habitat in an area not so affected. With wastes rich in organic materials, nitrogen, or phosphorus nutrients, the reduction in species is associated with a tremendous increase in the number of individuals representing a given species within the habitat. With dense silt or sediment loads, there is a corresponding decrease in the population of the species present. With the presence of acutely toxic materials, there is a decrease in the population of the species present, or the absence or near absence of species, depending upon the relative toxicity of the environment.

Organic or biodegradable wastes are attacked by bacteria upon entering the water environment. During this process of decomposition, the dissolved oxygen, so necessary for life within water, is used and reduced. When the organic load to the receiving waterway is heavy, all of the dissolved oxygen may be used up in this manner. The waterway becomes anaerobic (i.e., lacking in oxygen) and, from the conditions for existence of aquatic life, virtually dead. In addition to the oxygen-consuming properties associated with organic wastes, solids may settle to the waterway's bottom, forming sludge banks that not only continue to exert an oxygen demand during the decomposition process, but also furnish an ideal habitat for the development and reproduction of large numbers of sludgeworms. Organic wastes often are associated with nutrients, such as high concentrations of nitrogen and phosphorus. When the waterway has been cleansed of its visible signs of pollution through natural and biological actions, and the water becomes clear, the nutrients often persist and stimulate obnoxious growths of plants or animals in downstream areas.

Toxic wastes, even those that produce subtle chronic effects, may change the aquatic population balance by a number of processes:

1. Susceptible species of either fish or fish food organisms may gradually die off, thereby permitting tolerant species that are less desirable to humans to flourish because of a lack of competition.
2. If algae or invertebrate food organisms are killed by a low-level toxicity, fish may die or move out of the area because of an inadequate food supply.
3. Weakened individuals surviving near the threshold of their tolerance are more susceptible to attack by parasites and diseases such as the aquatic fungus, *Saprolegnia.*
4. The reproductive potential may be altered because eggs or very young individuals may be more susceptible to the low-level toxic substances than are the adults. The end result of such toxicity can be a slow and subtle alteration of the characteristics of the stream or lake inhabitants.

A water quality investigation provides a basis to understand the water environment and the manner in which the environment responds to conditions with which the water comes into contact. This investigation provides a basis for action and for determining if present controls are effective and adequate. Variances to many environmental regulations may be obtained by demonstrating a lack of significant change as a result of an ongoing or contemplated action. An investigation may provide this demonstration. The extent of the required investigation may vary considerably. Thus, in some cases, an experienced investigator may be able to examine a submersed rock or stick and form a general idea of the general health of the water environment. In other and more common situations, however, that same investigator may require many samples of water and organisms, sophisticated chemical analyses, and data interpretation to arrive at a similar conclusion.

A water quality investigation includes six essential, comparable, and separable components. These include developing a statement of objectives, planning the investigation, location of sampling areas and collecting of samples, sample analysis, data evaluation, and reporting the results. These topics will be discussed in the following pages.

OBJECTIVES

Why is the investigation being pursued? What are the requirements of the regulations that must be met by the water body being investigated? What is intended to be accomplished? When must it be completed to serve its purpose? Study objectives are a necessary and important beginning to any investigation. Careful thought and consideration should be given to their development. The objectives should encompass clear, concise, positive definitions of the investigation's purpose, its scope, and its boundary limits. Study objectives should be realistically oriented to the number, competencies, and disciplines of the investigators. They should be adjusted to budgetary limitations for the study, as well as to the length of time allocated for it, including the final report preparation. Ultimately, as the study progresses, and especially at its conclusion, the study's success and accomplishments will be judged on the extent to which it fulfilled the objectives stated at its instigation. Study objectives become important tools to guide subsequent investigations and to delineate avenues of approach toward problem solving.

Study objectives should be committed to writing as a first act in formulating an essential study plan. It is necessary that they include the standards or regulations that the water body has to meet. When properly developed, study objectives will ensure adherence to essential investigation and discourage pursuit of the interesting but nonessential bypaths or tangential considerations that so often dominate and defeat a well-intended purpose. Written objectives fix the responsibility of those charged with supervision of the study, and they provide a basis for judging the extent to which the results meet the needs that justified the initial undertaking.

PLANNING

Planning for an investigation involves a myriad of details that are essential for the completion of a successful study. The first essential activity is to become familiar with available information on the subject of the investigation. Seldom is the investigation of a waterway an original event. The results of past and perhaps related investigations and prognostications have been recorded either in published or unpublished reports, the latter of which may reside in a now obscure file of an appropriate state agency. Much time and effort in redoing what already has been done can be saved on the part of the investigator by searching out and becoming familiar with the past studies that relate to the waterway in question.

Good field maps of the watercourse under investigation must be secured and the points of access noted. The approximate location of known waste sources or other significant contributors to a decreased water quality should be marked. Tentative sampling locations should be selected from the maps based upon points of access and stream mile designations developed for major landmarks on the waterway and the location of waste sources.

Whenever time and opportunity permits, a reconnaissance survey of the area to be investigated should be undertaken. Certain judgments can be reached during the reconnaissance survey that will save much time and effort at a later date. A reconnaissance survey should provide the basis for determining the advantages and disadvantages of sampling by boat, as opposed to collecting samples from bridges and by wading, or by a car top or trailered boat that may be lowered into the water from several points of access along the waterway. The availability of boats for rental along the waterway and the availability of suitable access points for the types of samples to be collected should be ascertained during such a reconnaissance. Contacts may be made with local officials or local investigators, who may be encouraged to participate in some manner with the investigation. Arrangements should be made with landowners to cross private lands at times when samples are to be collected from the waterway, should this be a necessity.

Following the completion of a reconnaissance survey, and subject to modification during the course of the field sampling, decisions can be made on (1) types of samples necessary to meet the objective of the study (i.e., various physical, chemical, and biological samples), (2) sampling points for each of the selected types of samples, (3) periodicity of sampling and approximate time necessary for collection of a specific sample, and (4) approximate numbers of samples necessary to meet the objectives of the study.

The next aspect of study planning involves the details necessary to initiate the process of data collection. Decisions must be made on methods of sample handling between the time of collection and the time of analytical result, sample preservation, and transportation of samples to a base laboratory. Often biological samples may be preserved for examination at some future and more convenient time. Certain samples for chemical analysis also may be preserved for a short time until they can be analyzed at an appropriate laboratory where precision instruments are available. Sample collection containers must be obtained. The number of these will depend upon the relative number of samples to be collected during the investigation. Sampling equipment, data cards, notebooks, and all of the necessary paraphernalia associated with the collection, retention, and shipment of samples must be obtained and organized. Arrangements must be made to transport such equipment to the study site and to ensure that it is at hand when the field investigators arrive. Collecting and field analytical gear should be checked and rechecked to determine that no essential piece of equipment has been omitted from that necessary for the investigation and to determine that the equipment is operable and functions according to designed specifications.

If the study is some distance from a point of departure, a portion of the study planning involves the making of travel arrangements, room accommodations, transportation of samples and equipment to and from the sampling areas, and the arrangements for such items as transportation during the investigation, procurement of outboard motor gasoline, cartons or boxes for shipping collected samples, ice to keep certain samples cold if this is a prerequisite for analyses, and other considerations. Laboratories that will analyze collected samples should be alerted and given an estimate of the number and kinds of samples that will be submitted, the types of analyses required, how the samples will be shipped, and the approximate dates of arrival. The laboratory should also be advised of the dates their analytical results will be required to meet the investigator's deadline. Of significant importance to a field investigation is the development of a sound Quality Assurance Project Plan. The development of this plan will be discussed in Chapter 21.

A preliminary cost estimate can now be made of the investigation under consideration, and it may be that the first compromise of the initial plan will be necessary. The cost must be adjusted to the available budget. The compromise may be in a reduction in the number of sampling locations, in the types of analyses to be made, in the number of samples to be obtained from each sampling location, or in a combination of these factors. Realistically, the conceived ideal for a field investigation is seldom achieved because of resource limitation or an alteration in time schedule that must be imposed upon the study at some point in its course.

There are a number of sources of information concerning investigations or problems connected with water quality in waterways. One of the better sources is the state water pollution control or water resources agency. As would be expected, these agencies usually have the most complete collection of information and data on factors involved with water quality within a state. They have conducted surveys over a number of years and have received complaints and statements from citizens over a long period of time concerned with this subject. Other state agencies that may have important data include the State Health Department, which generally is responsible for supervising public water supplies; the State Fish and Game Department; the State Geological Survey, which cooperates with the U. S. Geological Survey in the stream gauging program; and the Public Service Commission, which usually has jurisdiction over dams and obstruction to navigation. In addition, interstate agencies such as the Interstate Commission on the Potomac River Basin, the Delaware River Basin Commission, and the Ohio River Valley Water Sanitation Commission usually have information similar to that in state files. Here, the information may be confined to a river system, rather than to a particular state boundary.

The U.S. EPA, with its 10 regional offices located in strategic cities throughout the United States, has a great deal of specific information on the waterways of the nation. The regional office associated with an investigation should be contacted for water quality information as it may pertain to a particular study. Federal river development agencies, such as the U.S. Corps of Engineers, the Bureau of Reclamation of the U.S. Department of the Interior, and the Tennessee Valley Authority are all fertile sources of information on streams for which they have responsibility. The U.S. Geological Survey operates stream gauging stations and reports daily stream discharges through-out the nation, usually in cooperation with the states. The U.S. Bureau of Sport Fisheries and Wildlife and the U.S. Marine Fisheries Service collect data on fish and fishing. Municipal water treatment plant operators have comprehensive records on the quality of water serving as their sources of raw water. Often these data include both chemical and biological constituents. The record of time for which these data have been collected extends through many years. Wastewater treatment plant operators often keep a log of the quality of their wastewater and may have data on stream water quality, both upstream and downstream from their discharge point.

SAMPLING LOCATIONS

Kittrell (1969) wrote that the ideal sampling station would be a cross section of a stream at which samples from all points on the cross section would yield the same concentrations of all constituents, and that a sample taken at any time would yield the same concentrations as one taken at any other time. The former occurs when vertical and lateral mixing of any upstream wastes or tributaries are complete at a sampling station. This is not uncommon. The latter occurs only if there is no variation in upstream waste discharges or there is complete mixing longitudinally of any variable waste discharge, and if there are no upstream variations in stream flow, time of water travel, temperature, biological activity, or other factors that contribute to variation in water quality. This situation never persists in nature for any appreciable period of time. Variations in water quality with time require that samples be collected at the proper frequencies and times of day to ensure results representative of the variations.

Usually, a series of sampling locations are selected on a stream to establish a course of pollution of water quality change throughout a given reach of river. When time-of-travel determinations can be made, a desirable interval for sampling locations is about one-half day time of travel for the first 3 days travel downstream from a source of waste and about 1 day throughout any remaining distance. On small streams that may be quite heavily polluted, the locations of longitudinal sampling locations should be at much closer intervals if one is to assess the damage of the waste load from an analyses of chemical constituents. Major points of water use, including recreational and water supply area, should be included in the sampling regimen.

Biological sampling locations to assess the reactions of benthos to stream water quality routinely should be located near the sampling locations selected for chemical and microbiological analyses to enhance the interpretation of water quality through the use of interrelated data. Sampling locations should be located upstream and downstream from suspected pollution sources, from major tributary streams, and at appropriate intervals throughout the stream reach under investigation. As a generality, the appropriate interval on a relatively large stream may be established as a distance of 5 miles during the initial investigative planning stages. On smaller streams, this distance would be considerably less. Many current discharge permits require a periodic assessment of water quality in the receiving water through the use of benthos and fish as indicators of water quality. In such cases, the fish population would need to be sampled upstream and downstream from the waste discharge and the benthos would need to be sampled upstream, downstream in the vicinity of the anticipated greatest impact, and at one or more locations farther downstream. The permit generally will specify the number of locations to be investigated.

Seldom is it necessary to sample at various depths in a stream because of incomplete vertical mixing. Sampling usually is either at 5 feet or mid-depth, whichever is lesser, except for certain biological samples, such as plankton, which may be sampled at a depth of about 1 foot, or bacteria, which usually are sampled just beneath the surface. Lateral mixing on a stream poses yet another problem. It is good practice to take samples at quarter points across the stream unless a predetermination of mixing has shown that a single sample at the midpoint of the main current is adequate.

One and preferably two upstream or control sampling locations should depict conditions unaffected by a pollution source or tributary. The nearest sampling point downstream from the pollution source or tributary should be located so that it leaves no doubt that conditions depicted by the sample can be related to the cause of any environmental change. The minimal number of downstream sampling locations from this point should be located in the most severe areas of active waste decomposition, downstream in an area depicting less severe conditions, near the upstream reach of stream recovery from pollution, near the downstream reach of such recovery zone, and lastly in the downstream reach that first shows no effect from the suspected pollution source. Precise locations will depend on the flow; the strength, volume, and type of pollution entering the stream; and the entrance of additional sources of pollution to complicate the definition of stream recovery.

When water in tributary streams is found to be polluted, or to influence water quality in a primary stream, these tributaries should be similarly investigated. The determination of the precise location of sampling areas can be aided through a cursory examination of the benthic fauna, which are excellent indicators, as a community, of the prevailing water quality.

A stream, especially a small stream, is usually composed of riffles and pools. These areas will vary in depth, velocity of flow, and types of substrata that form the stream bed. Because a biologist seeks to determine changes that occur in water quality, as depicted by aquatic organisms, and to relate the changes to particular sources, he or she must compare observations at a particular location within the stream reach that is unaffected by a suspected pollution source. To accomplish this, an effort should be made to collect samples from habitat types that are morphometrically similar. Riffle samples should be compared with riffle samples, and pool samples should be compared with pool samples. Both should be studied in a stream, where feasible, to determine the extent of each major environmental change produced. The biological investigator may need to choose a number of sampling locations, in addition to those selected for routine chemical or bacteriological sampling, to satisfactorily assess the extent of biological change.

Plankton samples usually are collected at one point within the sampling location, most commonly at midstream 1 to 2 feet below the water surface. Samples for bottom-associated organisms should be collected at a number of points on a transection line between the stream banks. Optimally, these samples should be collected at a minimum of five points across the stream: at the midpoint, two quarter points, and near zero water level with the banks. More than one sample may, at times, be collected from each point and retained separately. Realistically, the objectives of a particular survey and the number of locations at which bottom fauna are collected may dictate the number of samples from a particular location. Attached growths, such as slime or periphyton, may be sampled wherever they occur.

Within a lake or reservoir, a number of sampling sites may be chosen, depending upon the problem under investigation and the conditions to be studied. An investigation of the kinds and relative abundance of aquatic vegetation would naturally be limited to the littoral area. A mapping of aquatic plants often proves useful for future comparisons. Fish sampling also is often more profitable in shallow water areas, although gill nets set in the region of the thermocline and below may sample a fish population not usually observed in shallow water.

The use of transections in sampling a lake bottom is of particular value because there are changes in depth and because benthos concentration zones usually occur. Unless sampling is done systematically and at relatively close intervals along transections, especially those that extend across the zone between the aquatic plants and the upper extent of the hypolimnion, concentration zones may be missed entirely or inadequately represented. Maximum benthic productivity may occur in the profundal region. Because depth is an important factor in the distribution of bottom organisms, productivity is often compared on the basis of samples collected from similar depth zones, and a sufficient number of samples must be taken to make the data meaningful.

A circular lake basin should be sampled from several transections extending from shore to the deepest point of the basin. A long narrow basin is suitable for regularly spaced parallel transects that cross the basin perpendicular to the shore, beginning near the inlet and ending near the outlet. A large bay should be bisected by a transection originating near the shore and extending to the lake proper.

There are definite advantages in sampling the benthic population in winter beneath the ice cover in lakes. Samples can be collected at definite spaced intervals on a transection, and the exact location of sampling points can be determined. Also, collections in winter are at a time of peak benthic population, when emerging insects do not alter the benthic population.

Reservoirs located on a primary stream usually are long and narrow water bodies, with the widest portions occurring downstream. They are particularly suitable for the placement of imaginary transection lines that extend perpendicularly from one shore to the opposite shore. Sampling locations can be conveniently placed on these transections. In addition to the transections, samples should be obtained from areas designated for water use removals.

Estuaries combine the aspects of stream sampling with those of the more static lake environment. Water within the estuary is controlled by tides and the force of water discharged by a river. Particular constituents of water quality may remain localized in a given area for a considerable period of time before they are dispersed or carried out to sea. Thus, the flow characteristics of the water mass are extremely important in order to define water quality and prognosticate the effects of wastes discharged to it. The flowing water portion of an estuarine study should be attacked in a manner similar to that described for the stream environment. Sampling locations within the true estuary can be profitably developed along transection lines, or extended out into the estuary in two or more directions from a suspected point source of pollution. Whenever possible, samples should be collected from areas that represent the estuarine habitat unaffected by pollution, as well as areas that depict environmental changes produced by pollution.

SAMPLE ANALYSIS

Samples may be collected of the water, sediments, fish, benthos- or stream-bed associated organisms, plankton, periphyton or submersed attached community, or vascular aquatic plants. Sediment surface samples may be collected by any variety of dredge-type samplers that provide a small quantity of stream-bed or lake-bed surface sediments. To obtain a history of sediment deposition, or to allow selection of strata within the sediments, a core sampling devise is expedient. Much information can be obtained of a historical nature and can be related to the problem under investigation through chemical and biological examination of sediment cores.

Fish samples may be collected by nets, seines, poisons, electrofishing, or conventional fishing methods. Electrofishing is conducted by means of an alternating or direct electrical current applied to water that has a resistance different from the fish. This difference in resistance to pulsating direct current stimulates the swimming muscles for short periods of time, causing the fish to orient and be attracted to the positive electrode. An electrical field of sufficient potential to demobilize the fish is present near the positive electrode, but decreases in intensity with distance. After fish are identified, weighed, and measured, they may be returned to the water uninjured from the electrofishing experience.

Organisms associated with the stream bed are studied most often in the biological evaluation of water quality. If a discharge permit requirement addresses biological monitoring, generally it will require biological toxicity studies and an examination of the receiving water benthos. Benthic organisms are valuable to relate water quality because they are not equipped to move great distances through their own efforts and, thus, remain at fixed points to indicate tolerance of the organism community to the water quality. Because the life history of many of these organisms extends through 1 year or longer, their presence or absence is indicative of water quality within the past, as well as the present. Bottom-associated organisms are relatively easy to capture with conventional sampling equipment, and the amount of time and effort devoted to their capture and interpretation may not be as great as that required for other segments of the aquatic community.

An experienced investigator subconsciously asks three basic questions when in search of benthos in a waterway. These are

- Based upon a knowledge of preferred organism habitats, what bottom fauna should be expected at a particular sampling location?
- Specifically, where would one expect to find these creatures?
- What is the appropriate gear with which to capture them?

There are two commonly recognized methods of approach. One that is frequently used is a qualitative search; the other is a quantitative benthic sample.

The qualitative search for benthos should involve the collection of organisms from rocks, plants, submersed twigs or debris, or leaves of overhanging trees that become submersed and waterlogged. It should be mentioned that the latter also is a good habitat for snakes and wasps in some areas, which requires an investigator to beware of the hazards involved. It is often convenient to scrape and wash organisms from the above materials into a bucket or tub partially filled with water and then to pass this water through a standard 30-mesh sieve to concentrate and retain the organisms. The collected sample may be preserved for organism sorting and identification later. In a qualitative search, an investigator should search until a majority of the species have been collected that can tolerate the particular environment. Qualitative sampling determines the variety of species occupying a reach of waterway. Two convenient limiting sampling methods may be set on the sampling regimen. Presetting a time limit on the collector's effort at each sampling point with a minimum of 30 minutes and a maximum of an hour per sampling location may be helpful. Alternately, sampling in an area until new forms are encountered so infrequently that the "law of diminishing returns" dictates abandoning the sampling location may be used.

Quantitative benthic samples may be obtained through use of one of a variety of common dredge-type samplers that collect a given area of benthic materials. Drift nets may be suspended in flowing waters to capture invertebrates that have migrated into the water mass from the bottom substrates and are temporarily being transported by currents. Their principal uses have been to study migratory movements and to evaluate the effects of sublethal toxicants, especially insecticides, on the fauna. Before toxicants become lethal, the animals are weakened and cannot maintain their benthic position. Thus, they are swept away by the currents and carried into the nets. Artificial substrates also are successfully employed in studying bottom fauna in flowing water. The physical aspects of the sampling location dictate the type of equipment that may be most successfully used.

Samples collected for plankton analysis are most often similar to those collected for the analyses of chemical water quality. They may be collected with the aid of a Kemmerer sampler or a similar device that permits capture of a sample from a particular water strata.

Artificial substrates of the glass-slide holding variety may be employed in the capture of periphytic community growths. One week of submergence should be sufficient to establish a periphytic community in most sampling locations. Visible growths of aquatic fungi or attached algae may be qualitatively sampled by scraping the growths from the substrate where they occur.

Meaningful samples of littoral vegetation may be difficult to secure. Sampling often is not necessary, however. Usually it is sufficient to map, identify, and estimate the abundance of the principal components of the aquatic vegetation population.

Toxicity tests where organisms are exposed in the static or flow-through environment of undiluted or diluted wastewater for 96 hours or less to simulate acute exposure, or up to 7 or more days to simulate chronic exposure, are often used to indicate environmental conditions of existence. Sediment toxicity studies or ambient water toxicity tests may be employed. Various organisms are used as test organisms, but *Ceriodaphnia* is now in common usage for water toxicity tests. *In-situ* caged organisms, which are exposed at sampling locations for a period of 10 days or 2 weeks, often are helpful indicators of water quality.

Methods employed by states to determine water quality include studies and assessments related to macroinvertebrates, fishes, algae, periphyton, protozoa, primary productivity, sediment toxicity tests, fish flesh tainting, fish and mussel flesh analyses for bioaccumulated substances, caged organism toxicity, fish and invertebrate chronic toxicity tests, sediment analyses, and fish avoidance reactions. Thirty-three states conduct receiving water macroinvertebrate or fish assessments related either to special study pollution investigations or to provide trend monitoring determinations (U.S. EPA, 1987).

Because of a report deadline, limited personnel available, or particular permit conditions, the theory and practice of sampling location and sampling may not be the same. The objectives of a study may be met by investigating only benthic fauna and attached organisms in a stream, and these on only one occasion. Much can be learned from this minimal effort. An investigator should keep in mind that water quality effects from organic wastes, for example, will likely be at their worst during the warm weather low-flood period. However, when streams become covered with ice in northern climes during winter, another period with severe conditions of existence for benthic fauna occurs in late winter. The zone of active decomposition resulting from an organic waste source under these winter conditions will be transferred a considerable distance, perhaps as much as 50 mi, downstream under ice cover.

Investigators should be careful not to burden the sampling program with more than the kinds and numbers of samples and analyses that will be required to meet the stated objectives of a study. For example, little knowledge may be gained from only one or two series of plankton samples from a flowing stream. Because these organisms are carried by the currents, a given sample is representative of water quality at some undefined upstream point, rather than at the place where the sample was collected.

DATA EVALUATION

One who interprets data well continually tempers confidence with doubt. Doubt stimulates a search for new and different methods of confirmation for reassurance. Such reasonable doubt is directed toward each step in the investigative process:

- Were the sampling locations in the right areas to depict water quality within the stream or lake environments?
- Were a sufficient number of such locations used?
- Were the samples collected representative of water quality within the limits of available sampling technology?
- Were adequate measures employed to avoid contamination during the act of bacteriological sample collection?
- Were analyses completed for all water quality constituents vital to data interpretation?
- What would be the expected effects of the seasonal climate on the water quality sampled?

The correct expression in labeling data is vital to accurate data interpretation, as well as to later report preparation and to the reading of the report. The precise form of a water quality constituent must be accurately recorded. For example, phosphorus may be reported as the radical phosphate (PO_4), as elemental phosphorus (P), or, occasionally, and especially in soils literature, as phosphorus pentoxide (P_2O_5). The element has an atomic weight less than one-third the molecular weight of the phosphate radical. To convert from phosphate (PO_4) to phosphorus (P), the value must be multiplied by 0.326; to convert from phosphorus pentoxide (P_2O_5) to phosphorus (P), the value must be multiplied by 0.426. In addition, it frequently is not indicated whether the stated value is representative of total, soluble, or some other form of phosphate or phosphorus. The total to soluble phosphorus ratios in ambient water may vary from 2 to 17 or even 90, depending upon the particular water, season, aquatic plant populations, and probably other factors.

Data organization involves the least complex arrangement and display of the data that will aid in the interpretation of water quality and facilitate an understanding of conditions of existence within a waterway. Existing water quality standards and recorded water quality criteria are helpful benchmarks for data comparisons. Organization of data in some orderly form is a necessary first step in data interpretation.

REPORTING THE RESULTS

How many times have you received a letter, a set of instructions, or read a technical paper and had to call the author, or would have liked to call the author, to clarify a statement or find out what it was the author was trying to tell you? Reporting the findings of an investigation is at least equally as important as any other aspect of the investigation. A report represents the end product; it often is the only real contact between a field investigation, which may take considerable time, money, and effort, and the public or report recipient.

Good writing is systematic recording of organized thought; it involves a clear, concise, orderly presentation of an understandable message. Rarely in such writing is there more than one right word to express an idea exactly. A writer should search relentlessly to find that one right word to express a thought. Needless words always should be omitted.

When study objectives are crystallized, before the actual investigation commences, thoughts about the report should begin. The embryonic mental concept of the report should grow in organization and content as the investigation progresses, each phase of the study satisfying a part of an objective and fulfilling a part of the report.

A report is the end result of all the efforts expended on the investigation and should signal the beginning of any indicated remedial actions. A poor report frequently negates a meticulous field program; a good report often will ensure the success of a project. Any report should be planned as carefully as the field investigation. The report's style will depend on its intended purpose and the audience to which it is directed. It may be a record of the findings only. It may be an exposition of existing causes and effects and projections to other considerations that reasonably may occur. It may be a prediction of conditions to come and recommendations for actions to be taken. The report should be considered a document that records all essential facts in a study that will help meet the needs of those concerned, such as technical agencies and representatives of varied vested interests, as well as the public.

The first step in developing a good report is to prepare an outline. The outline should be considered carefully and should include all necessary items in logical continuity. An outline is a structural skeleton on which a good report may be built. It must have a beginning, a middle, and an end. It must avoid any omissions of necessary material. It will save much time in report writing.

A report's introduction should describe briefly the investigation and its location, the study objectives, the inclusive dates of the investigation, the authority for the study, and by whom the study was performed. The summary should briefly and concisely relate how the study was accomplished and what was found in the investigation. It should be as brief as possible and yet contain the essentials of the findings of fact. Stringent review and editing always should be employed. The summary should contain those particular facts that will be used to formulate the conclusions. The conclusions should be concise, positive, lucid statements that can be made from an evaluation of summarized data and other reported observations. Recommendations should be those conclusion-supported word combinations that will stimulate implementation of logical remedial actions to correct the concern that was the cause of instigating the study. The report's narrative and the data presented must support the conclusions.

Reading the manuscript aloud is a helpful adjunct to good report preparation. This procedure tends to accent the flaws in rhythm, as well as illogical approaches and conclusions.

The area description section should include a general area location map, as well as a specific map of the study reach showing sampling locations, principal populations centers, and principal waste sources. Insignificant streams, highway, railroads, towns that are not involved, symbols for types of land use, and similar features that are not pertinent to the investigation or to an understanding of the report by a reader should not clutter the base maps. However, any geographical feature that is mentioned in the text should be shown on the map.

It is the organization of data within the report where the ingenuity and imagination of the report writer will reap great rewards. Data first are organized in tables. Lengthy detailed tables should be placed in the report's appendix. When placed in a narrative, they detract from reading coherency. Easy-to-follow summary tables, prepared as a digest of the tabular data in the appendix, are helpful in the narrative to explain and substantiate discussions and conclusions. Graphs should be uncluttered, pertinent, and easy to follow. As an artist develops a painting with broad brush and bold strokes, the report's author should arrange graphs to portray essential information and should use them sparingly only to underscore principal points.

In developing a sentence or a paragraph, the who, what, why, when, where, and how questions must be answered at every opportunity. Answer these questions before a reader has an opportunity to think of them. Definite assertions should be made and noncommittal language avoided. The specific phrase should be chosen, rather than the general phrase, the definitive over the vague, the concrete rather than the abstract. Qualifying words should be avoided; without a quantitative bench mark they convey only an imprecise thought. Further, it is the writer's duty, not the reader's, to interpret the report's tabular and graphic materials. The narrative must contain a description and interpretation of the data presented in a report's tables.

What are the pitfalls in report writing? Is each sentence, clear, technically accurate, and devoid of a dual meaning? Do all tables support the narrative statements? Can a sentence be read to convey a meaning other than that obviously intended? Are any expressions redundant or unnecessarily vague? Are qualifying words overused, or are they supported by some quantitative bench marks? Are there obvious grammatical errors? Has sufficient information been provided for reader understanding? Have all acronyms been identified and are they used sparingly?

There are words that indirectly crease a reader's forehead. Frequently, a report will state that "Little data is available" when it is meant that "Few data are available." Quite often, a report will state that an agency "feels", which connotes a vague emotional conviction when a belief or consensus exists. Sometimes "varying data" is used incorrectly for "various data". The commonly used hyphenated expression "1988–1990" begs the question, did the writer mean a 2-year period to 1990, or a 3-year period through 1990?

Finally, a report should be checked for

1. Technical accuracy
2. Clarity and understandability
3. Dual meaning; is one meaning conveyed in one part of the report and another meaning in another part?
4. Format. Are the conclusions what they are meant to be rather than recommendations or summarizing statements?
5. Reference citations. Have all references been checked in the narrative against those cited in the references cited section to ensure that any reference appears both places, is accurate, and bears the correct date and spelling of the author's name?
6. Redundancies and repetition
7. Qualifying words. Have words such as *low*, *high*, *declining*, and *significant* been defined, or at least provided bench mark values for reader judgment?
8. Acronym definition
9. Grammatical errors

THE REPORT'S USERS

Often the investigations described in Chapters 6 and 7 will be made in compliance with an NPDES permit, as described in Chapter 5, in seeking a variance to an NPDES permit condition or a water quality standard, in association with litigation, to develop information for an Environmental Impact Statement, or for similar purposes. Where an investigation is completed because of a permit requirement or for some action related to a permit or water quality standard, appropriate state authorities will be the report's principal audience. The success of an effort will depend, in large measure, upon the findings of an investigation and the presentation of those findings in a report.

When an investigation shows degraded water quality downstream from a discharge, and all indications are that the cause of the degradation is the discharge, it generally will result in a requirement for a correction of the cause, or further investigation to determine the specific cause for corrective action. When there is no water quality degradation associated with a discharge, the investigation's report should strongly support a permittee's request for action.

States often conduct investigations of the type described in this chapter and in Chapter 7 as a means of assessing the quality of the state's waters. This type of an assessment is an ongoing and continuing process to maintain current information on water quality. Section 305(b) of the Clean Water Act mandates that states report biennially to the EPA on the quality of their waters.

REFERENCES CITED AND SELECTED READING

Bardach, J. 1966. *Downstream: A Natural History of the River from its Source to the Sea*. Grossett and Dunlap, New York.

Frey, D. G. 1963. *Limnology in North America*. University of Wisconsin Press, Madison.

Hutchinson, G. E. 1957. *A Treatise on Limnology*. John Wiley and Sons, New York.

Hynes, H. B. N. 1960. *The Biology of Polluted Waters*. Liverpool University Press, Liverpool.

Kittrell, F. W. 1969. "A Practical Guide to Water Quality Studies of Streams." U.S. Department of the Interior, Federal Water Pollution Control Administration, Washington, D.C.

Mackenthun, K. M. 1969. "The Practice of Water Pollution Biology." U.S. Department of the Interior. Federal Water Pollution Control Administration, Washington, D.C.

Ruttner, F. 1963. *Fundamentals of Limnology* (3rd ed.). University of Toronto Press, Toronto, Canada.

U.S. EPA. 1987. "Program Survey — Biological Toxicity Testing in the NPDES Permits Program." U.S. Environmental Protection Agency, Permits Division, Washington, D.C., August.

7 LAKES, RESERVOIRS, PONDS, AND WETLANDS

INTRODUCTION TO THE ECOSYSTEMS

A complex interaction of many physical, chemical, and biological factors, influenced by meteorological phenomena, occurs in the standing water environment. Lakes and reservoirs are well known by many people who live near their shores and enjoy the tranquil beauty and recreational activities they provide. Wetlands are less well known, but they are the nursery areas for life within lakes and for the estuaries in the coastal reaches. Lakes, reservoirs, and ponds are the settling basins of drainage areas via inflowing streams and rivers with their burden of pollution from the land. As a result, the potential productivity of a body of water is determined to a great extent by the natural fertility of the land through which the rivers flow, along with nutrient contributions that civilization abundantly provides. Along with providing a sanctuary and nursery for aquatic organisms, wetlands serve as natural filters removing nutrients, silt, and some pollutants from portions of the drainage basin and protect the lakes, rivers, and estuaries along which they are found.

The number of lakes or lake acres within the United States remains an unknown. Indeed, the definition of a lake is not precise. In a 1988 Report to Congress, the U.S. Environmental Protection Agency recorded that 40 states reported 131,615 lakes with a total acreage of 22,486,365 acres (U.S. EPA, 1990). The remaining states did not report information on this natural resource. In this same report, the most commonly reported cause of nonsupport of designated uses in lakes is nutrients, affecting 49% of impaired lake acres. Siltation and organic enrichment were other commonly cited causes of nonsupport, with each affecting 25% of impaired lake acres. Thirty percent of all lakes assessed for trophic status contained extremely enriched waters with high biological productivity.

Wetlands or marshes, swamps, bogs, and other frequently water saturated areas once covered over 200 million acres in the lower 48 states (U.S. EPA, 1990). In 1984, the U.S. Fish and Wildlife Service estimated that only 99 million acres remained. Wetland destruction was estimated to be continuing at the rate of 458,000 acres per year. The most notable causes of wetland losses are drainage, dredging and stream channelization, deposition of fill material, diking and damming, tilling for crop production, grazing by domestic animals, discharge of pollutants, mining, and alteration of wetland hydrology.

CONCEPTS OF THE STANDING WATER ENVIRONMENT

Nutrients are vital as a food supply for the ecosystem and dissolved oxygen is an essential component for aquatic life. Changes in the concentration of either of these factors will induce significant alterations in the complexity of life that inhabits the water. The pond or lake environment tends to be a vertical environment, as contrasted with the more horizontal environmental of the flowing stream. Because of this, factors such as temperature, light, dissolved oxygen, nutrients, inflows to and discharge from the system, and other considerations, such as density currents in reservoirs, assume roles of paramount importance and become controlling conditions to life in the vertical environment. These factors will be discussed in the pages that follow.

Temperature

The density of water as regulated by temperature induces a seasonal thermal stratification in many ponds and lakes. Water is the most dense when its temperature is 4°C (39.2°F). At this temperature, water weighs 62.4 lb/ft^3 or 8.345 lb/gal. Water becomes lighter or less dense as it either cools or warms. Because of this phenomenon, and in climates where seasons are distinct, lakes, ponds, and most reservoirs tend to stratify into three layers with different temperatures.

For a few weeks in the spring, water temperatures may be virtually the same from top to bottom in the standing water environment. Vertical water density is also homogeneous. During this time, it is possible for the wind to mix the water mass in the lake or pond, distributing nutrients and flocculant bottom solids from the deeper waters to the surface. Dissolved oxygen, which is abundant at this time, is also mixed, and tests will indicate that water quality characteristics are very similar from the surface to the bottom.

As atmospheric temperatures increase with the coming of summer, the surface waters become warmer. As they warm, they become lighter and rest over the cooler waters of greater density. Thus, a thermal stratification is formed for many months. In deep waters, three layers of various temperatures and densities are formed. The upper layer, or epilimnion, represents the more or less freely circulating waters of approximately uniform warm temperature. These waters come in contact with the atmosphere and generally are rich in dissolved oxygen, supporting a variety of fish, fish food organisms, algae, and rooted aquatic plants. The thickness of the epilimnion may vary from a few feet in shallow lakes to 40 feet or more in deeper lakes.

Near the bottom of the lake, a lower layer, or hypolimnion, represents the water region of uniform cold temperature. This may sometimes be referred to as the profundal region and represents a portion of the water body that is isolated from circulation with the upper waters. During stratification, this portion of the lake or pond is cut off from contact with the atmosphere and it receives no additional oxygen. When stratification first takes place, the water has the dissolved oxygen that it contained when it was a freely circulating mass of water. During stratification, however, it received a constant rain of dead algae, dead vascular plant particles, fecal pellets from fish and other aquatic organisms, occasional dead fish, and other organic materials to which it may be exposed. Because dissolved oxygen is not restored during stratification, it may be rapidly removed during the decomposition of organic materials, and its potential for supporting aquatic life becomes severely restricted or virtually eliminated.

The top and bottom water layers of approximately uniform temperatures are separated by a middle layer or thermocline. The thermocline is the region of rapid change in water temperature and is usually defined by a change of 1.8°F for each 3.28 ft, or 1 m, variance in depth. The thermocline represents a vertical temperature transition zone with the upper region representing warmer temperature conditions and the lower region representing cooler water conditions. The lower reaches of the thermocline may or may not contain dissolved oxygen during stratification, depending upon the organic enrichment of the water.

As atmospheric temperature cools and autumn approaches, the surface waters of a pond or lake also cool. The cooling process, with the corresponding increase in water density, increases the thickness of the epilimnion until the lake or pond becomes homothermous, and again, a period of complete water circulation aided by the wind begins. This phenomenon occurs from late September to December and depends upon the area and depth of the lake, its geographic location, and local climatological conditions. The period lasts until changes in density reestablish stratification, or until the lake is frozen over and a period of winter stratification follows.

Thus, the exchange of gases with those in the atmosphere is restricted during a greater part of the year for the entire lake environment. The water is saturated, or nearly so, with atmospheric gases in the spring and again in the fall. However, as soon as thermal stratification occurs, and lasting until the water again becomes homothermous, only the water of the epilimnion or upper portion has direct contact with the atmosphere. These conditions must be taken into account when planning a study of the standing water environment.

Water warms more rapidly and to a higher degree in the shallow areas near shore. Microscopic life, both plant and animal, accelerates first in standing crop in these areas following the cooler temperatures of winter and, if the food-supplying nutrients are abundant, localized plant nuisances may develop that could spread to other sectors of the water body. The factors that make wetlands the productive ecosystems that they are include shallow water, abundant light penetration, nutrients, and warm water.

The temperature gradient in reservoirs may be more complex than that found in ponds or lakes. A storage reservoir, often located at the headwaters of a stream, may have the characteristics of a lake because the water often is stored in the reservoir for a period of time extending for many months. Temperature gradients here are similar to those described for a lake. Main stream "run-of-the-river" reservoirs often have a small and fairly regular temperature gradient from top to bottom, however. In some situations, there may be a stream of inflowing cold water that tends to flow through the impoundment and is discharged by way of the penstock intake. This is termed a *density current*.

Reservoirs frequently have density currents that are caused by differences in temperature, differences in the concentration of electrolytes, such as carbonates, and differences in silt content. Density currents often extend from the inflowing area to the region of the penstock. In some instances, density currents have been detected from 60 to 80 ft below the surface. Density currents affect the fish populations, since game fish orient themselves both to the stratum of stagnant water caused by the density currents, as well as to the temperature range that suits them best. Often fish become trapped by a lack of oxygen within their chosen water.

Light

Another physical factor of significant importance in the standing water environment is that of light. Rooted, suspended, and floating aquatic plants require light for photosynthesis. Light penetration into water is exceedingly variable in different lakes. The principal factors affecting the depths of light penetration in natural waters include suspended microscopic plants and animals, suspended mineral particles such as mineral silts, stains that impart a color, foams, dense mats of floating and suspended debris, or a combination of these. The region in which light intensity is adequate for photosynthesis is often referred to as the *trophogenic zone*. This is a layer of water that contains 99% of the incident light reaching the surface. One percent generally is considered adequate for algal development; rooted aquatic plants require approximately 2.5% of the incident light for their development.

In winter, the presence of ice will limit light penetration. When snow covers the surface of the ice, the penetration is further reduced. It has been found that 7 in. of very clear ice permitted 84% light transmission, but only 22% of the light was transmitted through a similar thickness of cloudy ice. A 1 in. snow cover permitted only 7% light transmission through the ice and snow, and 2 in. of snow cover permitted only 1% light transmission. Without light, the plants die and instead of producing dissolved oxygen through photosynthesis, oxygen is used through the process of decomposition. Consequently, a fish mortality, known as *winter kill*, may result in shallow water bodies when the oxygen is reduced substantially. Mackenthun and McNabb (1961) found that less than 1% of light passed through 16 in. of ice covered by 2 in. of snow.

Dissolved Oxygen

Dissolved oxygen enters the water by absorption directly from the atmosphere or by plant photosynthesis. It is removed by the respiration of organisms and by the process of decomposition. Oxygen may be derived from the atmosphere through direct diffusion or by surface water agitation by wind and waves. Conversely, wind and waves may release dissolved oxygen under conditions of supersaturation. In photosynthesis, aquatic plants utilize carbon dioxide and liberate dissolved and free gaseous oxygen at times of supersaturation. Since energy is required in the form of light, photosynthesis is limited to the photic zone where light is sufficient to facilitate this process. During respiration and decomposition, animals and plants consume dissolved oxygen and liberate carbon dioxide at all depths where they occur. Because excreted and secreted products, dead animals, and plants sink, most of the decomposition takes place in the hypolimnion. Thus, during stratification, as discussed earlier, there is a gradual decrease of dissolved oxygen in this zone. After the dissolved oxygen is depleted, anaerobic decomposition continues with the evolution of methane and hydrogen sulfide gases.

Major Nutrients

Eutrophication now is a common term in our language. It is defined as the enrichment of waters by nutrients through either person-created or natural means. The fertilizing elements most responsible for lake or pond eutrophication are phosphorus(P) and nitrogen(N). Iron and certain "trace" elements are also important. Many organic wastes, such as sewage and effluents from sewage treatment plants, contain a generous amount of those nutrients necessary for algal development.

Lake eutrophication results in an increase in algal and aquatic weed nuisances, as well as midge larvae, whose adult stage has plagued people in many areas, including California, Wisconsin, and Florida. Dense algal growths form surface water scums and algal-littered beaches. Water may become foul smelling. Filter-clogging problems at municipal water installations can result from abundant suspended algae. When algal cells die, oxygen is used in decomposition, and fish kills have resulted. Rapid decomposition of dense algal scums, with associated organisms and debris, gives rise to odors and hydrogen sulfide gas, which creates strong local objections; in addition, the gas has stained the white lead paint on residences adjacent to the shore. Upon decomposition, certain forms of algae liberate toxic materials that have killed cows, birds, and other animals that have consumed the water during these dense algal growth conditions.

Evidence indicates that (1) high phosphorus concentrations are associated with accelerated eutrophication of waters, when other growth promoting factors are present; (2) aquatic plant problems develop in reservoirs or other standing waters at phosphorus values lower than those critical in flowing streams; (3) reservoirs and other standing waters collect phosphates from influent streams and store a portion of them within consolidated sediments; and (4) phosphorus concentrations critical to noxious plant growths vary and may produce such growths in one geographical area, but not in another.

Once nutrients are combined within the ecosystem of the receiving waters, their removal is tedious and expensive; removal must be compared to inflowing quantities to evaluate accomplishment. In a lake, reservoir, or pond, phosphorus is removed naturally only by outflow, by insects that hatch and fly out of the drainage basin, by harvesting an aquatic crop, such as fish, and by combination with consolidated bottom sediments where phosphorus is not easily released. Even should adequate harvesting methods be available, the expected standing crop of algae may exceed 2 tons/acre and contain only about 1.5 lb of phosphorus. Similarly, submerged aquatic plants could approach at least 7 tons/acre on a wet weight basis and contain 3.2 lb/acre of phosphorus. Probably only half of the standing crop of submerged aquatic plants can be considered harvestable. The harvestable fish population of perhaps 500 lb from 3 acres of water would contain only 1 lb of phosphorus.

Dredging has often been suggested as a means of removing the storehouse of nutrients contained within the lake bed sediments. These sediments usually are rich in nitrogen and phosphorus, for they represent the accumulation of years of settled organic materials. Some of these nutrients are recirculated within the water mass and furnish food for a new crop of organic growth.

Mackenthun (1968) published a considered judgment, suggesting that to prevent biological nuisances, total phosphorus should not exceed 100 µg/l P at any point within the flowing stream, nor should 50 µg/l P be exceeded where waters enter a lake, reservoir, or other standing water body. Those waters now containing less phosphorus should not be allowed to become degraded.

To properly assess a nutrient problem, consideration should be given all of those sources that may contribute nutrients to the watercourse. A partial list would include the nutrients in sewage effluents, septic drain fields, industrial wastes, land drainage applied fertilizers, precipitation, urban runoff, soils, and that which may be released from bottom sediments and from decomposing plankton. Nutrients contributed by transient ducks, falling tree leaves, and groundwater may be important additions to the nutrient budget. Flow measurements are paramount in a study to quantitatively assess the respective amounts contributed by various sources during different seasons and at different flow characteristics. In the receiving lake or stream, the quantity of nutrients contained by the standing crops or algae, aquatic vascular plants, fish, and other aquatic organisms are important considerations. A knowledge of those nutrients that annually are harvested through the fish catch, or that may be removed from the system through the emergence of insects, will contribute to an understanding of the nutrient budget.

Phosphorus occurs naturally in rocks and soils, primarily as calcium phosphate, $Ca_3(PO_4)_2$. Since the phosphate rock is sparingly soluble, leaching brings into solution small amounts of phosphorus. In natural waters, the element exists as secondary calcium phosphate, $CaHPO_4$, its form being determined by the pH of the water. The low concentration of phosphorus available from geologic sources is further reduced by biological systems, since the element is necessary for all life processes. Thus, in waters remote from human influence, phosphorus exists in very low concentrations as the secondary phosphate ion and as organic phosphorus incorporated into biomass. Seasonal changes in plant and animal production result in cyclic utilization and the release of phosphorus to the water.

Nitrogen comes into solution in water as a result of nitrogen fixation from the air, ammonia from rain-out, organic nitrogen from decomposing plants and animals, and land drainage. In water solution, the element exists as organic nitrogen, ammonium ion,

Table 7-1. Potential Pounds of Nutrients Contributed to Aquatic Ecosystems [from Mackenthun et al., 1964]

Nutrient Source	Basic Reference	Contribution N	P
Treated domestic contribution in sewage	Bush and Mulford, 1954	6–12* (9lb/yr)	2–4 (3lb/yr)
	Metzler et al., 1958	6** lb/yr	2.25 lb/yr
Domestic Duck	Sanderson, 1953	2.1 lb/yr	0.9 lb/yr
Wild Duck	Paloumpis and Starrett, 1960	1.0 lb/yr	0.45 lb/yr
Runoff - 20 % slope corn	Eck et al., 1957	38 lb/A/yr	1.8 lb/A/yr
Runoff - 8 % slope corn	Eck et al., 1957	18 lb/A/yr	0.5 lb/A/yr
Surface irrigation diversified farming	Sylvester, 1961	2.5–24.0 lb/A/yr	0.9–3.9 lb/A/yr
Rainwater	Hutchinson, 1957	5.5 lb/A	
Killed algae (summer maximum)	Birge and Juday, 1922	24 lb/yr	2.4 lb/A
Killed submerged plants	Rickett, 1922	32 lb/A	3.2 lb/A
Killed fish	Beard, 1926	50 lb/A	4 lb/ton

*   Normal range of domestic sewage for 15 California communities was given as 20 to 40   mg/1 N and PO_4.

**   The concentration in treated water was subtracted from the concentration in sewage to obtain domestic contribution.

nitrite ion, and nitrate ion. In the familiar nitrogen cycle, the proteinaceous material is decomposed by bacterial action, resulting in inorganic ions, which, in turn, are incorporated into new cell material. The relative concentrations of the various forms of nitrogen depend upon the biological systems involved, as influenced by environmental conditions.

When untreated domestic sewage is discharged to a watercourse, organic nitrogen (proteins) and ammonia are the principal nitrogen constituents. In the water, nitrifying organisms decompose the organic materials and oxidize the ammonia to nitrite and nitrate. Since the nitrite ion is a transient form, it usually is present in very low concentrations, if detectable at all. Treated sewage has undergone partial oxidation in the treatment process. Therefore, the nitrite and nitrate forms are increased in well-treated sewage, while the organic nitrogen and ammonia are reduced.

Potential contributing sources of nitrogen and phosphorus to the aquatic environment have been indicated in the literature (Table 7-1).

Although generally it is conceded that abundant major nutrients in the form of available nitrogen and phosphorus are important and necessary components of an environment in which excessive aquatic growths arise, algal production is influenced by many additional factors. Vitamins, trace metals, hormones and auxins, extracellular metabolites, autointoxicants, viruses, as well as predation and grazing by aquatic animals are factors that stimulate or reduce algal growths. Some of these may be of equal importance to the major nutrients in influencing nuisance algal bloom production.

Effects of Water Inflows and Discharges

The standing water environment receives its inflowing water from tributary streams, general land runoff, seepage from adjacent areas, and springs. The standing water basin is thus the first-line receptacle for those materials that may be washed or drained from the lands within the drainage basin, for those substances that are discharged as wastewater, and for those materials that may enter the water environment from the atmosphere and other sources. Those materials that are discharged from the pond, lake, or other standing water bodies into downstream waterways eventually reach the estuaries or the oceanic environment, which are the ultimate receptacles for the waste materials from all of the land.

The discharge from a lake or reservoir has an effect on downstream water quality. Water flowing from a natural lake should be expected to be of a quality similar to that of the water in the uppermost stratum of the lake. However, when water in a free-flowing stream is impounded in a large storage reservoir, marked changes are produced in the physical, chemical, and mineral quality of the water. In reservoirs operating for flood control and power production, discharge releases often are reduced over weekends and other periods of off-peak power loads. Discharges, likewise, may be increased substantially during the weekdays. The penstock usually is located deep within the reservoir, and the temperature of the water discharged to the receiving stream may be substantially lower than the natural receiving water temperature. Discharged water also may be low in dissolved oxygen concentration and release odors of hydrogen sulfide from decaying organic materials in the deeper portions of the reservoir.

The ecology of the receiving stream is drastically altered as a result of a low-level discharge characterized by low temperature and reduced dissolved oxygen concentrations. The warm-water fish habitat may be destroyed. A cold-water fish habitat may be created, providing dissolved oxygen is sufficient. Bottom fauna may be changed in the receiving waterway from an assemblage of stoneflies and hellgrammites to an assortment of cold-water species, such as immature midges, black flies, caddisflies, and scuds. Such a substantial alteration of the physical and chemical characteristics of the receiving stream can only produce a drastic change in the composition of the biota inhabiting the receiving water environment.

WETLANDS

Wetlands support a prevalence of vegetation typically adapted for life in a saturated soil condition. Wetlands are among the most productive natural ecosystems in the world. They are critical to the survival of a wide variety of animals and plants. They provide food and habitat, including that necessary for spawning and growth for fish and wildlife, improvement in water quality, flood protection, erosion control, natural products for human use, and opportunities for a variety of recreation and aesthetic enjoyment. A number of rare and endangered species depend upon wetlands for survival.

Once regarded as wastelands and an economic burden, wetlands were destroyed at random until the nation's wetlands resource was diminished by more than one half. Now recognized as among the most productive ecosystems and as essential to the survival of many fish and other species, they are being protected. Protection began after the enactment of the 1972 Clean Water Act, which mandated a permit for the discharge of dredged or fill materials into the waters of the United States. The most extensive wetlands losses have occurred in Louisiana, Mississippi, North Carolina, the Dakotas, Nebraska, Florida, and Texas.

Coastal wetlands are found along the Atlantic, Pacific, Alaskan, and Gulf coasts. They are closely linked to the nation's estuaries, where seawater mixes with fresh-water to form an environment of varying salinities. Inland wetlands occur throughout the nation's interior. They are most common on floodplains along rivers and streams, in isolated depressions surrounded by dry land, and along the margins of lakes and ponds. Inland wetlands include marshes and wet meadows dominated by grasses and herbs, shrub swamps, and wooded swamps dominated by trees, such as bottomland hardwood forests along floodplains.

Artificially created wetlands have shown promising potential as treatment areas for acid-mine drainage and for organic wastes. They remove nutrients, as well as provide environmental enhancement, especially wildlife areas. Phosphorus removals have attained 90%, ammonia nitrogen removals of 95% and biochemical oxygen demand 60%. Although wetlands are efficient in stabilizing organic wastes and removing suspended solids, they are affected by toxic and hazardous wastes in a manner similar to surface waters. Wetlands are particularly vulnerable because they are inhabited by the young of aquatic life. Persistent, bioaccumulative, toxic, organic chemicals head the list as destructive forces in this type of ecosystem. The food web in wetlands extends from small invertebrates through fish to predator animals and humans. There is a broad problem with contamination of wetlands. Irrigation return flows have introduced high toxic selenium levels in some western areas that have resulted in deformed ducks in refuges. Boron, heavy metals, and PCBs have been toxic pollution problems in many areas.

Agricultural drainage of wetlands was responsible for 87% of wetland losses between the mid-1950s and mid-1970s. Urban and other development accounted for the remaining 13% of the losses. Irrigation return flows in the West, as well as point and nonpoint source pollutant discharges, are responsible for the chemical pollutant concerns. Inland freshwater wetlands constitute 95% of the remaining wetland resource in the United States and 97% of the area lost each year to development. Agricultural activities had the greatest negative impact on forested wetlands, inland marshes, and wet meadows. Some of the agricultural activities are not regulated under the Clean Water Act Section 404 program that protects wetlands and is discussed in the next chapter. However, the 1985 Farm Bill contains provisions to reduce agricultural wetland destruction. It contains a "swampbuster" provision that denies a farmer's eligibility for all U.S. Department of Agriculture programs or subsidies if wetlands are converted to cropland or if wetlands are drained or planted to crops. In October of 1990, the Corps of Engineers declared that wetlands that had been drained for agriculture prior to 1985 no longer would be considered as wetlands subject to regulation by the Corps. A new wetland definition by EPA and the White House in the summer of 1991 substantially reduced the amount of wetlands in the U.S.

BIOTIC CONSIDERATIONS

Organisms respond to the aquatic environment by producing an aquatic crop that is suited best for the particular environment in which they exist. Organisms respond also to changes that take place within their environment with shifts in species dominance in the aquatic community and sometimes with dramatic changes in the population numbers of a single species or a group of species with similar habitat requirements. Because of this response, and because the response may be less evenly distributed in the standing water environment as compared to the flowing water environment, the quality of water at selected sampling locations will be influenced to a great extent by the standing crop of organisms in the vicinity of the sampling area. The consideration of this impact, therefore, becomes an important one in selecting the sampling site.

Daily climate may influence planktonic algal populations. Algae tend to rise to the surface during hot humid days and disperse in greater depths during rain storms or turbulent water conditions. Several successive dark or cloudy days may be sufficient to kill a portion of a dense algal population, and subsequent decomposition may bring about a localized dissolved oxygen reduction or oxygen depletion in a water stratum and may result in a fish kill from suffocation.

It is difficult to estimate the standing algal or plankton crop of a particular water body because of the diverse horizontal and vertical distribution of these organisms and their transportation by water movement. Early work on Lake Mendota, Wisconsin, indicated that, on a dry weight basis, the spring plankton crop was greatest and averaged 98 lb/acre in winter compared to 360 lb/acre in spring (Table 7-2). The dry weight of an algal mass is approximately 10% of its wet weight.

In Lake Sebasticook, Maine, the senior author found the wet-weight algal standing crop to reach a maximum of 2260 lb/acre on August 1, 1965. The filamentous alga, *Cladophora*, has been found to attain a population of 1 ton or more per acre.

In early studies in Wisconsin on submersed aquatic plant populations, it was found that the 1–3 meter zone contained the greatest density of plants, with lesser densities found both shoreward and lakeward. The population density averaged about 7 tons wet weight and 1800 lb dry weight per acre (Table 7-2). Other studies have indicated that various aquatic plant species have a substantially different population density; coontail populations have been found to approach 2500 lb/acre on a dry weight basis, whereas sago pondweed attained a population of 1700 lb/acre and duckweed, 240 lb/acre.

Bottom-associated organisms populations vary quantitatively and qualitatively with the seasons of the year and from year to year in the same lake. The population is

**Table 7-2. Lake Standing Crops with Tissue Nitrogen
and Phosphorous Content**

Constituent	Standing Crop (lbs/A)		%N	%P	Reference
	Wet	Dry			
Phytoplankton	1000–3600	100–360	6.8	0.69	Birge and Juday, 1922
			6.8	0.69	Gerloff and Skoog, 1954
			6.1	0.64	Mackenthun et al., 1968
Attached Algae	2,000	200			Neil, 1958
			2.8	0.14	Birge and Juday, 1922
Vascular Plants	14,000	1,800			Rickett, 1922, 1924
			1.8	0.18	Harper and Daniel, 1939
Myriophyllum			3.2	0.52	Birge and Juday, 1922
Bottom Organisms					
Midge Larvae	200–400	40–80			Dineen, 1953; Moyle, 1940
Chironomus			7.4	0.9	Borutsky, 1939
Fish	150–600				Swingle, 1950
			2.5	0.2	Beard, 1926
			2.8	0.18– 0.49	Borgstrom, 1961

not distributed evenly over the floor in any lake, but varies with depth and during different seasons. Investigators have found a zone of concentration of the organisms that shifts up and down the slope of the lake floor with seasonal changes.

Populations of bottom-associated organisms have been found to vary from 60 lb/acre on a wet-weight basis to 400 lb/acre in the Mississippi River system where no aquatic vegetation was associated. Where submersed plants were present in the Mississippi River areas, population densities as great as 1100 lb/acre were found, and one early study in New York indicated 3500 lb of such organisms in association with a *Chara* bed. Aquatic plants provide living space, food, and shelter for the invertebrates, and the invertebrates in turn tend to select a particular aquatic plant with leaves that are finely branched and compact. Coontail and water milfoil rank extremely high as being the most productive harbor for fish food organisms because of their finely divided and very compact leaves.

Standing crops of fish have been found to vary from 75 lb/acre on a wet-weight basis to more than 1000 lb/acre in the black soil ponds in the floodplains of central Illinois.

Earlier, mention was made of the nutrient-retaining capacity of wetlands. A lake or reservoir usually retains a portion, and sometimes a substantial portion, of those nutrients that it received from its various sources (Table 7-3). Nutrients are tied up at least temporarily within the collective biomass of the system, but retention of nutrients principally is within consolidated sediments. The amount or percentage of the nutrients that may be retained is variable and will depend upon (1) the nutrient loading to the lake

Table 7-3. Lake Nutrient Loadings and Nutrient Percentages Retained

Lake	State	Nitrogen (N) Loading lb/yr/A	Retention (%)	Phosphorus (P) Loading lb/yr/A	Retention (%)	Reference
Washington	Wash.	280	—	12	—	Anderson, 1961
Mendota	Wis.	20[1]	—	0.6[2]	—	Anon., 1949
Monona	Wis.	81[1]	48–70	7.5[2]	64–88	Lackey and Sawyer, 1945
Waubesa	Wis.	435[1]	50–64	62.8[2]	-26–25	Do
Kegonsa	Wis.	162[1]	44–61	35.9[2]	-21–12	Do
Tahoe	Calif.	2	89	0.4	93	Ludwig et al., 1964
Koshkonong	Wis.	90	80	40	30–70	Mackenthun, unpubl.
Green	Wash.	—	—	4.8	55	Sylvester and Anderson, 1964
Geist	Ind.	440[1]	44	28	25	F.W.P.C.A. Data
Sebasticook	Maine	—	—	2	48	Do
Ross R. Barnett	Miss.	—	—	32	—	Do

[1] Inorganic nitrogen only.
[2] Soluble phosphorus only.

or reservoir, (2) the volume of the euphotic zone, (3) the extent of biological activity, (4) the detention time within the basin or the time available for biological activity, and (5) the level of the penstock or the level of discharge from the lake.

A system with a near-surface discharge and a long retention time, which may extend into many years, such as Lake Erie, will retain the greatest amount of nutrients that enter the standing water system.

SAMPLING CONSIDERATIONS

The standing water environment adds new dimensions to sampling considerations. Generally, the horizontal dimension is increased over that of flowing water, and a vertical dimension is added to the sampling regimen. Lakes, reservoirs, and ponds serve as retention basins for some of the pollutants they receive. They also serve as reactors to use some of the inflowing materials in the production of increased biomass, as well as recycling basins where nutrients and some other constituents are recycled among the various biomasses and the lake or reservoir sediments. Those materials not retained by the basin are discharged downstream.

Thus, an effective sampling program for the standing water environment must provide information on a number of variable environmental factors. The sampling program must (1) isolate contributing impact sources in the upstream drainage basin, (2) determine the relative impact of each upstream pollutant source, (3) characterize the water quality within the standing water environment, and (4) determine the impact of the discharge of the lake, reservoir, or pond on downstream receiving waters.

Upstream Sources that Impact

Identification of pollution sources within the drainage basin includes a determination of the characteristics and volumes of wastewater discharges from municipalities and industries. If a thorough investigation of the wastewater components cannot be accomplished within the constraints of the study plan, the type of industry and its manufactured products, along with the number of persons connected to the municipal sewerage system, would be useful information in interpreting the data collected from the field investigation. Pertinent data on both municipal and industrial waste discharges to a particular drainage basin should be in the files of the state water pollution control agency.

Each upstream source of potential impact, or each segment of waterway containing more than one potential impacting source, may be a separate investigative entity. Areas that provide nonpoint source pollutants or land drainage must be approached as a contributing source of pollutants. Significant tributary streams to the system are potential sources to the system.

For each significant potential pollution source to the standing water system, a sampling and analyses regimen must provide information on water quality constituents that are pollutants of concern, as well as the relative quantities of such pollutants. To provide this information, samples are collected upstream from the potential source to provide background information and at one or more locations downstream from the source. The number of locations downstream will depend upon the relative distance that a source is separated from another downstream source or from the lake or reservoir being investigated. If such separation is in excess of 5 mi, an additional sampling location should be established. Regardless of the above, sampling must include the flowing water reach just before it enters the standing water environment. When discharges to the receiving water are involved, these effluents should be characterized in terms of the kinds and quantities of pollution constituents discharged.

When quantitative stream flow information can be obtained, stream flows should be determined at each of the sampling locations to allow quantitative calculations of the pollutant loads. Flow and waste constituent information should be available for each permitted discharge to the system in the Discharge Monitoring Reports that are filed routinely as a requirement of the discharge permit. Flow information should be obtained for the significant tributary flows to the standing water system.

The number of individual samples required at a sampling location will depend upon the relative size of the flowing water environment being sampled. A sufficient number of samples must be obtained to characterize the water environment at the location being sampled. When flowing water areas are adequately mixed, sample collection need not be extensive, as discussed in the previous chapter.

When eutrophication is of concern in the investigation, samples should be analyzed for organic nitrogen, ammonia nitrogen, nitrate and nitrite nitrogen, total phosphorus, and dissolved phosphorus. Analyses for other pollutants will depend upon the potential pollutant constituents from a contributing source of impact.

Thus, the lake, reservoir, or pond now has been isolated through a sampling program so that information is available on pollution sources contributing to the system. It may be possible to describe the relative contributions of individual point sources and the relative pollutant contribution of nonpoint sources. The significant tributaries discharging to the standing water environment and the downstream discharge from the lake or reservoir have been examined in a manner similar to that for the inflowing tributaries. The perimeter of the lake or reservoir should be examined for potential contributions of septic tank drain fields or other pollution sources discharging directly or indirectly to the system. Remaining for investigation is the complex ecosystem of the standing water environment.

Lake, Reservoir, or Pond

Whenever possible a contour map of the pond or lake basin will be of tremendous advantage to the investigators. When such a contour map is not available, one should be constructed for the waterway in question because the location of sampling points and the types of samples to be collected depend, to a large extent on the contour basin. A contour map provides also for the calculation of the volume of water within a particular depth stratum. This is important in ascertaining the volume that may be representative of a particular set of conditions found through sampling.

Physical information that will serve as essential background material for a lake investigation includes the following: area, mean depth, maximum depth, area of depth zones, volume of depth strata, shore length, shore development, littoral slope, number of islands, area of islands, shore length of islands, drainage area, rate of runoff, average inflow to the receiving pond or lake, average outflow, detention time within the pond, water level, and water level fluctuations.

The number of sampling locations will depend upon the relative size and configuration of the lake or reservoir. Without doubt, one location should be in the deepest portion. Other locations should involve major bays, as well as the mid-lake area if this area is not included in the deepest portion location.

Because of water density and stratification during summer and winter, sampling should be at vertical intervals sufficient to characterize water quality in the epilimnion, thermocline, and hypolimnion. Often it is desirable to calculate the quantity of a chemical constituent within appropriate contour segments of the basin. This may entail additional sampling. Generally, samples at a given depth from various locations within the standing water body are comparable and may be used to record or calculate constituent information for a particular water stratum.

A temperature and dissolved oxygen profile, top to bottom, should be developed, especially for the deepest portion of the lake or reservoir. If eutrophication is of concern, the nutrient analytical series should be examined at different sampling depths. Nutrients may be concentrated in the profundal region during stratification. As a minimum, two vertical samples should be collected for nutrient analyses in the epilimnion, one in the thermocline and perhaps three in the hypolimnion. One of the latter three should be about 5 ft from the lake or reservoir bottom.

Other water quality constituents may be required analyses to develop information for a particular problem. At the times of the spring and fall water mixing periods, the dissolved constituents in the bottom waters will be circulated through the water mass to impact the entire system.

Benthic sediments should be examined on transection lines to determine concentrations of important chemical constituents that may be released to the superimposed water. Sometimes it is important to have information on the characteristics of the sediments themselves. Sediment are best collected with a device that permits a core of the materials to be extracted, from which identifiable segments may be examined for pollen, diatom skeletons, or chitinized remains of cladocerans or midges to gain a historical perspective of sediment deposition. Sediment cores also may be analyzed for selected chemical constituents. Generally, carbon and nitrogen, and often phosphorus, are determined. The carbon, nitrogen, and phosphorus contents and their respective ratios are important values to aid in the characterization of sediment and to calculate the amount of major nutrients contained within a stratum of sediment. From this information, it should be possible to estimate the relative return of nutrients to the water mass when nutrients may be released.

Rooted aquatic plants in the littoral zone should be mapped with the predominant species identified and the relative abundance indicated. Algae and other planktonic forms should be sampled vertically within the water column to record predominant species and to ascertain the relative abundance. Benthos should be sampled on transects that will represent major portions of the lake or reservoir, and will include zones of benthic concentration. Fish populations, which generally represent the pinnacle of the aquatic food web, should be sampled to identify principal species present and to determine their relative condition. The resident duck population, if appropriate, should be estimated, and the pollution contribution from the bird population should be estimated. Aquatic organisms are the indicators of water quality. The health and well-being of the resident aquatic community reflects the health and well-being of the lake or reservoir environment.

Wetlands

There is not an abundant history upon which to base a sampling regimen for wetlands. Currently there is insufficient monitoring in wetlands to understand their environmental complexities. Satisfactory monitoring indicators to represent biological integrity need to be developed. The principles of sampling would remain the same as for lake and stream systems. A sampling location should represent a defined segment of the universe under investigation. Analyses performed at such a location should identify the kinds and amounts of constituents that would be expected to impact the universe under investigation.

REFERENCES CITED AND SELECTED READING

Anderson, G. C. 1961. "Recent Changes in the Tropic Nature of Lake Washington — A Review. Algae and Metropolitan Wastes," U.S. Public Health Service, SEC TR W61-3, 27–33.

Anon. 1949. "Report on Lake Mendota Studies Concerning Conditions Contributing to Occurrence of Aquatic Nuisances 1945–1947." Wis. Committee on Water Poll., Madison, 19 pp. (Mimeo).

Anon. 1989. "Federal Manual for Identifying and Delineating Jurisdictional Wetlands. An Interagency Cooperation Publication." U.S. Army Corps of Engineers, U.S. Environmental Protection Agency, U.S. Fish and Wildlife Service, and USDA Soil Conservation Service.

Beard, H. R. 1926. "Nutritive Value of Fish and Shellfish." Report, U.S. Commissioner of Fisheries for 1925, 501–552.

Birge, E. A. and C. Juday. 1922. The Inland Lakes of Wisconsin. The Plankton. I. Its Quantity Chemical Composition. *Wis. Geol. Natural History* Bull. No. 64, Scientific Series No. 13, 1–222.

Borgstrom, G. (Ed.) 1961. *Fish as Food.* Academic Press, New York.

Borutsky, E. V. 1939. "Dynamics of the Total Benthic Biomass in the Profundal of Lake Beloie." Proc. Kossino Limn. Sta. of the Hydrometeorological Service, U.S.S.R. 22:196–218. Trans. by M. Ochynnk, edited by R. C. Ball and F. F. Hooper.

Bush, A .F. and S. F. Mulford. 1954. "Studies of Waste Water Reclamation and Utilization." Calif. S.F. State Water Poll. Control Bd., Sacramento, Publication No. 9.

Corps Of Engineers. 1987. "Wetlands Evaluation Technique. Volume II Methodology." U.S. Army Corps of Engineers, Waterways Experiment Station, Vicksburg, MS.

Dineen, C. F. 1953. An Ecological Study of a Minnesota Pond. *Am. Midland Naturalist* 50(2):349–356.

Eck, P., M. L. Jackson, et al. 1957. "Runoff Analysis as a Measure of Erosion Losses and Potential Discharge of Minerals and Organic Matter into Lakes and Streams." Summary report, Lakes Investigation, University of Wisconsin, Madison, 13 pp. (Mimeo.).

Gerloff, F. C. and F. Skoog. 1954. Cell Content of Nitrogen and Phosphorus as a Measure of their Availability for Growth of *Microcystis aeruginosa. Ecology* 35(3):348–353.

Hammer, D. A. 1989. *Constructed Wetlands for Wastewater Treatment.* Lewis Publishers, Inc. Chelsea, MI.

Harper, H. J. and H. R. Daniel. 1939. Chemical Composition of Certain Aquatic Plants. *Bot. Gaz*. 96:186.

Hutchinson, G. E. 1957. *A Treatise on Limnology*. John Wiley and Sons, New York.

Lackey, J. B. and C. N. Sawyer. 1945. Plankton Productivity of Certain Southeastern Wisconsin Lakes as Related to Fertilization. I. Surveys. *Sew. Works. J.* 17(3):573–585.

Ludwig, H. F., E. Kazmierczak, and R. C. Carter. 1964. Waste Disposal and the Future of Lake Tahoe. *J. Sanit. Eng. Div., Proc. Am. Soc. Civil Engr*. 90(SA3):Paper 3947–:27–51.

Mackenthun, K. M. 1968. The Phosphorus Problem. *J. Am. Water Works Assoc.* 60(9):1047–1054.

Mackenthun, K.M., L. E. Keup, and R. K. Steward. 1968. Nutrients and Algae in Lake Sebaticook, Maine. *J. Water Poll. Control Fed*.40(2):R72–R81.

Mackenthun, K. M., and C. D. McNabb. 1961. Stabilization Pond Studies in Wisconsin. *J. Water Poll. Control Fed*. 33(12):1234–1251.

Metzler, D. F., et al. 1958. Emergency Use of Reclaimed Water for Potable Supply at Chanute, Kansas. *J. Am. Water Works Assoc*. 50(8):1021.

Moyle, J. B. 1940. A Biological Survey of the Upper Mississippi River System (in Minnesota). *Minn. Dept. Cons. Fish. Inv*. Report No. 10, 69 pp.

Neil, J. H. 1958. "Nature of Growth in a Report on Algae, *Cladophora*." Report of Ontario Water Resources Commission, 3–7.

Paloumpis, A. A. and W. C. Starrett. 1960. An Ecological Study of Benthic Organisms in Three Illinois River Flood Plain Lakes. *Am. Midland Naturalist* 64(2):406.

Rickett, H. W. 1922. A Quantitative Study of the Larger Aquatic Plants of Lake Mendota. *Trans. Wis. Acad. Sci., Arts Lett.* 20:501–522.

Rickett, H. W. 1924. A Quantitative Study of the Larger Aquatic Plants of Green Lake, Wisconsin. *Trans. Wis. Acad. Sci., Arts and Lett*. 21:381–414.

Sanderson, W. W. 1953. "Studies of the Character and Treatment of Wastes from Duck Farms." Proc. 8th Ind. Waste Conf., Purdue Univ. Ext. Ser., 83:170–176.

Swingle, H. W. 1950. "Relationships and Dynamics of Balanced and Unbalanced Fish Populations." Agr. Exp. Sta., AL Polytechnic Inst., Auburn, Bull. No. 274, 1–74.

Sylvester, R. O. 1961. "Nutrient Content of Drainage Water from Forested, Urban and Agricultural Areas." Algae and Metropolitan Wastes, U.S. Public Health Service, SEC TR W61-3, 80.

Sylvester, R .O and G. C. Anderson. 1964. A Lake's Response to its Environment. *J. San. Eng. Div., Proc. Am. Soc. Civil Engin*. 90(SA1):1–22.

Tiner, R.W, Jr. 1984. "Wetlands of the United States: Current Status and Recent Trends." U.S. Fish and Wildlife Service, Washington, D.C.

U.S. EPA. 1988. "America's Wetlands: Our Vital Link Between Land and Water." U.S. Environmental Protection Agency, Washington, D.C. (EPA-87-016).

U.S. EPA. 1990. "National Water Quality Inventory — 1988 Report to Congress." U.S. Environmental Protection Agency, Washington, D.C. (EPA-440-4-90-003).

8   DREDGED OR FILL MATERIAL

THE ISSUE AND THE LAW

Section 404 of the Clean Water Act regulates discharges of dredged or fill material into the waters of the United States. Dredged material means material that is excavated or dredged from the water bodies and placed elsewhere. Fill material means material that replaces portions of water with dry land or that changes the bottom elevation of a water body for any purpose. The waters of the United States in this definition include wetlands.

Section 404(a) provides that the U.S. Army Corps of Engineers may issue permits, after public notice and opportunity for a public hearing, for the discharge of dredged or fill material into waters of the United States, at specified disposal sites. Section 404(b) states that each disposal site shall be specified by the Corps through application of guidelines developed by the EPA in conjunction with the Corps. Where these guidelines would prohibit the specification of a disposal site, the Corps could specify a site because of the economic impact on navigation and anchorage. Lastly, the EPA is authorized to prohibit the specification of any disposal site and to deny or restrict the use of any disposal site. This prohibition or restriction is based, after public notice and opportunity for public hearing, on unacceptable adverse effect on municipal water supplies, shellfish beds and fishery areas, wildlife, or recreational areas.

Section 404(e) provides authority to the Corps to issue general permits for a period of up to 5 years provided the activities covered are similar in nature and will have only minimal adverse environmental effects individually and cumulatively. The general permit may be issued on a nationwide, regional, or statewide basis, and is subject to application of the Section 404(b) guidelines and public notice and opportunity for public hearing procedures. Certain discharges dealing with minor agricultural and silvicultural activities are exempt from requirements to obtain a permit. Discharges associated with activities that convert a water of the United States to upland use are not exempt.

Thus, the Section 404 program is coadministered by the U.S. Army Corps of Engineers and the EPA. The Corps bears the day-to-day administrative responsibilities for the program. These include reviewing permit applications and determining whether to issue or deny applications for dredge or fill permits. The EPA has extensive authority for determining how the program is implemented. The EPA develops, in conjunction with the Corps, the Section 404(b) guidelines, which are the environmental standards that the Corps must apply when evaluating permit applications. The EPA has discretionary authority to veto or restrict discharges upon a determination that a proposed discharge will have an unacceptable adverse effect. In addition, the EPA reviews permit applications and provides recommendations to the Corps regarding permit issuance, restriction, or denial; defines activities that may be exempt from permitting; and approves and oversees state assumption of the Section 404 program.

Pursuant to Section 309 of the Clean Water Act, the EPA has explicit authority to act against persons discharging dredged or fill material without a Corps- or state-issued 404 permit, and to enforce against violations of Corps-issued permits. Section 404(s) gives the Corps explicit authority of enforcement against violations of Corps-issued permits.

Discharges of dredged and fill material commonly are associated with activities such as port development, channel construction and maintenance, fills to create housing and other development, transportation improvements, and water resource projects, such as dams, jetties, and levees. Any activity having as its purpose bringing an area of the waters of the United States into a use to which it was not previously subject, where the flow or circulation of the water may be impaired or the reach reduced, is required to have a Section 404 permit. This would include changing a wetland into farmland for the growing of harvestable crops.

THE PERMIT PROCESS

Discharges of dredged or fill material can be authorized by either individual or general permits. In an individual permit, an application form describing the proposed activity is submitted to the Corps or to a state agency if the program has been assumed from the federal government. Once a complete application is received, the permitting agency issues a public notice containing the information needed to evaluate the likely impact of the proposed activity. This notice is sent to all interested parties, including adjacent property owners; appropriate government agencies at the federal, state, and local levels; and others as requested. Any person may request that a public hearing be held to consider the application.

General permits are developed through the same public notice and opportunity for public hearing process that is used for an individual permit. Once issued, a general permit may be modified or revoked if the permitted activities are found to have an adverse environmental impact. In some instances, the discharger must notify the Corps prior to discharging under the authority of the general permit. On a case-by-case basis, the permitting authority may invoke discretionary authority and require a discharger that would otherwise be covered by a general permit to apply for an individual permit.

The Corps' evaluation of a permit application is a two-part test that involves determining whether the project complies with the Section 404(b) guidelines, and a public interest review. A permit must be denied if the project fails to comply with the guidelines or is found to be contrary to the public interest.

The Corps' public interest review is a balancing test in which the public and private benefits of a project are weighed against its adverse impacts on the environment. It includes such considerations as aesthetics, recreation, historic values, economics, water supply, water quality, energy needs, and flood damage prevention. The Corps also considers all comments received in the permit process, whether in response to a public notice or a public hearing, in arriving at a final permit decision. As part of this evaluation, the Corps conducts an environmental assessment under the National Environmental Policy Act to determine whether the project has significant environmental impacts.

Section 401 of the Clean Water Act requires that a state in which an activity occurs must certify that the activity complies with the state's water quality standards or waive its right to so certify by not taking action within a specified time. This must be done before a permit can be issued. State 401 certificates will be discussed later in this chapter. Similarly, if the proposed project is within a coastal state, the state must concur that the activity meets the requirements of the coastal zone management program of the state or waive its right to concur by not taking action within a specified time. Coastal Zone management programs are developed by states under the Coastal Zone Management Act of 1972.

THE GUIDELINES

The Section 404(b)(1) guidelines are codified at 40 CFR 230. The guidelines are divided into eight subparts that provide the guidance and requirements, including testing procedures against which a proposed activity is judged in the process of permitting.

The policy is stated early in the guidelines, i.e., "(f)undamental to these Guidelines is the precept that dredged or fill material should not be discharged into the aquatic ecosystem, unless it can be demonstrated that such a discharge will not have an unacceptable adverse impact either individually or in combination with known and/or probable impacts of other activities affecting the ecosystem of concern. From a national perspective, the degradation or destruction of special aquatic sites, such as filling operations in wetlands, is considered to be among the most severe environmental impacts covered by these Guidelines. The guiding principle should be that degradation or destruction of special sites may represent an irreversible loss of valuable aquatic resources."

Several restrictions on the discharge of dredged or fill material are stated in the compliance evaluation procedures. Generally, no discharge of dredged or fill material is permitted if there is a practicable alternative to the proposed discharge that would have less adverse impact on the aquatic ecosystem, so long as the alternative does not have other significant adverse environmental consequences. No discharge of dredged or fill material is permitted if it violates water quality standards, toxic effluent standards, or critical habitat areas. No discharge is permitted if it will result in significant degradation of the waters of the United States, based upon appropriate evaluation as discussed further in the regulations. The permitting authority must determine in writing the potential short-term and long-term effects of a proposed discharge on the physical, chemical, and biological components of the aquatic environment.

A large section of the guidelines provides instructions on potential environmental effects that are necessary consideration areas in the permitting process. Environmental factors in this delineation process include the effect, individually and cumulatively, as a result of several similar discharges, on the characteristics of the substrate at the disposal site; on water current patterns and circulation, including downstream flows; on the structure and function of the aquatic ecosystem and organisms; and similar environmental factors. Secondary effects of the aquatic ecosystem also are to be considered. These secondary effects could include fluctuating water levels in an impoundment and downstream associated with the operation of dam, septic tank leaching and surface runoff from residential or commercial developments of fill, and leachate and runoff from sanitary landfill located in the waters of the United States.

The potential impacts on the physical and chemical characteristics of the aquatic ecosystem are to be considered, including potential impacts on the substrate; the effects of suspended particulates and turbidity; the effects on water clarity, nutrients and chemical content, dissolved gas levels, pH, and temperature; the effects on current patterns and water fluctuation; and the effects on salinity gradients. A basic description of expected environmental effects is provided within the regulations.

Another section of the regulations discusses the potential impacts of a proposed discharge on the biological characteristics of the aquatic ecosystem. These include potential effects on threatened and endangered species; fish, crustaceans, mollusks, and other aquatic organisms in the food web; and other wildlife. Again, a detailed description of potential effects that could be expected is provided in Subpart D of 40 CFR 230.

Subpart E of the regulations describes potential impacts on special aquatic sites, including sanctuaries and refuges, wetlands, mud flats, vegetated shallows, coral reefs, and riffle and pool complexes. The following section describes the potential effects on human use characteristics including municipal and private water supplies, recreational and commercial fisheries, water-related recreation, aesthetics, and parks and research sites.

Under evaluation and testing for potential damages associated with the discharge of dredged or fill material, guidance is provided for chemical, biological, and physical evaluation and testing. The regulations state that no single test or approach can be applied in all cases to evaluate the effects of proposed discharges of dredged or fill materials. Guidance is provided on obtaining an elutriate sample for chemical analyses to determine water column effects. When an analysis of biological community structure will be of value to assess the potential for adverse environmental impact at the proposed disposal site, a comparison of the biological characteristics between excavation and disposal sites may be required by the permitting authority. To determine the effects on benthos, the permitting authority may use an appropriate benthos bioassay, including bioaccumulation tests, when such procedures will be of value in assessing ecological effects and in establishing discharge conditions.

In yet another section of the regulation, there is a discussion of actions to minimize adverse effects. These include actions concerning the location of the discharge, controlling the material after discharge, affecting the method of dispersion related to technology, affecting plant and animal populations, and affecting human use. Other actions, in the case of dams, include designing water releases to accommodate the needs of fish and wildlife.

STATE CERTIFICATION

Any applicant for a federal license or permit to conduct any activity that may result in any discharge into the waters of the United States must provide the permitting agency a certification from the state in which the discharge originates or will originate stating that the discharge will not violate state water quality standards and will comply with certain other provisions of the Clean Water Act. State certification is a powerful tool to deter water pollution as a result of actions that require a permit or license. The EPA is promoting this concept as a tool on wetlands protection (U.S. EPA, 1989).

If a state grants water quality certification to an applicant for a federal license or permit, the state is affirming that the proposed activity will comply with state water quality standards. The state thus may deny certification because the applicant has not demonstrated that the project will comply with water quality and other applicable standards, or, the state may place whatever limitations or conditions on the certification it determines are necessary to ensure compliance. The state must take action on a request for certification within a reasonable time, which the law defines as not exceeding 1 year after the receipt of an application. If a state does not act within that time, it forfeits its authority to grant, grant conditionally, or deny certification.

If a state denies certification, the federal permitting or licensing agency is prohibited from issuing a permit or license. A state's decision ordinarily is subject to an administrative appeal, with review in the state courts designated for appeals of agency decisions. Court review typically is limited to the questions of whether the state agency's decision is supported by the record and is not arbitrary or capricious. The courts generally presume regularity in agency procedures and defer to agency expertise in their review.

A problem area that the EPA is attempting to overcome is the Section 401 certification process as it relates to wetlands. While all states have some form of water quality standards, not all states have standards that can be easily applied to wetlands. To overcome this problem, wetlands should be specifically designated as surface waters of the state and this has not uniformly been done.

REFERENCE CITED AND SELECTED READING

U.S. EPA. 1989. "Wetlands and 401 Certification. Opportunities and Guidelines for States and Eligible Indian Tribes." U.S. Environmental Protection Agency, Office of Wetlands Protection (A104F), Washington, D.C.

9   THE MARINE ENVIRONMENT

THE SETTING

EPA devoted its September-October, 1989 journal to the subject, "Can our coasts survive more growth?" Jack Lewis, Assistant Journal Editor, wrote that according to demographers, Americans have been moving in greater and greater numbers to the nearest major body of water since World War II. Already more than half of the U.S. population, 52.9% as of 1987, live within 50 mi of the coast, where people are densely congregated onto less than 10% of the nation's land.

The near-coastal development has resulted in few new cities being erected, but rather, many clusters of houses, stores, offices, and marinas. The sources of pollution within the immediate coastal environment are already enormous in scale and are constantly growing. Each day 900 sewage treatment plants discharge 9.5 billion gallons of effluent directly into estuaries and near-coastal waters. Another 3.2 billion gallons are discharged that same day by over 1300 commercial and industrial facilities. In some areas, non-point source pollution causes even greater problems in the form of toxic runoff from city streets, suburban developments, or agricultural land. In addition, the estuaries and oceans are the ultimate recipients of pollutants transported from the land by rivers.

BASIS IN LAW

The Marine Protection, Research, and Sanctuaries Act of 1972, better known as the Ocean Dumping Act, regulated the ocean dumping of all types of materials that may adversely affect human health, the marine environment, or the economic potential of the oceans. Title I of the act establishes a permit program to control ocean dumping. EPA is authorized to designate sites where ocean dumping may be permitted or prohibited. EPA issues permits for materials other than dredged materials. The U.S. Army Corps of Engineers is responsible for issuing permits to dump dredged material at sites designated by the EPA. The Coast Guard is given the responsibility for conducting surveillance and other appropriate enforcement activities to prevent unlawful ocean dumping and to ensure that the dumping occurs under a valid permit at the designated location and in the manner specified in the permit.

The Act prohibits the dumping of radiological, chemical, and biological warfare agents and high-level radioactive wastes. For other wastes, the EPA must determine, through applicable criteria, that their permitting for dumping will not unreasonably degrade or endanger human health, welfare, or amenities, or the marine environment, ecological systems, or economic potentialities.

In establishing criteria to regulate ocean dumping, the Act requires that consideration be given, but not necessarily limited to

1. The need for the proposed dumping
2. The effect of such dumping on human health and welfare, including economic, aesthetic, and recreational values
3. The effect of such dumping on fisheries resources, plankton, fish, shellfish, wildlife, shorelines, and beaches
4. The effect of such dumping on marine ecosystems, particularly with respect to the transfer, concentration, and dispersion of such material and its byproducts through biological, physical, and chemical processes; potential changes in marine ecosystem diversity, productivity, and stability; and species and community population dynamics
5. The persistence and permanence of the effects of dumping
6. The effect of dumping particular volumes and concentrations of such materials
7. Appropriate locations and methods of disposal or recycling, including land-based alternatives and the probable impact of requiring use of such alternate locations or methods upon considerations affecting the public interest
8. The effect on alternate uses of oceans, such as scientific study, fishing, and other living resource exploitation, as well as nonliving resource exploitation
9. In designating recommended sites, the Administrator shall utilize, wherever feasible, locations beyond the edge of the Continental Shelf

With respect to dredged material, the Act provides that the Secretary of the Army shall apply the criteria established by the EPA relating to the effects of the dumping in issuing permits for the transportation of dredged material for the purpose of dumping it into ocean waters. The Secretary of the Army is to make an independent determination of the need for dumping, other methods or disposal, and appropriate locations for the dumping. In determining the need for dumping, the secretary is directed by the Act to take into account the effects of permit denial on navigation, economic and industrial development, as well as foreign and domestic commerce.

Prior to issuing a permit for dumping of dredged material, the secretary is directed by the Act to notify the EPA of an intent to do so. If the EPA Administrator disagrees with the determination of the secretary as to compliance with the criteria established pursuant to Section 102 of the Act, or with restrictions relating to critical areas, the dredged material permit shall not be issued unless the EPA grants a waiver of requirements. In order to obtain a waiver, the Secretary of the Army must certify that there is no economically feasible method or site available other than a dumping site that would result in noncompliance of the criteria and he shall request a waiver from the Administrator of the specific requirements involved. The waiver shall be granted within 30 days unless the Administrator of EPA finds that the dumping of the material will result in an unacceptably adverse impact on municipal water supplies; shellfish beds; wildlife; fisheries, including spawning and breeding areas; or recreational areas.

Title II of the Act requires the National Oceanic and Atmospheric Administration (NOAA) and the EPA to conduct a comprehensive and continuing program of research and monitoring regarding the effects of the dumping of materials into ocean waters. Title III gives NOAA the authority to establish marine sanctuaries. The Act applies to the open ocean and coastal waters, but not to estuarine waters. It does not apply to wastes discharged through a pipeline or from a stationary drilling platform. The Clean Water Act regulates these wastes and all dumping in estuaries.

The Act is the domestic legislation for implementing the provisions of the Convention on the Prevention of Marine Pollution by Dumping of Wastes and Other Matter (London Dumping Convention), an international agreement for regulating ocean dumping. The United States is one of 58 contracting parties to the Convention. Technical aspects of the Convention regarding types of materials and other factors are contained in three annexes. Annex I establishes a list of substances whose dumping is prohibited, or prohibited unless they are present only as "trace contaminants" or would be "rapidly rendered harmless" in the marine environment. Such substances include cadmium and mercury and their compounds, organohalogen compounds, persistent plastics, and crude oil and petroleum byproducts. Dumping of high-level radioactive wastes, and chemical and biological warfare agents, is completely prohibited. Annex II contains a category of substances requiring special permits, as well as special care in dumping. Dumping of substances not listed in annexes I and II requires a general permit. Annex III sets forth factors to be considered regarding the characteristics and the composition of the material, method of disposal, and characteristics of the dumping site before a permit may be issued.

In 1988, the Congress passed the Ocean Dumping Ban Act to amend the Marine Protection, Research, and Sanctuaries Act. The primary purpose of this legislation is to end the dumping of sewage sludge and industrial waste in the oceans by December 1991. In addition, this Act regulates the operation of garbage barges and makes it illegal to dispose of medical wastes in coastal or navigable waters of the United States. The Ocean Dumping Ban Act directs the EPA to require the development of a compliance or enforcement agreement between the dumper, the governor of the appropriate state, and the EPA. This agreement must include a plan that will phase out the dumping no later than the December 1991 deadline and a schedule for implementing environmentally sound disposal alternatives. Through the agreement, dumpers are required to establish trust funds that will target money to aid the development of alternative systems. The legislation imposes two disposal fees on permitted dumpers, which include an administrative fee to cover the costs of carrying out the Act and a punitive fee to be paid by dumpers who cannot end ocean dumping by the end of 1991.

Section 320 of the Clean Water Act, established by the 1987 Water Quality Act Amendments, created a National Estuary Program. The purposes of the program are to identify nationally significant estuaries, protect and improve their water quality, and enhance their living resources. These goals are to be achieved through Comprehensive Conservation and Management Plans developed through the collaborative efforts of management conferences convened by the EPA Administrator.

Management conferences provide a mechanism for all interested parties to work together to develop a management plan that can be supported and carried out. The EPA provides technical and management experience, but it is the members of the conference who identify major problems in their estuaries, decide where to focus corrective actions, and bind themselves to specific political, financial, and institutional commitments.

The statutory purposes of a management conference are to

1. Assess trends in water quality, natural resources, and uses of the estuary
2. Collect, characterize, and assess data on toxics, nutrients, and natural resources within the estuarine zone to identify the causes of environmental problems
3. Develop the relationship between the in-place loads and point and nonpoint loadings of pollutants to the estuarine zone and the potential uses of the zone, water quality, and natural resources
4. Develop a comprehensive conservation and management plan that recommends priority corrective actions and compliance schedules addressing point and nonpoint sources of pollution to restore and maintain the chemical, physical, and biological integrity of the estuary, including restoration and maintenance of water quality; a balanced indigenous population of shellfish, fish, and wildlife; and recreational activities in the estuary, and to assure that the designated uses of the estuary are protected
5. Develop methods for the coordinated implementation of the plan by the states, as well as federal and local agencies participating in the conference
6. Monitor the effectiveness of actions taken pursuant to the plan
7. Review all federal financial assistance programs and federal development projects to determine whether such assistance programs or projects would be consistent with and further the purposes and objectives of the plan prepared under this section

THE ENVIRONMENT

The environment potentially affected by ocean dumping consists of ocean waters lying seaward of the baseline from which the territorial sea is measured. This vast and important marine area lies adjacent to a coastline in excess of 12,000 statue mi. Generally it can be described in terms of coastal waters and open ocean waters.

Coastal Waters

Coastal waters are those lying over the inner portion of the continental shelf and generally within the boundary of the territorial sea or within 3 mi of shore. They vary greatly in shape, size, and configuration. They include bays, sounds, and open waters along the shoreline. Coastal waters are influenced by tides, winds, ocean currents, upwelling of bottom waters, eddies, riptides, and, to some extent, rivers. These waters tend generally to be less productive than estuaries but more productive than open ocean waters. Ecologically and economically they are very important, however, and often they contain significant fishing grounds. Many organisms that inhabit coastal waters migrate into estuaries for spawning and food. Many birds and mammals also use and migrate though coastal waters for food.

Within the waters of the coastal area, there is an exchange among organisms, food, and dissolved nutrients. Submersed aquatic vegetation provides food and shelter for many organisms. Such plants can grow to depths of adequate light, which may range from 30 to 40 m. Light penetration, which is one of the most decisive environmental factors, may extend to a depth of 200 m, which is sufficient for photosynthesis in planktonic plants. Many animals from the ocean floor have free-swimming larval stages, and these and other organisms have vertical migration patterns through many meters of water. There is always a food web cycle extending from organic matter to bacteria to algae and protozoa to larger filter-feeding organisms to carnivorous animals to predator fish. The cycle repeats with death and decay and through fecal deposition.

Coastal waters are much used for various forms of recreation, including swimming and associated shore activities, picnicking and camping, sport fishing, boating, and aesthetic appreciation of the total environment.

Open Ocean

The open ocean includes waters overlying the outer portion of the continental shelf, the continental slope, and beyond. Open ocean waters are deeper, more open, and more saline than coastal waters. They are influenced less by tidal flow and more by ocean currents.

Typically, the open ocean is not as biologically productive as coastal waters because nutrient concentrations are less. Localized upwellings transport nitrogen and phosphorus to surface waters, however, and can result in increased productivity of phytoplankton. Areas of increased phytoplankton increase the fisheries potential. Water temperature, (controlled in part by ocean currents), the availability of nutrients in the form of nitrogen and phosphorus, and water density are major factors controlling the ecosystem.

Generally, the open ocean is less vulnerable to many impacts of pollution because of the vast volume of water and the mixing and turbulence that occurs. However, persistent metals and organic chemicals and pathogenic organisms are of concern. Substances that bioaccumulate or tend to increase in tissue concentration as they are passed up the trophic food web are of particular concern. Marine fish, mammals, and birds have been found to concentrate some of these toxic substances to very high tissue concentrations. Many of these animals have large amounts of fatty tissue, which is particularly prone to retain many toxic substances that bioaccumulate.

Ocean uses include commercial fishing, recreational fishing, commercial and recreational navigation; beach-going and other activities generated by the tourist trade in coastal areas, including swimming, waterfowl hunting, whale watching, bird watching; sand and gravel and other mineral extraction; oil and gas exploration and development, offshore marine terminals or other structure development; and scientific research and study. An Office of Technology Assessment study (1987) cited information to the effect that almost 12 million Americans fished recreationally in U.S. marine waters in 1980 and spent approximately $2.4 billion on food, lodging, transportation, equipment, licenses, tags, and permits. Thirty percent of all finfish landings used for human food in 1985 were caught by marine recreational fishermen within 3 mi of the shore. In Florida, over 13 million adults used the beaches in 1984. Direct and indirect beach-related sales amounted to $4.6 billion, which generated 180,000 jobs. A government survey found that wildlife alone attracted at least 5 million people to oceanside areas in 1980. Total commercial landings of fish and shellfish from all U.S. marine waters had a dockside value in 1985 of about $2.3 billion and a retail value several times greater. Added to the above, of course, is the not insignificant amount and value of residential property that has been and is being constructed overlooking oceanic waters.

POLLUTION THREATS

EPA has identified six areas of contaminants that threaten the estuaries and oceans. These include marine debris, medical waste, pathogens, eutrophication, toxic substances, oil contamination, and habitat loss or modification.

Marine debris is solid waste that floats or remains suspended in the ocean. It includes plastic bags, six-pack carriers, bottles, cans, driftwood, paper products, styrofoam products, plastic eating utensils, and other materials that can wash up on beaches, pose an aesthetic nuisance, and can injure or kill marine animals. Sources include illegal dumping of trash from shore or at sea, combined sewer overflows, and stormwater.

Medical waste includes used syringes, bandages and dressings, blood vials, and diseased body parts. Although there is a lack of a documented effect on human health, such wastes have created strong public revulsion when found on or near bathing beaches.

Fish are subject to contamination by pathogens such as disease-causing bacteria and viruses. Incidences of illness, including gastroenteritis, hepatitis A, and cholera, from eating contaminated fish are rising around the United States. In addition, about one third of the U.S. shellfish beds are closed because of pollution, resulting in millions of dollars in lost revenues. Over 4500 cases of shellfish-associated gastroenteritis, believed to be caused by viruses, have been documented in the United States since 1980.

Eutrophication is identified in increased plant biomass, generally in excessive amounts, which is stimulated by high concentrations of nutrients, principally nitrogen and phosphorus. The decomposition of aquatic vegetation uses dissolved oxygen from the water. Patches of water that have been almost totally depleted of oxygen are proliferating in the ocean. As many as one million fluke and flounder were killed in the summer of 1988 when they became trapped in oxygen-depleted water in New Jersey's Raritan Bay. Eutrophication is considered a problem in most estuaries in the National Estuary Program. Causes are believed to be excessive fertilizer use on cropland with associated runoff, high nitrogen and phosphorus content of treated sewage wastes, combined sewer overflows with untreated wastes, urban runoff from fertilizer-treated lawns, and in some cases the atmospheric deposition of nitrate.

Toxic substances are chemicals that lessen the ability of plants or animals to survive in nature or to adversely affect human health. Major adverse responses to toxic chemicals include death, a high incidence of tumors or cancer, bioaccumulation of a toxic chemical to a concentration that impacts human health when fish or shellfish are consumed, and reduced reproductive ability. Most heavy metals and many organic chemicals have toxic properties.

Oil contamination may be defined as the presence of crude oil or oil products in water, sediments, or organisms. Oil spills affect terrestrial and aquatic biota. Beaches, sea birds, and other wildlife are coated when oil slicks reach the shore. Chemicals toxic to aquatic life, including fish, are released from these events. Sources include tanker leaks, spills, and accidents; bilge pumping; improper domestic and commercial disposal in storm sewers, and on occasion offshore oil production.

Habitat loss and alteration still is of major concern. Wetlands continue to be lost each year, and the values that are lost with the wetlands include aquatic and wildlife habitat, flood control, and water quality. Channelization and river flow modifications because of dams have affected hydrologic regimes of estuaries, altering salinity regiments, and changing flushing patterns. In turn, these habitat changes affect the inhabitants of the ecosystem.

NATURE AND EXTENT OF DUMPING

The ocean dumping of sewage sludge has occurred under court order since 1981. Nine municipal sewage authorities that previously had held interim permits are dumping sewage sludge pursuant to court orders issued by U.S. district courts in New York and New Jersey. The amount of dumped sewage sludge increased from 4.8 million wet tons in 1973 to 7.9 million wet tons in 1986 (Figure 9-1). The largest amount of sewage sludge dumped occurred in 1983, and it was 8.3 million wet tons. Between 1973 and 1986 the amount of industrial waste dumped in the ocean declined steadily (Figure 9-1).

The relative amounts of sewage sludge placed in the ocean by the nine sewerage authorities is shown in Figure 9-2. In 1986, 45% was from the City of New York.

The industrial wastes disposed of in oceans from 1984 through 1986 range from drilling muds and cuttings to hydrochloric acid waste to fish wastes (Figure 9-3). In the 1970s and before the ocean disposal of industrial wastes and chemicals was practically

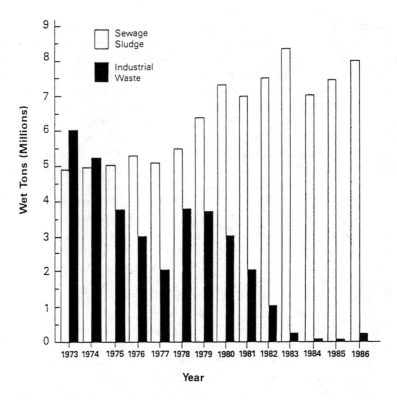

Figure 9-1.   Sewage sludge and industrial waste disposed of in ocean. (U.S. EPA, 1988.)

halted, they constituted a major problem in ocean pollution. As shown in Figure 9-1, the amounts were significant.

Fish wastes that have not been adulterated with additives are excluded from the requirement of a permit for ocean disposal. The fish wastes referred to in Figure 9-3, are, in essence, industrial wastes. They are wastes from the processing of fish for commercial use that have been pretreated through a dissolved air flotation process. Such wastes have a biochemical oxygen demand of approximately 150,000 mg/l, suspended solids of 130,000 mg/l, oil and grease of 14,000 to 18,000 mg/l, total nitrogen of 1900 mg/l, and total phosphorus of 1200 mg/l. Aluminum sulfate is added as a coagulant, resulting in an aluminum content of the waste that may range from 29 to 514 mg/l. The dissolved air flotation sludge, a major component of wastes destined for ocean disposal, has an average bulk density of 0.89 ± 0.08 g/ml to 1.00 ± 0.02 g/ml; sea water has a density of 1.025 g/ml. Thus, some of the waste tends to float on the ocean surface, at least until the air bubbles entrained within it are dispersed. Other solid particles within the waste sink.

Data from the U.S. Army Corps of Engineers indicate that dredged material

Quantities in Thousand Wet Tons

	1984	1985	1986
Sewage Authorities			
Bergen County Utilities Authority NJ	255	309	353
Joint Meeting of Essex and Union Counties NJ	385	341	238
Linden Roselle Sewerage Authority NJ	235	95	93
Middlesex County Utilities Authority NJ	966	1,039	1,018
Nassau County Dept. of Public Works NY	520	576	709
New York City Dept. of Environmental Protection NY	3,085	3,345	3,591
Passaic Valley Sewerage Commission NJ	854	884	1,317
Rahway Valley Sewerage Authority NJ	160	187	98
Westchester County Dept. of Environmental Facilities NY	539	470	506
	6,999	7,246	7,923

Figure 9-2.   Sewage sludge disposed of in ocean under court order, 1984–1986. (U.S. EPA, 1988.)

disposed of in the ocean in recent years has averaged about 49 million cubic meters per year. The amount of disposal has fluctuated from 29 million cubic meters to 56 million cubic meters over the last decade. The vast majority of this material was disposed of under corps project authority. About 50–60% of this material is dumped in the Gulf of Mexico and the remainder is distributed about equally between the Atlantic and Pacific oceans. The EPA tabulates the dumping data for sewage sludge and industrial wastes in wet tons and the Corps of Engineers tabulates dredged material disposal in cubic meters. For comparative purposes, an imprecise assumption was made that the average weight of the dredged material was 1500 g/l. On this assumed basis, a cubic meter of dredged material would equate to 1.65 wet tons; thus, the average weight of dredged material disposal for 1984 and 1985 would be about 81 million wet tons per year. On this basis, the dredged material makes up about 91% of the total disposed material; sewage sludge makes up 8.3% of the total; and the remaining industrial wastes make up less than 1% of the total amount disposed.

THE PERMIT PROGRAM

The ocean dumping regulations and criteria in 40 CFR Parts 220-229 identify five categories of permits under the Ocean Dumping Program. They are general, interim, special, emergency, and research permits.

General permits may be issued for the dumping of certain materials that will have

	Quantities in Thousand Wet Tons		
	1984	1985	1986
Region II			
Acid Waste Site (NY Bight Apex):			
Allied Chemical Corp.[1] NY	40	40	34
Deepwater Industrial Waste Site:			
DuPont — Edge Moor[2] DE	19	0	140
DuPont — Grasselli[3] NJ	146	100	73
Cellar Dirt Site (NY Bight Apex):			
Port Liberté, NJ	—*	—*	0
Region IX			
Fish Wastes Site			
Samoa Packing, American Samoa	8	4.6	21.4
Star Kist, American Samoa	7.9	20.3	24.1
Oil Drilling Muds and Cuttings			
THUMS Long Beach, CA	—*	2.7	13.6
	220.9	167.6	306.1

[1] Hydrochloric acid waste

[2] Aqueous iron and miscellaneous chlorides and hydrochloric acid wastes

[3] Solution of alkaline sodium wastes

*No permit issued

Figure 9-3.   Special permitted materials disposed of in ocean, 1984–1986. (U.S. EPA, 1988.)

a minimal adverse environmental impact and are generally disposed of in small quantities. Three general permits were established in the 1977 regulations. They are for burial at sea, transportation of target vessels by the U.S. Navy for the purpose of sinking the vessels in ocean waters in testing ordinance and providing related data, and transportation and disposal of vessels under specific conditions. No other general permits have been established since 1977.

According to the EPA (1988), the agency has used interim permits to control the burning at sea of wood debris collected from the New York Harbor area. Interim permits have an expiration date no later than 1 year from the date of issue. The burning is undertaken to dispose of driftwood, wood pilings, and other wood debris removed from New York Harbor and currently takes place at an interim designated site, known as the woodburning site. The agency currently is preparing an EIS, which incorporates monitoring results and other data, for use in evaluating a site for formal designation for this activity.

Special permits are used for the dumping of materials that satisfy the dumping criteria and have an expiration date no later than 3 years from the date of issue. The recently issued special permits are shown in Figure 9-3.

Emergency permits are designed for situations that pose an unacceptable risk relating to human health and admit of no other feasible solution to that of ocean disposal. EPA reports (1988) that one emergency permit was issued in 1984 for dumping 7000 canisters of aluminum phosphide pellets. The material had been brought into the United States as cargo. During unloading operations, a shipping container exploded, killing one person and damaging other parts of the shipment. When exposed to water vapor in the atmosphere, this material forms phosphine gas, an extremely toxic and unstable compound. The agency considered the potential impacts to the marine environment of dumping this material and concluded that after reacting with seawater, the effects of ocean dumping would be temporary and localized. Since the material in its existing state posed a major potential threat to public health and a review of other possible disposal measures indicated such alternatives were not feasible, an emergency ocean dumping permit was issued for disposal of the material in the Gulf of Mexico. No emergency permits were issued in 1985 or 1986.

Research permits are reserved for activities that are a part of a research project when it is determined that the scientific merit of the proposed project outweighs the potential environmental or other damage that may result from the dumping. Research permits specify expiration dates no later than 18 months from the date of issue.

Pursuant to 40 CFR 220.4(c), EPA regional administrators have the authority to review, approve, disapprove, or propose conditions upon dredged material permits for ocean dumping of dredged material at locations within the respective regional jurisdictions.

The regulations provide details for making application for a permit, providing public notice of the receipt of an application, entertaining requests for a public hearing on the merits of an application, and conducting a public hearing.

CRITERIA FOR DISPOSAL

The ocean dumping criteria are specified in 40 CFR Part 227. No permit will be issued when the dumping would result in a violation of an applicable water quality standards. Prohibited materials are identified, including persistent inert synthetic or natural materials that may float or remain in suspension in the ocean in such a manner that they may interfere materially with fishing or navigation.

Certain constituents are listed as prohibited in other than trace contaminants. The acceptability of trace contamination for ocean dumping is determined through a bioassay of the suspended particulate phase and solid phase, and a stipulation that the liquid phase does not contain the listed constituents in concentrations that will exceed applicable marine water quality criteria published by the EPA in 1976 (red book) or as amended in later official criteria documents. The criteria for evaluating environmental impact are complex. Generally, however, no wastes will be deemed acceptable for ocean dumping unless their dumping will not result in the limiting permissible concentrations being exceeded.

The limiting permissible concentration for a liquid waste is one that does not violate applicable marine water quality criteria after allowance for initial mixing or when such criteria are not available, will not exceed a toxicity threshold defined as 0.01 of a concentration shown to be acutely toxic to appropriate sensitive marine organisms. For a solid, the limiting permissible concentration is that concentration that will not cause unreasonable acute or chronic toxicity or other adverse effects based on bioassay results using sensitive marine organisms.

DISPOSAL SITE DESIGNATION

Section 102(c) of the act authorizes the EPA Administrator to designate recommended areas for dumping. This authority includes designation of ocean dumping sites for dredged material, as well as for sewage sludge, industrial waste, and other materials.

EPA has voluntarily adopted an EIS policy which provides that the agency will prepare an EIS for the designation of ocean dumping sites. The ocean dumping regulations at 40 CFR 228 set forth the criteria to be considered in designating ocean dumping sites. The site designation process is conducted to identify and select a location suitable for the type of material to be dumped. The designation of a site does not authorize actual dumping, however, as it may take place only if an ocean dumping permit is issued.

A large number of ocean dumping sites existed at the time of passage of the act in 1972 (U.S. EPA, 1988). Based on their historical use, the EPA designated 13 nondredged material dump sites and 127 dredged material dump sites on an interim basis, pending completion of environmental evaluation.

In February, 1980, the National Wildlife Federation filed suit against the agency challenging the interim designations. The court upheld the interim designations until settlement was reached. The suit resulted in a consent agreement wherein the EPA agreed to prepare and issue 22 EISs on 47 sites. Three of the EISs were for nondredged material disposal sites, and 19 were for dredged material disposal sites. Four additional sites were added through the site designation process, for a total of 51 sites.

According to the EPA (1988), as of December 31, 1986 there were 51 consent agreement sites needing designation and 109 nonconsent agreement sites needing designation. Of this total of 160 dumping sites, draft EISs had been completed on 75. To be designated, a site must go through a draft EIS, final EIS, proposed rule, and final rule of designation. Of the total 160 sites, 140 were designated as dredged material disposal sites and 20 were nondredged material disposal sites.

NATIONAL ESTUARY PROGRAM

The National Estuary Program currently includes 12 estuary projects. These are Buzzards Bay in Massachusetts; Narragansett Bay in Rhode Island; Long Island Sound in Connecticut and New York; New York-New Jersey Harbor in New York and New Jersey; Delaware Bay in New Jersey, Pennsylvania, and Delaware; Delaware Inland Bays in Delaware; Albemarle/Pamlico Sounds in North Carolina; Sarasota Bay in Florida; Galveston Bay in Texas; Santa Monica Bay and San Francisco Bay in California; and Puget Sound in Washington State.

These 12 estuaries were named by Congress to receive priority consideration to be included in the National Estuary Program. However, the EPA may select additional estuaries for the program in response to nominations from any state governor, or at its own initiative in the case of interstate estuaries. Estuaries are selected based on their potential to address issues of significant national concern, as well as their demonstrated commitment to taking protective measures. Once an estuary is selected, the EPA formally convenes a Management Conference. Each conference has up to 5 years initially to build the framework for future actions, as well as to begin some priority cleanup activities.

A concerted effort began on six of these estuaries about 5 years ago. The other six were nominated by the respective governors in 1988. Congress established the National Estuary Program to show how estuaries can be protected and their living resources enhanced through comprehensive, action-oriented management that

1. Identifies the probable causes of major environmental problems in estuaries of national significance
2. Promotes and sustains long-term state and local commitment to solving the problems
3. Generates meaningful public involvement and participation
4. Focuses existing regulatory, institutional, and financial resources to act on identified problems
5. Encourages innovative management approaches (U.S. EPA, 1990)

The water pollution problems associated with estuaries are similar to the water pollution problems associated with most of the nation's waters. The EPA (1990) has summarized the major problems to be corrected in the 12 designated estuaries. It is helpful to focus on those here because it reemphasizes water pollution control problems generally.

Buzzards Bay is located between Cape Cod and the southern coast of mainland Massachusetts. A long history of industrial discharge has resulted in an area of highly contaminated sediment on the western shores of Buzzards Bay. Industrial discharge of polychlorinated biphenyls in the Acushnet River area of New Bedford has contaminated the sediment to such an extent that the area is designated as a Superfund hazardous waste site. It has been closed to fishing for human consumption since 1979. Burgeoning development along the eastern shore of the bay has made it one of the fastest growing counties in New England, which is further degrading water quality. Since it was first organized in 1985, the Buzzards Bay Project has identified pathogens, toxic metals and organic compounds, and high nutrient inputs as the three major problems to be addressed. Buttermilk Bay, an embayment at the northern end of Buzzards Bay, has repeatedly been closed to shellfish harvesting because of high fecal coliform levels produced as a result of storm water runoff. To correct this problem, storm water retention systems based on inland treatment are being tested. In addition, nutrients enter the bay from a number of sources, including sewage treatment plant discharges, fertilizer runoff from residences and farms, precipitation, and groundwater. The results of a study suggest that groundwater is a major source of waterborne nutrients, probably originating in septic tanks surrounding the bay.

Narragansett Bay, with 420 mi of coastline, is 30 mi long and ranges in width from 3 to 12 mi. It accounts for approximately one third of the area of Rhode Island. A once valuable cultivated oyster fishery has virtually disappeared; crabs, scallops, and commercially important finfish have declined. Soft clam populations fluctuate. Approximately one third of the bay is closed to quahog (hard clam) shellfishing because of the bacterial pollution. Nutrient increase has led to phytoplankton changes, which in turn affect the bay's food chain. A brown tide (microscopic algal bloom) during the summer of 1985 killed 30% of the bay's mussels. Toxic contamination of important fishery species and the potential threat to human health from eating live fish have been identified as priority problems. Rhode Island has been and continues to be a national center for jewelry manufacture and metal finishing industries. Until recently, industrial wastes containing metals and solvents from these industries had been discharged directly into the bay or its tributaries, resulting in sediment contamination. Urban runoff may also contribute toxics to the bay. Discharges from treatment works and combined sewer overflows have added nutrients to the bay, affecting its ecosystem and perhaps causing shifts in phytoplankton communities.

Long Island Sound is 110 mi long and covers 1300 square mi of water bordered by 577 mi of coastline. Approximately 200,000 boats are registered and operated on Long Island Sound. The commercial catch of lobsters, finfish, and shellfish exceeds $20 million annually. The sound is surrounded by 14.6 million people. About 80% of the freshwater entering the sound comes from rivers that drain states as far north as Massachusetts, New Hampshire, and Vermont. The sound's two major water pollution problems are low levels of dissolved oxygen and toxic contamination. Many fish kills and shellfish losses have occurred as a result of low dissolved oxygen. Studies so far indicate that nutrients entering the sound from sewage treatment plants, storm water runoff, and atmospheric deposition contribute to the reduced oxygen. Nutrients grow algae, algae decompose, and dissolved oxygen is used.

Toxics of concern include metals such as copper, cadmium, and mercury, as well as organic compounds, such as polychlorinated biphenyls and polycyclic aromatic hydrocarbons. A study by the National Marine Fisheries Service found that winter flounder in contaminated regions of the New Haven harbor area produced eggs that developed smaller larvae with more physical defects than did fish in other areas of the sound.

New York-New Jersey Harbor has problems associated with combined sewer overflows, pathogen contamination, toxics contamination, changes in living resources, habitat loss and modification, eutrophication, and floatable debris.

The proposed goals of the Delaware Bay project are to restore living resources of the bay, reduce and control point and nonpoint sources of pollution, protect public water supplies, manage the economic growth of the estuary, and promote greater public understanding of the bay and public participation in decisions and programs affecting it.

Problems affecting the Delaware Inland Bays include increased population growth and land development, as well as nonpoint pollution from extensive agricultural activities, especially poultry farming.

The waters of Albemarle/Pamlico Sounds include more than 2000 square mi of lagoons and rivers bordered by beaches, marshes, and swamp forests. The watershed covers approximately 30,000 square mi in eastern North Carolina and southeastern Virginia. Albemarle and Pamlico Sounds are the region's key resource base for commercial fishing, tourism, recreation, and resort development. The 50% increase in harvested farm lands since the 1970s has often been at the expense of wetlands. Finfish fisheries have declined over the past 10 years, with particularly dramatic declines in catches of striped bass, shad, and river herring. Fish diseases, such as red sore disease and ulcerative mycosis, have occurred, as have large-scale fish kills due to low dissolved oxygen levels. Massive blue-green algal blooms take place almost annually in some of the area tributaries, and rooted aquatic plants have disappeared from the center of the Pamlico River. Between 1960 and 1980, a period of extensive agricultural clearing and drainage, the mean annual salinity within the estuary may have declined by almost 50%. The disappearance of some oyster beds may be related to this change in salinity, as well as to increased sedimentation. Agricultural best management practices to control excess nutrients from nonpoint sources is a major need.

Sarasota Bay is a small, subtropical, relatively pristine bay located in one of the nation's fastest growing areas. The goals proposed for the project are to improve water transparency, reduce the quantity and improve the quality of storm water runoff, prevent further losses of seagrasses and shoreline habitat, reduce dredging, and enhance the bay by coordinating beach-inlet-channel maintenance.

Galveston Bay is the seventh-largest estuary system in the United States. Surrounded by 203 mi of estuarine marsh, 14 square mi of forested wetlands, and 61 square mi of freshwater ponds and lakes, the bay's high freshwater inflow and low salinity provide ideal conditions for fish and shellfish. Issues identified for the project include maintenance of water quality and enhancement of estuary productivity; prevention of water quality deterioration in the Houston Ship Channel; evaluation of current wastewater treatment programs and methods of disposing of dredged spoils; development and analysis of baseline toxics data; and prevention of wetlands losses and shoreline erosion.

Santa Monica Bay is one of California's most heavily used recreational areas. Eight million people use it for swimming, boating, sport fishing, and other activities. Major problems include treated sewage discharges into the bay; contaminated sediments, including high levels of DDT, other organic compounds, and trace metals; and pathogen contamination.

The San Francisco Bay/Sacramento-San Joaquin Delta estuary encompasses more than 1600 square mi and drains more than 40% of California's surface. Six million people use it for drinking water, navigation, industry, and recreation. A key diversion point for water projects, tributaries to this estuary supply water for agriculture in the San Joaquin valley and for cities and industry in southern California. Since the 1850s, more than 150 square mi of the bay have been filled, an estimated 94% of its tidal marshes are gone, and some 65% of its freshwater inflow is diverted annually for agricultural, domestic, and industrial use. At times, the San Joaquin River flows backwards, its water reversed by export pumps, and saltwater intrudes farther inland. Populations of several commercially valuable fish species have declined, and individual fish often show signs of poor health, including parasites and lesions. Some fish and shellfish, especially striped bass and mussels, have been found with high levels of toxic contaminants in their tissues. To assess potential restoration strategies, a $1.575 million wetlands enhancement project at eight sites has been funded. The project will restore various categories of wetlands in difference locations by building levees, regrading channel bottoms, establishing water distribution systems, and controlling water flow. Several of the sites will be replanted, and at least four sites will use treated effluent as the water source.

With 2200 square mi of bays and inlets and over 2000 mi of shoreline, Puget Sound supports valuable commercial and sports fisheries, as well as commercial and recreational shellfishing, commercial and industrial activity, shipping, and international commerce. A major issue is the discovery of significant concentrations of toxic contaminants in the sediments of the sound's urban and industrial embayments. These pollutants include highly toxic and persistent materials, such as polychlorinated biphenyls, and heavy metals, such as mercury, arsenic, and lead. Field surveys have found abnormalities in bottom-dwelling organisms, increased incidence of disease in fish caught where sediments are contaminated, and high levels of chemicals in the edible tissues of fish and shellfish. Bacteria and other pathogens enter the sound from nonpoint sources, such as rural septic systems and farm operations, and storm water. Storm water control in highly urbanized, urbanizing, and rural environments is a management need. The project will test the use of simple detention and diversion systems in urban areas, and best management practices and other nonpoint controls in rural areas.

REFERENCES CITED AND SELECTED READING

Anikouchine, W. A. and R. W. Sternberg. 1981. *The World Ocean: An Introduction to Oceanography* (2nd Ed.) Prentice Hall, New York.

Executive Resource Associates. 1989. "Adulterated Fish Wastes, Ocean Dumping Operations." U.S. Environmental Protection Agency. Executive Resource Associates, Arlington, VA.

Gross, M. G. 1982. *Oceanography: A View of the Earth* (3rd Ed.) Prentice Hall, New York.

Harvey, J. W. 1957. "Treatise on Marine Ecology and Paleoecology." I. Physical and Chemical Characteristics by K.O. Emery and R.E. Stevenson. II. Biological Aspects by J.W. Hedgpeth. Geol. Soc. Amer., Memoir 67.

Hill, G. H., Ed. 1964. *The Sea, Volume II. The Composition of Sea Water; Comparative and Descriptive Oceanography*. Wiley Interscience, New York.

Lauff, G. H., Ed. 1967. *Estuaries*. Pub. 83, American Association for the Advancement of Science, Washington, D.C.

Sverdup, H. I., M. W. Johnson, and R. H. Fleming. 1946. *The Oceans, their Physics, Chemistry and Biology*. Prentice Hall, New York.

U.S. Congress. 1987. "Wastes in Marine Environment." U.S. Congress, Office of Technology Assessment, OTA-334. U.S. Government Printing Office, Washington, D.C. (April).

U.S. EPA. 1988. "Report to Congress on Administration of the Marine Protection, Research, and Sanctuaries Act of 1972, as Amended (P.L. 92-532) 1984-1986." U.S. Environmental Protection Agency, Washington, D.C. (EPA-503/8-88/002).

U.S. EPA. 1989. "Marine and Estuarine Protection, Programs and Activities." U.S. Environmental Protection Agency, Washington, D.C. (EPA-503/0-89-002).

U.S. EPA. 1989. *EPA Journal* (September/October). U.S. Environmental Protection Agency, Office of Communications and Public Affairs, Washington, D.C.

U.S. EPA. 1990. "Progress in the National Estuary Program, Report to Congress." U.S. Environmental Protection Agency, Washington, D.C. (EPA-503/9-90-005).

10   DRINKING WATER

BASIS IN LAW

The Safe Drinking Water Act protects drinking water sources by regulating persons who inject fluids into the ground, and public drinking water consumers by regulating the quality of water distributed by public water systems. Both surface and underground public drinking water sources are protected. A public water system is one that provides piped water for human consumption and that has at least 15 service connections or regularly serves at least 25 individuals.

EPA regulations establish "at-the-tap" primary and secondary water standards for public drinking water systems. National Interim Primary Drinking Water Regulations protect health to the extent feasible, using technology, treatment techniques, and other means, and taking costs into consideration. They are codified at 40 CFR 141. Secondary Drinking Water Regulations protect the public welfare and serve as guidelines to states for the non-health-related qualities of drinking water. They are codified at 40 CFR 143.

The 1986 amendments to the Safe Drinking Water Act required that the EPA set maximum contaminant level goals and national primary drinking water regulations for 83 specific contaminants and for any other contaminant in drinking water that may have any adverse effect upon the health of persons and that is known or anticipated to occur in public water systems (Figure 10-1). Maximum contaminant level goals are nonenforceable health goals that are to be set at levels at which no known or anticipated adverse health effects occur and that allow an adequate margin of safety.

The primary drinking water regulations contain maximum contaminant levels for specific contaminants. A maximum contaminant level is the maximum permissible level of a contaminant in water that is delivered to any user of a public system. The act requires that maximum contaminant levels be set as close to the maximum contaminant level goal as is feasible. Feasible is defined as the use of the best technology, treatment techniques, and other means that the EPA Administrator finds, after examination for efficacy under field conditions and not solely under laboratory conditions, are available (taking costs into consideration). For example, the Safe Drinking Water Act states that granular activated carbon is feasible for the control of synthetic organic

VOLATILE ORGANIC CHEMICALS	MICROBIOLOGY AND TURBIDITY
Benzene Carbon tetrachloride Chlorobenzene 1,2-Dichloroethane Dichlorobenzene 1,1-Dichloroethylene cis-1,2-Dichloroethylene trans-1,2-Dichloroethylene Dichloromethane Tetrachloroethylene Trichlorobenzene 1,1,1-Trichloroethane Trichloroethylene Vinyl chloride	Giardia lamblia Legionella Standard plate count Total coliform bacteria Turbidity Viruses
INORGANIC CHEMICALS	**ORGANIC CHEMICALS**
Antimony Arsenic Asbestos Barium Beryllium Cadmium Chromium Copper Cyanide Fluoride Lead Mercury Nickel Nitrate Nitrite Selenium Sulfate Thallium **RADIONUCLIDES** Beta particle and photo radioactivity Gross alpha particle activity Radium 226 Radium 228 Radon Uranium	Acrylamide Adipates Alachlor Aldicarb Aldicarb sulfone Aldicarb sulfoxide Atrazine Carbofuran Chlordane 2,4-D Dalapon DBCP 1,2-Dichloropropane Dinoseb Diquat EDB Endothall Endrin Eipchlorohydrin Ethylbenzene Glyphosate Heptachlor Heptachlor epoxide Hexachlorocyclopentadiene Lindane Methoxychlor PAHs PCBs Pentachlorophenol Phthalates Picloram Simazine Styrene 2,3,7,8-TCDD (Dioxin) Toluene Toxaphene 2,4,5-TP 1,1,2-Trichlorethane Vydate Xylene

Figure 10-1.   List of contaminants required to be regulated under 1986 Amendments.

chemicals and any technology or any other means found to be the best available for control of synthetic organic chemicals must be at least as effective in control as granular activated carbon. Maximum contaminant level goals and maximum contaminant levels must be proposed and promulgated simultaneously.

In the list of contaminants required to be regulated, Figure 10-1, seven substitutes were allowed if regulation of any seven other contaminants would be more protective of public health. Those contaminants removed from the list, for which other contami-

Aluminum	Cryptosporidium	Hypochlorite ion
Ammonia	Cyanazine	Isophorone
Boron	Cyanogen chloride	Methyl tert-butyl ether
Bromobenzene	Dibromoacetonitrile	Metholachlor
Bromochloroacetonitrile	Dibromochloromethane	Metribuzin
Bromodichloromethane	Dibromomethane	Molybdenum
Bromoform	Dicamba	Ozone byproducts
Bromomethane	Dichloroacetonitrite	Silver
Chloramine	1,1-Dichloroethane	Sodium
Chlorate	1,3-Dichloropropane	Strontium
Chlorine	2,2-Dichloropropane	2,4,5-T
Chlorine dioxide	1,1-Dichloropropene	1,1,1,2-Tetrachloroethane
Chlorite	1,3-Dichloropropene	1,1,2,2-Tetrachloroethane
Chloroethane	2,4-Dinitrotoluene	Trichloroacetonitrile
Chloroform	ETU	1,2,3-Trichloropropane
Chloromethane	Halogenated Acids,	Trifluralin
Chloropicrin	Alcohols, Aldehydes,	Vanadium
o-Chlorotoluene	Ketones, and other	Zinc
p-Chlorotoluene	Nitriles	

Figure 10-2.   Drinking water priority list.

nants were substituted, must be included on the drinking water priority list. The 1986 amendments require the EPA to publish a Drinking Water Priority List of drinking water contaminants that may require regulation under the Safe Drinking Water Act (Figure 10-2). The list is to be published every 3 years after the initial publication. Maximum contaminant level goals, national primary drinking water regulations, and monitoring requirements are to be set for at least 25 contaminants on the list initially, and this is to continue for subsequent triennial lists.

The EPA removed seven contaminants from the list of contaminants required to be regulated. These seven contaminants do not appear in Figure 10-1, but they are contained in Figure 10-2. The contaminants are aluminum, dibromomethane, molybdenum, silver, sodium, vanadium, and zinc. The EPA substituted seven contaminants in their place, which are on the list of contaminants required to be regulated. These contaminants are aldicarb sulfone, aldicarb sulfoxide, ethylbenzene, heptachlor, heptachlor epoxide, nitrite, and styrene.

National primary drinking water regulations can contain either maximum contaminant levels or treatment technique requirements for the contaminants regulated. Best available treatment technology is to be specified for each contaminant for which a maximum contaminant level is established.

The 1986 amendments banned the use of any pipe, solder, flux, or fittings that are not "lead free" in a public water system or in any building connected to a public water system. Flux and solder may not have more than 0.2% lead, and pipe and fittings not more than 8% lead.

The 1986 amendments substantially increased enforcement authority in the Safe Drinking Water Act. Added was the authority to issue administrative compliance orders, assess administrative penalties of up to $5000 for compliance order violation, and seek civil penalties of up to $25,000 per day of violation. The amendments also added civil and criminal penalties for persons who tamper or attempt to tamper with public water systems with the intention of harming persons. Further, the 1986 amendments provided that if a state that has been delegated primacy to manage the Safe Drinking Water Act program has not taken appropriate enforcement action within 30 days of notice from the EPA, the EPA is authorized to take the enforcement action.

SOURCE OF SUPPLY

As recorded by the U.S. EPA (1987), every day approximately 4.2 trillion gal of precipitation fall on the continental United States. About two-thirds of that precipitation evaporates, about 61 billion gal soaks into aquifers, and the rest runs off directly to streams and rivers. Estimates of the groundwater resources of the U.S. found within one-half mile of the land surface range from 15 to 100 quadrillion gal. These resources are 50-times greater in volume than all the nation's surface waters at any given point in time.

The richest groundwater resources are found in the mid-Atlantic, the Gulf Coast, the Great Plains, and the Central Valley of California. These resources are estimated to yield hundreds to thousands of gallons of fresh water per minute. Less extensive aquifers that yield smaller quantities of water are found throughout the country.

As recorded by the U.S. EPA (1987) from the Conservation Foundation's "Groundwater Protection," groundwater sources supply the fresh water needs of approximately 40% of the population receiving public water supplies. Of a population of 186 million served by public systems in 1980, 112 million received fresh water drawn from surface water and 73.7 million received fresh water drawn from groundwater. Data on rural fresh water use are difficult to obtain, but the USGS has determined the number of people served by self-supplied systems by subtracting the total number of people served by public supply systems from the total estimated U.S. population. This difference shows that approximately 44 million people obtained water through their own water supply systems in 1980. The combined usage of groundwater through public and rural supplies indicated that about 51% of the nation's population is dependent on groundwater for its drinking water and about 49% on surface waters.

Most large cities depend upon surface supplies because they are easier to get at and the quantities are less limited than from underground sources. Rivers, lakes, and impounded reservoirs generally are the sources for surface supplies. Many of these sources receive runoff and stormwater from the land, discharges from industries, treated sewage from cities, drainage from mines, or return flows from agricultural irrigation. Impounded water may result in the leaching of undesirable materials form flooded soils. The turbidity, mineral content, and degree of contamination may vary daily in a river and temperature may vary throughout the year. Most individuals find that water having a temperature between 50° and 60°F is most palatable. In a large lake or reservoir, the water intake structure may be 30 or more feet deep in order to obtain water of more consistent quality and temperature. A city often protects its water supply reservoir and upgradient watershed and may prohibit use or trespass to prevent contamination.

Groundwater depletion and contamination are localized problems. Groundwater availability is a significant issue in almost every state. Declining groundwater levels have occurred in a number of areas, including portions of California, the Dakotas, Illinois, Indiana, Iowa, and Wisconsin. Freshwater withdrawals from groundwater more than doubled between 1950 and 1980. Of the 150 billion gal of fresh water withdrawn every day to irrigate crops, approximately 40% or 60 billion gal comes from groundwater. Other major groundwater uses include public water supplies, rural water supplies, and industrial withdrawals from other than public supplies.

To reach an aquifer, water may percolate through mineral deposits from which hardness constituents, such as calcium and magnesium, are leached. Thus, well water may be excessively hard in some areas of the country. Except for hardness removal, well water often requires less treatment than a surface supply because of natural purification as the water passes through various underground soil formations.

CONTAMINANTS

The EPA (1987) lists 35 sources of contaminants to groundwater; they are subsurface percolation, injection wells, land application, landfills, open dumps, residential disposal, surface impoundments, waste tailings, waste piles, materials stockpiles, graveyards, animal burial, aboveground storage tanks, underground storage tanks, containers, open burning, radioactive disposal sites, pipelines, materials transport, irrigation, pesticide application, fertilizer application, animal feedlots, deicing, urban runoff, percolation of atmospheric pollutants, mine drainage, production wells, other wells, construction excavation, ground and surface water interaction, natural leaching, salt water intrusion, abandoned waste sites, and nuclear facilities.

The major sources of groundwater contamination reported by states in their Clean Water Act Section 305(b) reports in priority ranking included septic tanks, underground storage tanks, agricultural activities, on-site landfills, surface impoundments, municipal landfills, abandoned waste sites, oil and gas brine pits, salt water intrusion, underground injection wells, and construction activities. Septic tanks lead the list. As reported by the EPA, as of 1980 approximately 23 million domestic septic systems were in operation in the U.S., discharging about 820 to 1450 million gal of wastewater annually. One-half million new systems are installed each year. In addition to the domestic systems, approximately 25,000 commercial and industrial septic tanks discharge an estimated 1.2 to 1.9 billion gal per year.

As reported by the Conservation Foundation (1987), 37 inorganic substances have been found in groundwater in the U.S., including 27 metals. Between 1975 and 1985, about 1500 to 3000 public water supplies out of 40,000 using groundwater exceeded EPA's national primary or secondary drinking water standards for inorganic substances. The most common problems were fluoride and nitrates.

A 1985 study found trace levels of 33 organic chemicals in 18% of 3000 drinking water wells surveyed. However, only 165 of these wells had contaminant levels that exceeded state drinking water standards. The EPA found that the five most frequently detected organic compounds in their Ground Water Supply Survey were trichloro-ethylene, 1,1,1-trichloroethane, tetrachloroethylene, *cis/trans*-1,2-dichloroethylene, and 1,1-dichloroethane.

The EPA has found that normal agricultural usage has contributed to contamination from at least 17 pesticides in at least 23 states. California reported in 1985 that 57 different pesticides detected in the state's groundwaters were responsible for contaminating an estimated 2887 wells.

Approximately 20 different radionuclides have been detected in the nation's groundwater as reported by the Conservation Foundation (1987).

Contaminants, once they have entered groundwater, are difficult and expensive to treat or remove. Groundwater velocities are low in comparison to surface water velocities, thus, a contaminant introduced into a groundwater system does not mix rapidly with the existing water in the aquifer. Generally the flow paths, concentration, and chemical evolution of the contaminant are either unknown or difficult to ascertain. Identifying the source and extent of contamination is made problematical by the complex physics and chemistry of the flow system.

Naturally occurring iron bacteria in distribution systems or wells may cause turbidity and discoloration, unpleasant tastes and odors, and hard deposits that fill up pipes and reduce their water-carrying capacity.

Algae associated with surface water supplies have been the cause of corrosion of metal tanks and concrete reservoir walls. They have clogged sand filters in water supply treatment systems and are a principal concern in producing taste and odor problems. Other organisms that, on occasion, have caused concern to water purveyors include bloodworms (which are the immature forms of midges), as well as clams, snails, and nematodes in distributions systems and elsewhere.

TREATMENT

pH is a measure of the hydrogen ion activity, which indicates the degree of acidity. On a scale of 0 to 14, a pH of 7.0 is neutral. At low pH, water is acid and tends to be corrosive and dissolve materials. Lead, cadmium, iron, or copper may enter the water supply from pipes. At high pH, water is alkaline and may deposit calcium or magnesium carbonate scale in pipes. Sodium hydroxide, lime, soda ash, carbon dioxide, and sulfuric acid are often used as required to adjust pH to within a range of 6.5 to 8.5.

Sedimentation is a process of gravity settling and deposition of suspended material in water. Coagulation is treating the water with certain chemicals for the purpose of collecting slowly settleable and nonsettleable particles into larger or heavier aggregates that are more readily removed. These aggregates are termed *floc*, which is removed by sedimentation, filtration, or both. Aluminum sulfate or alum, sodium aluminate, or certain iron salts are often used as coagulating materials. In addition, low dosage levels of high molecular weight polymers (anionic, cationic, or neutral) may be added to speed up flocculation. The chemicals are mixed with the turbid water and then allowed to remain quiet. The sedimentation tank where this is done usually is designed with baffles to reduce high local velocities and short circuiting of the water. The cleaning and repairing of an installation can be facilitated by the use of a tank designed with two separated sections, each of which may be used independently. The flocculated material will settle to the bottom of the tank where the sludge so formed must be removed periodically.

Filtration is the process of removing suspended matter from water as it passes through beds of porous material. Sand, anthracite, and diatomite filters, or microstrainers remove particles too light or too finely divided to be removed by sedimentation. Filters often follow sedimentation units, so that the larger quantities of relatively coarse material are removed by sedimentation to avoid rapid clogging of the filters. Fine screens or microstrainers sometimes are used prior to sand filtration. The degree of removal in filtration depends on the character and size of the filter media, the thickness of the porous media, and the size and quantity of the suspended solids. The water is passed through the filtering material. As algae or debris collect on the filter surface, the process is slowed, and the filter must be taken out of service and backwashed to remove the collected debris. In a slow sand filter, water passes slowly through beds of fine sand at rates averaging 0.05 gal/min/ft^2 of filter area (U.S. EPA, 1982). In a pressure sand filter, water is applied at a rate at or above 2 gal/min/ft^2 of filter area, with provisions made for frequent backwashing of the filters to minimize clogging, which results in pressure drop.

Suspended solids are removed by passing the water through a layer of diatomaceous filter media supported by a rigid-base septum at rates approximately that of pressure sand filters. A microstrainer is a drum-shaped screen with uniform small openings through which water passes. A low-quantity jet spray on the opposite site of the screen removes the collected debris as the screen rotates.

The intent of disinfection is to destroy pathogenic organisms. A number of methods and materials have been used for disinfecting water. These have included ultraviolet light; organic chlorine-yielding compounds; bromine, iodine and iodine-yielding organics; ozone; hydrogen peroxide and peroxide-generating compounds; silver; nontoxic organic acids; lime and mild alkaline agents; supersonic cavitation; and heat treatment. Generally in the United States, chlorine is used as a water disinfectant, and it is applied as a gas or a solution, either alone or in conjunction with other chemicals. Free chlorine residual throughout the distribution system provides residual disinfection.

Aeration removes volatile substances and excess carbon dioxide. Aerators include cascades and sprays that expose water to the atmosphere. Aeration may be used to oxidize iron or manganese and to remove odors from water, such as those caused by hydrogen sulfide and algae. It is also effective in increasing the oxygen content of water deficient in dissolved oxygen. Carbon dioxide and other gases that increase the corrosiveness of water can be eliminated largely by effective aeration, although the increase in corrosion because of increased oxygen may partially offset the advantages of the decrease in carbon dioxide.

The basic water treatment operations described above are used in sequence or in combination, along with either treatment methods to produce a safe and aesthetically pleasing product. Iron and manganese may be controlled by aeration followed by filtration, lime and soda softening, ion exchange, or by adding polyphosphates or other organic sequestering agents. Corrosion protection may be achieved by good engineering design, proper selection of pipe materials, pH adjustment, reduction of oxygen, use of inhibitors such as phosphates and silicates, and lining of tank and pipe walls with coatings and paints.

STANDARDS AND REGULATIONS

The Safe Drinking Water Act provides for protection of underground sources of drinking water. Final regulations have been issued whereby states are to establish underground injection control programs to prevent endangering underground drinking water sources. For regulatory purposes, injection wells are divided into five classes. Construction and disposal standards are established for the permitting of Class I wells. Class I wells are wells used by generators of hazardous waste or industrial and municipal wastes that are injected below underground sources of drinking water. Class II wells are those for the injection of fluids that are brought to the surface in connection with conventional oil or natural gas production. Class III are wells that are injected for mineral extraction, such as the mining of sulfur, *in situ* production of uranium or other metals, and solution mining of salts or potash. Class IV wells are used for the disposal of hazardous wastes or radioactive wastes into a formation at least one-quarter mile from an underground source of drinking water. Class I and Class IV wells are subject to RCRA requirements. New Class IV wells are prohibited, and existing Class IV wells must be phased out within 6 months after approval or promulgation of an underground injection control program in a state. Class V wells are all other wells, and a regulatory program for them has not yet been developed.

National primary drinking water regulations protect health by specifying maximum contaminant levels allowed in drinking water at the tap for certain physical, microbiological, inorganic, organic, and radionuclide contaminants (Figure 10-3). In addition to the maximum contaminant levels, monitoring, reporting, recordkeeping, and public notification for certain regulatory noncompliance are required. Use of lead pipes, or lead in solder and flux is prohibited.

Community water systems and nontransient, noncommunity water systems must have a monitoring program for 36 volatile organic compounds, except that monitoring for ethylene dibromide and 1,1-dibromo-3-chloropropane is required only if a state determines that a system is vulnerable to contamination by either or both of these substances (Figure 10-4). For surface water systems, the minimum number of samples is 1 year of quarterly samples per water source. For groundwater systems, the minimum number of samples is one sample per entry point to the distribution system (40 CFR 141.40).

Although not federally enforceable, national secondary drinking water regulations are promulgated for contaminants in drinking water that primarily affect the aesthetic qualities relating to the public acceptance of drinking water (Figure 10-5). Currently, 13 contaminants are included in the secondary regulations, which are intended as guidelines for the states. These levels represent reasonable goals for drinking water quality (40 CFR 143.3). An additional nine contaminants have been proposed for national secondary drinking water regulations (Figure 10-6).

All but a very few states have been delegated primary enforcement responsibility to operate the public water systems supervision program under the Safe Drinking Water Act. To do so, a state must have a drinking water program in agreement with 40 CFR 142. These regulations require recordkeeping, reporting, a state laboratory certification program unless all compliance samples are analyzed in a state laboratory that is certified by the EPA, and certain additional administrative and approval matters.

In 1982, the U.S. Geological Survey began a national program to study toxic wastes and their behavior and fate in aquifer systems. At least eight separate federal statutes require groundwater monitoring for specific sources. Thirty-eight states monitor groundwater quality or are developing monitoring programs. In 1985, the EPA formulated a national groundwater monitoring strategy designed to coordinate many of these disparate monitoring efforts. The strategy contains an action plan designed to characterize the nation's groundwater resource, to identify new contaminate problems, to assess know problems, to assure compliance with regulations, to evaluate program effectiveness, to improve data quality, and to develop a groundwater data system for storing all groundwater quality and related well information. A minimum set of 22 elements necessary to use data from wells and springs across groundwater-related programs has been developed.

WELLHEAD PROTECTION

There are approximately 187,000 public drinking water well systems, including 47,000 community and 140,000 noncommunity facilities, such as campgrounds and truck stops. The wellhead protection program is designed to protect the surface and subsurface areas surrounding a well or wellfield that supplies a public water system. Because the groundwater around a pumping well is pulled down as water is drawn into a well, creating a cone of depression, wellhead areas are vulnerable to pesticides, fertilizers, road salts, and other contaminants that may enter near-surface groundwater. Management activities include land use regulations, land acquisition, and prohibition of specified activities in the vicinity of the wellhead. Funding for federal support of state programs has been authorized.

The potential for groundwater contamination is great (Figure 10-7). The EPA (1987a) provided an example of a leak in a gasoline storage tank in a community in Massachusetts, which made headlines in 1977 when it forced the shutdown of a nearby municipal wellfield, disrupting that community's only source of drinking water. When the tank was excavated, local officials estimated that between 2000 and 3000 gal of high-test unleaded gasoline had leaked into the ground less than 600 ft from the nearest well in the municipal wellfield. To address the problem, the town temporarily provided alternative water supplies, instituted a strict water conservation program, and began a two-phase cleanup process. The second phase, which began in 1985, consisted of

CONTAMINANT	MCLG	MCL
MICROBIOLOGICAL CONTAMINANTS		
Total coliform bacteria	0	1/100ml[a]
Giardia lamblia	0	TT[b]
Heterotrophic bacteria	-	TT[b]
Legionella	0	TT[b]
Virus	0	TT[b]
Turbidity	-	1-5NTU[c]
INORGANIC CONTAMINANTS		
Arsenic	-	0.05
Barium	-	1.00
Cadmium	-	0.010
Chromium	-	0.05
Fluoride	4.0	4.0
Lead	-	0.05
Mercury	-	0.002
Nitrate	-	10.0
Selenium	-	0.01
Silver	-	0.05

Figure 10-3.   National primary drinking water regulations as of May, 1990 (in milligrams per liter unless otherwise noted).

pumping and treating the contamination and then recharging the treated water back into the aquifer. This second phase will take 3 to 5 years to complete and will cost the town $1.1 million, the Massachusetts Department of Environmental Quality Engineering $1.2 million, the Massachusetts Executive Office of Community Development $750,000, and the U.S. Department of Housing and Urban Development $250,000. Many years of work, community disruption, and $3.3 million is the estimated price of this one incident.

Provisions for wellhead protection were part of the 1986 amendments to the Safe Drinking Water Act. This legislation established a nationwide program to encourage states to develop systematic and comprehensive programs within their jurisdictions to protect public water supply wells and wellfields from contamination from all anthropogenic sources. The purpose of the wellhead protection program is to prevent contamination of public water supplies, as contrasted to correction of existing situations.

ORGANIC CONTAMINANTS		
2,4-D	-	0.1
Endrin	-	0.0002
Lindane	-	0.004
Methoxychlor	-	0.1
2,4,5-TP	-	0.01
Benzene	0	0.005
Carbon tetrachloride	0	0.005
p-Dichlorobenzene	0.075	0.075
1,2-Dichloroethane	0	0.005
1,1-Dichloroethylene	0.007	0.007
1,1,1-Trichloroethane	0.20	0.20
Trichloroethylene	0	0.005
Vinyl Chloride	0	0.002
Total trihalomethanes	-	0.10
RADIONUCLIDES		
Gross alpha particle activity	-	15 pCi/l
Gross beta particle activity	-	4 mrem/yr
Radium 226 and 228 (total)	-	5 pCi/l

MCLG =   Maximum contaminant level goals; MCL = maximum contaminant level
a -   Revised regulations will be based on presence/absence
b -   Treatment technique requirements established in lieu of MCLs
c -   Revised regulations will establish treatment technique requirements

Figure 10-3.   (continued).

Generally, wellhead protection areas range from a few hundred feet to several miles from wells. The characteristics of the aquifer surrounding a well, the extent of pumping, the vulnerability of the aquifer to surface contamination, and the degree of development and activity surrounding the well are the primary criteria by which most states, counties, or municipalities have delineated protection areas. Management activities commonly employed within these protection areas include regulation of land use through special ordinances and permits, prohibition of specified activities, and acquisition of land.

Bromobenzene	trans-1,2-Dichloroethylene
Bromodichloromethane	2,2-Dichloropropane
Bromoform	1,2-Dichloropropane
Bromomethane	1,3-Dichloropropane
Chlorobenzene	1,1-Dichloropropene
Chlorodibromomethane	1,3-Dichloropropene
Chloroethane	Ethylene dibromide
Chloroform	Ethylbenzene
Chloromethane	Styrene
o-Chlorotoluene	1,1,1,2-Tetrachloroethane
p-Chlorotoluene	1,1,2,2-Tetrachloroethane
1,2-Dibromo-3-chloropropane	Tetrachloroethylene
Dibromomethane	Toluene
m-Dichlorobenzene	1,1,2-Trichloroethane
o-Dichlorobenzene	1,2,3-Trichloropropane
Dichloromethane	m-Xylene
1,1-Dichloroethane	o-Xylene
cis-1,2-Dichloroethylene	p-Xylene

Figure 10-4.   Unregulated volatile organic compounds subject to monitoring requirements.

CORROSION

Corrosion is one of the most important problems in the water utility industry. It can affect public health, public acceptance of a water supply, and the cost of providing safe water (U.S. EPA, 1984). Corrosion of distribution piping and of home plumbing and fixtures has been estimated to cost the public water supply industry more than $700 million per year. Two toxic metals that occur in tap water, almost entirely because of corrosion, are lead and cadmium. Three other metals, usually present because of corrosion, cause staining of fixtures, metallic taste, or both. These are copper, which causes blue stains and metallic taste; iron, which causes red-brown stains and metallic taste; and zinc, which causes metallic tastes (U.S. EPA, 1984).

The corrosion products in the distribution system also protect bacteria, yeasts, and other microorganisms. In a corroded environment, these organisms can reproduce and cause tastes, odors, and slimes; they also produce additional corrosion. The problems created include increased pumping costs due to clogging of pipes with corrosion products; holes in pipes, which cause loss of water and water pressure; leaks and

CONTAMINANT	MCL
Chloride	250
Color	15 Color Units
Copper	1.0
Corrosivity	Non-corrosive
Fluoride	2.0
Foaming agents	0.5
Iron	0.3
Manganese	0.05
Odor	3 threshold odor number
pH	6.5 - 8.5 units
Sulfate	250
Total dissolved solids	500
Zinc	5.0

MCL - Maximum contaminant level

Figure 10-5.   National secondary drinking water regulations as of May, 1990 (in milligrams per liter unless otherwise noted).

damage to dwellings; replacement of hot water heaters and other equipment where leaks occur; and responding to customer complaints of colored water, stains, or bad taste, which is expensive, both in terms of money and public relations for the water system.

Corrosion is commonly defined as an electrochemical reaction in which metal deteriorates or is destroyed when in contact with elements of its environment, such as air, water, or soil. Whenever this reaction occurs, there is a flow of electric current from the corroding portion of the metal toward the electrolyte or conductor of electricity, such as water or soil (U.S. EPA, 1982). Any characteristic of a water that tends to allow or increase the rate of this electrical current will increase the rate of corrosion.

Some of the characteristics of water that are important in corrosivity include:

1. **pH.** Low pH may increase corrosion; high pH may protect pipes and decrease corrosion rates. As pH values drop below 5, both iron and copper corrode rapidly and uniformly (U.S. EPA, 1984).
2. **Alkalinity.** Water with low alkalinity or buffering capacity tends to be corrosive. Hard waters generally are less corrosive than soft waters if sufficient calcium ions and alkalinity are present to form a protective calcium carbonate lining on the pipe walls.

CONTAMINANT	MCL
Aluminum	0.05
o-Dichlorobenzene	0.01
p-Dichlorobenzene	0.005
Ethylbenzene	0.03
Pentachlorophenol	0.03
Silver	0.09
Styrene	0.01
Toluene	0.04
Xylene	0.02

Figure 10-6. **Proposed secondary drinking water regulations as of May, 1989 (in milligrams per liter unless otherwise noted).**

3. **Dissolved oxygen.** When present, dissolved oxygen increases the rate of many corrosion reactions. The amount dissolved in water promotes corrosion by destroying the thin protective hydrogen film that is present on the surface of metals immersed in water.
4. **Conductivity.** Conductivity is a measure of the amount of dissolved mineral salts in water. An increase in conductivity promotes the flow of electrical current and increases the rate of corrosion.
5. **Water temperature.** The corrosion rate increases with increases in water temperature.
6. **Other factors.** Chlorine residual and high total dissolved solids increase metallic corrosion, as does hydrogen sulfide when present. Silicates and phosphates form protective films and inhibit or reduce corrosion. Iron-oxidizing and sulfate-reducing bacteria can induce corrosion.

When corrosion is caused by the acidity of the water supply, it can be effectively controlled by installing an alkaline neutralizing agent ahead of a water softener. Another method of controlling corrosion is that of feeding small amounts of commercially available film-forming materials, such as polyphosphates or silicates. Other methods for controlling corrosion are the installation of dielectric or insulating unions, reduction of velocities and pressures, removal of oxygen or acid constituents, chemical treatment to decrease the acidity, or the use of nonmetallic piping and equipment (U.S. EPA, 1982).

Scale is an associated problem. The occurrence of scale or sludge formation in industrial water systems may induce equipment failures, such as boiler tube ruptures or plugged heat-exchanger tubing. Such occurrences frequently result from increase

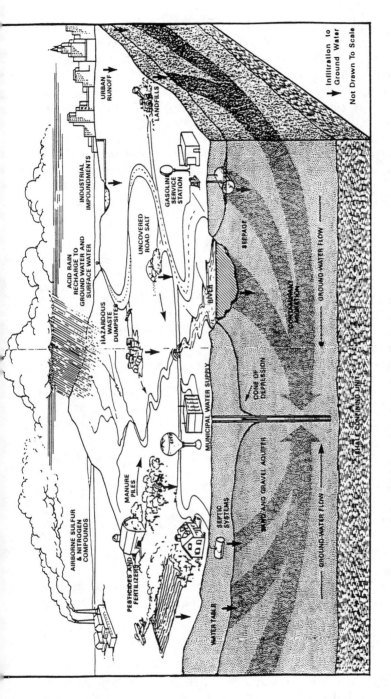

Figure 10-7.   Potential sources of groundwater contamination. (From U.S. EPA, 1987a.)

temperature evaporation, or aeration, which cause insolubility of some of the ionic combinations present. Common scale deposits may consist of calcium carbonate, phosphate, silicate, or sulfate, or of magnesium hydroxide, phosphate, and silicate. Others may be from oxides, silica, or related substances (Standard Methods, 1975).

Scale formation is prevented in boilers by ion-exchange or other hardness-reduction techniques or solubilizing methods in the feedwater. The residual hardness is then precipitated inside the boiler by the addition of phosphate or carbonate and organic sludge conditioning chemicals, producing a nonadhering sludge rather than a scale; or is reacted with chelating agents to form soluble complexes (Standard Methods, 1975). In cooling towers, acid is applied for alkalinity reduction and scale prevention; however, presoftening of make-up water is practiced in some cases. Polyphosphates and other chemicals are applied to control calcium carbonate, calcium phosphate, and silica deposit formation. Proper and adequate bleedoff is an important part of treatment of cooling water.

REFERENCES CITED AND SELECTED READING

Anon. (Not dated). *Manual of Instructions for Water Treatment Plant Operators.* New York State Department of Health, Albany, NY.

Canter, L. W., R. C. Knox, and D. M. Fairchild. 1987. *Ground Water Quality Protection.* Lewis Publishers, Chelsea, MI.

Conservation Foundation. 1987. *Groundwater Protection.* The Conservation Foundation, Washington, D.C.

Drew Chemical. 1977. *Principles of Industrial Water Treatment.* Drew Chemical Corporation, Boonton, NJ.

Fair, G. M., J. C. Geyer, and D. A. Okum. 1971. *Elements of Water Supply and Wastewater Disposal.* John Wiley & Sons, New York, NY.

Freeze, R. A. and J. A. Cherry. 1979. *Groundwater.* Prentice Hall, Englewood Cliffs, NJ.

Kemmer, F. N. (Ed.). 1977. *Water: The Universal Solvent.* Nalco Chemical Company, Oak Brook, IL.

Kerri, K. D. 1988. *Water Treatment Plant Operation.* California State University, Sacramento, CA (Vols. 1 & 2).

Larson, R. A. 1989. *Biohazards of Drinking Water Treatment.* Lewis Publishers, Chelsea, MI.

Office of Technology Assessment. 1984. "Protecting the Nation's Groundwater from Contamination." U.S. Congress, Office of Technology Assessment, Washington, D.C.

Riehl, M. L. 1976. *Hoover's Water Supply and Treatment* (11th Ed.). National Lime Association, Washington, D.C.

Standard Methods. 1976. *Standard Methods for the Examination of Water and Wastewater* (14th Edition). American Public Health Association, American Water Works Association, Water Pollution Control Federation, Washington, D.C.

Steel, E. W. 1960. *Water Supply and Sewerage*. McGraw-Hill Book Company, New York.

U.S. EPA. 1977. "National Interim Primary Drinking Water Regulations." U.S. Environmental Protection Agency, Washington, D.C. (EPA-570/9-76-003).

U.S. EPA. 1980. "National Secondary Drinking Water Regulations." U.S. Environmental Protection Agency, Washington, D.C. (EPA-570/9-76-000).

U.S. EPA. 1982. "Manual of Individual Water Supply Systems (Revised)." U.S. Environmental Protection Agency, Washington, D.C. (EPA-570/0-82-004).

U.S. EPA. 1984. "Corrosion Manual for Internal Corrosion of Water Distribution Systems." U.S. Environmental Protection Agency, Washington, D.C. (EPA-570/9-84-001).

U.S. EPA. 1985. "Ground-Water Monitoring Strategy." U.S. Environmental Protection Agency, Office of Ground-Water Protection, Washington, D.C.

U.S. EPA. 1987. "Improved Protection of Water Resources from Long-Term and Cumulative Pollution: Prevention of Ground-Water Contamination in the United States." U.S. Environmental Protection Agency, Office of Ground-Water Protection, Washington, D.C.

U.S. EPA. 1987a. "Wellhead Protection: A Decision-Maker's Guide." U.S. Environmental Protection Agency, Washington, D.C. (EPA-440/6-87-003).

U.S. EPA. 1988. "Developing a State Wellhead Protection Program." U.S. Environmental Protection Agency, Washington, D.C. (EPA-440/6-88-003).

U.S. EPA. 1988a. "EPA Workshop to Recommend a Minimum Set of Data Elements for Ground Water." U.S. Environmental Protection Agency, Washington, D.C. (EPA-440/6-88-005).

U.S. EPA. 1990. "Manual for Certification of Laboratories Analyzing Drinking Water, Criteria and Procedures and Quality Assurance (Third Edition)." U.S. Environmental Protection Agency, Washington, D.C. (EPA/9-90-008).

11   AIR QUALITY — STATIONARY SOURCES

THE CLEAN AIR ACT

The Clean Air Act was enacted to protect and enhance the nation's air quality as well as to safeguard public health and welfare and the productive capacity of its people. The Act is divided into three titles:

- Title I deals with control of pollution from stationary sources.
- Title II deals with control of pollution from mobile sources.
- Title III addresses general administrative matters.

The Act requires the EPA to promulgate national ambient air quality standards (NAAQS) for certain pollutants to protect the public health (primary NAAQS) and to protect the public welfare (secondary (NAAQS).

Each state is required to adopt a plan, called a State Implementation Plan (SIP), that limits emissions from air pollution sources to the degree necessary to achieve and maintain the NAAQS. The SIP provides emission limitations, schedules, and time-tables for compliance for stationary sources. The Act focuses on major stationary sources or major modifications of existing sources. Major sources are defined as sources that emit, or have the potential to emit, more than a prescribed amount of a designated pollutant.

States are also required to adopt measures to prevent significant deterioration of air quality (PSD) in "clean air areas". When a SIP is approved by the EPA, it is enforceable by both federal and state governments.

In addition to the SIP regulatory scheme, the Act establishes two other major regulatory programs for stationary sources. The New Source Performance Standards (NSPS) program establishes stringent emissions limitations for new sources in designated industrial categories, regardless of the state in which the program is located or the air quality associated with the area. The second program, the National Emissions

141

Standards for Hazardous Air Pollutants (NESHAP), regulates emissions of pollutants for which no NAAQS is applicable, but that causes increases in mortality or serious illnesses (U.S. EPA, 1989).

For existing sources, Section 109 of the Act requires that the EPA adopt national ambient air quality standards for so-called criteria pollutants to protect the public and welfare. They are called *criteria pollutants* because comprehensive air quality criteria documents support and provide the rationale for the regulated pollutants. There are six criteria pollutants — particulate matter, sulfur dioxide, carbon monoxide, ozone, nitrogen dioxide, and lead. The human health-related standards are designated *primary* ambient air quality standards, and the welfare-related standards are designated *secondary* ambient air quality standards.

Section 110 of the Act requires each state to submit to the EPA for approval on SIP for the implementation, maintenance, and enforcement of the NAAQS in each air quality control region or portion thereof within the state. Each plan must include source-specific emission limitations, and such other measures necessary to ensure attainment and maintenance of primary and secondary standards.

EPA has designated all areas of the country as either *attainment* or *nonattainment* for each of the criteria pollutants. SIPs must assure attainment of NAAQS by prescribed dates. SIPS must meet federal requirements, but each state may choose its own mix of emission controls for sources to meet the NAAQS. Controls may include stationary and mobile source emission limits; transportation plans; preconstruction review of new sources; nonattainment area (NAA); and prevention of significant deterioration (PSD) permits for construction of new sources; monitoring; and inspection and testing of vehicles. Other measures may include emission charges, closing and relocation of plants, changes in operations, and ways to reduce vehicular traffic, including taxes, staggered work hours, and mass transportation. The Clean Air Act provides that no SIP may be adopted without a public hearing, and sources affected by the SIP are entitled to participate.

For new or modified stationary sources of air pollution, the Act requires the EPA to promulgate uniform Federal New Source Performance Standards (NSPS) for specific pollutants in industrial categories based upon adequately demonstrated control technology. Rather than tying control levels to NAAQS, Congress required the EPA to base these uniform emission standards on strictly technological considerations.

The owner or operator of a new or modified source must demonstrate compliance with an applicable new source performance standard within 180 days of initial startup of the facility, and at other times as required by the EPA. The EPA has primary authority for enforcement of NSPS unless authority is delegated to the states. In such cases, the EPA and the states have concurrent enforcement authority.

Part C of Title I of the Act, prevention of significant deterioration (PSD) of air quality, applies in all areas that are attaining the national ambient air quality standards where a major source or modification is proposed to be constructed. Its purpose is to prevent the air quality in relatively clean areas from becoming significantly dirtier.

A clean air area is one where the air quality is attaining the ambient primary or secondary standard. The designation is pollutant specific so that an area can be nonattainment for one pollutant, but clean for another. It establishes three classifications of geographical areas for proposed emitters of sulfur dioxide and particulate matter:

- Only minor air quality degradation allowed — Class I.
- Moderate degradation allowed — Class II.
- Substantial degradation allowed — Class III.

In no case does PSD allow air quality to deteriorate below secondary air quality standards. *Baseline* is the existing air quality for the area at the time the first PSD is applied for. *Increments* are the maximum amount of deterioration than can occur in an attainment area over baseline. Increments in Class I areas are smaller than for Class II, and Class II increments are smaller than for Class III areas.

For purposes of PSD, a major emitting source is one of 26 designated categories that emits or has the potential to emit 100 tons/yr of the designated air pollutant. A source that is not within the 26 designated categories is a major source if it emits more that 250 tons/yr.

Any proposed major new source or major modification is subject to preconstruction review by the EPA, by a state to whom the program is delegated or by a state that has adopted PSD requirements in its SIP, so that a permit for increases will not be exceeded. The permit describes the level of control to be applied and what portion of the increment may be made available to that source by the state. Where the EPA has delegated such review, the EPA and the state have concurrent enforcement authority (U.S. EPA, 1989).

Nonattainment areas are those that are not in compliance with national air quality standards. For a proposed source that will emit a criteria pollutant in an area where the standards are presently being exceeded for that pollutant, even more stringent preconstruction review requirements apply. This review is the primary responsibility of the state where the source is proposed to be constructed, with overview authority vested in the EPA.

New construction of major sources or major modifications in an NAA is prohibited unless the SIP provides for the following:

- The new source will meet an emission limitation for the nonattainment pollutant that reflects the lowest achievable emission rate.
- All other sources within the state owned by the subject company are in compliance.
- The proposed emissions of the nonattainment pollutant are more than offset by enforceable reductions of emissions from existing sources in the nonattainment areas.
- The emissions offsets will provide a positive net air quality benefit in the affected areas.

The applying source in an NAA, therefore, must obtain a greater than 1:1 reduction of the pollutant or pollutants for which the area has been designated nonattainment. Emission offsets from existing sources may need to be obtained, especially if the new source will have emissions that would exceed the allowance for the NAA. In this situation, the source would need to obtain enforceable agreements from other sources in the NAA or from its own plants in the NAA.

Section 112 of the Clean Air Act defines hazardous air pollutants as those for which no air quality standard is applicable but that are judged to increase mortality or serious irreversible or incapacitating illness. National emissions standards for hazardous air pollutants (NESHAPs) are based on health effects, with strong reliance on technological capabilities. These standards apply to both existing and new stationary sources. The NESHAPs program can be delegated to any qualifying state.

Under NESHAPs, no person may construct any new source unless the EPA determines that the source will not cause violations of the standard. For existing sources, a standard may be waived for up to 2 years if there is a finding that time is necessary for the installation of controls and that steps will be taken to prevent the endangerment of human health in the interim (U.S. EPA, 1989).

THE CLEAN AIR ACT AMENDMENTS OF 1990

In Chapter 2, the chronology of the Hazardous and Solid Waste Amendments of 1984 was presented. Such chronologies are educational because they provide insight into the workings of Congress and how environmental legislation is developed. The U.S. Environmental Protection Agency has developed a similar chronology of the Clean Air Act Amendments of 1990. For the above reason, this latter chronology is presented here.

- June 12, 1989 — President Bush announces the administration's clean air proposal, which addresses three areas of environmental concern: acid deposition, toxic air pollution, and urban quality
- July 21, 1989 — the legislative language interpreting the President's proposal is submitted to Congress
- July 27, 1989 — the administration's bill is introduced by House Energy and Commerce Committee Chairman John Dingell (D-MI) as H.R.3030 with 146 cosponsors (eventually 166); the measure is subsequently referred to the Energy and Commerce Committee
- August 3, 1989 — the administration's bill is introduced in the Senate by Senator John Chafee (R-RI) as S.1490 with 24 cosponsors (eventually 25); the measure is subsequently referred to the Senate Environmental and Public Works Committee
- September 13, 1989 — Health and Environment Subcommittee of the House Energy and Commerce Committee holds first of 11 mark-ups on H.R.3030 that continued through October 11, 1989
- October 11, 1989 — Health and Environment Subcommittee of House Energy and Commerce holds their final mark-up of the administration's bill (H.R.3030); the measure as amended is sent to full Committee by a 21-0 vote

- October 26, 1989 — Environmental Protection Subcommittee of Senate Environment and Public Works begins process of marking up clean air legislation
- November 14, 1989 — Environmental Protection Subcommittee of Senate Environment and Public Works votes to include an acid rain title, which is based on the administration's original proposal; the subcommittee has no further action on S.1630
- November 16, 1989 — Senate Environment and Public Works votes out a Clean Air bill (S.1630) by a 15-1 margin
- January 23, 1990 — Floor debate begins in the U.S. Senate
- February 1, 1990 — a group of bipartisan senators begins meeting with administration officials in a month-long, closed-door negotiation session on amendments to S.1630 during which Senate floor debate is put on hold
- March 5, 1990 — Senator George Mitchell announces agreement with the administration on several key aspects of clean air; this measure is the product of the administration and bipartisan Senate negotiations during February and served as the vehicle for Senate floor deliberation (it would eventually become S.1630)
- March 14, 1990 — Energy and Power Subcommittee of House Energy and Commerce reports H.R.3030 out to full committee
- March 14, 1990 — House Committee on Energy and Commerce begins public mark-up of H.R.3030
- April 3, 1990 — the Senate votes out the Clean Air Act Amendments of 1990; the measure was passed by a vote of 89-11
- May 17, 1990 — House Committee on Energy and Commerce reports H.R. 3030 out of committee by a vote of 42-1; the measure then moved to the entire House of Representatives
- May 17, 1990 — House Committee on Public Works and Transportation and the House Committee on Ways and Means are given sequential referral of certain aspects of H.R.3030; both committees report the bill out on May 21, 1990
- May 17, 1990 — House Committee on Ways and Means receives sequential referral of H.R.3030 for a period ending no later than May 21, 1990
- May 23, 1990 — the House of Representatives votes to pass a new Clean Air Act by a vote of 401-21
- June 6, 1990 — the Senate announces their conferees for the Clean Air Act Amendments of 1990
- June 28, 1990 — the House of Representatives announces their conferees for the Clean Air Act Amendments of 1990
- July 13, 1990 — House and Senate Clean Air Conferees hold their first joint conference
- October 22, 1990 — House and Senate Clean Air Conferees reach final agreement on Clean Air Authorization and thus conclude conference negotiations
- October 26, 1990 — the House of Representatives considers the conference report and passes the measure with a 401-25 roll call vote
- October 27, 1990 — the Senate considers the conference report and passes the measure with an 89-10 roll call vote

- November 13, 1990 — S.1630, "The Clean Air Act Amendments of 1990" is submitted to the President
- November 15, 1990 — the President signs the Clean Air Act Amendments

Titles I, III, IV, and V of the 1990 amendments relate to stationary sources. Title I addresses nonattainment areas. For the pollutant ozone, the new law establishes nonattainment area classifications for metropolitan areas ranked according to the severity of the air pollution problem. These five classifications are marginal, moderate, serious, severe, and extreme. The EPA assigns each nonattainment area one of these categories, thus triggering various requirements the area must comply with in order to meet the ozone standard. They will be required to conduct an inventory of their ozone-causing emissions and institute a permit program. Moderate areas and above must achieve 15% volatile organic compounds reduction within 6 years of enactment. For serious and above, an average of 3% volatile organic compounds reduction per year is required until attainment. For the City of Los Angeles, for example, this translated to a 20-year ozone-reduction program to achieve attainment (U.S. EPA, 1990). The law established similar programs for areas that do not meet the federal health standards for the pollutants carbon monoxide and particulate matter.

Title III addresses emissions of toxic pollutants. The amendments list 189 hazardous air pollutants. Within 1 year, the EPA must list the source categories that emit one or more of the 189 pollutants. Within 2 years, the EPA must publish a schedule for regulation of the listed source categories. For all listed major point sources, the EPA must promulgate maximum achievable control technology standards. These standards must address 40 source categories plus coke ovens within 2 years, 25% of the remainder of the list within 4 years, and additional 25% in 7 years, and the final 50% in 10 years. The maximum achievable control technology regulations are emission standards based on the best demonstrated control technology and practices in the regulated industry. For existing sources, they must be as stringent as the average control efficiency or the best controlled 12% of similar sources. For new sources, they must be as stringent as the best controlled similar source.

Title IV is designed to reduce acid rain. It is intended to result in a permanent 10 million ton reduction in sulfur dioxide emissions per year from 1980 levels. The first phase, effective January 1, 1985, will affect 100 power plants and will provide them with certain reduction allocations. The second phase will become effective January 1, 2000 and will affect 2000 utilities. In both phases, affected sources will be required to install systems that continuously monitor emissions in order to track progress and to assure compliance. The law allows utilities to trade emission allowances within their system or to buy or sell allowances to and from other affected sources.

Title V establishes a clean air permit program similar to the NPDES permit program in water, which was discussed in Chapter 5. EPA must issue program regulations within 1 year. Within 3 years, each state must submit to the EPA a permit program meeting these regulatory requirements. After achieving the state submittal, the EPA has 1 year to accept or reject the program. The EPA must levy sanctions against a state that does not submit or enforce a permit program.

All sources subject to the permit program must submit a complete permit application within 12 months. The state permitting authority must determine whether or not to approve an application within 18 months of the date it receives the application. Each permit issued to a facility will be for a fixed term of up to 5 years. The new law establishes a permit fee system whereby the state collects a fee from the permitted facility to cover reasonable direct and indirect costs of the permitting program.

Title VI relates to stratospheric ozone and global climate protection. The law requires a complete phaseout of certain chemicals that affect the ozone layer. Leading up to a phaseout there will be stringent interim reductions placed upon the specific chemicals. Within 60 days of enactment, the EPA must list all regulated substances, along with their ozone-depletion potential, atmospheric lifetimes, and global warming potential.

Enforcement, research, and other clean air-associated issues are addressed in other titles of the new act.

AIR QUALITY TRENDS

In 1987, 88.6 million people were living in counties with measured air quality levels that violated the national ambient air quality standard for ozone. This compares with 29.4 million people for carbon monoxide, 21.5 million people for particulate matter, 7.5 million people for nitrogen dioxide, 1.7 million for lead, and 1.6 million for sulfur dioxide. Overall, 107 million people lived in counties where one of the criteria pollutant standards was exceeded in 1987. Sixty-six air quality areas failed to attain the ozone standard, and 50 areas failed to attain the carbon monoxide standard (U.S. EPA, 1990a).

Based upon monitoring sites that recorded at least 8 of the 10 years of data in the period 1978 to 1987, all of the criteria pollutants showed improvement in air quality and emissions. Annual average total suspended particulate air quality levels, measured at 1726 sites, decreased 21% between 1978 and 1987. This corresponds to a 23% decrease in estimated particulate emissions for the same period from 9.1 to 7.0 million metric tons per year. Between 1986 and 1987, ambient total suspended particulate levels increased 2%, and emissions increased 3%.

Annual average sulfur dioxide air quality levels measured at 347 sites with continuous sulfur dioxide monitors decreased 35% from 1978 to 1987, improving at a rate of approximately 4% per year. There was a 17% drop in sulfur dioxide emissions during this 10-year period from 24.6 to 20.4 million metric tons per year.

Nationally, the 8-h average carbon monoxide air quality levels at 198 sites decreased 32% between 1978 and 1987. The median rate of improvement has been about 4% per year. The estimated number of exceedances of the 8-h national ambient air quality standard decreased 91% in this same period.

The annual average nitrogen dioxide air quality levels, averaged over 84 sites, increased from 1978 to 1979 and decreased through 1987, except for a slight increase in 1984. The 1987 composite nitrogen dioxide air quality average, however, was 12% lower than the 1978 level, indicating a downward trend during the overall period.

The composite average of the second highest daily maximum 1-h ozone air quality values, recorded at 274 sites, decreased 16% between 1978 and 1987. However, there was a calibration change in the monitoring in the 1978 and 1979 period. In the postcalibration period, the ozone levels decreased 9%. Volatile organic compound emissions decreased 17% for the 10-year and 17% for the post calibration 1979–1987 period. The 10-year change was from 23.7 to 19.6 million metric tons per year.

The composite maximum quarterly average of ambient lead levels, recorded at 97 urban sites, decreased 88% between 1978 and 1987. Lead emissions declined 94% during the same period from 127.9 to 8.1 thousand metric tons per year. This long-term improvement is largely due to the reduction of the lead content of leaded gasoline.

All of the above information on air quality trends was extracted from EPA's "Report to Congress" (U.S. EPA, 1990a).

AMBIENT AIR QUALITY CONTROLS

National ambient air quality standards are based upon medical and other scientific evidences of health and environmental effects for six pollutants. These standards apply to ozone, oxides of nitrogen, carbon monoxide, particulate matter, sulfur dioxide, and lead. Ozone and smog are formed when volatile organic compounds and oxides of nitrogen interact in the presence of sunlight. Ozone irritates the eyes, aggravates respiratory problems, and causes crop damage. Oxides of nitrogen affect the respiratory system and can cause bronchitis, pneumonia, and lung infections. Lead, which can come from battery manufacturing and nonferrous smelters, is a dangerous pollutant because it accumulates in body tissues, particularly in children, and can cause neurological impairment and behavioral disorders. *Particulate matter* is a general term for airborne particles, some of which are seen in the form of smoke or dust; some are too small to be seen. Particulates can irritate the respiratory system and may carry metals, sulfates, and nitrates. Sulfur oxides, and particularly sulfur dioxide, come primarily from the burning of coal and oil and various industrial processes. In the atmosphere, they react to form sulfuric acid, sulfates, and sulfides. They can affect the respiratory system, especially when the sulfuric acid settles on a fine particle that is inhaled.

State and local agencies are required to develop, set up, maintain, and operate the State and Local Air Monitoring Stations (SLAMS) network to provide year-round measurements of the six NAAQS pollutants. A subset of these monitors, specifically designated as National Ambient Monitoring Stations (NAMS), is used by the EPA for national trend analyses, such as discussed in the preceding section of this chapter. The NAMS and SLAMS monitoring must adhere to very specific network design, probe siting, monitoring method and equipment, and quality assurance requirements stated in the EPA regulations. In 1988, there were 3967 SLAMS monitors and 957 NAMS monitors nationwide. The resulting data are used by the EPA and the states to determine the attainment status of specific geographic areas, to evaluate air quality trends, and as the basis for the development of air pollution control strategies and regulations to reduce or maintain ambient air quality concentrations of specific constituents.

State implementation plans (SIPs) form the basis for all state air pollution assessment and control activities as well as management of emerging problems. They contain a state's plans, policies, regulations, and schedules for controlling air pollution. They result from a formal requirement for a state to determine if national air quality standards are being attained. States must develop and enforce SIPs that detail measures to be undertaken to achieve compliance with national air quality standards for any nonattainment areas. The EPA approves these plans. If a state plan is not acceptable, the EPA is required to provide a federal implementation plan that the EPA itself must then enforce. When a state has not shown that it can achieve air quality standards by an acceptable date, the EPA must disapprove the SIP and propose bans on construction in the area or take other measures. A SIP is federally enforceable.

The prevention of significant deterioration (PSD) program and regulations is designed to ensure that new or modified air pollution sources constructed in clean air areas will not cause ambient air concentrations to rise over the NAAQS. The regulations require that a potential source demonstrate that the processes and controls that will be employed will achieve the desired ambient air concentrations. PSD is oriented toward ambient air quality impacts.

POINT SOURCE EMISSION CONTROLS

NESHAPs, or national emission standards for hazardous air pollutants, currently control arsenic, benzene, asbestos, beryllium, mercury, vinyl chloride, coke oven emissions, and radionuclides. They are developed for a particular source category and currently regulate about 25 source emissions categories. Several more substances are under consideration for NESHAPs action. It is a federal permit program, delegatable to the states, that is designed to control emission of particular hazardous materials without regard to NAAQS. For specific stationary source sampling, the analytic procedures are included in quality assurance project plans, which often are called *stack test protocols* in this program. These project plans must be approved ahead of time and must be followed during the testing. In addition, EPA and state personnel are able to arrange for performance evaluation audit samples to improve confidence in the analytical results.

New source performance standards (NSPS) is a federal program that requires permits for new sources of air pollution in specific source categories. The program may be delegated to any state that demonstrates its ability to enforce a program at least as stringent as the federal program. Any new or modified facility in one of the specific source categories is required to install control equipment along with the process construction. The level of control required depends upon the current air quality in the area for the pollutant in question. If the area to be affected by the source is currently attaining the NAAQS, the source is required to install the best available control technology, while a source in a nonattainment area must meet the lowest achievable emission rate for that source category. Source testing and monitoring requirements, along with a quality assurance program, are specified in the regulations.

INDOOR AIR

Many sources of potential irritants and toxicants may be found in residential and commercial buildings. Frequently, these are of greater concern indoors than out because of the close proximity, closed environment, fertile breeding grounds for organisms, and extended time of exposure. Many of these concerns and means of testing and control are discussed in Chapter 19. This is an emerging program within the federal government. Certain responsibilities related to indoor air are assigned to many agencies. The Congress has not yet established a comprehensive national program.

Title IV of the 1986 Superfund Amendments and Reauthorization Act (SARA) mandated that the EPA carry out a program aimed at conducting research into the scientific and technical questions concerning the various facets of indoor air quality and at disseminating information to the public. In addition, SARA required the EPA to coordinate federal, state, local, and private section activities related to indoor air quality.

Implementation of SARA Title IV by the EPA has focused on three objectives: (1) performing the policy analyses needed to make recommendations with respect to the long-term federal role in indoor air quality issues, (2) developing mechanisms of coordination of government and private-sector indoor air programs and activities, and (3) developing a wide spectrum of information on indoor air pollution problems and mitigation strategies.

EPA has informed the Congress (U.S. EPA, 1990a) that it will implement the following objectives:

1. "The Agency will conduct research and analysis to further refine its assessment of the nature and magnitude of the health and welfare problems posed by individual air pollutants as well as pollutant mixtures indoors.
2. The Agency will identify and assess the full range of mitigation strategies available to address high priority indoor air pollution problems.
3. For identified high risk, high priority problems, the Agency will adopt and execute appropriate mitigation strategies. These mitigation strategies may involve one or more of the following:

   • Issuing regulations under existing regulatory authorities (e.g., the Toxic Substances Control Act, the Federal Insecticide, Fungicide and Rodenticide Act, and the Safe Water Drinking Act).
   • Building state and local government and private section capability to address indoor air quality problems through non-regulatory programs of information dissemination, technical assistance, guidance, and training.
   • Referring problems to other Federal Agencies with appropriate statutory authority (e.g., the Consumer Products Safety Commission and the Department of Housing and Urban Development).
   • Requesting separate indoor air regulatory authority from Congress if deemed necessary."

REFERENCES CITED AND SELECTED READING

Cross, F. L. 1973. *Handbook on Air Pollution Control.* Technomic Publishing Co., Westport, CT.

Stern, A. C. 1976. *Air Pollution*, 3rd edition, in 8 volumes. Academic Press, New York. *Vol. 1. Air Pollutants: Air Transformation and Transport. Vol. 2. Effects of Air Pollution.*

U.S. EPA. 1989. "Basic Inspectors Training Course: Fundamentals of Environmental Compliance Inspection." U.S. Environmental Protection Agency, Office of Compliance Monitoring, Washington, D.C.

U.S. EPA. 1989a. "Progress in the Prevention and Control of Air Pollution in 1987." Report to Congress. U.S. Environmental Protection Agency, Research Triangle Park, NC (EPA-450/2-89-009).

U.S. EPA. 1989b. "Status of Selected Air Pollution Control Programs." U.S. Environmental Protection Agency, Office of Air Quality Planning and Standards, Research Triangle Park, NC.

U.S. EPA. 1990. "The Clean Air Act Amendments of 1990. Summary Materials." U.S. Environmental Protection Agency, Office of Air and Radiation, Washington, D.C.

U.S. EPA. 1990a. "Progress in the Prevention and Control of Air Pollution in 1988." Report to Congress. U.S. Environmental Protection Agency, Washington, D.C. (EPA-450/2-90-007).

12   AIR QUALITY — MOBILE
SOURCES

THE CLEAN AIR ACT

Title II of the Clean Air Act establishes the federal motor vehicle emission control program, which is designed to regulate and control emissions from all classes of motor vehicles and engines throughout their useful life. Under Section 202 of the Act, the EPA establishes standards for various pollutants by model year for classes of motorcycles, passenger vehicles, trucks, and truck engines that must be met for a prescribed useful life period. Section 206 on new vehicle testing authorizes oversight and enforcement authorities to ensure that new vehicles and engines are designed and built to comply with the applicable standards.

The EPA has authority under Section 211 to regulate fuels and fuel additives that would contribute to air pollution or impair motor vehicle emissions performance.

In-use compliance tests are to be administered through state or local emissions inspection and maintenance (I/M) programs. Title I of the Act requires I/M for any area that does not meet the national ambient air quality standard (NAAQS) for carbon monoxide or ozone by 1987. There are a number of states and local areas that administer these tests (U.S. EPA, 1989).

Section 203 contains a number of prohibitions pertaining to motor vehicle manufacturing and sale. The sale or importation of any vehicle not covered by a certificate of conformity is prohibited. Tampering with emission control devices or fuel switching from non-leaded to leaded gasoline likewise is prohibited. The law does not authorize the EPA to enforce prohibitions against tampering or fuel switching against individual vehicle owners at this time.

THE 1990 AMENDMENTS

The Clean Air Act of 1990 establishes tighter pollution standards for emissions from automobiles and trucks. These standards will reduce tailpipe emissions of hydrocarbons, carbon monoxide, and nitrogen oxides on a phased-in basis beginning with the model year 1994. Automobile manufacturers also will be required to reduce vehicle emissions resulting from the evaporation of gasoline during refueling.

Fuel quality also will be controlled. Scheduled reductions in gasoline volatility and sulfur content of diesel fuel, for example, will be required. New programs requiring cleaner gasoline will be initiated in 1995 for the nine cities with the worst ozone problems. Other cities can "opt in" to the reformulated gasoline program. Higher levels of alcohol-based oxygenated fuels will be produced and sold during the winter months in 41 areas that exceed the federal standard for carbon monoxide.

The new law also establishes a clean-fuel-car pilot program in California, requiring the phase-in of tighter emission limits for 150,000 vehicles in model year 1996 and 300,000 by model year 1999. These standards can be met with any combination of vehicle technology and cleaner fuels. The standards become stricter in 2110. Other states can "opt in" to this program, but only through incentives and not through sales or production mandates.

Twenty-six of the dirtiest areas of the country will have to adopt programs limiting emissions from centrally fueled fleets of 10 or more vehicles beginning as early as 1998 (U.S. EPA, 1990).

POLLUTION CONCERNS AND SOURCES

The power to move a car comes from burning fuel and air in the car's engine. Gasoline and diesel fuels are mixtures of hydrocarbons, which are compounds containing hydrogen and carbon atoms. Air is composed primarily of nitrogen and oxygen. In the combustion process, the pollutants that are emitted in the exhaust of automotive engines are hydrocarbon fuel molecules that do not get burned in the engine, carbon monoxide that results from partially oxidized carbon in the fuel, and nitrous oxide and nitrogen dioxide, which are formed from the nitrogen and oxygen atoms in the air under the high pressure and temperature conditions in the engine.

Hydrocarbons and nitrogen oxides react in the presence of sunlight to form ground-level ozone, a major component of smog. Ozone irritates the eyes, aggravates respiratory problems, and can damage lungs. It is the most widespread and intractable urban air pollution problem. Carbon monoxide is a poison that reduces the flow of oxygen in the bloodstream and is particularly dangerous to persons with heart problems.

Hydrocarbon pollutants also escape into the air through fuel evaporation. This can occur when the car is parked, when the fuel tank heats up during the day, or as fuel in the engine compartment vaporizes after a hot engine is turned off. Fuel evaporation can occur when the car is running, when gasoline fumes exceed the capacity of the vapor control system. Fuel evaporation also takes place during refueling, when vapors in the gasoline tank are displaced by the new liquid fuel. Because of significant improvements in exhaust emission control systems, evaporative losses now account for about two thirds of the total hydrocarbon pollution from current-model cars.

Ozone is a form of molecular oxygen that consists of three oxygen atoms linked together. Ozone in the upper atmosphere occurs naturally and protects life on Earth by filtering out ultraviolet radiation from the sun. However, ozone at ground level is a dangerous pollutant.

Ozone is a severe irritant. It is responsible for the choking, coughing, and stinging eyes associated with smog. Ozone damages lung tissue, aggravates respiratory disease, and makes people more susceptible to respiratory infections. Elevated ozone levels also inhibit plant growth and can cause widespread damage to crops and forests. Nearly half the residents of the United States live in areas with unhealthy ozone levels.

Carbon monoxide consists of a carbon atom and an oxygen atom linked together. A product of incomplete burning of hydrocarbon-based fuels, carbon monoxide is a colorless, odorless poisonous gas. When inhaled, carbon monoxide enters the bloodstream and forms carboxyhemoglobin. This compound disrupts the delivery of oxygen to the body's tissues. Persons with certain types of heart disease are especially sensitive to this effect and may experience chest pain if they are exposed to carbon monoxide while exercising. Others likely to be susceptible to carbon monoxide include young infants, the elderly, anyone with severe cardiac or other severe diseases, and individuals with chronic bronchitis or emphysema. In addition, carbon monoxide impairs visual perception, manual dexterity, learning ability, and performance of complex tasks in healthy individuals.

Two thirds of the nationwide carbon monoxide emissions are from transportation sources, with the largest contribution coming from highway motor vehicles. In urban areas, the contribution from highway motor vehicles is often greater. Carbon monoxide emissions from automobiles increase dramatically as the temperature decreases. This is because cars require more fuel to start at cold temperatures, and some emission control devices operate less efficiently when they are cold. Under these conditions, the fuel is only partially converted to carbon dioxide, resulting in higher carbon monoxide emissions.

Several probable or definite cancer-causing compounds also are associated with motor vehicle emissions. These include benzene, formaldehyde, soot from diesel buses and trucks, and 1,3-butadiene. Benzene is a component of gasoline. Cars can emit benzene as unburned fuel or as fuel vapors that simply evaporate. Most automotive benzene emissions come from the incomplete combustion of compounds, such as toluene and xylene, that are chemically very similar to benzene. These compounds are added to gasoline to increase octane.

Similarly, formaldehyde, soot, and 1,3-butadiene are not present in fuel but are byproducts of incomplete combustion. Formaldehyde also forms in the atmosphere in the same reactions that form ozone.

CONTROL PROGRAMS

Ozone Control

EPA's attempts to further control ozone include several actions. One is controlling excess evaporative emissions through regulation of in-use gasoline volatility. Running losses and excess evaporative emissions account for more than 20% of volatile organic compound emissions, which makes evaporative emissions the single largest uncontrolled volatile organic compound emissions sources. Efforts are underway to develop on-board diagnostic systems for ozone and carbon monoxide control. Current on-board vehicle computers have the capacity to monitor emission control system components for malfunctions, notify the driver if a malfunction has occurred, and assist mechanics in diagnosing malfunctions. In addition, the standards for light-duty truck exhaust hydrocarbon and carbon monoxide are being tightened.

Preproduction Compliance

Before a manufacturer can offer a motor vehicle for sale in the United States, a certificate of compliance with emission standards must be obtained. This program intensively evaluates each vehicle design to assure that only those designs reasonably likely to comply in use are certified and allowed to be sold. Initiated in 1968, the program involves EPA staff doing selective engineering review and testing of engine families representing new vehicles that are to be sold in the United States. This process includes the submission of technical data from manufacturers about prospective production vehicles, emissions testing of prototypes by manufacturers, a review of engineering data and test results by EPA personnel, and confirmatory testing of prototypes at EPA's National Motor Vehicle Emissions Laboratory in Ann Arbor, Michigan. This procedure identifies and resolves potential problems that could result in excessive in-use emissions. Correcting these problems at the preproduction stage assures maximum environmental benefits and reduces the compliance cost to the industry compared to correcting the problems when discovered in use (U.S. EPA, 1990a).

Assembly-Line Testing

As cars are produced at a manufacturer's facilities, EPA representatives randomly select some of them for emissions testing by the manufacturer. For every car randomly selected for the manufacturer's test during this audit, over 100 cars are voluntarily tested by auto producers to assure that the audits do not result in failures that could affect vehicle production. If enough of the vehicles tested fail to meet standards, the manufacturer must make a change in the design of the vehicle to correct the problem. Quality assurance is built into this program because confirmatory tests are made by the EPA testing laboratory at Ann Arbor, Michigan on some of the same vehicles that the manufacturer tested. EPA personnel audit all testing procedures from the selection of the vehicles to be tested to the completion of the tests and the recording of the data.

Surveillance of In-Use Vehicles

Randomly selected vehicles in use are chosen to determine their emission levels after they have been purchased and driven by their owners. The results of this EPA program, conducted with the cooperation and consent of the vehicle owner, serve two purposes. First, the data are used to estimate emission rates for air-quality planning purposes and are entered into a computer modeling program to project future emissions levels and to suggest whether new or different control programs are necessary. Second, Section 207(c) of the Clean Air Act authorizes the EPA to order the recall of vehicles if a substantial number of any class do not conform to emission standards during their useful lives. During 1987, a total of 1.5 million vehicles were recalled as a result of EPA investigations. In the same period, manufacturers voluntarily recalled an additional 1.4 million vehicles to correct emission problems. During 1988, a total of 2,364,200 vehicles were recalled by the EPA, and manufacturers voluntarily recalled an additional 904,100 vehicles to correct emissions problems.

Vehicle Inspection Programs

An effective strategy for dealing with in-use emissions problems is the establishment of motor vehicle inspection and maintenance (I/M) programs. The EPA's basic approach was determined by the 1977 amendments to the Clean Air Act. Urban areas of the country that obtained an extension to the deadline for attaining the ambient air quality standards for ozone and carbon monoxide beyond 1982 are required by the Clean Air Act to implement an I/M program. The EPA has also interpreted the Act to require areas that do not achieve the predicted attainment in 1982 to implement I/M programs unless they could otherwise prospectively demonstrate attainment by 1987. In 1988, 64 areas had initiated I/M programs and implementation was underway in five other areas.

To ensure that operating I/M programs achieve the planned emission reductions, EPA has initiated a systematic I/M auditing plan. Auditing and thorough follow-up by federal, state, and local officials will pinpoint and lead to the correction of any major deficiencies in individual programs. Many states are switching to computerized analyzers in the inspection networks.

Tampering and Fuel Switching

The EPA is also responsible for carrying out programs designed to deter tampering with vehicle emissions control systems or using leaded fuel in vehicles that require unleaded fuel. Surveys undertaken by the EPA have shown tampering and fuel switching to be continuing serious problems that undermine the emissions control performance of many in-use vehicles. A motor vehicle tampering audit indicated that about 19% of the vehicle fleet is subject to gross tampering, and about 6% to fuel switching. The enforcement of tampering and fuel-switching activities resulted in 215 notices of violation with proposed penalties of over $2 million. There were 298 settlements obtained, which included some notices of violation issued in previous years, from which just under $1 million was obtained in civil penalties and approximately $800,000 in alternative projects (U.S. EPA, 1989a). Tampering or the removal of emission control equipment is a federal offense for repair shops, while fuel switching is a federal offense for fleet and gas station owners.

Alternative Fuels

Alternate fuels are being examined as an opportunity for further vehicle emissions reduction. Alternative fuels currently being studied include ethanol, methanol, natural gas, propane, reformulated gasoline, and electricity. Ethanol is the primary automotive fuel in Brazil and ethanol-gasoline blends (gasohol) have been used in this country for many years. Currently they are more expensive than gasoline. Methanol is a high-performance liquid fuel that emits low levels of toxic and smog-forming compounds. It can be produced at prices comparable to gasoline from natural gas and from coal and wood. All major auto manufacturers have produced cars capable of running on a blend of 85% methanol and 15% gasoline. Natural gas currently is used as motor fuel in some fleet vehicles. It costs about the same or slightly less than gasoline. However, the cost of converting or manufacturing vehicles to accommodate heavy tanks of natural gas must be considered.

The petroleum industry is modifying gasoline to produce formulations that emit less hydrocarbons and toxic pollutants than today's gasolines.

The driving range of today's electric cars is limited by the amount of the power the batteries can provide; the cost of electric vehicles is high and current batteries take hours to recharge.

Many steps must be taken before the use of clean fuels becomes widespread. Technology must be further developed so that vehicles can achieve optimum performance and emissions characteristics. Consumers must be willing to accept the new vehicles and fuels, and government and industry must cooperate to ensure their availability.

REFERENCES CITED AND SELECTED READING

Patterson, D. J. and N. A. Henein. 1972. *Emissions from Combustion Engines and their Control*. Ann Arbor Publishers, Ann Arbor, MI.

U.S. EPA. 1989. "Basic Inspectors Training Course: Fundamentals of Environmental Compliance Inspection." U.S. Environmental Protection Agency, Office of Compliance Monitoring, Washington, D.C.

U.S. EPA. 1989a. "Progress in the Prevention and Control of Air Pollution in 1987." A Report to Congress. U.S. Environmental Protection Agency, Research Triangle Park, NC, (EPA-450/2-89-009).

U.S. EPA. 1989b. "Status of Selected Air Pollution Control Programs." U.S. Environmental Protection Agency, Office of Air Quality Planning and Standards, Research Triangle Park, NC.

U.S. EPA. 1989c. "Fundamentals of Air Pollution and Motor Vehicle Emissions Control. Training Manual." U.S. Environmental Protection Agency, Office of Mobile Sources, Washington, D.C.

U.S. EPA. 1990. "The Clean Air Act Amendments of 1990, Summary Materials." U.S. Environmental Protection Agency, Office of Air and Radiation, Washington, D.C.

U.S. EPA. 1990a. "Progress in the Prevention and Control of Air Pollution in 1988." Report to Congress. U.S. Environmental Protection Agency, Washington, D.C. (EPA-450/2-90-007).

13   THE WORKER ENVIRONMENT

THE LAW AND THE AGENCY

The Occupational Safety and Health Administration (OSHA) was established by the Occupational Safety and Health Act of 1970. Following 100 years of intensive industrial growth in the United States, OSHA was the first comprehensive nationwide attempt to insure occupational safety and health for America's workers. In large measure, American society of the 19th century accepted occupational deaths and injuries as an integral part of the job.

OSHA develops and promulgates occupational safety and health standards, develops and issues regulations, conducts investigations and inspections, issues citations, and proposes penalties for noncompliance with safety and health standards and regulations. It has regional offices in the standard federal regions, which are the same cities in which EPA regional offices are located.

The Act requires virtually every private employer to furnish each employee a place of employment free from recognized hazards likely to cause death or serious physical harm. It establishes a process for the development of standards to protect employee health. For toxic substances, the Act specifically requires that standards assure health by limiting the length of toxic exposure. The purposes of the Act are to

1. Encourage employers and employees to reduce hazards in the workplace and to implement new, or to improve existing, safety and health problems
2. Establish separate but dependent responsibilities and rights for employers and employees for the achievement of better safety and health programs
3. Establish reporting and recordkeeping procedures to monitor job-related injuries and illness
4. Develop mandatory safety and health standards and enforce them effectively
5. Encourage the states to assume the fullest responsibility for establishing and administering their own occupational safety and health programs, which must be at least as effective as the federal program

The Act authorizes OSHA's inspectors to enter any workplace without prior notice. Both employer and employee representatives are allowed to accompany OSHA compliance officers on their inspections. Specified penalties are presented for any violation. Employers are able to contest violations and penalties by appealing to the Occupational Safety and Health Review Commission, an independent body composed of three presidentially appointed members provided by the Act. Judicial reviews of penalties by the U.S. Court of Appeals are also guaranteed. With federal oversight, states are authorized to establish their own programs for worker protection.

In addition, the Act provides for the establishment of a National Institute for Occupational Safety and Health (NIOSH) in the Department of Health and Human Services to carry out research and related activities on occupational safety and health. Employer recordkeeping to aid in uncovering the causes of occupational accidents and illnesses is mandated.

The Occupational Safety and Health Review Commission is charged with ruling on cases forwarded to it by the Department of Labor when disagreements arise over the results of safety and health inspections performed by OSHA. Employers have the right to dispute any alleged job safety or health violation found during the OSHA inspection, the penalties proposed, and the time given to correct any hazardous situation.

The review commission was created to adjudicate enforcement actions initiated under the Act when they are contested by employers, employees, or representatives of employees. A case arises when a citation is issued against an employer as a result of an OSHA inspection and it is contested within 15 working days. The commission is more of a court system than a simple tribunal. Within the review commission there are two levels of adjudication. All cases that require a hearing are assigned to a review commission administrative law judge, who decides the case. Ordinarily, the hearing is held in the community where the alleged violation occurred or as close as possible. At the hearing, the government generally will have the burden of proving the case. After the hearing, the judge must issue a decision, based on finding of fact and conclusion of law. A substantial number of the decisions of the judges become final orders of the commission. However, each decision is subject to discretionary review by the three members of the review commission upon the direction of any one of the three, if done within 30 days of the filing of the decision. When that occurs, the commission issues its own decision.

Once a case is decided, any person adversely affected or aggrieved thereby, may obtain a review of the decision in the U.S. Court of Appeals. The principal office of the review commission is in Washington, D.C. There are nine regional offices where review commission judges are located.

The National Institute for Occupational Safety and Health (NIOSH) is one of nine operating components of the Center for Disease Control, Atlanta, Georgia, established as an operating health agency within the Public Health Service. The center is the federal agency charged with protecting the public health of the nation by providing leadership and direction in the prevention and control of diseases and other preventable conditions. NIOSH conducts research, provides technical assistance to OSHA, and recommends standards for OSHA adoption. OSHA promulgates standards and conducts inspections and provides for their enforcement. NIOSH evaluates all known and available medical, biological, engineering, chemical, trade, and other information relevant to a potential hazard. The purpose is to formulate recommendations on limits of exposure to potentially hazardous substances or conditions in the workplace and appropriate preventive measures designed to reduce or eliminate adverse health effects. These recommendations then are published and transmitted to OSHA and the Mine Safety and Health Administration for use in promulgating legal standards.

HAZARD INFORMATION

NIOSH publishes a *Pocket Guide to Chemical Hazards*. About 790 chemicals and conditions are addressed in the publication. In order to maximize the amount of data provided within a limited amount of space, extensive use is made of abbreviations and symbolic codes; however, these are fully explained in appropriate tables.

For each chemical addressed in the publication, the following information is provided in 14 separate columns:

1. **Chemical name and formula**. This includes the chemical name; Chemical Abstract Service Registry number, NIOSH Registry of Toxic Effects of Chemical Substances number, and the U.S. Department of Transportation UN or NA identification number and corresponding guide number. The identification number indicates that the chemical is regulated by DOT. The guide number refers to actions to be taken to stabilize an emergency situation.
2. **Synonyms**. All common synonyms, if any, are listed for each chemical.
3. **Exposure limits.** The OSHA permissible exposure limit (PEL), which is a time-weighted 8-h concentration to which employees may be exposed without adverse health effects for an 8-h working day, is provided. Chemicals for which NIOSH has published recommended exposure limits (RELs) are also listed. The American Conference of Governmental Industrial Hygienists (ACGIH) time-weighted average and ceiling threshold limit values are also noted when they are less than the OSHA PEL. Carcinogenic substances and suspected carcinogens are indicated.
4. **IDLH**. The immediately dangerous to life or health (IDLH) level defined for the purpose of respirator selection represents a maximum concentration from which, in the event of respirator failure, one could escape within 30 min without experiencing any escape-impairing or irreversible health effects. The IDLH level is listed where one has been assigned.
5. **Physical description**. A brief description of the appearance and odor of each substance is provided.
6. **Chemical and physical properties**. A number of important chemical and physical properties are given for each substance, e.g., molecular weight, boiling point, solubility, flash point, ionization potential, vapor pressure, melting point, upper explosive limit in air, lower explosive limit in air, and minimum explosive concentration for a dust in air.

7. **Incompatibilities**. Potentially hazardous incompatibilities of each substance are listed.
8. **Measurement methods**. A key word description of the suggested sampling and analytical method is provided.
9. **Personnel protection and sanitation**. This information is provided in six categories, including clothing, goggles, wash, change, remove, and special features that should be provided for a specific substance.
10. **Respirator selection**. A table of allowable respiratory use is provided. All respirators selected must be approved by NIOSH and the Mine Safety and Health Administration.
11. **Route of health hazard**. The toxicology important routes of entry for each substance are listed, including inhalation, skin absorption, ingestion, and skin or eye contact.
12. **Symptoms**. Potential symptoms as a result of exposure are given.
13. **First aid**. First aid procedures are listed for response to eye and skin contact, inhalations, and ingestion of the toxic substance.
14. **Target organs**. Target organs that are affected by exposure to each substance are listed.

The ACGIH adopts and publishes threshold limit values and biological exposure indices. Threshold limit values (TLVs) are airborne concentrations of substances that represent conditions under which it is believed that nearly all workers may be repeatedly exposed day after day without adverse effect. They are issued as recommendations and should be used as guidelines for good practice.

Three categories of TLVs are specified. The TLV-TWA is the time-weighted average concentration for a normal 8-h workday and a 40-h workweek to which nearly all workers may be repeatedly exposed without effect. A short-term exposure limit (STEL) is a 15-min time-weighted average exposure that should not be exceeded at any time during a workday. A STEL exposure should not be repeated more than four times during the day and there should be at least 60 min between successive exposures. STEL exposures should not result in irritation, chronic or irreversible tissue damage, or narcosis of sufficient degree to increase the likelihood of accidental injury. The third TLV category specified by the ACGIH is TLV-C, which is the concentration that should not be exceeded during any part of the working exposures. This information is provided for about 600 substances. In addition, heat stress, wind chill, and other physical and biological exposure indices are provided.

NIOSH, OSHA, EPA, and the U.S. Coast Guard published an Occupational Safety and Health Guidance Manual for Hazardous Waste Site Activities (1985). Chemical exposure, explosion and fire, oxygen deficiency, ionizing radiation, biologic hazards, safety hazards, electrical hazards, heat stress, cold exposures, and noise were considered. Oxygen deficiency may result from the displacement of oxygen by another gas or the consumption of oxygen by a chemical reaction. Confined spaces or low-lying areas are particularly vulnerable to oxygen deficiency and should always be monitored prior to entry.

The oxygen content of normal air is approximately 20.5%. Physiological effects of oxygen deficiency in humans are readily apparent when the oxygen concentration in the air decreases to 16%. These effects include impaired attention, impaired judgment and coordination, and increased breathing and heart rate. Oxygen concentrations lower than 16% can result in nausea and vomiting, brain damage, heart damage, unconsciousness, and death. To take into account individual physiological responses and errors in measurement, concentrations of 19.5% oxygen or lower are indicative of oxygen deficiency (NIOSH et al., 1985). Sixteen percent equates to 16,000 ppm. Consider for a moment that in the aquatic environment, an organism functions well in dissolved oxygen concentrations of 5–9 ppm, but experiences physiological responses similar to the above when the dissolved oxygen drops to the 3–5 ppm range or lower.

STANDARDS AND REGULATIONS

The legally binding standards and regulations promulgated by OSHA that are of most direct interest to this book are the occupational safety and health standards codified at 29 CFR Part 1910. Selected standards from this group will be examined in the material that follows. 29 CFR Part 1910 has 21 subparts and nearly 500 sections. It addresses such divergent subjects as employee exposures and medical records, portable wood and metal ladders, means of egress, vehicle-mounted elevating and rotating work platforms, ventilation, hazardous materials, compressed air equipment, mechanical power presses, powered tools and equipment, bakery equipment, electric utilization systems, commercial diving operations, and toxic and hazardous substances.

There are occupational safety and health standards that have been found to be national consensus standards or established federal standards. In this context, *standard* means a standard that requires conditions, or the adoption or use of one or more practices, means, methods, operations, or processes, reasonably necessary or appropriate to provide safe or healthful employment and places of employment. National consensus standard means any standard that (1) has been adopted and promulgated by a nationally recognized standards-producing organization under procedures whereby it can be determined that persons interested and affected by the scope or provisions of the standard have reached substantial agreement on its adoption, (2) was formulated in a manner that afforded an opportunity for diverse views to be considered, and (3) has been designated as such a standard by the Secretary of Labor after consultation with other appropriate federal agencies. An established federal standard means any operative standard established by any federal agency in effect on the date of enactment of the Occupational Safety and Health Act.

Employee Exposure and Medical Records (29 CFR 1910.20)

Medical records for each employee shall be preserved and maintained for at least the duration of employment plus 30 years. Each employee exposure record shall be preserved and maintained for at least 30 years. An exposure record may consist of a record that measures or monitors the amount of a toxic substance or harmful physical agent to which an employee is or has been exposed.

Employee Emergency Plans and Fire Prevention Plans (20 CFR 1910.38)

Where more than 10 employees are involved, a written emergency action plan must contain the following elements:

1.   Emergency escape procedures and emergency escape route assignments
2.   Procedures to be followed by employees who remain to operate critical plant operations before they evacuate
3.   Procedures to account for all employees after emergency evacuation has been completed
4.   Rescue and medical duties for those employees who are to perform them
5.   The preferred means of reporting fires and other emergencies
6.   Names or regular job titles of persons or departments who can be contacted for further information or explanation of duties under the plan

Hazardous Waste Operations and Emergency Response (20 CFR 1910.120)

For those within the scope of this section, each employer shall develop and implement a safety and health program for employees involved in hazardous waste operations. The program shall be designed to identify, evaluate, and control safety and health hazards and provide for emergency response for hazardous waste operations. The program entails the identification of hazards and IDLH conditions monitoring, engineering controls and work practices, employee training, medical surveillance, and the selection and use of personal protective equipment. All employees are to receive a minimum of 40 h of initial instruction off the site and a minimum of 3 d of actual field experience under the direct supervision of a trained, experienced supervisor. An 8-h refresher training course is required annually.

A medical surveillance program, including medical and work history, the ability to wear any required personal protective equipment, and a physical examination, must be maintained for employees who are or may be exposed to hazardous substances of health hazards at or above the established permissible exposure limits for those substances for 30 d or more a year, or employees who wear a respirator for 30 d or more a year. Medical examination and consultation are to be provided an employee annually and upon termination of employment or reassignment.

Particular requirements dealing with eye and face protection and permissible practices dealing with respiratory protection are to be found at 29 CFR 1910.133 and 1910.134, respectively. Respirators are to be provided by the employer when such equipment is necessary to protect the health of the employee. Instructions and training on the use and fitting of respirators are required.

Toxic and Hazardous Substances (Subpart Z of Part 1910)

Subpart Z of the regulations beginning with 40 CFR 1910.1000 presents standards for a number of chemical carcinogens, asbestos, coal tar pitch, cotton dust, and similar hazardous materials. To serve as an example of this series of standards, and for the purposes of this discussion, the standard for asbestos at 40 CFR 1910.1001 will be considered. The asbestos standard begins with definitions, including an action level, the establishment of a permissible exposure limit, and exposure monitoring requirements. Engineering controls and work practices associated with asbestos-containing materials are presented. The employer must provide respirators at no cost to the employee, when required, and ensure that they are used, where required. Generally, there is a requirement for respirators in areas where the permissible exposure limit is not attained. Provisions are stated for performance and the frequency of respirator fit testing. Guidance is provided on the communication of asbestos warning and hazards to employees.

When conditions exist at or above the action level, an annual employee training program and medical surveillance of employees must be instituted. The training program includes health effects, engineering controls and work practices, use and limitations of respirators and protective clothing, purpose and description of the medical surveillance program, and other relevant issues. The annual medical surveillance requirement includes a medical and work history, a complete physical examination, a chest roentgenogram, and a pulmonary function test. In addition, the physician must provide any recommended limitations related to the use of personal protective equipment, including respirators. An employee's medical record shall be maintained for the duration of employment plus 30 years.

The appendices to the standard provide mandatory sampling and analytical procedures for asbestos air sampling and mandatory qualitative and quantitative fit testing procedures for respirators. Nonmandatory work practices and engineering controls for automotive brake repair operations and nonmandatory medical surveillance guidelines are also provided, in addition to other related procedures.

Hazard Communication (29 CFR 1910.1200)

"The purpose of this section is to ensure that the hazards of all chemicals produced or imported by chemical manufacturers or importers are evaluated, and that information concerning their hazards is transmitted to affected employers and employees within the manufacturing sector. This transmittal of information is to be accomplished by means of comprehensive hazard communication programs, which are to include container labeling and other forms of warning, material safety data sheets and employee training." This is not only a federal program, but several of the states have adopted their own version of it.

Each container of hazardous chemicals in the workplace must be labeled, tagged, or marked with the identify of the hazardous chemical and with appropriate hazard warnings. Chemical manufacturers and importers shall obtain or develop a material safety data sheet (MSDS) for each hazardous chemical they produce or import. Each employer shall have an MSDS for each hazardous chemical which they use. Each material safety data sheet shall contain

1. The identity used on the label or the chemical and common names of all health-hazard ingredients that comprise 1% or greater of the composition
2. Physical and chemical characteristics of the hazardous chemical, such as vapor pressure, and flash point
3. The physical hazards of the chemical, including the potential for fire, explosion, and reactivity
4. The health hazards, including signs and symptoms of exposures, and any medical conditions that are generally recognized as being aggravated by exposure to the chemical
5. The primary route or routes of entry
6. The OSHA PEL, ACGIH TLV, and any other exposure limit used or recommended by the chemical manufacturer, importer, or employer preparing the material safety data sheet
7. Whether the hazardous chemical has been found to be carcinogenic
8. Any generally applicable precautions for safe handling and use, including appropriate hygienic practices, protective measures during repair and maintenance of contaminated equipment, and procedures for cleanup or spills and leaks
9. Any generally applicable control measures, such as appropriate engineering controls, work practices, or personal protective equipment
10. Emergency and first aid procedures
11. The date of preparation of the material safety data sheet
12. The name, address, and telephone number of the responsible party preparing or distributing the material safety data sheet

Often, an informative material safety data sheet is arranged to occupy the front and back of one page and may be divided into the following nine sections:

1. Material identification, with synonyms and the name and address of the supplier
2. Ingredients and hazards, including applicable hazard data
3. Physical data, including boiling point, vapor pressure, vapor density, water solubility, specific gravity, volatiles, melting point, evaporation rate, molecular weight, appearance, and odor
4. Fire and explosion data with flash point and method and flammability limits in air, including extinguishing information
5. Reactivity data, including thermal decomposition or burning products
6. Health hazard information, including first aid procedures

7. Spill, leak, and disposal procedures
8. Special protection information, including personal protective equipment
9. Special precautions and comments, including storage guidance and information not covered in the above categories

The MSDSs are to be kept in a location that is readily accessible to employees in an emergency. In addition, employees are to be trained in their use. Records must be kept of the training.

REFERENCES CITED AND SELECTED READING

Government Manual. Latest Edition. "The United States Government Manual." Office of the Federal Register, General Services Administration, U.S. Government Printing Office, Washington, D.C.

ACGIH. 1987–1988. "Threshold Limit Values and Biological Exposure Indices for 1987–1988." American Conference of Governmental Industrial Hygienists, Cincinnati, OH.

NIOSH. 1985. "Pocket Guide to Chemical Hazards." U.S. Department of Health and Human Services, Public Health Service, Center for Disease Control, National Institute for Occupational Safety and Health, Atlanta, GA.

NIOSH, et al. 1985. "Occupational Safety and Health Guidance Manual for Hazardous Waste Site Activities." National Institute for Occupational Safety and Health, Occupational Safety and Health Administration, U.S. Coast Guard, and U.S. Environmental Protection Agency, U.S. Government Printing Office, Washington, D.C.

OSHA. 1976. "All About OSHA." U.S. Department of Labor, Occupational Safety and Health Administration, Washington, D.C.

14 SOLID AND HAZARDOUS WASTES

ENVIRONMENTAL CONCERNS AND SOURCES

In the last 25 years, municipal solid waste has risen from 87 million tons per year to nearly 158 million tons per year (U.S. EPA, 1989). Paper and paperboard make up 41% of this waste. Other nonhazardous solid wastes include yard wastes, 18%; glass, 8.2%; food wastes, 7.9%; plastics, 6.5%; and miscellaneous inorganic wastes, 1.6%. Sources of these wastes include residences, institutions, commercial businesses, municipalities, and industry. The EPA estimates that about 3.6 lb of municipal solid waste were generated per person per day in 1986. At present about 11% of all solid waste is recycled. The full recyclable potential of such solid waste could be as high as 50%.

For these nonhazardous wastes, EPA's goal, which was established in 1988, is a 25% reduction in solid waste by 1992. This is to be achieved through source reduction, including reuse of products, recycling of materials, and composting, with special emphasis on yard wastes. On-line and already permitted incinerators are projected to handle about 20% of the total waste stream, and the remaining 55% is projected for disposal in landfills. The EPA intends to reach these goals through increasing its available information in the form of guidance and materials on the technical aspects of source reduction, combustion, recycling, landfilling, composting, and collection; and through encouraging state and Indian tribe strategies and planning for managing the waste problem. Yard wastes and paper products have been given high priority because these products contribute significantly to the filling of landfills.

A hazardous waste may be a solid, semisolid, liquid, or contained gas. It may be listed as a hazardous waste in the regulations, or it may be hazardous because it meets one of four characteristics of a hazardous waste. These four characteristics include *ignitable* wastes, such as solvents and friction-sensitive substances, which can flash and create fires under certain conditions; *corrosive* wastes, which include those that are acidic and those that can corrode metals; *reactive* wastes, which can create intense heat, explosions, or toxic fumes when mixed with water; and *toxic* wastes, which have the potential to pollute ground and surface waters.

There were 271 million tons of hazardous waste generated in the United States in 1985 by 21,728 large-quantity generators (Table 14-1). The state of Texas ranked number one, with 38,767,600 tons of hazardous waste generated. California has the most individual large quantity generators, with 3972. A large quantity generator is one that generates 13.2 or more tons annually.

The top 50 generators in 1985 accounted for approximately 217 million tons of hazardous waste or 80% of the nation's total, and the top 100 generators accounted for 87% of the total (U.S. EPA, 1989). There were 4944 regulated treatment, storage, and disposal facilities in the United States in 1985. Of these facilities, the state of Texas had 23% or 1153 such facilities (U.S. EPA, 1989). There are 12,500 firms that transport hazardous waste from one place to another.

Waste generators include chemical manufacturers, vehicle maintenance shops, the printing industry, the leather products manufacturing industry, the paper industry, the construction industry, cleaning agents and cosmetic manufacturing, furniture and wood manufacturing and refinishing, metal manufacturing, electroplating, and others. Source reduction, recycling, incineration, and land disposal are the four principal waste management means.

The treatment, storage, and disposal facilities are subject to an EPA permitting system that ensures their safe operation. There is a major concern with pollution of groundwater, and many of the standards that these facilities have to meet are designed to protect groundwater. Some of the requirements for a permitted facility include:

- Analyzing the waste prior to treatment, storage, or disposal
- Preventing the entry of unauthorized personnel into the facility
- Periodically inspecting the facility to determine if there are any problems
- Adequately training employees
- Preparing a contingency plan for emergencies
- Complying with the manifest system and with various reporting and recordkeeping requirements
- Complying with technology requirements, such as installing double lines and leachate detection and collection systems

Underground storage tanks represent another concern of the hazardous waste program. The estimated number of underground storage tanks that recently came under regulation because of a 1986 amendment to the law is at least one million. The EPA estimates that between 5 and 20% of these are leaking.

THE LAW

The purpose of the Resource Conservation and Recovery Act (RCRA) was to provide "cradle to grave" management of hazardous wastes, management of solid wastes, and regulation of underground storage tanks containing chemical and petroleum products.

Hazardous wastes are subject to regulation in their generation, transport, treatment, storage, and disposal under Subtitle C of RCRA. A waste is hazardous if it exhibits hazardous characteristics, such as corrosivity, reactivity, ignitability, or extraction procedure toxicity, or it is specifically listed in a regulation by the EPA. Wastes excluded from regulation as hazardous wastes are household wastes, crop or animal wastes, mining overburden, wastes from processing and benification of ores and minerals, fly ash, bottom ash, slag waste, flue gas emission control waste, and drilling fluids from energy development.

Solid wastes, if land disposed, are regulated through state programs under Subtitle D of RCRA. Solid waste includes garbage, refuse, and sludge, and other solid, liquid, semisolid, or contained gaseous material that is discarded. Exclusions from solid waste include domestic sewage, irrigation return flow, material defined by the Atomic Energy Act, *in situ* mining waste, and NPDES point source wastes.

Subtitle I was added to RCRA by the 1984 amendments. It enables national regulation of underground storage tanks for the first time. In practice, the individual states presently do most of the regulating. Underground storage tanks subject to Title I are those containing chemical and petroleum products. Underground storage tanks containing hazardous wastes are regulated under Subtitle C.

Section 3001 requires the EPA to develop criteria for identifying the characteristics of hazardous waste and for listing hazardous waste. The criteria are to take into account "toxicity, persistence, and degradability in nature, potential for accumulation in tissue, and other related factors such as flammability, corrosiveness, and other hazardous characteristics." EPA then is to identify hazardous waste characteristics and to list particular wastes.

Section 3002 requires the promulgation of standards applicable to generators of hazardous waste. The 1984 amendments require that each manifest include a certification by generators that they have a program of waste minimization, and that the proposed method of treatment, storage, or disposal minimizes the present and future threat to human health and the environment.

Section 3003 requires the EPA to promulgate standards applicable to transporters of hazardous waste. It requires the transportation of hazardous waste to a treatment, storage, or disposal facility only if the waste is properly labeled and in compliance with a manifest system that provides a permanent record of the waste at all times.

Section 3004 requires the EPA to promulgate standards applicable to owners and operators of hazardous waste treatment, storage, and disposal facilities. The 1984 amendments added several significant provisions to this section, including bans on liquids in landfills, the development of standards for facilities that produce fuel from hazardous waste, and corrective action at permitted facilities and beyond facility boundaries.

Section 3005 provides permit requirements for facilities that treat, store, or dispose of hazardous waste.

Table 14-1. State, Rank According to Quantity of Hazardous Waste Generated, and Number of Hazardous Waste Regulated Generators (U.S. EPA, 1989)[a]

State	Rank (Quantity)	Quantity Generated	No. of Generators 000 tons
Alabama	12	7406.2	217
Alaska	49	2.6	9
Arizona	23	846.7	160
Arkansas	38	57.2	114
California	09	9657.8	3972
Colorado	29	295.0	90
Connecticut	30	178.0	364
Delaware	36	94.5	25
District of Columbia	51	1.9	6
Florida	24	833.7	273
Georgia	02	37,324.8	330
Guam	53	0.4	4
Hawaii	46	7.3	26
Idaho	50	2.0	24
Illinois	18	2141.4	760
Indiana	16	2517.0	395
Iowa	33	120.8	123
Kansas	20	1324.7	131
Kentucky	11	7661.9	187
Louisiana	07	13,672.1	302
Maine	47	7.1	69
Maryland	25	698.3	206
Massachusetts	34	114.4	1013
Michigan	14	4076.9	542
Minnesota	28	328.6	291
Mississippi	17	2507.9	109
Missouri	37	68.1	191
Montana	40	25.2	17
Nebraska	26	543.4	65
Nevada	35	94.8	34
New Hampshire	41	19.0	102
New Jersey	10	8999.5	1480
New Mexico	45	8.8	56
New York	06	15,969.2	652
North Carolina	21	1285.3	384
North Dakota	48	3.2	8
Ohio	15	2986.3	688

Table 14-1, Cont'd.

Oklahoma	19	1591.2	118
Oregon	39	30.8	505
Pennsylvania	04	31,307.2	2607
Puerto Rico	31	149.0	115
Rhode Island	43	11.6	403
South Carolina	13	5300.8	171
South Dakota	52	0.9	9
Tennessee	03	33,199.0	556
Texas	01	38,767.6	2450
Utah	22	1134.8	220
Vermont	44	9.8	124
Virginia	05	24,995.5	532
Washington	27	439.2	188
West Virginia	08	12,077.1	57
Wisconsin	32	123.4	240
Wyoming	42	15.8	14
Totals		271,037.3	21,728[a]

[a] These are large-quantity generators with 13.2 tons or more annually (1000 kg/month) of hazardous waste.

LAND DISPOSAL

The 1984 amendments to RCRA prohibit the continued land disposal of untreated hazardous waste beyond specified dates, unless a petitioner demonstrates that the hazardous constituents will not migrate from the land disposal unit for as long as the waste remains hazardous. The amendments require EPA to (1) rank all listed hazardous wastes so that wastes with high intrinsic hazard and volume would be restricted from land disposal first, and wastes with low intrinsic hazard and volume would be dealt with last; (2) separate the list of wastes into a schedule of thirds; and (3) set treatment standards for all hazardous wastes that will diminish the toxicity of the wastes or reduce the likelihood of the migration of their hazardous constituents. The amendments require that if the EPA fails to set treatment standards for a particular waste by the specified deadline, that waste is automatically prohibited from land disposal.

Treatment standards are expressed as concentrations in the leachate of the waste. The leachate is obtained by use of the toxicity characteristic leaching procedure provided in the regulations. For example, the Congress, in amending RCRA, provided guidance related to concentrations for certain metals in liquids for land disposal. Congress also stated that, when necessary to protect human health and the environment, the EPA shall substitute more stringent concentration levels than the levels specified. Land disposal is prohibited if the concentration in the prescribed filtrate exceeds the following levels:

Free cyanides	1000 mg/L
Arsenic (As)	500 mg/L
Cadmium (Cd)	100 mg/L
Chromium (CrVI)	500 mg/L
Lead (Pb)	500 mg/L
Mercury (Hg)	20 mg/L
Nickel (Ni)	134 mg/L
Selenium (Se)	100 mg/L
Thallium (Ti)	130 mg/L

In order to be land disposed, wastes containing the above constituents must either be treated to levels below the statutory prohibition level or be rendered nonliquid.

For purposes of restriction, Congress defined land disposal under RCRA to include any placement of hazardous waste in a landfill, surface impoundment, waste pile, injection well, land treatment facility, salt dome or salt or salt-bed formation, or underground mine or cave. An applicant, such as the owner or operator of a treatment, storage or disposal facility, may petition the EPA to allow land disposal of a specific waste at a specific site. The applicant must prove that the waste can be contained safely in a particular type of disposal unit, so that no migration of any hazardous constituents occurs from the unit for as long as the waste remains hazardous. If the EPA grants the petition, the waste is no longer prohibited from land disposal in that particular type of unit.

REGULATIONS

Codification of hazardous waste regulations begins at 40 CFR Part 260. Part 261 provides the definition for a hazardous waste, the exclusions and those materials that are not hazardous waste, the characteristics of a hazardous waste, and the list of specific hazardous wastes.

Part 262 specifies standards applicable to generators of hazardous waste. A generator must prepare a manifest before transporting the hazardous waste off site. The manifest must contain:

1. A manifest document number
2. The generator's name, mailing address, telephone number, and EPA identification number
3. The name and EPA identification number of each transporter
4. The name, address, and EPA identification number of the designated facility and an alternate facility, if any
5. The description of the waste
6. The total quantity of each hazardous waste by units of weight or volume, and the type and number of containers as loaded into or onto the transport vehicle
7. A certification related to proper classification, labeling, and other factors

The generator signs the manifest by hand. The generator will receive a copy of the manifest signed by the owner or operator of the facility receiving the waste, which must be retained for 3 years. Thirty-five days from shipment, if a generator has not received a copy of the manifest with the signature of the owner or operator of the designated receiving facility, the generator must contact the transporter and the operator of the facility to determine the status of the hazardous waste. If a copy of the manifest has not been received in 45 d by the generator, an Exception Report must be filed with the EPA.

Part 263 provides standards applicable to transporters of hazardous waste and Part 264 provides standards for hazardous waste treatment, storage, and disposal facilities. The latter provides for contingency plans and emergency procedures. There are groundwater protection standards and groundwater monitoring provisions. There are conditions for closure and postclosure care related to the facility, as well as financial assurance for closure operations. Part 264 addresses containers, tanks, surface impoundments, waste piles, land treatment, landfills, and incinerators.

Part 270 addresses treatment, storage, and disposal permits. The permit is of two parts. The Part A application requires identification and other general information about the facility, including the types of the hazardous wastes to be treated, stored, or disposed of and an estimate of the quantity of such wastes to be treated, stored, or disposed of annually. In addition, Part A requires a listing of all permits obtained and a topographic map extending 1 mi beyond the property boundaries of the source.

Part B of the permit application requires both general and specific information. These requirements include

1. A general description of the facility
2. Chemical and physical analyses of the hazardous waste to be handled at the facility
3. A copy of a waste analysis plan
4. A description of the security procedures and equipment
5. A copy of the schedule for facility inspections of malfunctions or discharges to the environment
6. A copy of the contingency plan in the event of fires, explosions, or any unplanned release of hazardous waste to the air, soil, or surface water
7. A description of procedures, structures, or equipment used at the facility to prevent hazards in unloading operations; to prevent runoff from hazardous waste handling areas; to prevent contamination of water supplies; to mitigate effects of equipment failure and power outages; and to prevent undue exposure of personnel to hazardous waste
8. A description of precautions to prevent accidental ignition or reaction of ignitable, reactive, or incompatible wastes
9. A description of traffic patterns at the facility, estimated volume and control of traffic, and description of access road surfacing and load-bearing capacity
10. Information related to facility location, and seismic zones and 100-year floodplain

11.   An outline of both the introductory and continuing training programs by owners or operators to prepare persons to operate or maintain the facility in a safe manner
12.   A copy of the closure plan and the postclosure plan where applicable
13.   Information on the most recent closure cost estimate for the facility
14.   A topographic map showing a distance of 1000 ft around the facility at a scale of 1 in. to not more than 200 ft. Contours must be shown on the map. The contour interval must be sufficient to clearly show the pattern of surface water flow in the vicinity of and from each operational unit of the facility.

For owners or operators of hazardous waste surface impoundments, waste piles, land treatment units, and landfills, additional information regarding protection of groundwater is required. This information includes

1.   A summary of groundwater monitoring data
2.   Identification of the uppermost aquifer and aquifers hydraulically interconnected beneath the facility property, including groundwater flow direction and rate, and the basis for such identification
3.   Detailed plans and an engineering report describing the proposed groundwater monitoring program to be implemented
4.   If the presence of hazardous constituents has been detected in the groundwater at the point of compliance at the time of permit application, the owner or operator must submit sufficient information, supporting data, and analyses to establish a compliance monitoring program, and submit an engineering feasibility plan for a corrective action program.

THE HAZARDOUS WASTE AUDIT

The objective of an audit is to establish the degree of compliance with applicable laws, regulations, permits, and good management practices related to an operation. An audit provides management with knowledge of the degree of compliance with applicable laws and regulations; a list of needs or adjustments necessary to attain full compliance with applicable laws and regulations; and insight into staff's ability to provide information in a timely fashion. Generally, the conduct of an audit entails a solicitation of responses to questions designed to uncover inadequacies in the system; an evaluation of responses and other information obtained as a result of the questioning; and a statement of findings of fact and needs for compliance.

In preparation for an audit, potential audit, or for self-examination, audit-type review questions may be helpful. Some of these relating to hazardous waste management follow:

- Does the facility generate, store, transport, treat, or dispose of a hazardous waste?
- What are the federal and state identification numbers? (40 CFR 262.12)

- Describe and identify by hazardous waste number the hazardous wastes generated. (40 CFR 261.3)
- List and describe the manufacturing processes producing the waste.
- Provide schematic diagrams of all such manufacturing processes.
- Provide a complete list of raw materials used in the manufacturing process.
- Identify and describe any other substances used in the manufacturing processes, including solvents, cleaners, degreasers, and coating or painting materials; indicate maximum total weekly usage. [40 CFR 261.3(a)(2)(iv)(A)]
- What is the average weekly flow of wastewater into the headworks of the facility's wastewater treatment or pretreatment system?
- Provide material safety data sheets for all substances used.
- Provide health-effects data sheets for all substances used.
- What are the average and maximum volumes of waste generated per month and per year? (40 CFR 261.5)
- Describe any waste treatment system connected with hazardous waste management.
- Provide a schematic diagram of the waste treatment system.
- Provide a general description of hazardous waste management facility.
- What were disposal methods and where was disposal undertaken for wastes generated prior to November 1980?
- Provide a copy of laboratory testing results related to the facility's hazardous waste.
- Have there been any process or product changes that would alter the waste since the last laboratory result?
- Provide a copy of laboratory's quality assurance program and procedures.
- What has been the procedure for disposing of commercial chemical products? (40 CFR 261.33)
- What has been the practice for disposal of empty containers that previously held hazardous waste? (40 CFR 261.7)
- Describe any packaging, labeling, or marking of hazardous waste prior to transportation.
- Provide a file of the generator's copies of transportation manifests. (40 CFR 262.21)
- Provide a file of the generator's annual report — Part A. (40 CFR 262.41)
- Provide a file of the generator's exception report file. (40 CFR 262.42)
- How long are hazardous wastes accumulated on site? (40 CFR 262.34)
- Do you transport your own hazardous waste? What are necessary actions relating to spills during transportation? (40 CFR 263.30 &.31)
- Provide copies of facility's waste analyses plan. [40 CFR 265.13(b)]
- What security measures are provided to prevent unauthorized entry or human or other animal contact with waste? (40 CFR 265.14)
- What security measures are provided to protect employees from areas where hazardous wastes are stored? (40 CFR 265.14)
- Provide in writing the facility's inspection schedule and file on any such inspections performed. (40 CFR 265.15)

- Describe the program for personnel training. (40 CFR 265.16)
- Have police, fire department, and emergency response teams been made familar with layout and properties of the hazardous waste? (40 CFR 265.37)
- Provide a contingency plan to minimize hazards to humans. (40 CFR 265.51,.52,.53)
- Have copies of the contingency plan been submitted to local police, fire, and other emergency officials? (40 CFR 265.53)
- Who is the identified emergency coordinator for the contingency plan? (40 CFR 265.55)
- Provide a file of operating record for the facility. (40 CFR 265.63)
- Describe container or tank storage management practices.
- Provide plans for container or tank storage areas.
- Provide a Best Management Plan for controlling runoff and leachates from plant site.
- Provide an SPCC plant or container-tank storage and other appropriate areas.
- Has the groundwater monitoring program been implemented? Provide a copy of laboratory results.
- Provide a groundwater sampling and analyses plan. [40 CFR 265.92(a)]
- Provide an outline of the groundwater quality assessment program. [40 CFR 265.93(a)]
- Provide a plan for the facility's closure. (40 CFR 265.112)
- Have adequate financial assurances for closure and postclosure operations and liability protection been provided?
- Provide the employee accident report file.
- Provide the citizen complaint file.
- Provide the federal-state comment-correspondence file.
- Describe the employee supervision structure.
- Are employees provided job descriptions? Does each have a copy of same?
- Provide copies of transporters' Certificates of Liability Insurance.
- Provide copies of logs of inspections of above-surface or underground hazardous waste containers or storage facilities.

As a minimum, a hazardous waste information file with provision for at least the following identified information would be helpful in responding to hazardous waste information needs:

- Accident information
- Air quality
- Complaints: citizen
- Complaints: employee
- Contingency plan
- Correspondence: state
- Correspondence: EPA
- Delisting records
- Disposal: state authorization
- Facility closure plan

- Groundwater analyses
- Groundwater sampling and analyses plan
- Groundwater quality assessment program outline
- Health effects data
- Inspection logs
- Material safety data sheets
- Manufacturing process: schematic diagram
- Manifests
- Manifests: exception reporting
- NPDES monitoring
- Operating records: facility
- Pretreatment permit
- Pretreatment monitoring
- Reports: generator's
- Runoff BMP plan
- Security
- Spills
- Spill prevention and countermeasure plan
- Training: employee
- Transporters liability insurance certificates
- Waste analyses plan
- Waste analyses laboratory reports
- Waste treatment system: schematic diagram

UNDERGROUND STORAGE TANKS

The Superfund Amendments and Reauthorization Act of 1986 amended RCRA to provide for further regulation of underground storage tanks that store useful materials, as well as wastes. The law was passed because there was a growing concern over the increasing number of incidents where gasoline vapors were detected in houses and where drinking water was contaminated by leaking petroleum tanks. The original Superfund statute excludes petroleum releases from its jurisdiction. Thus, until this law was passed, there was no way to clean up leaks of petroleum products from underground tanks.

An underground tank is defined as any tank with at least 10% of its volume buried below ground, including any pipes attached. Thus, overground tanks with extensive underground piping may now be regulated. Certain tanks are excluded from the law. These include farm and residential tanks holding less than 1100 gal of motor fuel, on-site heating-oil tanks, septic tanks, systems for collecting stormwater and wastewater, and liquid traps or gathering lines related to oil and natural gas operations.

The law gives the EPA and states that enter into cooperative agreements with the EPA the authority to issue orders requiring owners and operators of underground storage tanks to undertake corrective action where a leak is suspected. This corrective action could include testing tanks to confirm the presence of a leak, excavating the site to determine the exact nature and extent of contamination, and cleaning contaminated soil and water. It may also include providing an alternative water supply to affected residences or temporary or permanent relocation of residents.

A $500 million Leaking Underground Storage Tank Trust Fund (LUST Trust) has been set up under EPA control, which, over the next 5 years, can be used to clean up leaks from underground petroleum storage tanks. These funds are supported by a 0.10¢ federal tax on certain petroleum products, primarily motor oils. Where LUST Trust funds are used, owners and operators of underground storage tanks, as well as any other responsible parties, are liable to the EPA or the state for the costs incurred. They will be pursued in court to recover costs.

The Congress believes that payment of cleanup costs can be satisfied by pollution liability insurance maintained by tank owners and operators. The EPA is directed by the law to publish regulations requiring all tank owners and operators, including those owning chemical tanks, to maintain the financial capability to clean up leaks. For petroleum production, refining, and marketing facilities, Congress has set minimum coverage levels at $1 million per occurrence.

A regulation banning underground installation of unprotected new tanks went into effect on May 7, 1985. After that date, an underground storage tank may not be installed unless:

1. It will prevent release of the stored substance due to corrosion of structural failure for the life of the tank.
2. It is protected against corrosion, constructed of noncorrosive material, or designed to prevent the release of the stored substance.
3. Construction or lining materials are electrolytically compatible with the substance to be stored.

The law specifies that leak detection, prevention, and corrective action regulations must require owners and operators of underground storage tanks to

1. Be able to detect releases
2. Keep records of release detection methods
3. Take corrective action when leaks occur
4. Report leaks and corrective action
5. Provide for proper tank closure
6. Provide evidence, as EPA deems necessary, of financial capability to take corrective action and compensate third parties for injury or damages from instant or continuous releases. States may finance corrective action and compensation programs by a fee levied on owners and operators.

REFERENCES CITED AND SELECTED READING

Dawson, G. W. and B. W. Mercer.1986. *Hazardous Waste Management*. John Wiley & Sons, New York.

Minnesota Pollution Control. 1987. "Environmental Risk Discussion of Solid Waste Management Systems." Minnesota Pollution Control Agency, St. Paul, MN.

Relis, P. and A. Dominski. 1987. "Beyond the Crisis: Integrated Solid Waste Management." Community Environmental Council, Santa Barbara, CA.

U.S. EPA. 1985. "The New RCRA: A Fact Book." U.S. Environmental Protection Agency, Washington, D.C. (EPA/530-SW-85-035).

U.S. EPA. 1985. "Solving the Hazardous Waste Problem: EPA's RCRA Program." U.S. Environmental Protection Agency, Washington, D.C. (EPA/530-SW-86-037).

U.S.EPA. 1988. "Report to Congress on Solid Waste Disposal." U.S. Environmental Protection Agency, Washington, D.C.

U.S. EPA. 1989. "The Solid Waste Dilemma: An Agenda for Action." U.S. Environmental Protection Agency, Washington, D.C. (EPA/530-SW-89-019).

U.S. EPA. 1989a. "1985 National Biennial Report of Hazardous Waste Generators and Treatment, Storage and Disposal Facilities Regulated under RCRA." U.S. Environmental Protection Agency, Washington, D.C. (EPA/530-SW-89-033A).

U.S. EPA. 1989b. "Decision-Maker's Guide in Solid Waste Management." U.S. Environmental Protection Agency, Office of Solid Waste, Washington, D.C.

WHHM. 1988. "Hazardous Wastes and Hazardous Materials." Proceedings of the 5th National Conference. The Hazardous Materials Control Research Institute, Silver Spring, MD.

15 SUPERFUND — ABANDONED HAZARDOUS WASTE SITES

THE PROBLEM AND ENVIRONMENTAL CONCERNS

Hazardous waste is produced in the United States at the rate of 700,000 tons per day or over 250 million tons per year (U.S. EPA, 1987). Because of uncontrolled deposition of hazardous wastes in the past, thousands of abandoned or inactive sites containing hazardous waste have been identified nationwide. Many of these sites are located in environmentally sensitive areas, such as floodplains or wetlands. Rain and melting snow seep through the sites, carrying chemicals that contaminate underground waters and nearby streams and lakes. At some sites, the air also is contaminated as toxic vapors rise from evaporating liquid wastes or from uncontrolled chemical reactions.

Superfund, the abbreviated name for the Comprehensive Environmental Response, Compensation and Liability Act of 1980, was created to clean up the hazardous waste mistakes of the past and to cope with the emergencies of the present. The objectives of Superfund are to develop a comprehensive program to set priorities for cleaning up the worst existing hazardous waste abandoned or uncontrolled sites; to make responsible parties pay for cleanup wherever possible; and to operate under a trust fund for the purposes of performing remedial cleanup in cases where responsible parties cannot be held accountable, as well as responding to emergency situations involving hazardous substances. By contrast, solid and hazardous waste programs discussed in Chapter 14 were designed to provide guidelines for prudent hazardous waste management and disposal in the present and in the future, and to provide a tracking system for the regulation of hazardous waste from its generation to disposal.

Many Superfund sites were created by the chemical and petroleum industries. Others were once municipal landfills that may have become hazardous as a result of accumulated pesticides, cleaning solvents, and other chemical products discarded in household trash. Many sites are the result of transportation spills or other accidents, and others are the final resting place of persistent toxic pollutants contained in industrial wastewater discharge or air pollution emissions (U.S. EPA, 1987).

EPA has established a National Priorities List (NPL), which is a list of priority sites for long-term remedial response and cleanup. Only those sites included on the NPL are eligible for financed remedial action with funds supplied by the Trust Fund. EPA has identified about 1200 sites as proposed or final on the NPL and has determined that about 16,000 are not candidates for the list.

There are about 31,000 sites still to be evaluated for possible inclusion on the NPL, with an average of 2000 new sites added each year to the potential site list. Cleanup action may take 4–5 years at some sites and decades at others. In cases of extensive groundwater contamination, long-term pump and treatment response actions are often projected to take 20–30 years, and in some cases up to 50 years. The cost of cleanup now approaches $25 million for construction costs at each site. The current projected total cost of construction for all sites on the current NPL is $30 billion.

EPA's overriding goal is to protect human health and the environment. To accomplish this goal with the formidable cleanup task, the EPA adopted a 1989 eight-element strategy (U.S. EPA, 1989b). That strategy identifies the following components:

1. Control acute threats immediately.
2. Initiate remedial work on worst sites, worst problems, first, which may involve cleanup of sites in stages.
3. Carefully monitor and maintain sites over the long run.
4. Emphasize enforcement to induce private-party cleanup.
5. Expand the research, development, and demonstration of new technologies for more effective cleanup.
6. Improve efficiency of program operation.
7. Encourage full participation by the public and involved communities.
8. Foster cooperation with state agencies, natural resource trustees, and the Agency for Toxic Substances and Disease Registry.

THE FEDERAL LAW

The Comprehensive Environment Response, Compensation and Liability Act (CERCLA or Superfund) was enacted December 11, 1980 and amended October 17, 1986. It authorizes the federal government to clean up hazardous substances at closed and abandoned hazardous waste sites that endanger public health and the environment, to establish a cleanup trust fund to be funded by a system of fees, and to provide for liability of persons responsible for releases of hazardous waste at such sites.

Section 104 is the cleanup response section. It grants authority to eliminate the current danger posed by the release of a hazardous substance and to provide long-term solutions to prevent future threats. The EPA can act to remove, arrange for removal, provide for remedial action, or take any other response measure consistent with the National Contingency Plan when necessary to protect the public health or the environment. Conditions for action include the release of a hazardous substance, a substantial threat that a hazardous substance will be released, an imminent and substantial danger to the public health or welfare from the release of a hazardous substance, or a substantial threat that a pollutant may be released and such a release may present an imminent and substantial danger to the public health or welfare. Cleanup responses must be terminated after either 12 months have passed or $2 million has been spent, unless it is determined that continued response actions are immediately required to prevent or mitigate an emergency; there is an imminent risk to the public health, welfare, or the environment; or an added expenditure of time or money would be consistent with the long-term goals of a planned remedial action. Before providing remedial action, the EPA must enter into an agreement with the affected state or states. Even after such an agreement has been reached, the EPA still has the power to select the appropriate remedial action.

The EPA is authorized to use investigation, monitoring, surveys, testing, and other information gathering that may be needed to determine the source and the extent of danger from hazardous substances. Federal facilities are under the jurisdiction of CERCLA. The selection of a remedy at a federal facility can be through joint efforts between the EPA and the federal agency, or by the EPA if the joint action does not end in agreement on the remedy. The EPA is required to establish a special docket open to the public that lists all federal-agency hazardous waste facilities.

Section 121 requires remedial actions to comply with applicable or relevant and appropriate requirements (ARARs), which include federal and state standards, requirements, criteria, or limitations, unless such requirements are waived. ARARs include the Toxic Substances Control Act, Safe Drinking Water Act, Clean Air Act, Ocean Dumping Act, Solid Waste Disposal Act, and others. Remedial actions must consider recommended maximum contaminant levels, and water quality criteria, where such requirements are relevant and appropriate under the circumstances.

The transfer of hazardous substances or contaminants to an off-site land disposal facility is authorized only if the unit to which the materials are being taken is not releasing hazardous waste into surface or groundwater or soil, and releases from any other unit at that facility are controlled through RCRA corrective action. CERCLA provides a strong recommendation that remedial actions, where possible, utilize permanent solutions and alternative treatment technologies or resource recovery technologies. There is a stated preference for remedial actions that utilize treatments that permanently and significantly reduce the volume, toxicity, or mobility of hazardous substances.

The 1986 amendments to the act increased the size of the Hazardous Response Trust Fund to $8.5 billion. The source of revenue for the trust fund is a tax on crude oil and 42 different commercial chemicals. State governments are to pay 10% of the cost of Superfund work at privately owned sites and 50% at those sites that are publicly owned. Examples of commercial chemicals that are taxed to provide funds for hazardous waste cleanup include benzene, toluene and xylene, ammonia, arsenic, cadmium, chromium, a number of different acids, nickel, zinc, sulfate, and others.

It is illegal under Section 103 for any person to knowingly fail to notify the EPA of the existence of any hazardous waste facility for hazardous waste disposal. The 1986 amendments authorized increased criminal penalties for failure to report releases of hazardous waste and made the providing of false or misleading information a criminal offense. Other enforcement authorities were likewise strengthened. Statutory authority was given to the use of settlement agreements and the establishment of specific procedures for reaching them. The powers of EPA access to hazardous waste sites for the completion of investigations and cleanup were increased. Enforcement authorities are required to keep an administrative record of enforcement actions at NPL sites.

State involvement is a requirement of the 1986 amendments. EPA must ensure that states participate in identifying NPL sites; the review of all preliminary documents related to Superfund remedial actions, as well as final plans for the action; all enforcement negotiations and concurrences in settlement agreements; and the deletion of sites from the NPL, such as by agreement among the EPA and responsible parties that a Suprfund cleanup is complete.

STATE PROGRAMS

Since CERCLA became law, many states have enacted laws and developed programs with authorities and capabilities similar to the federal Superfund program. Twenty-five states are actively involved in managing removals and remedial actions at non-NPL sites. Some of these states also manage or oversee cleanups at NPL sites as well. Fourteen states with funds and enforcement authorities have limited Superfund activities at present. Generally, this is because of insignificant fund balances or inadequate staffing levels. The remaining 11 states have limited cleanup capabilities or enforcement authorities (U.S. EPA, 1989).

Approximately 20 state statutes require the development of a priority list. At least 21 states reported compiling such a list, however. Generally, a priority list requires prioritization of sites through a ranking, scoring, or formal screening procedure. Many states report a less formal listing of sites, called an *inventory* or *registry,* which generally contains all identified, investigated, unconfirmed, and potential sites. At least 28 states reported a registry or inventory of sites (U.S. EPA, 1989).

The NPL has 881 final sites, 279 proposed sites, and a total of 1160 total and proposed sites (Figure 15-1). Nevada has no Superfund sites. Alaska and South Dakota each have one site. New Jersey is the state with the greatest number of sites, 107 in all; Pennsylvania ranks second, with 95 total sites. According to state reports, there are about 31,239 hazardous waste sites being investigated for proposal to the NPL. These sites include those listed for the individual states in Figure 15-1. These sites are those in the state CERCLIS lists, unconfirmed sites, and in some cases, estimates of hazardous waste sites for some states. The states with the fewest sites include Arkansas, New Mexico, and Oklahoma. The states with over 2000 hazardous waste sites include California, Michigan, and Pennsylvania. California lists the most sites of any state, with 4000 sites. The geographic distribution of NPL sites is shown in Figure 15-2.

NATIONAL CONTINGENCY PLAN

A National Contingency Plan (NCP) initially was published in response to a mandate of the Clean Water Act. Section 105 of CERCLA required that the NCP be revised and republished to include

1. Methods for discovering and investigating facilities at which hazardous substances have been disposed
2. Methods for evaluating, including analyses of relative cost, and remedying any releases or threats of releases that pose substantial danger to the public health or the environment
3. Methods and criteria for determining the appropriate extent of removal, remedy, and other measures
4. Appropriate roles and responsibilities for the federal, state, and local governments
5. Provision for identification, procurement, maintenance, and storage of response equipment and supplies
6. A method for and assignment of responsibility for reporting the existence of facilities on federally owned or controlled properties and any releases of hazardous substances from these facilities
7. Means of assuring that remedial action measures are cost effective over the period of potential exposure to the hazardous substances
8. Criteria for determining priorities among releases or threatened releases for purposes of taking remedial action
9. Specified roles for private organizations and entities in preparation for response and in responding to releases of hazardous substances

The NCP is the regulation governing Superfund and emergency response for oil and hazardous wastes; it is codified at 40 CFR Part 300. Oil spills are discussed in Chapter 16. The NCP defines four operations response phases for oil removal:

*   Discovery and notification
*   Preliminary assessment and initiation of action
*   Containment, countermeasures, cleanup, and disposal
*   Documentation and cost recovery

The preliminary assessment evaluates the magnitude and severity of the discharge, assesses the feasibility of removal, determines the existence of potential responsible parties, and ensures that jurisdiction exists for undertaking additional response actions. In the cleanup phase, defensive actions should begin as soon as possible to prevent, minimize, or mitigate damage. Actions may include analyzing water samples to determine the source and spread of oil, controlling the source of discharge, measuring and sampling, damage control or salvage operations, placement of physical barriers to deter the spread of the oil or to protect endangered species, control of water discharged from upstream impoundments, use of chemicals, and waterfowl conservation activities. Documentation is collected and maintained to support all actions taken under the Clean Water Act and to form the basis for cost recovery.

STATES	FINAL	PROPOSED	TOTAL	STATE LISTS [1]
Alabama	10	2	12	500+
Alaska	1	0	1	277
Arizona	5	4	9	700
Arkansas	10	0	10	26
California	52	36	88	4000
Colorado	13	3	16	400
Connecticut	8	6	14	567
Delaware	12	8	20	200
Florida	32	15	47	500+
Georgia	7	6	13	753
Hawaii	0	6	6	---
Idaho	4	0	4	175
Illinois	23	16	39	1325
Indiana	30	7	37	1200
Iowa	9	15	24	384
Kansas	9	2	11	489
Kentucky	12	5	17	500
Louisiana	9	2	11	506
Maine	6	2	8	317
Maryland	7	3	10	300
Massachusetts	21	1	22	1634
Michigan	65	15	80	2500
Minnesota	40	0	40	300
Mississippi	2	1	3	347

Figure 15-1.   National priorities list of hazardous waste sites. (From U.S. EPA, 1989.)

SITE CLEANUP

Federal cleanup results from a series of identifiable actions (Figure 15-3). The principal actions in the remedial response process will be discussed in the paragraphs that follow.

Site discovery or notification may take place through reports submitted in regulatory compliance, investigations by government authorities, inventory or survey efforts or random or incidental observation reported by government agencies or the public, citizen petition to the EPA or the appropriate federal facility requesting a preliminary assessment, or other sources. The EPA is authorized to begin response actions immediately using trust fund monies. Responsible parties can undertake a response action as a result of the EPA's enforcement authorities. States can act using trust fund monies pursuant to a cooperative agreement with the EPA.

STATES	FINAL	PROPOSED	TOTAL	STATE LISTS [1]
Missouri	14	7	21	1400
Montana	8	2	10	149
Nebraska	3	2	5	40
Nevada	0	0	0	115
New Hampshire	15	0	15	175
New Jersey	100	7	107	1200
New Mexico	6	4	10	10
New York	73	3	76	1091
North Carolina	15	7	22	781
North Dakota	2	0	2	47
Ohio	29	3	32	1047
Oklahoma	8	3	11	30
Oregon	6	1	7	750
Pennsylvania	71	24	95	2182
Rhode Island	8	3	11	258
South Carolina	14	7	21	410
South Dakota	1	0	1	56
Tennessee	10	3	13	850
Texas	24	4	28	1000+
Utah	5	7	12	191
Vermont	4	4	8	130
Virginia	12	9	21	140
Washington	25	17	42	700
West Virginia	5	1	6	304
Wisconsin	35	4	39	173
Wyoming	1	2	3	110
TOTALS	881	279	1160	31239

[1] State CERCLIS lists; potential hazardous waste sites; unconfirmed sites; estimates.

Figure 15-1.   (continued).

Removal may take place at any time during the remedial response process where prompt action is required because of an emergency or time-critical situation for the protection of human health or the environment. It begins with a preliminary evaluation to determine the identity of the source and nature of the release or threat of release, an evaluation of the threat to public health and the magnitude of the threat, an evaluation of factors necessary to make the determination of whether a removal is necessary, and whether a nonfederal party is undertaking proper response. Where it is found that fire, explosion, contamination of drinking water, or other hazardous releases are potentials, removal action may be instituted.

Figure 15-2.   Geographical distribution of national priorities list sites. (From U.S. EPA, 1989.)

To determine the appropriateness of a removal action, consideration is given to

1. Actual or potential exposure to nearby human populations, animals, or the food chain from hazardous substances
2. Actual or potential contamination of drinking water supplies or sensitive ecosystems
3. Hazardous substances in drums, barrels, tanks, or other bulk storage containers that may pose a threat of release
4. High levels of hazardous substances in soils largely at or near the surface that may migrate
5. Weather conditions that may cause hazardous substances to migrate or be released
6. Threat of fire or explosion
7. The availability of other appropriate federal or state response mechanisms to respond to the release
8. Other situations or factors that may pose threats to public health or welfare or the environment

Removal actions may include

1. Fences, warning signs, or other security or site control precautions
2. Drainage controls, where needed to reduce migration of hazardous substances off site or to prevent runoff or flooding from precipitation

THE REMEDIAL RESPONSE PROCESS

● SITE DISCOVERY OR NOTIFICATION

● PRELIMINARY ASSESSMENT   (REMOVAL[1])

● SITE INSPECTION

● APPLY HAZARD RANKING SYSTEM

● PLACE ON NATIONAL PRIORITIES LIST

● CHOOSE LEAD; FUND OR ENFORCEMENT;   (ENFORCEMENT)
    FEDERAL OR STATE

● REMEDIAL INVESTIGATION-   (EXPEDITED RESPONSE ACTION[1])
    FEASIBILITY STUDY

● RECORD OF DECISION

● REMEDIAL DESIGN

● REMEDIAL ACTION

                                  (COST RECOVERY ACTION)

● OPERATION AND MAINTENANCE

[1]May occur at any time.

Figure 15-3.   Federal-lead remedial response process. (From U.S. EPA, 1987.)

3. Stabilization of berms, dikes, or impoundments where needed to maintain the integrity of the structures
4. Capping of contaminated soils or sludges where needed to reduce migration into soil, groundwater, or air
5. Using chemicals and other materials to retard the spread of the release or to mitigate its effects
6. Excavation, consolidation, or removal of highly contaminated soils from drainage or other areas
7. Removal of drums, barrels, tanks or other bulk containers that contain or may contain hazardous substances

8. Containment, treatment, disposal, or incinerations of hazardous materials, where needed to reduce the likelihood of human, animal, or food chain exposures

9. Provision of alternative water supply until such time as local authorities can satisfy the need for a permanent remedy (40 CFR 300.415)

Remedial site evaluation is a more structured evaluation, where immediate removal is not a requirement, to assist in determining whether a site should be included on the NPL. Information, data, and samples are obtained to fully characterize the site and to substantiate a recommendation of whether further action is warranted. Quality assurance is built into the site-specific sampling plan that is a part of a site evaluation. One purpose of this assessment is to eliminate from further consideration those sites that pose no threat to public health or the environment. A remedial preliminary assessment consists of a review of existing information about a release, such as information on the pathways of exposure, exposure targets, and source and nature of the release.

A recommendation is made on whether further action is warranted, which lead agency should conduct further action, and whether removal action should be undertaken.

Any person may petition the EPA or the appropriate federal agency to perform a preliminary assessment of a release or suspected release from a federal facility when such a person is or may be affected by a release of a hazardous substance (40 CFR 300.420).

The NPL is EPA's list of hazardous waste sites for long-term remedial action. Only those sites included in this list are eligible for trust fund financed remedial action. The NPL identifies the worst abandoned sites according to type, quantity, toxicity of wastes, number of people potentially exposed, likely pathways of exposure, and importance and vulnerability of groundwater. The NPL is updated once each year. A site may be included on the NPL if it meets one of the following criteria:

1. The release scores sufficiently high pursuant to EPA's hazard ranking system.
2. A state has designated a release as its highest priority. States may make only one such designation.
3. The release satisfies all of the following criteria: (1) the Agency for Toxic Substances and Disease Registry has issued a health advisory that recommends dissociation of individuals from the release, (2) the EPA determines that the release poses a significant threat to public health, and (3) the EPA anticipates that it will be more cost effective to use its remedial authority than to use removal authority to respond to the release.

Enforcement is a significant effort on the part of the EPA and the states to identify potentially responsible parties and to compel them to undertake the required cleanup activities, through legal action if necessary. If this cannot be done, the EPA will proceed with the cleanup, using trust fund resources, and will attempt to recover the costs later.

Alternately, the state may be asked to take the lead in the cleanup. Thus, maintaining complete and detailed records of site activities is essential for the purposes of enforcement activities. Enforcement actions involve settlement agreements with responsible parties, administrative orders against potentially responsible parties, and civil actions in which the EPA and the Department of Justice are involved.

Expedited response action may take place at any time during the remedial response process and is initiated when threats or potential threats to the public health or the environment are determined. This is a removal action and must comply with the regulations, procedures, and policies of the removal program. It starts with an engineering evaluation and cost analysis. It may address such issues as alternative public water supplies and should address permanent solutions and alternative treatment techniques to the maximum extent practicable. An expedited response action must meet National Environmental Policy Act equivalency and must undergo a public comment period.

A *remedial investigation/feasibility study* (RI/FS) has as its purpose to characterize the nature and extent of contamination, the likely exposure pathways at a site, the extent of risk raised by the contamination, and the selection and evaluation of potential remedies to mitigate the extent of damage. The development of an RI/FS includes project scoping, data-collection risk assessment, and analysis of alternatives. In addition to other alternatives, the no-action alternative must be developed.

To the extent sufficient information is available, the short- and long-term aspects of the following three criteria must be used to guide the development and screening of remedial alternatives. The *effectiveness* criterion focuses on the degree to which an alternative minimizes residual risks and affords long-term protection, and minimizes short-term impacts, and how quickly protection can be achieved. Alternatives that do not provide adequate protection of human health and the environment must be eliminated from further consideration. The *implementability* criterion focuses on the technical feasibility and availability of the technologies each alternative would employ and the administrative feasibility of implementing the alternative. The *cost* criterion requires consideration of construction and any long-term costs to operate and maintain the alternatives. A detailed analysis is conducted on the limited number of alternatives that represent viable hazardous-waste management approaches.

All remedial action will require evaluation of the nine evaluation criteria (40 CFR 300.430). These criteria are

1. **Overall protection of human health and the environment.** Alternatives must be assessed to determine whether they can adequately protect human health and the environment from unacceptable risks posed by hazardous substances by eliminating, reducing, or controlling exposures to levels established during development of remediation goals.
2. **Compliance with ARARs.** Alternatives must be assessed to determine whether they attain applicable or relevant and appropriate requirements of other federal and state environmental public health laws and regulations.

3.   **Long-term effectiveness and permanence**. This criterion includes the degree of certainty that the alternative will prove successful. It includes also a consideration of the nature and magnitude of total residual risks in terms of amounts, potential for exposures, concentrations of hazardous substances, persistence, toxicity, mobility, and propensity to bioaccumulate hazardous substances; and the type, degrees, and adequacy of long-term management required, including engineering controls, institutional controls, monitoring, and operation and maintenance are matters of consideration. Long-term reliability of the engineering and institutional controls and potential need for replacement of the remedy, as well as the continuing need for repairs to maintain the performance of the remedy, are additional matters of consideration.

4.   **Reduction of toxicity, mobility, or volume**. The degree to which alternatives employ treatment that reduces the toxicity, mobility, or volume must be assessed.

5.   **Short-term effectiveness**. This includes short-term risks that might be posed to the community during implementation of an alternative, potential impacts on workers during remedial action, and the effectiveness and reliability of protective measures, potential environmental impacts of the remedial action, and the effectiveness and reliability of mitigative measures during implementation.

6.   **Implementability**. The ease or difficulty of implementing the alternatives must be assessed, including uncertainty associated with construction and operations of the technology, expected operational reliability, ability and time required to obtain any necessary approvals and permits from other agencies, availability of necessary equipment and specialists, and available capacity and location of needed treatment, storage, and disposal services.

7.   **Costs**. These include capital costs, contingency and engineering fees, and operation and maintenance costs.

8.   **State acceptance**. This criterion includes the state's position and key concerns related to the preferred alternative and other alternatives, as well as state comments on ARARs or the proposed use of waivers for certain requirements.

9.   **Community acceptance**. This acceptance includes determining which components of the alternatives interested persons in the community support, have reservations about, or oppose.

The evaluation of potential remedial alternatives may involve bench or pilot-scale treatability studies to determine if an alternative can attain the expected or needed cleanup levels.

The *Record of Decision* (ROD) documents the selection of a remedy. The ROD contains all facts, analyses of facts, and site-specific policy determinations considered in the course of carrying out activities related to the response effort. The documentation must explain how the nine evaluation criteria discussed above were used to select the remedy. The ROD must describe how the selected remedy is protective of human health and the environment; the federal and state requirements that are applicable or relevant and appropriate to the site that the remedy will attain; the applicable or relevant and appropriate requirements or other federal and state laws that the remedy will not meet, the waiver invoked, and the justification for invoking the waiver; how the remedy is cost effective; how the remedy utilizes permanent solutions and alternative treatment technologies or resource recovery technologies to the maximum extent practicable; and whether the preference for remedies employing treatment that permanently and significantly reduces the toxicity, mobility, or volume of the hazardous substances is or is not satisfied by the selected remedy.

Remedial design includes the preparation of detailed engineering plans, drawings, and specifications to implement the chosen remedial alternative. It specifies the requirements necessary for construction or other remedial action activities to meet the objectives of the remedial alternative.

Remedial design includes site cleanup, as specified in the engineering design. This generally involves treatment, disposal, or containment of the hazardous waste, as well as cleanup, restoration, or replacement of the affected resources. The final step in the remedial process is *operation and maintenance* subsequent to the cleanup. This is designed to ensure continued functioning and effectiveness of the remedial response action. Operation and maintenance generally is the responsibility of the states. To complete, the total remedial response process may take 4–6 years, or more, and may cost millions of dollars.

GROUNDWATER REMEDIAL ACTION

One of the principal concerns associated with hazardous wastes, and especially those that are in association with the land, is groundwater pollution. One of the most difficult environments to clean up is that of contaminated groundwater.

Before collecting data, it is useful to conduct two planning activities. One is site management planning, which involves identifying the types of analyses and actions that are appropriate to address site problems and their optimal sequence. The other is project planning, which includes such activities as scoping, data collection efforts, initiating the identification of ARARs, and work plan preparation (U.S. EPA, 1989c).

Data collection activities include characterization of the hydrogeology, characterization of the contamination, and evaluation of plume movement and response. The site geology should be determined through the collection of sediment samples from soil borings and monitoring wells. Groundwater movement should be determined. Any seasonal fluctuation should be detected. Choosing one or a few chemicals for monitoring will reduce analytical costs and will simplify modeling. The horizontal and vertical extent of the contaminant plume would be determined through monitoring at various locations and depths. The concentrations of the contaminants should be determined to aid in assessing their behavior in groundwater. Contaminant-soil interactions should be determined to aid in assessing the effectiveness of a groundwater extraction system.

An investigation should identify sources of uncertainty, such as predicting the nature, extent, and movement of contamination; estimating the rate and direction of the groundwater flow; and weighing the costs and benefits of reducing uncertainty by collecting additional information.

Cleanup levels generally will be set at health-based levels, reflecting current and potential use and exposure. Here, ARARs include the drinking water maximum contaminant levels, as discussed in Chapter 10, or promulgated state standards. Other potential levels of quality include proposed maximum contaminant levels, risk-specific doses, reference doses, lifetime health advisories, or water quality criteria.

A range of remedial technologies can be combined under a particular general response action. Process options for extraction include extraction wells, extraction-injection systems, and interceptor drains and trenches. Treatment options include biological, chemical, physical, thermal, or *in situ* methods. Treated groundwater can be discharged to surface water or a publicly owned treatment works, reinjected to the aquifer, or used. There are various options for containment, monitoring effectiveness, and institutional controls. Alternatives are developed by combining these various process options into a comprehensive response approach.

EMERGENCY PLANNING AND COMMUNITY RIGHT-TO-KNOW

The Emergency Planning and Community Right-to-Know Act of 1986 is Title III of the Superfund Amendments and Reauthorization Act of 1986. Title III requires federal, state, and local governments and industry to work together in developing emergency plans and reporting on hazardous chemicals. These requirements build on EPA's Chemical Emergency Preparedness Program and numerous state and local programs aimed at helping communities deal with potential chemical emergencies. The community right-to-know provisions allow the public to obtain information about the presence of hazardous chemicals in their communities and releases of these chemicals into the environment.

Title III has four major sections: emergency planning, emergency notification, community right-to-know reporting requirements, and toxic chemicals release reporting.

The emergency planning section is designed to help state and local governments develop emergency response and preparedness capabilities through better coordination and planning, especially within the local community. It requires the governor of each state to designate a state emergency response commission. This state commission should represent state organizations and agencies with expertise in emergency response, such as state environmental, emergency management, and public health agencies.

Private sector groups and associations may also be included. The state commission must designate local emergency planning districts and appoint local emergency planning committees for the districts. The local emergency planning committees must include elected state and local officials; police, fire, civil defense, public health professionals; environmental, hospital, and transportation officials; community groups; and the media.

The state commission supervises and coordinates the activities of the local emergency planning committees, establishes procedures on how to handle requests for information, and reviews local emergency plans. The local emergency planning committee has primary responsibility in developing a plan that will

- Identify facilities and transportation routes of extremely hazardous substances
- Describe emergency response procedures
- Designate a community coordinator and facility coordinator to implement the plan
- Outline emergency notification procedures
- Describe community and industry emergency equipment and facilities, and who is responsible for them
- Describe and schedule a training program to teach methods for responding to chemical emergencies
- Establish methods and schedules for exercises to test emergency response plans

Emergency notification requires that facilities where a listed hazardous substance is produced, used, or stored must immediately notify the local emergency planning committee and the state emergency response commission if there is a release of any such substance to the environment. The listed substances are those on the list of 360 extremely hazardous substances as published in the *Federal Register* (40 CFR 355) or on a list of 725 substances subject to the emergency notification requirements under CERCLA Section 103(a), 40 CFR 302.4. Some chemicals are common to both lists.

Under the community right-to-know reporting requirements, facilities are required to prepare or have available material safety data sheets (MSDS) and under the regulations of OSHA and must submit copies of them or a list of MSDS chemicals to the local emergency planning committee, the state emergency response commission, and the local fire department. In addition, the facility must submit an emergency and hazardous chemical inventory form to the same groups. The hazardous chemicals are the same as those for which facilities are required to submit MSDS or a list of MSDS chemicals under the first reporting requirement. The inventory form must record

- An estimate of the maximum amount of covered chemicals present at the facility at any time during the preceding calendar year
- An estimate of the average daily amount of covered chemicals present
- The general location of covered hazardous chemicals

The toxic chemical release reporting affects owners and operators of facilities that have 10 or more full-time employees, that are in Standard Industries Classification Codes 20 through 39 (which include basically all manufacturing industries), and that manufacture, process, or otherwise use a listed toxic chemical in excess of specified threshold quantities. The toxic chemical release form must be submitted to the EPA, as well as to state officials designated by each governor. Submission is on an annual basis. The report contains information on whether a chemical is manufactured, processed, or otherwise used; estimates of the maximum amounts of the toxic chemical present at the facility at any time during the preceding year; waste treatment and disposal methods for dealing with the chemical and the efficiency of the methods for each waste stream; and the quantity of the chemical entering the environment annually.

REFERENCES CITED AND SELECTED READING

U.S. EPA. 1987. Looking Back, Looking Ahead. *EPA J.* U.S. Environmental Protection Agency, Office of Public Affairs, Washington, D.C. (January/February).

U.S. EPA. 1987a. "The New Superfund: What It Is, How It Works." U.S. Environmental Protection Agency, Washington, D.C. (August).

U.S. EPA. 1989. "An Analysis of State Superfund Programs: 50-State Study." U.S. Environmental Protection Agency, Washington, D.C. (EPA/540/8-89/011).

U.S. EPA. 1989a. "A Management Review of the Superfund Program, Implementation Plan, The Superfund 90-Day Study." U.S. Environmental Protection Agency, Washington, D.C.

U.S. EPA. 1989b. "A Management Review of the Superfund Program, A Comprehensive Statement of Program Philosophy." U.S. Environmental Protection Agency, Washington, D.C.

U.S. EPA. 1989c. "A Guide to Remedial Action for Contaminated Ground Water." U.S. Environmental Protection Agency, Solid Waste and Emergency Response, Washington, D.C.

Wagner, T. 1988. *The Complete Handbook of Hazardous Waste Regulations. A Comprehensive Step by Step Guide to the Regulation of Hazardous Wastes Under RCRA, TSCA, and Superfund.* Perry-Wagner Publishing Co., Brunswick, ME.

16   SPILLS — OIL AND OTHER HAZARDOUS SUBSTANCES

HISTORY AND LAW

Section 311 of the Clean Water Act prohibits discharges of oil or hazardous substances in quantities that may be harmful to waters of the United States. There must be immediate notification to the appropriate authorities of any spill of a reportable quantity as defined in the Act. Section 311 also provides for cleanup of spills and requires the preparation of Spill Prevention, Control and Countermeasure Plans for facilities that conceivably could have spills.

A person or corporation who properly notifies the designated appropriate agency, which is the Coast Guard, as designated in Executive Order 11735, of the discharge of a reportable quantity of oil or hazardous substance is immune from criminal prosecution, but is liable for civil penalties. Additionally, those who cause the spill are liable for the costs of cleanup and removal. If the federal government must clean up the spill, the discharger of the spill is liable for cleanup costs. There are maximum liability limits, depending upon the type of facility and spill.

Control of spills began with the Water Quality Improvement Act of 1970. Section 11 of that act addressed the control of pollution by oil. The Congress declared that it is the policy of the United States that there should be no discharges of oil into or upon the navigable waters of the United States, adjoining shorelines, or into or upon the waters of the contiguous zone. Regulations were to be promulgated to determine those quantities of oil, the discharge of which, at such times, locations, circumstances, and conditions, will be harmful to the public health or welfare. Section 12 of that act addressed the control of hazardous polluting substances.

With the passage of the Federal Water Pollution Control Act Amendments of 1972, Section 311 was modified so as to focus on oil and hazardous substance liability. It required eight significant regulations to be developed by the EPA for the control of hazardous substances spills:

1. The designation of hazardous substances, which, when discharged in any quantity, present an imminent and substantial danger to the public health or welfare
2. A determination whether any such designated hazardous substance can actually be removed
3. A unit of measurement based upon the usual trade practice for the purpose of determining discharge penalties
4. The determination of quantities not to be harmful where permitted in quantities, times, location, or under designated circumstances or conditions
5. The determination of quantities that will be harmful to the public health or welfare at such times, locations, circumstances, and conditions
6. The establishment of reasonable and equitable classifications of onshore facilities that, because of size, type, and location, do not present a substantial risk of violating the nonharmful quantities regulation
7. The establishment of methods and procedures for removal of discharged oil and hazardous substances
8. The establishment of procedures, methods, and equipment to prevent discharges of oil and hazardous substances

An array of penalties were provided in Section 311. Whenever a discharge was a result of willful negligence or willful misconduct, a civil penalty in such amount as the Administrator of the EPA would establish, based upon the toxicity, degradability, and dispersal characteristics of the discharged substance, was to be sought. Much depended upon the removability regulations, because penalties were assessed only on those substances determined not to be removable.

Following prolonged deliberation, the EPA promulgated regulations, which were immediately brought into the U.S. District Court in St. Charles County, Louisiana. The regulations were virtually vitiated by the court. The court found that the one-pound method set forth in the regulations for determining hazardous quantities in chemical substances and thereby triggering a comprehensive reporting, liability, and cleanup scheme is arbitrary, capricious, and contrary to statutory mandate in that such factors as times, locations, circumstances and conditions are not met and their influence cannot be found in the method as promulgated. The treatment of certain substances as being removable and not subject to relevant penalty provisions because they have characteristics similar to oil, which is actually removable from water under certain circumstances, was ruled to be arbitrary, and hence, invalid. Further, the court found that it is not practicable to develop a totally accurate scheme for determining mitigability of harm for all substances, under all circumstances, and for every conceivable type of spill or receiving body. It was a case where the initial law could not be implemented in regulation, therefore making it necessary to modify the initial law.

Section 311 was modified by the Congress in Public Law 95-576, which was enacted on November 2, 1978. The penalty provisions of the 1972 law were changed and the required regulations were changed and reduced in number. The hazardous substances designation regulation, the first of eight specified above, remained, and the regulation promulgated for this section of the law was not vitiated by the district court. The harmful quantities regulation, the fifth of the eight regulations specified above, became a reportable quantities regulation. The law was changed to require a determination of those quantities of a hazardous substance the discharge of which *may be* harmful to the public health or welfare. Formerly, the law required the designation of substances the discharge of which, at such times, locations, circumstances, and conditions, *will be* harmful to the public health or welfare.

REGULATIONS

Over 300 elements and compounds have been designated as hazardous substances in 40 CFR Part 116. The reportable quantities for these hazardous substances are found in 40 CFR Part 117. The reportable quantity is that quantity that may be harmful, the discharge of which is a violation of Section 311(b)(3) of the Act. For this purpose, the elements and compounds are placed in five groups with reportable quantities of 1, 10, 100, 1000, and 5000 pounds, respectively. Except when a discharge (spill) is in compliance with a valid permit or permit application, a discharge of a substance addressed in these regulations equal to or exceeding the reportable quantity in any 24-h period must be reported to the U.S. Coast Guard. Failure to so notify makes the discharger subject to a fine of up to $10,000 and imprisonment for not more than 1 year. There are penalties for such discharges, even when reported. The responsible party is liable for the actual costs incurred by the government in the removal of a discharged substance.

The quantity of discharged oil that has been determined to be harmful to the public health or welfare at all times and locations, and under all circumstances and conditions, is that which will violate applicable water quality standards or cause a film or sheen upon or discoloration of the surface of the water (40 CFR 110.3).

The requirements for preparation and implementation of Oil Spill Prevention Control and Countermeasure Plans and guidance for their preparation are codified at 40 CFR Part 112. A facility that has experienced one or more spill events in the past 12 months must include a written description of each such spill, corrective action taken, and plans for preventing recurrence within the plan. Where experience indicates a reasonable potential for equipment failure, the plan should include a prediction of the direction, rate of flow, and total quantity of oil that could be discharged from the facility as a result of each major type of failure.

The Spill Prevention Control and Countermeasure Plans should discuss appropriate containment or diversionary structures to prevent discharged oil from reaching a watercourse. These structures may include dikes, berms, or retaining, curbing, spill diversion ponds, retention ponds, or other preventive devices. The regulation specifies that all bulk storage tank installations should be constructed so that a secondary means of containment is provided for the entire contents of the largest single tank plus sufficient freeboard to allow for precipitation. Buried piping installations should have protective wrappings and coatings, and should be cathodically protected if soil conditions warrant. Whenever possible, such piping should be examined for corrosion and deterioration. No tank should be used for the storage of oil unless its material and construction are compatible with the material stored and the conditions of storage.

All above-ground valves and pipelines should be examined periodically on a scheduled basis for the general condition of items such as flange joints, valve glands and bodies, drip pans, pipeline supports, pumping well polish rod stuffing boxes, and bleeder and gauge valves. All plants handling, processing, and storing oil should be fully fenced, and entrance gates should be locked or guarded when the plant is not in production or is unattended. The regulation provides additional instructions and guidance for Spill Prevention Control and Countermeasure Plans.

17 PESTICIDES AND OTHER TOXIC CHEMICALS

ENVIRONMENTAL CONCERNS

By definition, pesticides are toxic chemicals. They are designed to kill specific or general pests, including terrestrial and aquatic plants, insects, fungi, bacteria, nuisance snails, clams, barnacles, selected fish, and other organisms. Some pesticides have been found to cause cancer, birth defects, skin, eye, and other health effects.

Pesticides are used in agriculture and silviculture, in industry as slimicides and for incorporation into a commercial product, as an antifouling paint on ships and boats, in hospitals, in greenhouses, and for a variety of home and garden uses. Pesticide use in the United States more than doubled in the 21-year period from 1964 to 1985, increasing from 540 million pounds of active ingredients to over one billion pounds. Agricultural uses of pesticides accounted for 77% of the consumption in 1985, costing the farming industry $4.6 billion. Pesticides are used on as many as two million farms, in 75 million households, and by 40,000 commercial pest control firms. Thirty major and 100 minor companies produce active pesticide ingredients, 3000 companies formulate pesticides, and there are 29,000 distributors (U.S. EPA, 1986).

Pesticides are one of the leading groundwater contaminants of concern in reports submitted by states in compliance with Section 305(b) of the Clean Water Act (U.S. EPA, 1990). Of 500 water well and drinking water samples collected, 38% had detectable levels of one or more pesticides in Minnesota. Connecticut recently sponsored investigations of pesticides in groundwater and detected concentrations of 1,1-dichloroethylene and atrazine at several sites above state drinking water standards and EPA advisory levels.

The most important properties determining whether a pesticide represents a threat to groundwater are its persistence and mobility. For pesticides not yet on the market, the EPA is using sophisticated environmental chemistry and mathematical models to predict whether a new pesticide has the potential to reach the groundwater. All prospective registrants of pesticides intended for use outdoors must submit a range of test data to assist in assessing the fate of a new pesticide when used as proposed. Where possible groundwater contamination is identified, the EPA may take regulatory action ranging from selective restrictions to an outright ban against the manufacture and use of a pesticide.

There are also environmental concerns with toxic chemicals other than pesticides. After 5 years of public hearings and debate, Congress enacted the Toxic Substances Control Act (TSCA), with its defined coverage as the manufacture, distribution, processing, use, or disposal of a chemical substance or mixture that may present an unreasonable risk of injury to health or the environment. As a result of this law, programs have been implemented to evaluate chemicals prior to their appearance on the market through premanufacture notification for new chemical substances and significant new uses of existing chemical substances, evaluation of existing chemicals by requiring testing and reporting of unpublished health and safety data, and control of unreasonable risks of existing chemicals by regulatory action. Asbestos, formalde-hyde, methylene chloride, and polychlorinated biphenyls (PCBs) are among the more toxic chemicals regulated under this act.

Congress singled out PCBs for both immediate regulation and phase withdrawal from the market. PCBs are of concern because tests on laboratory animals show that long-term exposure to PCBs may cause reproductive failures, gastric disorders, skin lesions, and tumors. PCBs are persistent and tend to accumulate in the tissues of living organisms. Standards for the cleanup of spilled PCBs have been published, as have other regulations involving their manufacture, use, and disposal. Efforts continue for a phase-out, leading to total prohibition.

An aggressive asbestos reduction program likewise is underway. The EPA has issued a rule to protect state and local government employees from the potential hazards of asbestos-abatement work. In addition, all schools must conduct inspections for asbestos to determine if protective corrective action is necessary. The manufacture, import, and processing of certain asbestos products have been banned. Labeling of nonbanned asbestos products has been proposed. Asbestos-abatement training courses have been sponsored by the EPA, and certification requirements have been developed by the EPA, states, and some cities for personnel involved in the surveying and removal of asbestos.

FEDERAL INSECTICIDE, FUNGICIDE, AND RODENTICIDE ACT

General Requirements

The Federal Insecticide, Fungicide, and Rodenticide Act (FIFRA) regulates the manufacture, distribution, sale, and use of pesticides to minimize risks to human health and the environment. A pesticide is defined as any substance intended to prevent, destroy, repel, or mitigate any pest. It includes plant regulators, defoliants, or desiccants. The Act requires the registration of all pesticides, restricts the use of certain pesticides, establishes requirements for the certification of pesticide applicators, authorizes experimental use permits, creates the conditions for cancellation of pesticides, requires the registration of pesticide manufacturers, and sets standards for the disposal of pesticides.

The EPA regulates pesticides under both FIFRA and the Pesticide Amendment to the Federal Food, Drug, and Cosmetic Act. Under FIFRA, the EPA is responsible for registering specified uses of pesticide products on the basis of both safety and benefits. A pesticide must perform its intended function without causing unreasonable adverse effects on human health or the environment when balanced against the potential benefits of the proposed use. This balancing of risks and benefits underlies all basic regulatory decisions.

Manufacturers of pesticides are required to provide data on the potential for skin and eye irritation; hazards to nontarget organisms, including fish and wildlife; the possibility of acute poisoning, tumor formation, birth defects, reproductive impairments, or other serious health effects; the behavior of the chemical in the environment after application; and the quantity and nature of residues likely to occur in food or feed crops.

The EPA is required to classify and certify all pesticide products for either general or restricted use. General use pesticides are considered safe for use by anyone, provided label directions, restrictions, and precautions are observed. Restricted-use pesticides may be used only by persons who have been certified as trained applicators. Training and certification is administered through EPA-approved state pesticide programs.

Under the provisions of the Federal Food, Drug, and Cosmetic Act, the EPA establishes tolerances for pesticide residues on feed crops and raw and processed foods. Tolerances are established at levels below amounts that might cause harm to people or the environment. For agricultural commodities, tolerances are enforced by the Food and Drug Administration. In meat, poultry, and fish products, tolerances are enforced by the U.S. Department of Agriculture.

FIFRA's Section 3 prohibits the distribution and sale of pesticides that have not been registered with the EPA and establishes procedures and data requirements for registration. The Section also provides the requirement for classification of pesticides for general use, restricted use, or both.

Section 4 requires reregistration of each registered pesticide containing any active ingredient first registered before November 1, 1984. Where there are no outstanding data requirements, the pesticide and its label must meet the requirements of the Act, that "when used in accordance with widespread and commonly recognized practice it will not generally cause unreasonable adverse effects on the environment." Provision is made for phases and priorities for reregistration.

Section 5 allows experimental use of a pesticide, under a permit issued by the EPA or an authorized state, to enable a manufacturer to develop the data necessary to register the pesticide under Section 3. When an experimental use permit is issued for a pesticide containing any chemical that has not been included in any previously registered pesticide, studies may be required to detect whether the use of the pesticide may cause unreasonable adverse effects on the environment.

Section 6 provides for the registration of any pesticide to be canceled at the end of

5 years unless the registrant requests that the registration be continued in effect. If it appears that a pesticide or its label does not comply with the provisions of FIFRA, or "when used in accordance with widespread and commonly recognized practice, generally causes unreasonable adverse effects on the environment," EPA may issue a notice of intent: (1) to cancel its registration or change its classification or (2) to hold a hearing to determine whether or not its registration should be canceled or its classification changed. In the event of imminent hazard, there is provision to suspend the registration of a pesticide immediately. This section also provides that EPA shall have jurisdiction over the place of pesticide storage for any pesticide that has had its registration cancelled or suspended.

Section 11 provides for the certification of applicators for restricted-use pesticides. To become certified, a person "must be determined to be competent with respect to the use and handling of pesticides." Separate certification standards are provided for private applicators, such as farmers and homeowners, and commercial applicators, such as pest-control operator employees, aerial applicators, and government employees who apply pesticides as part of their employment.

Section 12 enumerates 22 unlawful acts. Section 13 authorizes the EPA to issue an administrative order to stop the sale, use, or removal of any pesticide that is reasonably believed to be in violation of the Act; has been, or is intended to be, distributed or sold in violation of the Act; or has been canceled or suspended. The section also authorizes seizure of any pesticide that has been adulterated or misbranded, has not been registered; bears inadequate or improper labeling; has not been colored or discolored if required; differs in its claims or use directions compared to those in the registration application; or causes unreasonable adverse environmental effects when used in accordance with applicable requirements and restrictions.

Section 14 authorizes the imposition of civil administrative penalties and criminal sanctions. Criminal penalties may be imposed on those who knowingly violate any provision of the Act, or who, with intent to defraud, use or reveal information relative to formulas of products acquired under registration authorities. Registrants, commercial applicators, wholesalers, dealers, and other distributors are subject to more stringent civil and criminal penalties than are private applicators.

Federal pesticide legislation began in 1910 with the Federal Insecticide Act, which protected consumers against fraudulent goods. In 1947, FIFRA required federal registration of pesticides prior to marketing, but it was limited to interstate commerce. In 1954, the Miller amendment to the Federal Food, Drug, and Cosmetic Act required the establishment of tolerances for residues of pesticides on food, feed, and fiber crops. Amendments to FIFRA have occurred on an average of one every 5 years.

Registration of New Pesticides

Pesticides are registered on the basis of their active ingredients. In making pesticide registration and labeling decisions, the EPA is required to take into account the economic, social, and environmental costs and benefits or pesticide uses. For the 50,000 pesticide products already registered on the basis of their active ingredients, the

EPA can (1) continue registration with no changes where risks already are in balance; (2) modify the terms and conditions of the registration to lower the risk by requiring protective clothing for application, including gloves, hats, respirators, and protective outer clothing; restricting use to persons who have been certified by a state as qualified; prohibiting certain formulation uses; prohibiting certain application methods; and other constraints; (3) cancel the use of a pesticide; or (4) suspend use of a pesticide on a regular or emergency basis.

Pesticide registration is a premarket review and licensing program for all pesticides marketed in the United States. The EPA annually reviews about 15,000 registration submissions of various kinds. Only about 15 new active ingredients chemicals are registered each year. The agency bases registration decisions for new pesticides on its evaluation of test data provided by applicants. Required studies include testing to show whether a pesticide has the potential to cause adverse effects in humans, fish, wildlife, and endangered species. Data on environmental fate and effects also are required so that the EPA can determine whether a pesticide poses a threat to ground or surface water. The EPA reviews, evaluates, and validates data submitted on toxicological and adverse effects on humans and domestic animals and on their effects on fish and wildlife, as well as their ultimate fate. Human and nonhuman risk assessments are made. Economic analyses on the impacts of regulatory options are developed. Registration standards are issued for new active ingredients. Registration standards include a comprehensive review of all available data on a chemical, a list of additional data needed for full registration, and the agency's current regulatory position on the pesticide. For a new active ingredient that has not been marketed before, it may take 6–9 years and $2–4 million to comply with all registration data requirements. The EPA may issue experimental use permits or temporarily authorize state or federal agencies to combat emergencies with pesticide uses not permitted by existing federal registrations.

Registration of a new formulation containing an active ingredient already registered with the EPA requires far less time and expense. Such new product registrations may be completed within 6–9 months.

The EPA considers three types of pesticide application. These include an application for registration of a pesticide containing an active ingredient that is not a constituent of a product currently registered; an application for registration of a use for an active ingredient not currently included in the directions for use of any product that contains such active ingredient or ingredients; and an application for registration of a pesticide product that is substantially similar or identical in its uses and formulation to products that are currently registered.

Detailed requirements for registering a pesticide are provided in the regulations. The applicant's name, address of record, and authorized agent, if applicable, must be specified. A Confidential Statement of Formula must be completed and submitted with each application for registration. Copies of the proposed draft label with ingredients statement, warnings, and precautionary statements are required. The application must contain all applicable data required to support the registration, including product-specific chemistry data, acute toxicity data, and product chemistry data on the technical grade of the active ingredient, as well as on the pesticide formulated product. There must be a demonstration that the product performs in accordance with its labeling claims. There also must be certification that the packaging that will be used for the product meets the child-resistant packaging standards in 40 CFR 157.32. For those products that are believed to be substantially similar or identical to a product already registered, the EPA registration number of the currently registered product must be included. Such applications for registration require minimal supporting product chemistry, acute toxicity and, if applicable, efficacy data.

By the late 1960s, the amount of scientific data that was required to support the registration of a pesticide began to increase rapidly. Applicants and registrants who were required to generate these data, which were quite costly, asked Congress to provide protection for their investment, since by the time they obtained their registration or amended registration, most or all of the pesticide's patent life had expired. Other registrants were then able to obtain a registration for the same type of product by relying on the data generated by the original data submitter, without sharing the cost burden of generating the data. In response to this concern, the Congress added Section 3(c)(1)(D) to the amended FIFRA, placing data compensation obligations on those applicants for registration of a pesticide who would use the data submitted by another applicant or registrant in support of their own application for registration. In 1978, a second amendment to FIFRA granted "exclusive use rights" rights, for a 10-year period, to the original data submitter for certain data that were submitted to support the first registration of a product containing a new active ingredient.

An applicant must satisfy the above data compensation requirements to obtain a registration or reregistration, or to amend the registration of a registered product. One category of data pertains to those data submitted in support of the registration of a pesticide containing active ingredients that were first registered after September 30, 1978. These data were termed *exclusive use* data and the EPA may not consider these data to support another application for registration for a period of 10 years after the date of initial registration, unless there is written authorization from the original data submitter authorizing the agency to use these data. After the 10-year "exclusive use" period has expired, the applicant requesting use of these data must still offer to compensate the data submitter for use of the data, but written authorization is no longer needed.

Reregistration of Existing Pesticides

The Federal Insecticide and Rodenticide Act, amended in 1988, requires the reregistration of all existing pesticides within an approximate 9-year time. For reregistration, a pesticide must meet the same no-unreasonable-adverse-effects criteria that apply to new pesticides. Through its registration standards program, the EPA is reexamining, by current scientific standards, the health and environmental safety of the active ingredients contained in registered products. Under the registration standards program, the agency evaluates the scientific database underlying each active ingredient and identifies missing data, as well as regulatory and labeling restrictions needed to protect health and the environment. These measures are set forth in a registration standard, which essentially is a document that describes EPA's regulatory positions and rationales. From the period 1980 through 1988, the EPA issued 194 registration standards, covering 350 chemical substances used in pesticide products. This is about one third of the number currently required.

Depending on how the existing data measure up to current registration requirements, the manufacturer of a major active ingredient may incur first-time registrations costs ranging from $2.4 to 4.0 million to comply with data requirements for registration (U.S. EPA, 1986). If existing data largely satisfy registration requirements, the costs of complying with a registration standard will be considerably less.

The 1988 FIFRA amendments require an accelerated pace for the reregistration of existing pesticides. They set a sequence of deadlines for pesticide registrants, who are responsible for supplying the test data that the EPA needs to make pesticide reregistration decisions. The EPA must meet specific deadlines in analyzing data submissions and deciding whether or not to reregister currently registered pesticides. The process requires five phases. In Phase I, the EPA must publish four lists of pesticide active ingredients subject to reregistration. Phase II requires registrants to declare their intent to seek reregistration for the active ingredients listed, identify applicable data requirements, and commit to generate missing studies.

Phase III requires registrants to submit existing studies that have been reformatted and the data summarized for each active ingredient to be reregistered. Phase IV requires the agency to review the Phase II and III submissions and to notify registrants of additional data requirements. Phase V requires the agency to review all data concerning a pesticide and to determine if products containing a specific active ingredient may be reregistered.

Special Review

If a registered pesticide shows evidence of posing a potential safety problem, the EPA can conduct a special review of risks and benefits in which all interested parties can participate. Depending on the EPA's findings during the Special Review process, the agency may implement various regulatory options, including cancellation or suspension proceedings, restricting pesticide use to certified applicators, requiring protective clothing when applying the chemical, prohibiting certain application methods, or prohibiting certain uses. The EPA may decide to continue the pesticide's registration if risk-reduction measures are found unnecessary.

If the pesticide is found to cause unreasonable adverse effects on human health or the environment, the EPA may issue a notice of intent to cancel registration. The registrants and others who would be adversely affected are given 30 d to request a hearing. If there is no such appeal, all pertinent registrations are automatically canceled. If a hearing is requested, cancellation proceedings may take 2 years or more, and during that interval marketing may continue. However, if the EPA finds that continued registration of the pesticide for a given use presents an imminent hazard to human health, suspension actions may ensue. Such action requires evidence that the risks of continued use outweigh benefits during the 2 or more years necessary to complete a cancellation hearing.

There are two kinds of suspensions under FIFRA. Under an ordinary suspension, a registrant has a right to request a hearing before the suspension goes into effect. An ordinary suspension may take about 6 months. If the EPA determines that the risks of continued use outweigh benefits during the 6 months it would take to hold an ordinary suspension hearing, an emergency suspension order may be handed down. An emergency suspension is immediate and absolute.

Since the program began in 1975, the time required from start to conclusion of a Special Review has generally been from 2 to 6 years.

FFDCA TOLERANCE LEVELS FOR PESTICIDE RESIDUES

Under the Federal Food, Drug, and Cosmetic Act (FFDCA), the EPA is responsible for regulating the amount of pesticide residues that can remain in or on food or feed commodities as a result of pesticide application. A tolerance is the legal maximum residue concentration of a pesticide chemical allowed in food or feed. If residues of a pesticide exceed the established tolerance, or no tolerance has been established, the crop may be considered adulterated and may be seized by the Food and Drug Administration, the United States Department of Agriculture, or a state enforcement agency (U.S. EPA, 1989).

40 CFR Part 180 provides comprehensive information on definitions and interpretative regulations, procedures for filing petitions, temporary tolerances, exemptions from the requirement of a tolerance, residue data, fee requirements, specific tolerances, and exemptions that have been established for raw agricultural commodities. 40 CFR Part 185 provides tolerances for residues of pesticides in foods and food additives resulting from pesticide application during the growing process, direct application to the end food product, or indirect application to the end food product by treating the processing or storage area. 40 CFR 186 provides tolerances for residues of pesticides in animal feeds.

Before a pesticide can be registered for use on a food or feed crop or for use in a food processing or storage area, a tolerance or the exemption from the requirement of a tolerance must be established. A petition requesting the establishment of a tolerance requires the following information:

1. Name, chemical identity, and composition of the pesticide chemical
2. The amount, frequency, and time of application of the pesticide chemical
3. Full reports on investigations made with respect to the safety of the chemical, including toxicological data
4. The results of tests on the amount of residue remaining, including a description of the analytical method used to test for the pesticide
5. Accurate and precise analytical methods for identifying and measuring the amount of pesticide residues in the agricultural commodity and processed foods
6. Information on practical methods for removing residue that exceeds any proposed tolerance, such as washing or some other means

7. A proposed tolerance for the pesticide that best represents the total toxic residue on the raw agricultural commodity
8. A rationale of how the residue data support the proposed tolerance, a brief discussion on the adequacy of the analytical method with respect to sensitivity and determination of total toxic residues, an explanation of any aberrant residue values reported, an explanation for the omission or substitution of required data or information, a discussion of fate of the pesticide in the environment, and any residue considerations applicable to the proposed use

TOXIC SUBSTANCES CONTROL ACT

General Requirements

The Toxic Substances Control Act provides the EPA with broad authority to regulate chemicals and chemical substances whose manufacture, processing, distribution in commerce, use, or disposal may present an unreasonable risk of injury to health or the environment.

Section 4 authorizes the EPA to require product testing of any substance that may present an unreasonable risk of injury to health or the environment.

Under Section 5, manufacturers are required to provide the EPA with a premanufacture notification 90 d prior to manufacture or import of a new chemical substance or prior to a new use for an existing chemical. If the EPA does not make a declaration within 90 d to restrict the product, then full marketing can begin, and the chemical is added to the existing chemicals inventory. If information available to the EPA is insufficient to permit a reasoned evaluation of the chemical, and the EPA determines that the activities may present an unreasonable risk to human health or the environment, the EPA may issue an order to limit or prohibit manufacture, import, processing, distribution in commerce, use, or disposal of the substance, pending development of the test data needed to evaluate the potential hazard.

Section 6 provides that the EPA may ban, prohibit, or restrict the manufacture, processing, distribution in commerce, or use of chemicals or chemical substances when there is reason to believe that the manufacture, processing, distributing, use, or disposal of a chemical substance may cause an unreasonable risk or injury to health or the environment. Actions may be taken to prohibit the manufacturing, processing, or distribution; to limit the amount that may be manufactured, processed, or distributed; to regulate the concentration for a particular use; to require specific markings or warnings; to require specific disposal requirements; and to provide that such actions be limited in application to specified geographic areas.

In the event of an imminent and unreasonable risk of serious or widespread injury to health or the environment, Section 7 authorizes civil action in a U.S. District Court for seizure; notice of risk to the affected parties; or recall, replacement, or repurchase of a substance.

The EPA is provided inspection authority and subpoena authority to investigate any activity that the act prohibits. The prohibited actions are provided in Section 15. Civil penalties are provided for any person who violates a provision of Section 15, and criminal penalties are provided for those who knowingly or willfully violate any provision of Section 15.

Pesticides, tobacco, nuclear materials, firearms and ammunition, food additives, drugs, and cosmetics are excluded from action under the Toxic Substances Control Act.

Testing Rules

A test rule specifies the chemical to be tested, health and environmental effects for which testing is required, test standards, schedules for submission of data, and who is responsible for conducting the testing. To require testing, the EPA must find that a chemical may present an unreasonable risk, that there are insufficient data available with which to reasonably determine or predict the effects of the chemical, and that testing is necessary to generate such data. A test rule may also be based on a finding of substantial production and exposure to humans and the environment. Procedures are included for using enforceable consent agreements to require testing. This allows the EPA to negotiate with manufacturers, processors, and other interested parties to establish testing programs that satisfy the EPA testing needs.

New Chemical Substances

Of the more than 60,000 chemical substances that are manufactured or processed for commercial use in the United States, nearly 2000 new chemical substances are introduced each year.

Manufacturers are required to provide the EPA with a premanufacture notification 90 d prior to the manufacture or import of a new chemical substance or a significant new use of an existing chemical substance. The premanufacture notification must include the identity of the chemical, its molecular structure, proposed use, an estimate of amount to be manufactured, byproducts, exposure estimates, and test data related to human health and environmental effects. If the EPA determines that insufficient information is in a notification to evaluate potential risks, it may order that the manufacture or importation of the chemical be limited or prohibited until adequate data are developed.

Many of the new chemical substances reviewed do not require regulatory action. In this event, a Notice of Commencement of Manufacture, when actual manufacturing begins, must be submitted to the EPA and the new substance is then added to the existing Chemical Substances Inventory.

The EPA is responsible for regulating microorganisms used as pesticides, or for general industrial or environmental purposes. Special consideration is given to microorganisms that contain new combinations of traits or that are new to the environment in which they are to be used, microorganisms that are pathogens or that contain genetic material from pathogens, and microorganisms that are deliberately released.

As with all toxic substances, the EPA must be notified by manufacturers, processors, or distributors if they become aware of new information that suggests that microorganisms or any chemical substance present a substantial risk of injury to human health or the environment.

Existing Chemical Substances

The goal of the existing chemicals program is to reduce unreasonable risks of injury to health or the environment from chemicals already in commerce. The objectives of the program include identifying potential risks, evaluating those risks, and addressing them with regulatory action under this or another relevant authority. The EPA makes a risk assessment of a given chemical based upon an analysis of exposure data and health and environmental effects data. From the available information and the risk assessment, a decision is made regarding the need for risk management actions. Alternative risk management actions are identified and evaluated, with a consideration of effectiveness and cost factors. The focus of effort is on the potential risks of greatest concern.

Nonregulatory tools, such as chemical advisories, can be used to monitor or warn of situations that raise some concern, but do not necessitate immediate regulation. The EPA can control unreasonable risks through regulatory action or require the immediate elimination of any imminent hazards. To aid in this effort, manufacturers and importers must report general production, use, and exposure information. These data are important for priority testing considerations.

REFERENCES CITED AND SELECTED READING

Kamrin, M. A. 1988. *Toxicology: A Primer of Toxicology Principles and Applications*. Lewis Publishers, Chelsea, MI.

National Research Council. 1987. *Regulating Pesticides in Foods: The Delaney Paradox*. National Academy Press, Washington, D.C.

U.S. EPA. 1985. "National Pesticides Monitoring Plan." U.S. Environmental Protection Agency, Office of Pesticides and Toxic Substances, Washington, D.C.

U.S. EPA. 1986. "Pesticides Fact Book." U.S. Environmental Protection Agency, Office of Public Affairs, Washington, D.C. (A-107/86-003).

U.S. EPA. 1987a. "Toxic Substances Control Act (TSCA) Report to Congress for Fiscal Year 1986." U.S. Environmental Protection Agency, Office of Pesticides and Toxic Substances, Washington, D.C.

U.S. EPA. 1987b. "The Layman's Guide to the Toxic Substances Control Act." U.S. Environmental Protection Agency, Washington, D.C. (EPA-560/1-87-001).

U.S. EPA. 1989. "General Information on Applying for Registration of Pesticides in the United States." U.S. Environmental Protection Agency, Office of Pesticides Programs, Washington, D.C.

U.S. EPA. 1990. "National Water Quality Inventory — 1988 Report to Congress." U.S. Environmental Protection Agency, Washington, D.C. (EPA-440-4-90-003).

U.S. EPA. 1987b. "The Layman's Guide to the Toxic Substances Control Act." U.S. Environmental Protection Agency, Washington, D.C. (EPA-560/1-87-001).

U.S. EPA. 1989. "General Information on Applying for Registration of Pesticides in the United States." U.S. Environmental Protection Agency, Office of Pesticides Programs, Washington, D.C.

U.S. EPA. 1990. "National Water Quality Inventory — 1988 Report to Congress." U.S. Environmental Protection Agency, Washington, D.C. (EPA-440-4-90-003).

18   ENFORCEMENT

INTRODUCTION

Enforcement is the ultimate action to seek compliance with law or regulations and to assess damages for past noncompliance. It may involve compliance inspection or monitoring, sampling and analyses, gathering of other evidence, administrative actions, civil actions, or criminal actions. Compliance with federal and state statutes and regulations is the foremost goal of a regulatory agency. Obtaining compliance and deterring the regulated party from future violations are the major purposes behind penalties and related enforcement actions. Deterrence may foster compliance and prevent an individual from committing a violation or allowing it to reoccur, as well as deter others in the regulated community from committing a violation.

Successful deterrence is an important first goal in enforcement because it provides the best protection for the environment and it reduces resources necessary for program administration. If a penalty is to achieve deterrence, both a potential violator and the general public must be convinced that a penalty places a violator in a worse position than those who have complied in a timely fashion. The second goal of penalty assessment is fair and equitable treatment of the regulated community. This goal is tempered by factors such as degree of willfulness or negligence in the violation, history of noncompliance, ability to pay, degree of cooperation or noncooperation, and other unique factors specific to a violator or a case. The third goal of penalty assessment is swift resolution of an environmental problem.

Inspection or monitoring activities may uncover permit or law violations. In such an event, the EPA may take one of four legal actions pursuant to the appropriate statute. Generally, the first action is an informal notice of noncompliance or a warning letter that seeks corrective action. If corrections are not forthcoming as a result, the second stage may be an administrative action under an administrative law judge. Usually, these actions result in an order to correct the deficiencies plus a penalty assessment. The vast majority of actions that the EPA takes are through this process. For more serious or recalcitrant cases, the EPA can use the U.S. Court system in civil or criminal actions. In these cases, the actions are taken by the Department of Justice at the request of and with assistance by the EPA. Criminal cases, which can include incarceration as one of the penalties, have been the least used of the potential legal actions, historically, with the majority of the cases being civil. However, this situation is changing for two reasons:

- The most recent environmental laws passed by Congress allow more criminal cases to be filed.
- The U.S. Department of Justice believes that the most effective deterrent is to find "the person who turned the valve" and perhaps his superiors guilty of criminal conduct and send them to jail. This impresses corporations much more than low to moderate corporate fines in civil cases.

Penalties are associated with most EPA statutes, including the Clean Air Act, Safe Drinking Water Act, Stationary Source Air, Mobile Source Air, Hazardous Waste, Pesticides, and Toxic Substances. Cash penalties are only one element of the EPA's overall enforcement effort. The EPA and states use other sanctions, in addition to penalties, such as revoking permits, imposing additional compliance conditions, and publicizing enforcement actions to create deterrence.

Specific enforcement actions by the EPA are taken against relatively few violators at specific sites where inspections have revealed violations, but these actions are capable of fostering compliance at facilities throughout the country. Enforcement casts a wide shadow of deterrence, which dissuades people from violating the laws (U.S. EPA, 1989).

A credible enforcement presence gives facility managers a substantial incentive to comply. Many managers have concluded that it is good business strategy to comply with environmental regulations and to take the credit for good community citizenship. The alternative is noncompliance and the unfavorable publicity associated with violations and penalties for them. What is a credible enforcement presence? It is one that maintains the likelihood of violation detection, provides serious consequences of violation detection, ensures swift and sure response to detection, and results in a fair and consistent response to violation detection.

AUTHORITY

Section 113 of the Clean Air Act provides the basic enforcement mechanisms for stationary source violations. Administrative orders generally are available only for requiring new or existing sources to comply within 30 d from receipt of an order, or to provide delayed compliance orders for existing sources that can comply with State Implementation Plan requirements by a specific time. Civil actions are provided against any owner or operator of a major stationary source, for a permanent or temporary injunction, or to assess and recover a civil penalty of not more than $25,000 per day of violation, or both, for violation of a number of different standards or other actions. Where knowing violation of the Act occurs, criminal prosecution may result in fines of up to $25,000 per day of violation, or imprisonment for up to 1 year, or both.

Sections 205 and 211 provide civil enforcement authority for violations of the motor vehicle emission control program. Section 304 allows citizen civil actions against sources violating emission limitations or standards, or federal or state administrative orders.

The Clean Water Act authorizes states to be the first-line enforcers, although the EPA retains independent authority to take enforcement action in both authorized and unauthorized states. Section 309 provides for administrative compliance orders, administrative penalties, civil penalties of up to $25,000 per day of each violation of the act or permit limitation, and criminal penalties for negligent violations, knowing violations or personal endangerment. Section 505 provides for citizen civil suits against any person who is alleged to be in violation of an effluent standard of limitation under the act or an administrative order. Section 311 (b)(6)(B) provides guidance on the gravity of the violation in determining the amount of a penalty for the discharge of oil or hazardous substances. Associated with the gravity of the violation is the standard of care manifest by the owner or operator, the size of the business, the effect on the ability to continue in business, and the nature, extent, and degree of success of any efforts to minimize or mitigate the effects of a discharge.

The Resource Conservation and Recovery Act provides the authority to issue compliance orders, to initiate civil litigation for injunctive relief, and to assess penalties for violations and criminal penalties for specified violations. Section 3013 provides the authority to issue administrative orders requiring owners and operators of hazardous waste facilities to undertake monitoring, testing, analysis, and reporting regarding their facility whenever the EPA determines that the release of any hazardous waste from such a facility may present a substantial hazard to human health or the environment. Citizen suits are provided for in Section 7002.

The Comprehensive Environmental Response, Compensation, and Liability Act provides for administrative or court orders to force a responsible party to clean up a site, settlement agreements, and cost recovery actions where the government performs the clean up, and then seeks court-imposed liability on responsible parties for response costs.

The Toxic Substances Control Act provides inspection authority under Section 11, subpoena authority, civil penalties, criminal penalties, and particular enforcement and seizure authority under Section 17. The EPA may ban, prohibit or restrict the manufacture, processing, distribution in commerce, or use of chemicals or chemical substances.

Section 13 of the Federal Insecticide, Fungicide, and Rodenticide Act authorizes the EPA to issue an administrative order to stop the sale, use, or removal of any pesticide that is reasonably believed to be in violation of the act. It authorizes seizure of any pesticide that has been adulterated or misbranded. Civil administrative penalties and criminal sanctions are provided.

Section 1445 of the Safe Drinking Water Act provides inspection and information-gathering authority. An EPA inspector may inspect each public water supplier or other person subject to a national primary drinking water regulation, applicable underground injection control program, or any requirement under the act to monitor an unregulated contaminant. The 1986 amendments to the Act provided authority to issue administrative compliance orders, to assess administrative penalties of up to $5,000 for compliance order violation, and to seek civil penalties of up to $25,000 per day of violation. The amendments also added civil and criminal penalties for tampering or attempting to tamper with public water systems with the intention of harming persons.

COMPLIANCE

For each environmental law and regulatory program, the EPA has developed a systematic program to achieve high compliance levels. Each program is different, taking advantage of the unique opportunities presented by the nature of the regulated community and the provisions of the law. One element of a compliance strategy is a compliance monitoring plan, which sets out the priorities and rationale for conducting on-site inspections and other types of compliance monitoring. Another element is an enforcement response policy, which details the appropriate level of enforcement action associated with the many ways that a regulation can be violated, and the principles and rationale for determining the seriousness of various types of violation as a factor in assessing penalty amounts.

A fundamental principle of the EPA environmental policy is that regulated parties should keep track of their compliance status and report all of the resulting data to the responsible regulatory authority. An inspection provides an examination of the environmental affairs of a single regulated facility to determine if it is in compliance with applicable environmental requirements. Inspections may be routine, as a result of a reason to believe that a violation exists, to support the development of a case, or as a follow-up to determine whether a facility found to have been in violation is in compliance with an administrative order or a consent decree.

Self-monitoring and reporting requirements identify potential violations and provide an inspector with a complete history of the compliance behavior of a facility. The Discharge Monitoring Reports required to be filed by all NPDES permittees provide information generally on a monthly or quarterly basis for all of the constituents designated for monitoring as a condition of the discharge permit. While required self-monitoring and submission of reports are key features of the compliance program, regulated sources also receive periodic on-site inspections. Part of the on-site inspection is a review of monitoring reports, recordkeeping, compliance status, and reasons for noncompliance. Owners or operators of facilities that submit incomplete, inaccurate, or false information are subject to civil or criminal sanctions. There have been cases where citizen's suits have been filed against facilities with several noncompliance records, as shown by the discharge monitoring reports, which are available for public viewing. Area monitoring is another method used in compliance monitoring, although it is less used than self-monitoring and inspections. It consists of using ambient monitoring or remote sensing to monitor environmental conditions in the vicinity of a facility or over a large area. Area monitoring is used to assess impacts of activities, to assess trends, to provide data useful in assessing risks and health impacts, and to provide a screening device for identifying potential violations and areas where compliance problems may be found.

There are several inspection levels. One could be termed a walk-through where a tour of a facility would include noting the existence of pollution-control equipment, observing work practices and housekeeping, and checking the records repository. A compliance evaluation inspection, in addition to the above, would include a review and evaluation of records, interviews with facility personnel, determining the details about process and control devices in place, and perhaps collecting a grab sample of the effluent for an analytical check.

A sampling inspection could include the activities above and would include, in addition, preplanned sample collection. The sample collection might be done to duplicate sampling and analyses performed by the owner or operator, or to document the extent of a contaminated area or environmental damages.

In addition, inspections and inspectors serve other useful purposes. They promote voluntary compliance through consultation and the provision of information and technology transfer. They serve as a visible manifestation of the regulatory process and foster compliance by establishing a regulatory presence. Further, data gathered during inspections may support the permit issuance or standards setting processes.

EVIDENCE

Evidence is the means by which any alleged fact that is being investigated may be established or disproved. Documentation of evidence must be accurate, authenticated by signature or initials of the documentor, and complete. The chain of custody for sampling and analyses must be complete and unbroken. The concepts of quality assurance, as described in Chapter 21, prevail throughout the gathering of evidence. A universal rule is that hearsay is inadmissable. Hearsay is evidence that is based not on a witness' personal knowledge or direct involvement, but on matters told to him by another.

Evidence includes everything an individual does that is relevant to an issue at hand. It may include inspections, personal observations during inspections, examination of self-monitoring reports, field notes appropriately dated and signed or initialed, specific conversations with identified individuals, the collection of samples at a particular time and on a particular day, and similar information. Preferably, field notes should be recorded in a bound notebook, with each page dated, numbered, and signed or initialed by the recorder. Anyone, after being sworn, may present evidence. All who have participated in any relevant way in the events of a matter at issue are in a position to present evidence. For example, all who have signed the chain-of-custody document may be called to testify individually regarding their management of the samples during the interval of time that they were in control.

Expert testimony is evidence presented by a person where both sides and the court agree that the person is an expert on the subject at issue because of education, training, or knowledge of the subject matter. An expert may testify on the alleged facts presented in the case or on personal judgment or conclusions based upon similar situations elsewhere with which the witness is familiar in a professional way.

SAMPLING AND ANALYSES

Sampling and analyses to be used for evidence may involve the air, land, or water; aquatic sediments or sludges; bacteria, plants, or animals; waste effluents or waste sludges; containers; or water supply systems. There should be a quality assurance project plan for the sampling operation and a quality control plan for laboratory analyses, as discussed in Chapter 21. Standard operating procedures should be recorded and followed. Where it is necessary to deviate from the above plans or procedures, the deviation should be recorded and the reason for the deviation noted. The controlling word is *documentation*. All aspects of the sampling and analyses procedures should be recorded, dated, and signed or initialed by the person who will be in a position to testify regarding personal participation in the action and personal knowledge of the facts presented on the signed note page.

As with all evidence, a witness must describe what was done, when, how, by whom, and what the results were, because the witness saw these occurrences or personally performed the act. As stated earlier, a witness cannot testify on something the witness has heard someone else say because this is based on the veracity and competence of someone other than the witness.

DETERMINING THE DETERRENCE AMOUNT

The EPA has developed internal policy on items to consider in determining the civil penalty that will provide deterrence. In most cases, these items for consideration are designed to ensure that penalties remove any significant economic benefit of noncompliance (U.S. EPA, 1984). In many instances, the economic advantage to be derived from noncompliance is the ability to delay making the expenditures necessary to achieve compliance. Noncompliance examples of these types may include the following:

1. Failure to install equipment needed to meet discharge or emission control standards
2. Failure to affect process changes needed to eliminate pollutants from products or waste streams
3. Failure to test where testing must be done to demonstrate achieved compliance
4. Improper storage or disposal where such is required to achieve compliance

Many kinds of violations enable a violator to avoid certain compliance costs, such as

1. Cost savings from operation and maintenance of required equipment that was not installed
2. Failure to properly operate and maintain existing environmental control equipment
3. Process, operational, or maintenance savings from removing pollution control equipment

There are some situations where goods or services are not available elsewhere or are more attractive to a consumer. Examples of these violations are

1.   Selling banned products
2.   Selling products for banned use
3.   Selling products without required labelling or warnings
4.   Removing or altering pollution control equipment

A penalty should include an amount reflecting the seriousness or gravity of the violation. Factors of consideration here include:

1.   Actual or possible harm caused by the violation
2.   Importance to the regulatory scheme
3.   Relative impact of a penalty on the violator
4.   Amount of pollutant
5.   Toxicity of the pollutant
6.   Sensitivity of the environment
7.   The length of time a violation continues

In addition to the above, some additional adjustment factors are considered by the EPA to promote flexibility for a particular case (U.S. EPA, 1984). These include:

1.   The degree of willfulness or negligence
2.   The degree of cooperation or noncooperation in reporting of noncompliance and prompt correction of environmental problems
3.   History of noncompliance
4.   Ability to pay

ADMINISTRATIVE ACTIONS

Administrative actions may either be informal or formal. Informal administrative actions are notices of noncompliance or warning letters, which are advisory in nature. In these actions, the manager of a facility is advised that a violation has been found, the corrective action needed, and the time within which an action to correct the problem must be instituted. Generally, informal actions carry neither penalty nor power to compel action. The record of an informal action can be used to support more severe legal actions when a situation is not satisfactorily corrected.

Formal administrative actions are legal actions that result in an order requiring the violating party to correct the violations and, in most cases, to pay a civil penalty that is commensurate with the seriousness and the circumstances of the violation. These administrative actions are strong enforcement tools; if a person violates the terms of an administrative order, a U.S. court action may be obtained to force compliance with the order. Generally, administrative actions are the most expedient means of requiring correction, and they are used in lieu of civil or criminal actions whenever appropriate.

Administrative actions are taken under EPA's internal administrative litigation system, which is comparable to any court system, except that it is presided over by EPA's administrative law judges, whose salaries are paid by the EPA. All administrative actions have the potential to be challenged in the U.S. court system. Therefore, conduct of these actions is governed by an extensive set of procedural rules designed to provide due process to the alleged violator and to ensure the integrity of the system. Violators may appeal the initial rulings of the administrative judge to the EPA Administrator and may appeal the Administrator's final decision to the U.S. courts.

CIVIL JUDICIAL ACTIONS

Civil actions are taken in the U.S. court system by the U.S. Department of Justice at the request of the EPA. Typically, they are used against more serious or recalcitrant violators of environmental laws. Generally, they are intended to seek prompt correction of imminent hazard situations posing an immediate threat to human health or the environment. Preparation of civil judicial cases is resource intensive because of the Department of Justice involvement and the more formalized procedures required for court action as compared to administrative actions. Sometimes judicial litigation may take several years to complete. Civil cases often result in penalties and court orders requiring correction of the violation and also requiring specific actions, such as specialized monitoring to prevent future noncompliance.

CRIMINAL JUDICIAL ACTIONS

Criminal actions are taken when a person or company has knowingly and willfully committed a violation of the law. In a criminal case, the Department of Justice prosecutes an alleged violator in the U.S. court system, seeking criminal sanctions, usually including fines and incarceration. Criminal actions are taken for flagrant, intentional disregard for environmental laws and deliberate falsification of documents or records. Criminal cases usually are brought by the Department of Justice at the request of the EPA, but the Department of Justice can initiate them on its own. Criminal cases are the most difficult to pursue. They require special investigation and case development procedures, and they involve the highest standard of proof, including proof of the intent of the violator to commit the violation.

STATE-EPA AGREEMENTS

Virtually every environmental statute provides for the EPA delegation to, or approval of, state programs to implement national standards and regulations through state-specified rules, permits, and enforcement activities. Although delegated states have primary responsibility for compliance and enforcement action, the EPA retains oversight and overall responsibility for ensuring fair and effective enforcement of federal requirements and a credible national deterrent to noncompliance. States conduct 80–90% of all compliance inspections in a delegated or approved program state. To ensure a complete understanding and definition of responsibility related to programs, plans, and activities, agreements or contracts are negotiated between the EPA and a state. State-EPA enforcement agreements reflect the criteria for direct enforcement in delegated states, protocol for advance notification and consultation, and the data the state will report to the EPA.

The EPA may conduct inspections in a delegated or approved program state. The EPA may take direct enforcement action under the following conditions: at the request of a state; when state enforcement response is not timely or appropriate; when there are national legal or program precedents involved; or when there is a violation of an EPA order or consent decree.

CITIZEN'S SUITS AND NUISANCE SUITS

Citizen's suits in the U.S. court system may be made by a citizen or group of citizens using the provisions of federal applicable law and the penalty system prescribed by such law for violation. Citizen's suits may be instituted for violations of law, such as discharging without a permit, or violation of permits, compliance requirements, or other regulations or standards. Often the self-monitoring reports, such as the discharge monitoring reports related to discharges to water in the NPDES permit program, are used to show that the preparer of the report violated permit conditions.

Nuisance suits, which are designed to show damage to property because of environmental action, are brought under nuisance laws. Generally, they seek corrective action and monetary damages. Often the citizen's suit and a nuisance suit may be combined into one court action. The court procedures for each virtually are the same as in civil judicial action.

THE PROCEEDINGS

Among the early events in the litigatory process is discovery. This is the phase during which each side works at obtaining the facts and at understanding the theory of the case from the point of view of the opposition. Discovery is a time to gather information and to avoid trial by surprise, to pin down witnesses and parties on the record through written responses or statements, and to evaluate the other side's evidence and tactics.

Discovery is enhanced through three principal mechanisms. These are interrogatories, requests for documents and data, and depositions. If something has been written down, that information potentially is available to the other side, unless it is exempted or protected through attorney-client privilege. This is the reason that many attorneys request that certain information not be written or transmitted in writing.

Interrogatories are written questions formed by one side to which answers must be provided by the opposite side. Requests for documents may include any written or printed information of which an attorney is sufficiently aware to permit its identification in a request. A deposition is a statement by a witness under oath, transcribed by a court reporter, in the presence of an attorney, that has relevancy to a case. A deposition may be filed by either side of a case.

Once a deposition is filed, attorneys for the opposite side may question the witness under oath regarding the statements presented in the deposition, or a deposition may be taken of opposing witnesses or expert witnesses. In the latter case, the lawyers may explore the field of expertise of an expert witness to arrive at a sense of the depth of knowledge of a particular witness. In this regard, carefully phrased questions by an attorney will attempt to limit the field of expertise, because once a witness admits to a lack of specific knowledge about a particular subject matter, that witness will be rapidly disqualified when attempting to testify on that particular subject matter during the trial proceedings.

Often a deposition is a verbal fishing trip seeking information on

1. Specific areas of expertise of a witness
2. Specific fields that the witness expects to testify to
3. Activities that the witness has begun, completed, or anticipates that are related to the case
4. Depth of knowledge by the witness about areas related to anticipated testimony
5. The information and backup literature, reports, facts, and data that the witness intends to use to support the anticipated testimony
6. Details of any visits to a physical location that are relevant to the case
7. Details of any contacts with persons during such site visits
8. Knowledge by the witness of any written communications with the witness' attorney or with litigants on the site that the witness represents
9. Knowledge of any studies or investigations completed or being considered with relevancy in the case
10. Always, there is an effort by the questioning attorney to limit the expertise of the witness, or to get the witness to admit to not being an expert in a particular field that would be a potential arena for testimony

The trial begins with opening remarks by the opposing attorneys; first the plaintiff, then the defense. The attorneys present legal arguments of law applicable to the case and follow with a statement of what the respective sides expect to prove in the case. This is followed by the presentation of the plaintiff's case, witness by witness. For each witness, there is opportunity for direct examination with questions presented by the attorney representing the witness and cross-examination by the opposing attorney. There may be redirect examination to clarify responses made to the cross-examination questions, but no new information is to be introduced into the record by this witness at this time. The opposing attorney has an opportunity to continue with re-cross-examination questioning to attempt to counter any facts that may have been restated in some way as a result of the redirect examination.

The trial continues with the defense presenting its case with the same order of examination, except that the defense attorney becomes the direct examiner of witnesses for the defense. This is followed with closing remarks being presented by the opposing attorneys and assignments by the judge. Generally, a judge will require the attorneys to present a summary of the relevant law and their interpretation of it, as well as their arguments for judgment in the case. A judge usually renders a decision after an opportunity to reflect on the final submissions and arguments by the opposing attorneys.

An attorney has many duties during the course of litigation. One is obtaining the relevant facts. These include the literature of the case in the form of letters, memos, reports, legal and other documents; the published technical literature with relevancy to the case; depositions; information from retained experts; and information from special studies to obtain data.

The organization of the information collected to support a case is extremely important to the success of the attorney representing the facts. Information must be instantly at hand. Often a report must be obtained and read while a witness is being cross-examined by another attorney in order for a specific question to be phrased or a fact to be substantiated. This organization of information may take the form of

1. A chronological file of every memo, letter, handwritten note, or other piece of information even remotely relevant to the case, with each piece of information separated by tabs in a notebook or in separate file folders
2. A separate cross-referenced subject file with each subject identified that may be relevant to the case
3. A personnel file for each person associated with either side of the case, including expert witnesses, which contains resumés and other information related to expertise or particular function in the case
4. An alphabetical file containing the deposition of each individual deposed by either side in the case

A successful attorney is one who trains to become generally knowledgeable of the technical issues associated with the case. Of course, an attorney must present the facts of the case through direct and cross-examination of the witnesses.

An expert witness has a number of duties for the side of the case that the witness represents. Among these are to

1. Provide technical competence in all activities associated with the case
2. Critique depositions, reports, and other related information that will be presented by the opposition for technical accuracy and correct technical judgment related to data interpretations
3. Provide the attorney with alternative conclusions to the data presented in 2 (above) that are applicable
4. Develop and advise on any technical study or investigation that may be required to develop needed data

5.   Assist the attorney, if applicable, with potential questions and possible answers to those questions to be used in taking depositions, or in cross-examination, of opposing expert witnesses
6.   Assist the attorney, if applicable, with potential questions and answers to be directed to the expert witness in direct examination
7.   Remember, when on the witness stand, that the audience to convince is the judge or jury, and not the attorney asking the questions; face the judge or jury when answering all questions
8.   Speak truthfully, calmly, clearly and professionally
9.   Make certain that the question is fully understood before a response is provided

THE PUBLIC'S ROLE

The public can have an important role in helping to stop pollution; the EPA has published guidance on the public's role (U.S. EPA, 1990). The most important things to do when you see a potential pollution problem are to make careful observations of the problem, write the observations down, and then report these observations to the proper authorities.

What observations would be written down? They are

1.   The date and time the observation occurred
2.   Where the pollution was observed
3.   How the pollution came to be noticed
4.   Has the problem occurred more than once?
5.   Can a person or source be identified?
6.   If a truck is involved, note the license number, type of truck, and any signs or emblems on the truck
7.   If a camera is available, a picture of the pollution is helpful
8.   If another person is able to make similar observations, that too is helpful

The appropriate authority to contact probably would be the county or state environmental or pollution control official. Often a state will maintain several regional offices. Make sure to obtain the contact's name and telephone number in the event that additional contacts become necessary.

In general, discharging a waste without a permit is illegal; discharging a waste without certain testing or monitoring activities is illegal, and the results of testing or monitoring must be reported to state authorities. The results of such tests are available to the public through state environmental offices or EPA regional offices. Demolition of a building containing asbestos without proper measures to keep the asbestos contained is a violation of the Toxic Substances Control Act, as is improper storage or disposal of asbestos or of transformers containing PCBs. Use of pesticides in a manner inconsistent with the direction on the label or the application of a restricted-use pesticide by an unlicensed applicator is a violation of the Federal Insecticide, Fungicide, and Rodenticide Act. Many other illegal actions become apparent in reading the preceding chapters of this book.

REFERENCES CITED AND SELECTED READING

U.S. EPA. 1984. "Memorandum: Courtney M. Price, Assistant Administrator for Enforcement and Compliance Monitoring, New Civil Penalty Policy." U.S. Environmental Protection Agency, Washington, D.C. (February 16).

U.S. EPA. 1985. "Study of Literature Concerning the Roles of Penalties in Regulatory Enforcement." U.S. Environmental Protection Agency, Office of Enforcement and Compliance Monitoring, Washington, D.C. (September).

U.S. EPA. 1986. "Memorandum: A. James Barnes, Deputy Administrator, Revised Policy Framework for State/EPA Enforced Agreements." U.S. Environmental Protection Agency, Office of the Administrator, Washington, D.C. (August 25).

U.S. EPA. 1988. "FY 1988 Enforcement Accomplishments Report." U.S. Environmental Protection Agency, Office of Enforcement and Compliance Monitoring, Washington, D.C.

U.S. EPA. 1989. "Basic Inspector Training Course: Fundamentals of Environmental Compliance Inspection." U.S. Environmental Protection Agency, Office of Enforcement and Compliance Monitoring, Washington, D.C.

U.S. EPA. 1990. "The Public's Role on Environmental Enforcement." U.S. Environmental Protection Agency, Office of Enforcement, Washington, D.C.

19 ENVIRONMENTAL REAL PROPERTY AUDITS

NEED AND PURPOSE

Land developers, owners, lenders, buyers, and sellers have been made abundantly aware of liability associated with land contamination as a result of recent hazardous waste legislation. The latin phrase, *caveat emptor*, let the purchaser beware, has created a new need for the identification of potential environmental problems associated with real property transfers.

Before money is loaned on apartment buildings, vacant lots on which homes will be built, commercial or industrial properties, either for their purchase or renovation, lending institutions generally require that environmental audits of the facility in question be performed. These environmental audits address such toxic materials as asbestos, radon, PCBs, hazardous wastes, and underground storage tanks. If any of these toxic materials are discovered on or near the site in quantities that could have liability implications, either the borrower or the seller must make arrangements to have them removed before the lending institution will provide the borrower with funding. The purpose of this requirement is to prevent the lender from becoming a responsible party in a law suit for impairment of health by a resident or worker in the facility for which the funding is sought.

A number of court cases have held a purchaser liable for hazardous waste contamination caused by a prior owner or hazardous waste that simply has been dumped on the land. However, a landowner who unknowingly acquires contaminated property may now have a defense afforded by the "innocent landowner" provision of the Superfund Amendments and Authorization Act of 1986. To establish this defense, a landowner must demonstrate that, at the time of the purchase, he or she undertook all appropriate inquiry into the previous ownership and uses of the property consistent with good commercial or customary practice. Thus, it is advantageous for a buyer or a lending institution to determine, before the close of escrow, whether a given piece of property may have been contaminated.

The need for an environmental real property audit is clear; it is to provide a defense for liability that may be associated with any contamination of the property. The purpose is to identify the existence or nonexistence of such contamination. The need and purpose are fulfilled through a comprehensive physical inspection of the property, an examination of records and historical use, and possibly sampling and laboratory analysis.

BACKGROUND INFORMATION

There are certain items that are helpful and often essential to a site investigation. These include:

1. Specific site location map and plat
2. U.S. Geological Survey quadrangle map of area that includes the site
3. Survey records with drawing of site and notes
4. Blueprints or drawings of buildings on the site
5. Legal description
6. The most recent appraisal
7. Records of past ownership and land use practices
8. National Priority List of hazardous waste sites
9. CERCLIS list of state potential hazardous waste sites
10. List of known underground storage tanks in area of site
11. Wetlands map of area
12. Any aerial photographs of the site

Obviously, it is essential that the investigator know the precise location of a site and the precise boundaries of a site prior to the site investigation. The above items will ensure that these factors are known. The past history of the site may reveal the presence of toxics in the ground. The existence of hazards close to the site being investigated may raise the potential for the migration of those hazards into the site itself.

SITE INVESTIGATION

The site investigation entails walking the property with notebook in hand to ensure that every part of it is visible to the investigator. The investigator should be alert for discarded containers, labels, packing material, or any other discarded or dumped materials. The soil, ground vegetation, and trees should be examined for signs of stunting, ill health, or discoloration. Anything considered by the investigator to be unusual should be noted and investigated. The location, condition, and storage method of any solid, liquid, gaseous, or other contaminants should be determined. Any contained material must bear a label and the label contents should be noted by the investigator.

Wetlands and their integrity are important investigative considerations. Any land condition that potentially may be defined as a wetland should be noted. An outline map of the property with various field observations noted on it will be useful in developing a report on the investigation and, when redrawn, will be an important part of the final report. An investigator should be cognizant of special zoning restrictions. For example, the Chesapeake Bay Critical Area Law, passed by the state of Maryland in 1984, created the Chesapeake Bay Critical Area Commission, which established criteria for local critical area program development. A minimum 100-ft buffer landward from the mean high-water line of tidal waters, tributary streams, and tidal wetlands is required. A minimum 25-ft buffer around identified nontidal wetlands, where development activities or other activities that may disturb the wetlands or the wildlife are contained therein, is also required (Chesapeake Bay Critical Area Commission, 1986).

The existence of underground storage tanks (USTs) must be reported, as this creates a potential toxic hazard. This applies to both USTs on the property or close enough to it so that they could contaminate groundwater in the property. Any tank having greater than 10% by volume of its capacity beneath the surface is an underground tank. New underground tanks must be equipped with leak detectors, devices to prevent spill or overflow, and have corrosion protection. Existing tanks must undergo leak detection tests and have associated notification and recordkeeping activities. Farm and residential tanks holding 1100 gal or less of motor fuel are exempt from the above, as are septic tanks (40 CFR Part 280 and 281). In addition, most states have specific requirements for existing USTs.

The previous and historical ownership of the property and previous land-use practices should be investigated. If there was industrial or commercial ownership over the past 40–50 years, the housekeeping practices of that period should be determined, if possible. Often chemicals were discarded via the back door of the building or warehouse. Local persons with a long-time knowledge of the property should be interviewed to determine if there is knowledge of land use practices of a historic nature. Obviously, the name and address of the individual providing this knowledge should be retained. Is a groundwater well located on the property, or nearby, being investigated?

GOVERNMENT FILES AND RECORDS

The National Priority List of hazardous waste sites, the state CERCLIS list of potential hazardous waste sites, and the state list of underground storage tanks should be examined to determine the nearest such site or tank to the property being investigated. Examining the files and records of government agencies, especially the state regional environmental agency, often is of great help in producing information. One can determine areas where complaints have been filed near the property of interest, areas of nearby state inspections or investigations, and generally areas of nearby environmental concern as recorded in state records. This information may be color coded on pins in an enlarged wall map that is maintained by the state agency. The quality of the water in well samples from on-property or nearby wells would provide useful information.

WATER AND SOIL TESTING

The nature and extent of pollution or contamination are terms basic to and associated with environmental laws and regulations. Defining and creating boundaries for such terms are the objectives of any environmental investigation, however small or complex. The nature of a potential problem embodies a definition of cause, or of something introduced into the environment; the extent of such embodies concentration, quantity, size and space, and potential risk or damage to human health and the environment. Although regulations may require certain implicit actions, industries especially would be well served to consider carefully the potential or actual nature and extent of environmental damage from operating a facility and the potential risks or damages to human health and the environment of such action.

Water and soil testing of a property requires advance planning. It can be expensive; it should result in data-supportable conclusions. It may be the first step in a remediation program if contamination is found. Any monitoring program should not be made more complex than necessary. Often basic questions can be answered with relatively few data, providing care has been exercised in how and where such data have been developed and in their interpretation.

Water

Sampling and analysis of water is relatively routine. If there are water wells on the property or nearby water wells, they may be sampled easily. The distance from the property and their locations relative to being upgradient or downgradient from the property should be noted. If there is a stream that may receive surface drainage or groundwater from the vicinity, it could be sampled at locations upstream and downstream from the expected effects from the property. The complexity of soil sampling, however, is another matter.

Soil

Murrmann and Koutz (1972) characterized soil chemistry in relation to wastewater renovation. They stated that a sample of any soil can be considered in simplest terms to contain inorganic solids, organic solids, solution, and vapor. A typical mineral soil may contain by volume about 45% inorganic solids and from 2 to 6% organic material. The vapor phase varies from 15 to 35% with time, depending upon soil moisture content. The normal vapor phase of soil contains nitrogen, oxygen, carbon dioxide, water vapor, and many other trace gas components, but differs in composition from the normal atmosphere because of utilization of oxygen and production of carbon dioxide, as well as other volatile compounds during biological processes. It is not unusual for the carbon dioxide content to increase from 0.03% to more than 5%, while the oxygen concentration may decrease from 20% to a few percent.

The sand and silt soil fractions are composed mostly of primary materials, the identity and amounts of which reflect the parent material from which the soil originated. The most abundant mineral classified as sand and silt is quartz, followed in importance by feldspars, which are sodium, potassium, and calcium aluminum silicates. The native organic fraction of soils results primarily from the decomposition of plant material. Plant tissue has many components that fall into groups, such as lignins, fats, oils, resins, cellulose, starches, sugars, and proteins. Eventually, as a consequence of biological activity, components of the organic fraction are degraded to carbon dioxide, water, nitrates, sulfates, and orthophosphate (Murrmann and Koutz, 1972).

Often, the relative size of the property being sampled constrains the placement of soil sampling locations to demonstrate land pollution or lack thereof. There is a wide range in concentration of soil constituents. There is a necessity to determine background soil constituent concentrations for the area of interest because background concentrations are the key to defining pollution. Following are the questions related to soil sample collection: How many samples should be collected? Where should they be collected? How deep within the soil should the sample be collected? Where should the control or background sample be collected? What analyses should be conducted on the soil samples?

The question most easily answered may be the last one. Knowledge of the past property ownership and land use should provide a clue regarding the types of contaminants expected if land pollution exists. The most difficult question to answer may be the next-to-last question. As will be shown later in this chapter, the wide variation in soil constituent concentrations necessitates data from a local area against which to compare results of analyses to determine if a problem exists or if a sample result is within the realm of natural variation.

A minimum of three control or background samples should be analyzed, even if only a similar number of samples are collected in a suspected area of pollution on a small parcel of property. Two of the control samples should be collected within the confines of the property but as far removed and upgradient from a suspected area of pollution as it is possible to get. The third control sample may be nearby and substantially removed from the property of interest, but from an area believed to be uncontaminated. Often, a nearby city park may serve as an excellent control area. The control samples should represent the same soil strata as the remaining samples collected from a parcel of property. Generally, the initial sampling and analyses will involve surface soils down to a depth of about 3 in. within the soil.

The objective of this investigation, as it is with most other environmental investigations, is to determine the nature and extent of soil pollution. If there is indication through research on past ownership or land use practices that containers of toxic materials were at one time stored on a particular spot or that chemicals had been discarded in a particular area, that would be an area upon which to focus initial sampling. How many samples to collect? The EPA, in its simplified sampling scheme for friable surfacing materials to identify asbestos in buildings, recommends collecting nine samples, but never less than three samples, per homogeneous sampling area (U.S.

EPA, 1985). There is logic in transferring that recommendation to soil sampling. Never less than three samples from a possible contaminated area should be taken, plus three control or background samples. An additional six samples taken from a sampling grid around a suspected area of contamination would be most useful in data interpretation, but the cost of sample analysis may be a factor in decisionmaking. However, if the area of concern to be sampled exceeds approximately 0.5 acre, the number of samples required would increase.

How deep within the soil should a sample be taken? The initial sampling would be surface soil sampling to a depth of 3 in. If toxic materials are found in any of these samples, removal of the contaminated soils may be indicated. Under these circumstances, it would be necessary to sample vertically to a depth where background concentrations of the toxic chemical or chemicals again are found. Generally, a state will require that contaminated soils be removed to a depth of background concentrations. Obviously, this results in an expensive testing and removal operation.

If, after sample analysis, the soil contaminant is found to be an organic chemical, the chances are great that this was something introduced by the activities of people. However, if the soil concentration of a heavy metal or metals is high, the cause may be either natural or the result of industrial activities. In the following paragraphs, selected heavy metals and cyanide are discussed along with their concentrations that have been documented in the Earth's crust.

Arsenic

Arsenic is found in air and all living organisms; it is a naturally occurring element in concentrations reported as 1.5–2 parts per million (ppm) in the Earth's crust (U.S. EPA, 1976). Concentrations of arsenic in igneous rocks average 2–3 ppm and range upward to 113 ppm; in sedimentary rocks, the range in shales and clays is 0.3–490 ppm; in coal, up to 2000 ppm; and in sedimentary manganese ores, it is up to 1.5% (U.S. EPA, 1976). The natural arsenic content in virgin soils varies from 0.1–40 ppm. Soils overlying sulfide ore deposits commonly contain arsenic at several hundred parts per million; the reported maximum is 8000 ppm. The arsenic may be present in unweathered sulfide minerals or in an inorganic anion state. In Tennessee phosphorite blue rock, the arsenic average is 20.4 ppm; in such brown rock, it is 14.6 ppm; and in Tennessee white rock, it is 10.6 ppm (U.S. EPA, 1976).

Beryllium

Beryllium occurs in most soils. The beryllium content in the Earth's crust is reported at 10 ppm (U.S. EPA, 1978). Shacklette et al. (1971) report an average of 1 ppm and a range of 1–7 ppm beryllium in surficial materials of the conterminous United States. Mineral soils have been reported to contain 0.2–10 ppm beryllium (Murrmann and Koutz, 1972). The main beryllium ore is beryl, which contains about 5% beryllium metal (Heindel, 1970). Major beryllium deposits are found in Kentucky, Texas,

Arizona, Nevada, and Idaho. Kopp and Kroner (1967) reported that for 1577 surface water samples collected at 130 sampling station in the United States, 85 or 5.4% contained from 0.01–1.22 µg/L (parts per billion), with a mean of 0.19 µg/L beryllium.

Cadmium

Cadmium is a soft, white, easily fusible metal that always is found in nature in association with zinc (U.S. EPA, 1975). Biologically, cadmium is a nonessential, nonbeneficial element that has been shown to be toxic to humans when ingested or inhaled. It is naturally present in trace amounts in most environmental media including soil, water, air, and food. Plants used as food grown on cadmium-contaminated soils concentrate the cadmium. Food, therefore is the single largest environmental source of cadmium exposure to most humans.

Uncontaminated soils may range from 0.01 to about 1.0 ppm cadmium; contaminated soils near smelters or zinc metallurgical factories may exceed 100 ppm and have been reported as high as 450 ppm (Fleischer et al., 1974). In urban soils of Pittsburgh, Pennsylvania, the mean of 51 soil samples was 1.21 ppm and the range was 0.0–4.95 ppm cadmium (Gowen et al., 1976). The use of phosphate fertilizers or municipal sewage sludges on land may contribute substantially to the soil's cadmium content. Dressing land with phosphate fertilizers has been found to increase the soil cadmium content to 3.38 ppm (U.S. EPA, 1979).

Chromium

Chromium is the 17th most abundant nongaseous element in the Earth's crust (Schroeder, 1970); its concentration range in the continental crust is 80–200 ppm, with an average of 125 ppm (NAS, 1974). Chromium rarely is found in natural waters. Kopp and Kroner (1967) reported that for 1577 surface water samples collected at 130 sampling locations in the U.S., 386 samples contained from 1–112 µg/l; the mean was 9.7 µg/l chromium.

Chromium is recognized as an essential trace element for humans and is found in air, soil, some foods, and most biological systems. Microgram amounts of chromium are essential for the maintenance of normal glucose metabolism, and some animal studies indicate that chromium deficiencies may induce arteriosclerosis. Hexavalent chromium, however, is irritating and corrosive to mucous membranes; it is absorbed via ingestion, through the skin, and by inhalation. Hexavalent chromium is toxic when introduced into laboratory animals systemically.

Copper

Copper occurs as a natural or native metal and in various mineral forms, such as cuprite and malachite. The copper content of soils varies considerably with the parent rock, weathering, drainage, pH, and organic content. The copper concentration in the continental crust generally is about 50 ppm. Sandstones contain 10–40 ppm; shales, 30–150 ppm; and marine black shales, 20–300 ppm (U.S. EPA, 1977).

Copper is an essential trace element for the propagation of plants. It performs vital functions in several enzymes and a major role in the synthesis of chlorophyll. The copper concentration in commonly consumed vegetables and leafy plants seldom exceeds 25 ppm and usually is 10–15 ppm. Grains and seeds contain about 20–40 ppm copper (NAS, 1977). A shortage of copper in soil may lead to chlorosis, which is characterized by a yellowing of plant leaves.

Copper is required in animal metabolism. It is important in invertebrate blood chemistry and for the synthesis of hemoglobin. Oysters, clams, crustacea, and the liver and kidneys of animals may contain 200–400 ppm copper. The human intake of copper in food is estimated to be 2–5 mg/day (NAS, 1977).

Cyanide

Cyanide ions are not strongly absorbed or retained by soils. The cyanide salts of most cations are soluble, except for silver cyanide, AgCN, and move only a short distance through soil before being biologically converted under aerobic conditions to nitrates or fixed by trace metals through complex formation. Under anaerobic conditions, cyanides denitrify to gaseous nitrogen compounds, which enter the atmosphere. The cyanide ion is not involved in oxidation-reduction reactions (Murrmann and Koutz, 1972). Cyanide has a low degree of persistence in the environment. It is not mutagenic, teratogenic, or carcinogenic, and it is not bioaccumulated. Cyanide may complex irreversibly with heavy metals and thereby become biologically inactivated.

Lead

Lead is a natural constituent of the Earth's crust. The usual concentration in rocks and in soils from natural resources ranges from 10–30 mg/kg. The normal concentration of lead in rural vegetation ranges from 0.01–1.0 mg/kg dry weight, or 2–20 mg/kg ash weight (U.S. EPA, 1980). The lead content of rural U.S. soils is 10–15 μg/g (Chow and Patterson, 1962), but the range of lead-in-soil concentrations is 2–200 ppm, exclusive of areas near lead ore deposits (Motto et al., 1970). Urban soils may be higher in lead concentration. In a survey of 77 midwestern U.S. cities, it was found that the average lead concentration in the street dust of residential areas was 1636 μg/g, and that in commercial and industrial areas the average concentrations were, respectively, 2413 and 1512 μg/g (Hunt et al., 1971). Within 1 mile of an El Paso, Texas smelter, the soil had a mean lead concentration of 1791 ppm and that of house dust was 4022 ppm (Landrigan et al., 1975).

Mercury

Mercury concentrations of unpolluted, nonmineralized soils in the United States range from 0.01–4.7 µg/g and average 0.071 (Shacklette et al., 1971a). Although highly variable, the mercury content of soils in mineralized areas can exceed 500 µg/g. Cinnabar ore deposits usually contain from 0.5 to 1.2% mercury. The mercury contents of nonmineralized freshwater sediments exhibit ranges of 0.01–1200 µg/g, although the available data indicate a mean of about 0.3 µg/g. Concentrations of 800–1000 µg/g have been observed in polluted sediments, usually in close proximity to chloralkali plants. The mercury content of unpolluted U.S. rivers from 31 states where natural mercury deposits are unknown is less than 0.01 µg/l (Wershaw, 1970).

Nickel

Soils normally contain nickel in a wide range of levels, 5–500 ppm, and soils from serpentine rock may contain as much as 5000 ppm. The nickel content of soils is less important for plant uptake than such factors as soil composition, pH, and organic content (U.S. EPA, 1980a).

Nickel probably is essential for animal nutrition, but there has not yet been unequivocal demonstration that nickel deprivation produces consistent abnormalities in experimental animals that can be prevented or cured by the administration of nickel (NAS, 1977). Toxicity studies have demonstrated that nickel and nickel salts have relatively low toxicity to various species of animals when administered orally. There appears to be a mechanism that limits the intestinal absorption of nickel in mammals.

Selenium

Selenium in the Earth's crust has been reported at 0.09 mg/kg (CRC, 1970). Turekian and Wedepohl (1961) and Taylor (1964) revised downwards the selenium concentration in igneous rocks to 0.05 mg/kg, based on a revised sulphur content of these rocks (down 300 from 600 mg/kg) and the accepted sulphur to selenium ratio in igneous rocks of 6000. Actual analyses of igneous rocks showed a selenium concentration range from 0.004–1.5 mg/kg (Larkin, 1973). Some sandstones, limestones, and shales contain selenium concentrations of over 100–200 mg/kg. Selenium concentrations in soils have been reported to range between 0.1 mg/kg in a selenium-deficient area of New Zealand, and 1200 mg/kg in an organic soil in Ireland (Johnson, 1976). Phosphate rocks, and consequently some phosphate fertilizers, have been reported to contain 1–300 mg/kg selenium (NAS, 1976). Biologically, selenium is an essential, beneficial element recognized as a metabolic requirement in trace amounts for animals but is toxic to them when ingested in amounts ranging upward to 10 mg/kg in food. An acceptable daily intake of selenium from food for humans is 0.7 mg for protection against low toxic response effects, assuming a 70-kg person (U.S. EPA, 1980b).

Silver

Silver has been estimated in the Earth's crust to be 0.07 mg/kg (Taylor, 1964). In igneous-type rocks, the average silver content varies from 0.04 (granite) to 0.12 mg/kg (gabbros, diabase), while in sedimentary rocks the average silver content ranges from 0.05 (anhydrite, gypsum) to 0.10 mg/kg (normal shale) (MRI, 1975). Deep-sea sediments contain an estimated 0.11 mg/kg silver (Turekian and Wedepohl, 1961). In normal soils, the silver content ranges from less than 0.1 to 5 mg/kg, with an average concentration of 0.3 mg/kg. Near lead-zinc-silver deposits, the silver content of most soils commonly reaches 10 mg/kg or higher (Boyle, 1968). Biologically, silver is a nonessential, nonbeneficial element recognized as causing localized skin discoloration in humans and as being systematically toxic to aquatic life.

Zinc

The Earth's crust's average zinc concentration has been estimated at 70 mg/kg, ranking zinc 24th among the elements found there (Taylor, 1964; Bowen, 1966). Other estimates of zinc concentration in the Earth's crust range from 5 to 200 mg/kg (Aylett, 1973; Brooks, 1977). Turekian and Wedepohl (1961) estimated the zinc concentration in sedimentary rocks as follows: shales, 95 mg/kg; sandstone, 16 mg/kg; and limestones, 20 mg/kg. Deep-sea sediments contain an average of 165 mg/kg. Zinc never is found free in nature, but occurs as the sulfide, oxide, or carbonate (Lange, 1956).

The mean zinc concentrations of groundwater samples from the nonmineral and mineral regions of Front Range, Colorado were 200 and 310 µg/l, respectively (Klusman and Edwards, 1977). The average zinc concentrations in the sediments of the Grand Calumet River system were between 750 and 2060 mg/kg (Romano et al., 1977). Concentrations ranged from 2.5 to 393 mg/kg in the sediments of Lake Michigan (Hutchinson and Fitchko, 1974). The mean value for zinc concentration in precipitation in the United States has been estimated at 110 µg/l (Kramer, 1976). Zinc is an essential and beneficial element in human metabolism (Vallee, 1957). The daily requirement of preschool-aged children is 0.3 mg Zn/kg body weight; deficiency leads to growth retardation. The daily human intake should average 15 mg (Vallee, 1957).

INSIDE A BUILDING

Indoor air sources can emit the products of combustion from appliances, dirt, dust, asbestos, radon, fabric fibers, insect parts, and environmental tobacco smoke that may cause eye and respiratory irritation, respiratory function impairment, allergic and infectious diseases, asbestosis, and cancer. In many cases, indoor air is of greater concern than outdoor air because of the close proximity to people for long time periods and the closed environment.

Many chemicals are emitted within a building from household or commercial products by evaporation, combustion, volatile breakdown, degassing, or intentional use. Inorganic gases, such as nitrogen dioxide, carbon monoxide, and sulfur dioxide, can cause eye and respiratory irritation, neurotoxicity, blood effects, and respiratory function impairment. Volatile organic compounds, such as kerosene and mineral spirits, can cause neurotoxicity. Aromatic hydrocarbons, such as toluene, styrene, ethylbenzene, benzene, and xylenes, can cause liver and kidney effects, blood effects, leukemia, and anemia. Halogenated carbons, such as methylene chloride, 1,1,1-trichloroethane, chlordane, ethylene dichloride, freon, PCBs, carbon tetrachloride, and chloroform, can cause liver and kidney effects, neurotoxicity, and cancer. Alcohols, such as ethanol, methanol, ethylene glycol, phenol, and cresol, can cause developmental effects, neurotoxicity, and liver and kidney effects. Ketones, such as acetone, methyl ethyl ketone, and methyl isobutyl ketone, can cause developmental effects and eye and respiratory irritation and cancer. Organic pesticides such as malathion can cause neurotoxicity.

Bacteria and viruses can cause Legionnaire's disease and pneumonitis. Animal dander and excreta, molds and mildews, can cause respiratory irritation, allergic and infectious diseases, and produce immune effects. Radon found in soils and rocks beneath a building can cause cancer. Electromagnetic radiation from nearby high-voltage powerlines, appliances, and television sets is suspected of causing reproductive, developmental, and neurobehavioral effects, as well as cancer.

Sources of these air pollution problems include gas stoves, kerosene heaters, building materials, human activities, pets, insects, arachnids, pesticides, combustion fuels, painting supplies, hobby supplies, solvents, cleaners, tobacco smoke, toilet deodorizers, fabric protectors, adhesives, certain cosmetics, some tap water, motor vehicles in attached garages, facilities such as damp basements, and air conditioning cooling towers that serve as bacterial, viral, and fungal breeding grounds, the soils and rocks beneath a building, and nearby powerlines. Many of the chemicals may be present as the volatile breakdown products of materials of construction, dry cleaning, pressed wood, insulation, carpets, and sprayed-on materials.

The effects described above may not occur at indoor exposure levels. In many cases, the exposure data are insufficient to determine the levels at which these effects will occur. Research and case studies are needed in a great many areas to better define the nature and extent of indoor air pollution problems and mitigative measures.

Radon

Isolated incidents of elevated indoor radon levels were reported in the 1960s and 1970s in houses built with materials contaminated with uranium mine tailings and in several houses built in reclaimed phosphate lands. It was not until early 1985 that naturally occurring indoor radon problems were reported.

At that time, extremely high radon levels were discovered in houses located along a geological formation, known as the Reading Prong, which extends from Pennsylvania, through New Jersey and into New York. Numerous homes were found with levels of radon as high as 130-times the federal occupational exposure standard for underground uranium miners. Of 20,000 samples taken by the state of Pennsylvania in the Reading Prong area, more than 60% reported levels above 4 picocuries/liter (pCi/l), which is the action level recommended by the EPA. More than 20% were over 20 pCi/l and some were as high as 2000 pCi/l. In terms of cancer risk, regular exposure to 4 pCi/l is the equivalent of smoking about 10 cigarettes a day, or enough to cause cancer in 13–50 of every 1000 persons exposed to that level for a lifetime. Exposure to 20 pCi/l is equivalent to smoking about $1^1/_2$ packs of cigarettes per day or enough to cause cancer in 60–210 of every 1000 persons exposed (U.S. EPA, 1989). Since the findings in the Reading Prong, radon problems have been identified in nearly every state. The EPA estimates that about 20,000 lung cancer deaths each year may be attributable to indoor radon, and as many as 8 million houses may be affected, with radon levels reaching or exceeding 4 pCi/l.

In addition to soil, radon may also be found in groundwater and can enter the building through the water supply. Of 1000 public water systems surveyed for radon, levels from 100 to 25,700 pCi/l were found in the water, with a median of 289 pCi/l and a mean of 881 pCi/l. It is EPA's estimation that over 20,000 of the 45,000 community groundwater systems have radon levels above 200 pCi/l in their water (U.S. EPA, 1989).

Standardized measurement protocols for radon in buildings have been issued. The EPA current program consists of four main elements; problem assessment, mitigation and prevention, capability development, and public information. Problem assessment relates to determining the national distribution of radon occurrences in schools, houses, the workplace, and the associated health risks that go with those locations. Mitigation and prevention includes demonstrations and evaluations of cost-effective methods to reduce radon levels. Capability development includes radon diagnostic and mitigation techniques, training courses, implementation of regional radon training centers, a radon measurement proficiency program, and a radon contractor proficiency program. Public information includes the dissemination of information through brochures and technical reports.

Asbestos

Asbestos became a popular commercial product because it is strong, will not burn, resists corrosion, and insulates well. In the United States, its commercial use began in the early 1900s and peaked in the period from World War II into the 1970s. The EPA began regulating many asbestos-containing materials, which by EPA definition are materials with more than 1% asbestos, under the Clean Air Act of 1970.

In 1973, the Environmental Protection Agency issued a ban on the use of sprayed-on asbestos-containing materials in buildings for insulation or fireproofing purposes, except for equipment and machinery. Methods of removing friable asbestos from buildings during demolition were also regulated at this time. The ban was amended in 1975 to include molded and wet-applied insulation. In addition, rules governing asbestos removal were broadened to include building renovation, and procedures for disposal of removed materials were defined. Finally, the ban on spraying asbestos-containing materials was broadened in 1978 to include decorative applications.

On June 20, 1986, the U.S. Occupational Safety and Health Administration (OSHA) published new regulations concerning asbestos. The regulations stated that "All [asbestos] fiber types, alone or in combination, have been observed in studies to induce lung cancer, mesothelioma and asbestosis." The document went on to say that "OSHA is aware of no instance in which exposure to a toxic substance has more clearly demonstrated detrimental health effects on humans than has asbestos exposure." Exposure to high levels of airborne asbestos is associated with a debilitating lung disease called *asbestosis*; a rare cancer of the chest and abdominal lining, called *mesothelioma*; and cancer of the lung, esophagus, stomach, colon, and other organs.

The use of asbestos in the construction or repair of buildings was common in the period starting after World War II and lasting through the mid-1970s. Sources of potential exposure to asbestos fibers from asbestos-containing friable materials include those materials sprayed or trowelled onto ceilings, rafters, beams, and other structural building parts for fireproofing, insulation, sound deadening or decoration, or used as pipe and boiler insulation. Friable materials are those that can be crumbled, pulverized, or reduced to powder by hand pressure. The EPA has found that approximately 20% of U.S. buildings contain friable asbestos. They estimated that there are 1.2 billion square feet of sprayed-on or trowelled-on asbestos materials, with an average asbestos content of 14% in 192,000 buildings. Buildings built since the 1950s are more likely to have these materials than other buildings. About 593,000 buildings are estimated to have asbestos-containing pipe and boiler insulation, with an average asbestos content of 70% (U.S. EPA, 1990).

In July 1989, the EPA promulgated the Asbestos Ban and Phasedown Rule. The rule applies to new product manufacture, importation, and processing, and essentially bans almost all asbestos-containing products in the United States by 1997. This rule does not require the removal of asbestos-containing materials currently in place in buildings.

Intact and undisturbed asbestos-containing materials do not pose a health risk. The presence of asbestos in a building does not mean that the health of building occupants is endangered. Asbestos-containing materials that are in good condition, and are not damaged or disturbed, are not likely to release asbestos fibers into the air. However, asbestos materials can become hazardous when, due to damage, disturbance, or deterioration over time, they release fibers in building air.

Studies of laboratory animals, as well as of asbestos workers and their families, have demonstrated that several life-threatening diseases, such as lung cancer, asbestosis, and mesothelioma, can be caused by exposure to airborne asbestos. Three laws give the EPA authority to control asbestos in schools: the Asbestos Hazard Emergency Response Act, the Asbestos School Hazard Abatement Act, and the Toxic Substances Control Act. Together these laws direct the EPA to establish a comprehensive program to control asbestos-containing materials in schools and a loan and grant program to assist eligible school districts in abating asbestos problems in their schools.

In October 1987, the EPA promulgated the Asbestos Containing Materials in Schools rule. It requires the inspection of schools for asbestos-containing materials, the development of an asbestos management plan that includes the results of the inspections, and plan implementation. The rule requires the use of trained, accredited persons to conduct the inspections and develop the plan, the training of custodial and maintenance staff prior to conducting activities that may disturb asbestos, the transportation and disposal of asbestos by approved transporters in approved landfills, and the maintenance of records. The following approaches are used to control exposure to asbestos (Bregman, 1988):

- **Removal**. Asbestos material is removed and disposed by burial at an approved landfill site.
- **Encapsulation**. Asbestos material is coated with a bonding agent called a sealant.
- **Enclosure**. Asbestos material is separated from the building environment by barriers such as walls.
- **Deferred Action**. No action is taken; the area is inspected periodically for changes in exposure potential under an operations and maintenance program.

Removal, encapsulation, and enclosure are corrective methods and can be used separately or in combination. Removal completely eliminates the source of exposure to asbestos and is, therefore, a permanent solution. Both enclosure and encapsulation are containment methods.

Removal is today's method of choice because it presents a permanent solution to the asbestos. In addition, it becomes more likely that, as time goes by, the regulations governing asbestos will become more stringent and what is acceptable today for encapsulation or enclosure will be changed to require removal of the material that has already cost money to encapsulate or enclose. Finally, and perhaps most important, many lenders are insisting on complete removal in all cases where more than a trace of asbestos is present.

Several asbestos-related regulations have been issued under the Clean Air Act, including regulations specifying workplace procedures to use in demolitions and renovations where asbestos is present. Under the Toxic Substances Control Act, a rule was issued to extend worker protection in abatement activities, to ban certain asbestos products and phase out others. A model accreditation plan to provide for training and accreditation of persons who inspect school buildings, development management plans, or design or conduct response actions was published in 1987. At least 18 states have passed legislation for contractor accreditation programs similar to the EPA mode.

The requirements for asbestos removal vary from state to state. Some states impose stringent requirements on asbestos removal contractors, while others specify that they must follow EPA and OSHA procedures. Generally, a permit or license for asbestos removal also requires the employment of properly trained workers, financial stability of the firm, and adequate liability insurance coverage. Among the standards the laws impose are notification of local and federal environmental agencies, documenting the work done, and maintaining records for a specified number of years.

Technical requirements cover isolation of the work area, the use of air respirators by the employees doing the removal, cleanup facilities, and monitoring the air in the work area and its surroundings. The laws show special concern for protection of the public, tenants, and workers during the removal and disposal.

Finally, the removed asbestos must be packaged properly and disposed of in approved landfill sites. The air at the sites from which the asbestos has been removed must be monitored according to specified procedures to prove that no dangerous concentration of asbestos exists any longer (Bregman, 1988).

Formaldehyde

The EPA has classified formaldehyde as a probable human carcinogen. The current focus is on developing the technical basis for decisionmaking on the need for, and the nature of, additional federal regulations affecting formaldehyde emissions for urea formaldehyde pressed-wood particleboard, hardwood plywood paneling, and medium- density fiberboard.

Chlorinated Solvents

Chronic exposure to some volatile organic compounds is suspected to contribute to mortality from cancer. Common sources include building materials and furnishings, paints and related products, cleaning, disinfecting and odor-control products, and pesticides. Research is being conducted by the EPA to define the risks from methylene chloride, perchloroethylene, trichlorethylene, and 1,1,1-trichloroethane when used in dry cleaning, solvent cleaning, aerosols, and paint stripping. Preliminary risks assessments and economic analyses are being performed to determine the most appropriate control options.

Pesticides

The EPA has taken a series of actions that have led to the withdrawal from the marketplace of a family of termiticides known as the cyclodienes, which are aldrin, dieldrin, chlordane, and heptachlor. Short-term effects to high levels of these pesticides are associated with symptoms, such as headaches, dizziness, muscle twitching, weakness, tingling sensations, and nausea. Potential long-term effects include damage to the liver and the central nervous system, as well as increased risk of cancer. For a long time it was thought that these chemicals, when correctly applied to the soils surrounding homes or into house foundations, would not cause significant exposure to the household occupants. However, recent studies demonstrate that air samples taken, even in homes where chlordane is properly applied, may contain measurable chlordane residues. The sales of chlordane and heptachlor have been banned until an application method is demonstrated that will not result in any measurable exposure to household occupants. Sales of aldrin and dieldrin have been ended voluntarily (U.S. EPA, 1990).

Lindane was formerly used as a general purpose insecticide against indoor pests. Because of concerns over the potential long-term risks of cancer, the EPA canceled the registrations of all indoor fumigating devices containing lindane in 1986. In 1984, all indoor uses of pentachlorophenol and creosote, with certain limited exceptions, were banned.

Building Ventilation

Indoor workplace air can affect job performance, comfort, general sense of well-being, and health. With millions of people working in buildings with mechanical heating, ventilation, and airconditioning systems, the efficient and effective operation of the system can determine the indoor air quality. The EPA has no regulatory authority in building ventilation.

The American Society of Heating, Refrigerating, and Air Conditioning Engineers in the ASHRAE 62-1981R standard, specified a ventilation rate of 20 ft³/min/person for office environments. Building Officials and Code Administrators International (SBCCI), the Council of American Building Officials (CABO), and other code-writing organizations often incorporate ventilation requirements into their model codes. Ventilation standards are applicable to new and renovated buildings, and may not be applicable to the normal operation of existing buildings. Thus, while design standards may be adequate, subsequent operation and maintenance of the system may compromise the standards and reduce their potential to control indoor air quality.

REFERENCES CITED AND SELECTED READING

Aylett, B. J. 1973. Group IIB. In: *Comprehensive Inorganic Chemistry*, Vol. 3. J. C. Bailar et al. (Eds.), Pergamon Press, Oxford, pp. 187–328.

Bowen, J. J. M. 1966. *Trace Elements in Biochemistry*. Academic Press, NY.

Boyle, R. W. 1968. "The Geochemistry of Silver and Its Deposits." Geol. Surv. Can. Bull. No. 160. Department of Energy, Mines and Resources, Ottawa, Canada.

Bregman, J. I. 1988. Environmental Financial Liabilities in Real Estate Transactions. *Area Development*, May, 1988. pp. 146–156.

Brooks, R. R. 1977. Pollution through Trace Elements. In: *Environmental Chemistry*. J. O'M. Bockris (Ed.), Plenum Press, New York, pp. 429–476.

Chesapeake Bay Critical Area Commission. 1986. "Law Amendments, and Final Regulation." Department of Natural Resources, Annapolis, Maryland.

Chow, T. J. and C. C. Patterson. 1962. The Occurrences and Significance of Lead Isotopes in Pelagic Sediments. *Geochim. Cosmochim. Acta.* 26:263.

CRC. 1970. *Handbook of Chemistry and Physics*, 51st ed. The Chemical Rubber Company, Cleveland, OH.

Fleischer, M., et al. 1974. Environmental Impact of Cadmium: A Review by the Panel on Hazardous Trace Substances. *Environ. Health Persp.* 7:253–323.

Gowen, J. A., et al. 1976. Residues in Soil: Mercury and 2,4-D Levels in Wheat and Soils from Sixteen States. *Pestic. Monitor. J.* 10:111–113.

Heindel, R. A. 1970. Beryllium. In: *Mineral Facts and Problems*. U.S. Bureau of Mines Bulletin 650, pp. 489–501.

Hunt, W. F., Jr., et al. 1971. A Study in Trace Element Pollution of Air in Seventy-Seven Midwestern Cities. In: *Trace Substances in Environmental Health. IV.* D.D. Hemphill (Ed.), University of Missouri Press, Columbia, MD.

Hutchinson, T. C. and J. Fitchko. 1974. Heavy Metal Concentrations and Distributions in River Mouth Sediments Around the Great Lakes. In: *Proc. Int. Conf. on Transport of Persistent Chemicals in Aquatic Ecosystems*, Ottawa, Canada, pp. I-69–77.

Johnson, C. M. 1976. Selenium in the Environment. *Residue Rev.* 62:101–130.

Klusman, R. W. and K. W. Edwards. 1977. Toxic Metals in Ground Water of the Front Range, Colorado. *Ground Water* 15:160.

Kopp, J. F. and R. C. Kroner. 1967. "Trace Metals in Waters of the United States." U.S. Department of the Interior, Federal Water Pollution Control Administration, Cincinnati, OH.

Kramer, J. R. 1976. "Assessment of the Ecological Effects of Long-Term Atmospheric Material Deposition." Unpublished Manuscript.

Landrigan, P. J., et al. 1975. Epidemic Lead Absorption Near an Ore Smelter. The Role of Particulate Lead. *N. Engl. J. Med.* 292:123.

Lange, N. A. 1956. *Handbook of Chemistry*. Handbook Publishers, Sandusky, OH.

Larkin, J. W. 1973. Selenium in Our Environment. In: *Trace Elements on the Environment*. E. L. Kothny, (Ed.), Advances in Chemistry Series No. 123. American Chemical Society, Washington, D.C.

Lindberg, P. 1973. Selenium Determination in Plant and Animal Material in Water. *Acta. Vet. Scand.* Suppl. 32, Stockholm.

Meyer, B. 1983. *Indoor Air Quality*. Addison Wesley Publishing, Reading, MA.

Motto, H. L., et al. 1970. Lead in Soils and Plants: Its Relationship to Traffic Volume and Proximity to Highways. *Environ. Sci. Tech.* 4:231.

MRI. 1975. "Silver. An Appraisal of Environmental Exposures." Midwest Research Institute, Technical Report No. 3.

Murrmann, R. P. and F. R. Koutz. 1972. Role of Soil Chemical Processes in Reclamation of Wastewater Applied to Land. In: *Wastewater Management by Disposal on the Land*. S.C. Reed, Coordinator. U.S. Army Cold Regions Research and Engineering Laboratory, Hanover, NH, pp. 48–76.

NAS. 1974. "Chromium." National Academy of Sciences. U.S. Government Printing Office, Washington, D.C.

NAS. 1976. "Selenium. Medical and Biological Effects of Environmental Pollutants." D. D. Hemphill (Ed.), Division of Medical Sciences, National Academy of Sciences, Washington, D.C.

NAS. 1977. "Drinking Water and Health. A Report of the Safe Drinking Water Committee." National Academy of Sciences, Washington, D.C.

Romano, R. R., et al. 1977. Trace Metal Discharges of the Grand Calumet River. *J. Great Lakes Res.* 3:144.

Schroeder, H. A. 1970. "Chromium. Air Quality Monograph No. 70–15." American Petroleum Institute, Washington, D.C.

Shacklette, H. T., et al. 1971. "Elemental Composition of Surficial Materials in the Conterminous United States." Geological Survey Professional Paper 574-D, Washington, D.C., pp. D3–D17.

Taylor, S. R. 1964. Abundance of Chemical Elements in the Continental Crust: A New Table. *Geochim. Cosmochim. Acta* 28:1273–1285.

Traversy, W. J., et al. 1975. "Levels of Arsenic and Selenium in the Great Lakes Region." Environment Canada, Inland Waters Directorate, Scientific Series No. 58, Burlington, Ontario.

Turekian, K.K. and K. H. Wedepohl. 1961. Distribution of the Elements on Some Major Units of the Earth's Crust. *Geol. Soc. Am. Bull.* 72:175–192.

U.S. EPA. 1975. "Scientific and Technical Assessment Report on Cadmium." U.S. Environmental Protection Agency, Washington, D.C. (EPA-600/6-75-003).

U.S. EPA. 1976. "Arsenic." U.S. Environmental Protection Agency, Research Triangle Park, NC (EPA-600/1-76-036).

U.S. EPA. 1977. "Copper." U.S. Environmental Protection Agency, Research Triangle Park, NC (EPA-600/1-77-003).

U.S. EPA. 1978. "Review of the Environmental Effects of Pollutants: VI. Beryllium." U.S. Environmental Protection Agency, Health Effects Research Lab., Cincinnati, OH (EPA-600/1-78-028).

U.S. EPA. 1979. "Health Assessment Document for Cadmium." U.S. Environmental Protection Agency, Research Triangle Park, NC (EPA-600/8-79-003).

U.S. EPA. 1980. "Ambient Water Quality Criteria for Lead." U.S. Environmental Protection Agency, Washington, D.C. (EPA-440/5-80-057).

U.S. EPA. 1980a. "Ambient Water Quality Criteria for Nickel." U.S. Environmental Protection Agency, Washington, D.C. (EPA-440/5-80-60).

U.S. EPA. 1980b. "Ambient Water Quality Criteria for Selenium." U.S. Environmental Protection Agency, Washington, D.C. (EPA-440/5-80-070).

U.S. EPA. 1985. "Asbestos in Buildings: Simplified Sampling Scheme for Friable Surfacing Materials." U.S. Environmental Protection Agency, Washington, D.C. (EPA-560/5-85-030a).

U.S. EPA. 1985a. "Guidance for Controlling Asbestos-Containing Materials in Buildings." U.S. Environmental Protection Agency, Washington, D.C. (EPA-560/5-85-024).

U.S. EPA. 1986. "A Citizen's Guide to Radon: What It Is and What To Do About It." U.S. Environmental Protection Agency, Office of Radiation Programs, Washington, D.C.

U.S. EPA. 1987. "Radon Reference Manual." U.S. Environmental Protection Agency, Washington, D.C. (EPA-520/1-87-020).

U.S. EPA. 1989. "Report to Congress on Indoor Air Quality." Executive Summary and 3 Volumes. U.S. Environmental Protection Agency, Washington, D.C. (EPA-400/1-89-001).

U.S. EPA. 1990. "Managing Asbestos in Place. A Building Owner's Guide to Operations and Maintenance Programs for Asbestos-Containing Materials." U.S. Environmental Protection Agency, Pesticides and Toxic Substances, Washington, D.C. 2OT-2003.

Vallee, B. L. 1957. Zinc and its Biological Significance. *Arch. Indust. Health.* 16:147.

Walsh, P. J. et al. (Eds.). 1984. *Indoor Air Quality.* CRC Press, Boca Raton, FL.

Wershaw, R. L. 1970. "Mercury in the Environment." Geological Survey Professional Paper No. 713. U.S. Government Printing Office, Washington, D.C.

WHO. 1972. *Health Hazards of the Human Environment.* World Health Organization. Geneva.

20 ENVIRONMENTAL ASSESSMENTS AND IMPACT STATEMENTS

THE NATIONAL ENVIRONMENTAL POLICY ACT

The National Environmental Policy Act (NEPA) took effect in 1970. It requires that all federal agencies study the environmental impacts of all major actions, including permits, policy, and programs, before final action is taken. The Council on Environmental Quality (CEQ) then issued regulations that spelled out how to accomplish this. Each federal agency, in turn, developed procedures to implement the CEQ regulations.

NEPA is the basic national charter for protection of the environment. That law establishes policy, sets goals, and provides a means for carrying out the policy. The Council on Environmental Quality regulations, 40 CFR Part 1500, notify federal agencies of what they must do to comply with the procedures and achieve the goals of the act. These regulations provide guidance on the necessity for environmental impact statements (EIS), as well as the recommended procedures and format for their development and issuance for public review. An EIS is a documented thought process for public review to consider environmental consequences of a major federal action and to discuss mitigative measures to reduce or eliminate adverse environmental effects should the action be implemented. An action by the federal government includes projects and programs entirely or partly financed, assisted, conducted, regulated, or approved; new or revised rules and regulations; plans, policies, or procedures; and legislative proposals.

NEPA allows the preparation of abbreviated EISs, known as Environmental Assessments (EAs) as the first step in the EIS process. As a result of the findings of the EA, either an EIS is then prepared or else a document known as a Finding of No Significant Impact (FONSI) is issued. About 10,000 environmental assessments for projects with minimal environmental impact are prepared annually by federal agencies. About 450 environmental impact statements are prepared annually for projects that the proposing agencies view as having significant potential for environmental impact.

THE EPA ROLE IN NEPA

The EPA has a key role in assuring that NEPA will be carried out faithfully by federal agencies. It has far-reaching oversight, environmental review, and comment authority for virtually all major federal actions that are subject to the NEPA process. In addition, Section 309 of the Clean Air Act made the EPA a central clearinghouse for ensuring an on-the-record review of proposed actions by other federal agencies that might adversely affect the environment. It further requires that if the EPA determines that any proposal, including an EIS, is "unsatisfactory from the stand point of public health or welfare or environmental quality," EPA's Administrator is to make public that determination and refer the matter to the Council on Environmental Quality.

Procedural compliance by the EPA with NEPA is required for municipal waste-water treatment construction grants, EPA-issued NPDES permits for discharges subject to new source performance standards, research and development projects, and EPA facility construction. Voluntary development of an EIS pursuant to EPA policy applies to radiation and portions of the clean air program, ocean dumping regulations and ocean dump-site specifications. The remainder of EPA's programs are deemed to provide reviews that are "functionally equivalent" to NEPA reviews. EPA's NEPA compliance involves the preparation of an EA, a finding of no significant impact, or the preparation of an EIS, as well as overview of state programs under delegation of the construction grants program and under the State Revolving Fund. The EPA has been delegated the management of the official filing system for all federal EISs.

Under OMB circular A-106, the EPA reviews all federal agency annual pollution-abatement plans and environmental budgets and provides comments to the Office of Management and Budget. In 1988, there were 758 proposed federal pollution-abatement projects that totaled nearly $1.1 billion.

Federal environmental statutes require that facilities of the federal government comply with federal, state, and local pollution-control requirements to the same extent as nonfederal entities. Executive Order 12088 established the executive program for carrying out these legislative mandates. Disputes regarding compliance by federal facilities are resolved through administrative procedures specified in the executive order.

40 CFR 1500–1508

The Council on Environmental Quality regulations provide the procedures and the processes through which federal agencies comply with the NEPA. The stated purpose of the regulations is to integrate the NEPA process into early planning of federal projects, in order to ensure appropriate consideration of NEPA's policies and to eliminate delay. They emphasize cooperative consultation among federal agencies before the EIS is proposed. NEPA procedures must ensure that environmental information is available to public officials and citizens before decisions are made and before actions are taken.

The regulations require that a lead agency supervise the development of an EIS. The criteria for determining the responsible lead agency are as follows: magnitude of agency's involvement, project approval or disapproval authority, expertise concerning the action's environmental effects, duration of the agency's involvement, and sequence of the agency's involvement. If any governmental entity or person is affected by the absence of a lead agency designation for a project, a request may be made to the Council on Environmental Quality that a lead agency be designated.

The EIS process includes the following activities:

1. Publication in the *Federal Register* of a notice of intent to prepare an EIS.
2. Holding a scoping meeting.
3. Preparing and publishing a draft EIS for public comment. Public hearings or meetings may be held to solicit discussion of issues and comments.
4. Preparation of the final EIS with a response to comments received on the draft EIS and a discussion of opposing views to the preferred alternative action. Supplements to either the draft or final EIS may be prepared.

The stated purposes of an EIS are to serve as an action-forcing document to ensure that the policies and goals of the NEPA are infused into the ongoing programs and actions of the federal government, to provide full and fair discussion of significant environmental impacts, and to inform decisionmakers and the public of the reasonable alternatives that would avoid or minimize adverse impacts or enhance the quality of the human environment. The regulations require that "Statements shall be concise, clear and to the point, and shall be supported by evidence that the agency has made the necessary environmental analysis." Advice is provided on good writing in 40 CFR 1502, which states that EISs shall be analytic rather than encyclopedic. Impacts shall be discussed in proportion to their significance. They shall be written in plain language and may use appropriate graphics so that decisionmakers and the public can readily understand them. The text of the final EIS shall normally be less than 150 pages. For proposals of unusual scope or complexity, the text shall normally be less than 300 pages.

NOTICE OF INTENT

A Notice of Intent should be published in the *Federal Register* as soon as a decision is reached to prepare an EIS. The Notice of Intent declares that an EIS will be prepared and considered; it describes the proposed action and possible alternatives, describes the agency's proposed scoping process, and states the name and contact information of a person within the agency who can answer questions. The notice should state when, and where any scoping meeting will be held.

SCOPING

The purposes of a scoping meeting are to determine the scope of issues to be addressed in the EIS, to identify the significant issues related to a proposed action, and to eliminate environmental issues that are not significant. A scoping meeting should be held as soon after the publication of the Notice of Intent as convenient. The participation and views of affected federal, state, and local agencies; Indian tribes, proponents of the action; opponents of the action on environmental grounds; and other interested persons should be invited.

A preliminary environmental analysis document often is prepared to serve as background for the scoping process. It is made available to those who attend the scoping meeting, as well as to the invitees to the meeting in the event that they are unable to attend. This document provides a brief description of alternative actions that are proposed to be considered, a discussion of the environmental issues relating to the affected environment, and the possible impacts on them as a result of the proposed action. These environmental issues generally include water quality, air quality, noise, land use, historic preservation and archaeology, demography, housing, hazards and nuisances, aesthetics and urban design, infrastructure, community services, transportation, climatology, topography, geomorphology, geology, soils, and biotic systems.

A scoping meeting should be held early in the EIS process before EIS preparation has begun. It should involve the public in the process at an early stage to ensure their opportunity to provide comments in the EIS development process.

EIS RECOMMENDED FORMAT

A recommended format for an EIS is provided in 40 CFR 1502.10. This format includes:

1. Cover sheet
2. Summary
3. Table of contents
4. Purpose of and need for action
5. Alternatives including proposed action
6. Affected environment
7. Environmental consequences
8. List of preparers
9. List of agencies, organizations, and persons to whom copies of the statement are sent
10. Index
11. Appendices (if any)

The cover sheet presents a list of the responsible agencies, including the lead agency and any cooperating agencies; the title of the proposed action; the name, address, and telephone number of the person at the agency who can supply further information; a designation of the statement as a draft, final, or draft or final supplement; a one-paragraph abstract of the statement; and the date by which comments must be received.

Each EIS shall contain a summary that adequately and accurately summarizes the statement. The summary should stress the major conclusions, areas of controversy, and the issues to be resolved, including the preferred choice of alternatives.

The purpose and need should detail the underlying purpose and need to which the agency is responding in proposing the alternatives, including the proposed action.

The alternatives section should present the environmental impacts of the proposal and the alternatives in comparative form, thus sharply defining the issues and providing a clear basis for choice among options by the decisionmaker and the public. Each reasonable alternative to the action should be identified, described, and discussed. The no-action alternative should be discussed. The agency's preferred alternative or alternatives, if one or more exist, should be identified and the rationale to support the preference presented.

The existing environment of the area or areas to be affected or created by the alternatives under consideration should be described. The affected environment will be discussed later in this chapter as a separate section.

The environmental consequences section forms the scientific and analytic basis for the comparisons of alternatives. This section, likewise, will be discussed later in this chapter as a separate section.

The list of preparers includes the names and qualifications of the persons who were primarily responsible for preparing the EIS or significant background papers, including basic components of the statement.

The appendix normally consists of material that substantiates any analysis fundamental to the impact statement and may be analytic and relevant to the decision to be made. It could include affidavits of publication of the notice of the scoping meeting, draft agenda for the scoping meeting, a copy of the preliminary environmental analysis, minutes of scoping meetings, a list of attendees at the scoping meeting, and copies of data, correspondence, or other information related to the development of the EIS.

RECORD OF DECISION

At the time of its decision related to an EIS, an agency is required to prepare and publish a concise record of decision. The record of decision is to

1. State what the decision was
2. Identify alternatives considered
3. Specify the alternative or alternatives considered to be environmentally preferable
4. State whether all practicable means to avoid or minimize environmental harm from the alternative selected have been adopted and if not, why not
5. Adopt and summarize, where applicable, a monitoring and enforcement program for any mitigation to be achieved

Until the record of decision is issued, an agency is required to take no action related to the proposal that would have any adverse environmental impacts or limit the choice of reasonable alternatives.

ENVIRONMENTAL ASSESSMENT

An Environmental Assessment (EA) is an abbreviated version of an EIS. Where there may be doubt as to the need for an EIS, an EA provides the evidence for determining whether to prepare an EIS or a Finding of No Significant Impact (FONSI). It is a concise public document for which a federal agency is responsible. It facilitates the preparation of an EIS when one is necessary.

A FONSI is a document that may be published in the *Federal Register* by a federal agency that briefly presents the reasons why an action will not have a significant effect on the human environment and for which an EIS will not be prepared. It should include the environmental assessment or a summary of it, and note any other environmental documents related to the proposed action.

COLLECTING THE INFORMATION

An initial task associated with the preparation of an EIS is to develop a comprehensive outline that includes in logical sequence all of the items that should be addressed in the EIS. When an outline is completed, there follows the task of collecting the information from which to prepare the discussions for the various listed topics. Reports and data associated with a proposed action should be collected from the lead agency and all cooperating agencies. Historic as well as current data should be solicited. Other information will need to be obtained from state, county, and local agencies.

A listing of hazardous waste sites on the National Priority List (NPL) may be obtained from the appropriate state agency, as well as a listing of potential hazardous waste sites under study to determine if they should be recommended for inclusion on the NPL. The potential of underground storage tanks to affect an area in which a proposed action would be located should be determined and a listing of these is maintained by the appropriate state and county agency. A listing of endangered and threatened species may be obtained from the state endangered species board or agency.

Archaeological and historical site preservation information may be obtained from the State Historical Preservation Agency. Soils information, generally organized by county, may be obtained from the Soil Conservation Service for the county of interest and may be available from the Soils Department of the state university.

Information on wetlands may be obtained from the appropriate U.S. Army Corps of Engineers district. Where wetlands have been mapped, appropriate maps may be obtained from the U.S. Fish and Wildlife Service. Flood insurance rate maps are necessary to determine floodplains and the potential for flooding. These may be obtained from the Federal Emergency Management Agency. Generally, it is necessary to first obtain an index map for a county in order to select the map panels required for a particular study.

In seeking assistance or corresponding with an agency related to a particular study or question, it is helpful and virtually necessary to clearly delineate the area of concern on an U.S. Geological Survey quadrangle map. To do so leaves no question regarding the boundaries of an area of concern.

THE AFFECTED ENVIRONMENT

If there is an existing installation that has not previously been discussed in the EIS and if the proposed action relates to that installation, the affected environment section of the EIS could begin with a description that presents the installation's location and history. Under the above circumstances, the environment of the installation may be affected to a greater extent than the environment beyond the installation.

The affected environment may conveniently be discussed in terms of the natural environment and the person-impacted environment. The natural environment would include a discussion of climate, soils, geology, geomorphology, topography, seismicity, flood hazards and floodplains, wetlands, fish, and wildlife. The person-impacted environment would discuss water quality, including surface water and groundwater; air quality; solid and hazardous wastes; pesticides; noise; transportation; land use; historic and cultural resources; endangered species; recreation; and socioeconomic considerations. These issues will be discussed briefly in the paragraphs that follow.

Climate

The National Oceanic and Atmospheric Administration provides summaries with comparative data for a large number of locations throughout the United States from its National Climatic Data Center in Asheville, North Carolina. Climate should be discussed in terms of temperature, precipitation, snowfall, occurrence of thundershowers, and other climatic events associated with the area of interest.

Soils

Soil is a result of the interaction of soil-forming processes on materials deposited by geologic agents. The properties of the soil at any given place are determined by five factors: (1) the physical and mineralogical composition of the parent materials; (2) the climate under which the soil material has accumulated and has existed since accumulation; (3) living organisms on and in the soil; (4) the topography or lay of the land; and (5) the length of time the forces of soil formation have acted on the soil materials.

County soil survey maps and descriptive reports are published by the U.S. Department of Agriculture Soil Conservation Service in cooperation with a State Agricultural Experiment Station. These reports contain much useful information. Not only do they identify and describe the different soils and formations associated with a particular parcel of earth, but they also provide useful information related to each soil type.

Information is presented on depth to seasonal high-water table; permeability;

shrink-swell potential; corrosion potential for untreated steel; suitability as a source for topsoil, high subgrade material, foundations for low buildings, septic tank filter fields, and sewage lagoons; building site development for shallow excavations, dwellings without basements, and dwellings with basements; potential frost action; depth to bedrock; and flooding potential.

Geology, Geomorphology, and Topography

This section deals with the subsurface geology and slope of the land. The geology of the site may influence construction activities, as well as groundwater contamination.

Seismicity

Seismic risk related to structural damage in the United States generally is represented by a relative scale of 0 through 4, with Zone 0 not expected to encounter earthquake damage and Zone 4 expected to encounter the greatest risk. Building codes require that the design and construction of a building comply with the requirements for the seismic zone in which the building is located, with the required strength increasing as the zone classification goes from 0 to 4. The area of greatest risk is in the southwestern United States generally, and the area of least risk is in northcentral and southcentral United States.

Floodplains

The 100-year flood boundary is easily determined with the aid of a Federal Emergency Management Agency flood insurance rate map.

Wetlands

There are four federal agencies with jurisdictional interest in wetlands. They are the U.S. Army Corps of Engineers, Environmental Protection Agency, Fish and Wildlife Services, and Soil Conservation Service. Definitions of wetlands have been developed by each agency. The Fish and Wildlife Service's definition encompasses both vegetated and nonvegetated areas; definitions for the other agencies include only areas that are vegetated under normal circumstances. All definitions have three basic elements for identifying wetlands, which are hydrology, vegetation, and soil characteristics. Basically, the Fish and Wildlife Service's definition includes mud flats, sand flats, rock shores, gravel beaches, and sand bars. The Soil Conservation Service emphasizes a predominance of hydric soils in their wetlands definition.

The Environmental Protection Agency and Army Corps of Engineers, in the administration of the Clean Water Act Section 404 permit program for the introduction of fill material into the waters of the United States, have adopted the following definition for wetlands:

> Those areas that are inundated or saturated by surface or groundwater at a frequency and duration sufficient to support, and that under normal circumstances do support, a prevalence of vegetation typically adapted for life in saturated soil conditions. Wetlands generally include swamps, marshes, bogs, and similar areas.

> A Section 404 permit, issued only after review and public comment, would be required to introduce fill material into a wetland. Wetlands and soil classification are closely related; hydric soils are suggestive that conditions are suitable for the occurrence of wetlands.

Wildlife

Birds, mammals, fish, and reptiles found in the vicinity of the proposed action should be listed and briefly described. Information of this nature for a general area may be available from appropriate state authorities.

Water Quality

Surface water quality includes lakes, reservoirs, rivers, and streams in the general vicinity of or in a location to be affected by the proposed action. Water quality studies or reports on fish or other aquatic life are helpful to document surface water conditions.

Groundwater is part of the natural hydrologic cycle, or the continuous circulation of water between the atmosphere and the Earth. The amount of rainfall infiltrating into the unsaturated zone varies, depending on the duration and intensity of precipitation, topography, and the moisture content and physical properties of the soil as modified by plant material and the work of soil organisms. The soil zone absorbs water until it has reached its capacity for holding water by molecular action, and only then does water move downward. The water table, or the top of the saturated zone, generally undulates with the topography in response to hydrologic conditions. The water table rises as water enters the groundwater system and falls as water drains to the lower part of the system or is discharged. Water that reaches the water table and the saturated zone moves downgradient and laterally to be discharged by springs or in wetlands, or is confined by clay beds located downdip.

An examination of several well logs in the vicinity of the proposed action is helpful in determining the distance to a water supply source. A well log provides information on the soils that are penetrated during the drilling operation. The potential for groundwater contamination from surface activities can be ascertained through a determination of the amount of impervious materials, such as clays, that separate the surface from the groundwater aquifer.

Air Quality

The appropriate state agency will have information on air quality standards for a particular area and whether a specific area is in attainment or nonattainment with those standards.

Hazards

Hazards include conventional hazards, as well as solid and hazardous waste sites. The Federal NPL and the State CERCLIS list of potential hazardous waste sites should be consulted to determine the location of the nearest site to the proposed action area. Any ongoing solid or hazardous-waste management practices within the proposed action area should be discussed in this section.

Noise

The state may or may not have laws or regulations related to noise in the ambient environment. The effects of noise are related to the magnitude of the noise level generated by an activity and the existence of noise-sensitive receptors nearby. These issues are discussed in this section.

Transportation

Transportation arteries and mass transit are discussed in this section, along with relative traffic volume. The State Department of Transportation will have annual average traffic volumes for major roads within the state.

Land Use

The current land use of the proposed action area is described in this section.

Endangered Species

Any endangered or threatened species associated with the proposed action area or in the vicinity of it should be noted with information regarding location and sitings of the species.

Recreation

Current recreational activities that the proposed action area affords should be described and discussed.

Historical and Cultural Resources

The National Historic Preservation Act's Section 110(a)(2) states

> With the advice of the Secretary and in cooperation with the State Historic Preservation Officer for the state involved, each Federal agency shall establish a program to locate, inventory, and nominate to the Secretary all properties under the agency's ownership or control by the agency, that appear to qualify for inclusion on the National Register in accordance with the regulations promulgated under Section 101(a)(2)(A). Each Federal agency shall exercise caution to assure that any such property that might qualify for inclusion is not inadvertently transferred, sold, demolished, substantially altered, or allowed to deteriorate significantly.

Section 106 of the National Historic Preservation Act requires a federal agency to take into account the effects of the agency's undertakings on properties included in or eligible for the National Register of Historic Places and, prior to approval of an undertaking, to afford the Advisory Council on Historic Preservation a reasonable opportunity to comment on the undertaking. An undertaking includes construction, repair projects, demolition, licenses, permits, loans, grants, and other types of federal involvement. The National Register is the basic inventory of historic resources maintained by the Secretary of the Interior. A memorandum of agreement or a finding of no adverse effect by the responsible federal agency begins the Section 106 review process, which may take 30 days.

Any known historic, prehistoric, or archaeological site related to the proposed action area would be described and discussed in this section.

Socioeconomic Considerations

In this section, those social and economic issues that have a bearing on the proposed action area would be discussed. These would include such items as population, population density, net change in population during the past 5 years, number of households, persons per household, sources of income for area residents, per capita income, percentage change in per capita income over the last 5 or 10 years, mean household income, unemployment, available housing, number or physicians per segment of the population, hospital beds, nursing home beds, school accommodations, and other community services.

ENVIRONMENTAL CONSEQUENCES

In Section 102 of NEPA, the Congress mandated that an EIS be prepared "for legislation and other major federal actions significantly affecting the quality of the human environment ...." The Council on Environmental Quality defined the term *significantly* in 40 CFR 1508.27. It states that the word *significantly* requires considerations of both context and intensity. Context requires an analysis of effect on society as a whole, the affected region, the affected interests, and the locality. With a site-specific action, significance would usually depend upon the effects in the locale. The following should be considered in evaluating intensity:

1. Impacts may be beneficial or adverse
2. The degree to which the proposed action affects public health or safety
3. Unique characteristics of the geographic area, such as proximity to historic or cultural resources, park lands, prime farmlands, wetlands, wild and scenic rivers, or ecologically critical areas
4. The degree to which the effects on the quality of the human environment are likely to be highly controversial
5. The degree to which the possible effects on the human environment are highly uncertain or involve unique or unknown risks
6. The degree to which the action may establish a precedent for future actions with significant effects or represents a decision, in principle, about a future consideration
7. Whether the action is related to other actions with individually insignificant but cumulatively significant impacts
8. The degree to which the action may adversely affect districts, sites, highways, structures, or objects listed in or eligible for listing in the National Register of Historic Places, or may cause loss or destruction of significant scientific, cultural, or historic resources
9. The degree to which the action may adversely affect an endangered or threatened species or its habitat that has been determined to be critical under the Endangered Species Act of 1973
10. Whether the action threatens a violation of federal, state, or local law or requirements imposed for the protection of the environment

These issues are relevant to a discussion of environmental consequences.

This is the section of the EIS where the potential effects or impacts of a proposed action on each facet of the affected environment are discussed. An outline for this section might have the following arrangement:

1.1   Direct Impacts
    1.1.1   Water
            1.1.1.1   Surface Water
            1.1.1.2   Groundwater
            1.1.1.3   Wetlands
    1.1.2   Air
    1.1.3   Noise
    1.1.4   Transportation
    1.1.5   Recreation
    1.1.6   Wildlife
    1.1.7   Endangered Species
    1.1.8   Land Use
    1.1.9   Cultural and Historic Resources
    1.1.10   Waste Disposal
    1.1.11   Solid and Hazardous Wastes
1.2   Indirect Impacts
    1.2.1   Socioeconomic Considerations
    1.2.2   Energy Requirements and Potential for Energy Conservation
    1.2.3   Natural and Depletable Resource Requirements
1.3   No Action Alternative
1.4   Mitigation
    1.4.1   Measures to be Taken to Mitigate Effects
    1.4.2   Impacts that Can be Minimized or Eliminated
    1.4.3   Impacts that Cannot be Mitigated
1.5   Advantages and Disadvantages of Each Alternative (including the no-action alternative)

If the proposed action has a construction phase and an operations phase, the direct impacts may be discussed under a subhead of construction and a subhead of operations.

Considering the proposed action, what is the possibility for pollution of area streams, ponds, or lakes? Will the existing subsurface clay barrier prevent groundwater contamination in the event of a chemical spill? Will wetlands be impaired or partially destroyed as a result of construction? Will air pollution be increased? Will traffic be increased significantly to affect transportation routes? Will traffic noise, construction noise, or operational noise present a problem? Will any standards or regulations be violated, thus suggesting the need for an application for variance, as a result of the proposed action? Some impacts may have both an adverse and a beneficial effect; they may impact transportation adversely but be most beneficial to the area economy or to job opportunities. In such case, is it projected that the benefits outweigh the adverse effects or vice versa?

In preparing a summary of environmental impacts, it is helpful to include a matrix table or checklist showing the alternative actions at the top and the facets of the affected environment to the left of the page. Qualitative descriptors, such as *None*, *Low*, *Moderate*, and *High,* may be used to indicate the relative impact. This presents a tabular chart to the reader to enhance the narrative description.

In the event that farmland is impacted as a result of the proposed action, there is an additional realm of consideration and coordination involved. Section 1539 of the Farmland Protection Policy Act, Pub. L. 97-98 (December 22, 1981), has as its purpose to minimize the extent to which federal programs contribute to the unnecessary and irreversible conversion of farmland to nonagricultural uses and to ensure that federal programs are administered in a manner that, to the extent practicable, will be compatible with state, local government, and private programs and policies to protect farmland. Section 1547(a) of this Act states that, "(t)his subtitle does not authorize the Federal government in any way to regulate the use of private or non-Federal land, or in any way affect the property rights or owners of such land." The Act pertains to prime, unique, and statewide or locally important farmland.

Pursuant to this Act, the Soil Conservation Service promulgated 7 CFR 658. The preamble to this rule states, "(n)either the act nor this rule requires aFederal agency to modify any project solely to avoid or minimize the effects of conversion of farmland to nonagricultural uses. The act merely requires that before taking or approving any action that would result in conversion of farmland as defined in the Act, the agency examines the effects of the action using the criteria set forth in the rule, and if there are adverse effects, consider(s) alternatives to lessen them. The agency would still have discretion to proceed with a project that would convert farmland to nonagricultural uses once the examination required by the Act has been completed."

The federal rule provides criteria for establishing a numeric score to the value of a farmland parcel. Farmland states have comparable laws and programs. A Farmland Conversion Impact Rating form is supplied by the U.S. Department of Agriculture. This form is completed partially by an applicant, partially by the Soil Conservation Service District Office in which the farmland resides, and partially by the applicable state agency for the state in which the farmland resides. Using the criteria in the federal rule, the highest attainable score on the form is 260 points. Some states use criteria with slightly higher point scores. Typical assessment criteria in the federal rule include: area in nonurban use, percent of site being farmed, distance from urban builtup area, size of present farm unit compared to average, effects of conversion on farm support services, and compatibility with existing agricultural use.

7 CFR 658.4 provides guidelines for use of the criteria. Once this score is computed, USDA recommends:

> "(1) Sites with the highest combined scores be regarded as most suitable for protection under these criteria and sites with the lowest scores, as least suitable.

(2) Sites receiving a total score of less than 160 be given a minimal level of consideration for protection and no additional sites be evaluated.

(3) Sites receiving scores totaling 160 or more be given increasingly higher levels of consideration for protection.

(4) When making decisions on proposed actions for sites receiving scores totaling 160 or more, agency personnel consider:

   (i) Use of land that is not farmland or use of existing structures.

   (ii) Alternative sites, locations and designs that would serve the proposed purpose but convert either fewer acres of farmland or other farmland that has a lower relative value.

   (iii) Special siting requirements of the proposed project and the extent to which an alternative site fails to satisfy the special siting requirements as well as the originally selected sites."

The next portion of the environmental consequences section deals with mitigation of the impacts identified above. Environmental consequences may result from actions of employees, facilities and equipment, management of solid and liquid wastes, construction activities, and facility operation. Environmental degradation prevention, to a considerable degree, involves doing things in accordance with laws, regulations, and established policies at the federal, state, and local governmental levels. The application of so-called best management practices adds a further substantial measure of pollution prevention.

Mitigation activities are enhanced through advanced planning. A detailed plan should be developed to control erosion, sedimentation, slope stability, and disposal and storage of excavated materials during construction activities. Best management practices to reduce sediment pollution of nearby waterways during construction activities include hay filters staked in place, temporary stormwater catchment and settling basins, gravel dams supported by wire mesh, or a combination of these. Buffer zones of native vegetation are protective of sensitive areas.

Adherence to state and local requirements for the minimization of fugitive dust emissions during construction activities should be rigorously maintained. These requirements include mitigation measures, such as wetdown of soil and excavated materials, graveling access roads, covering soil and debris piled into open trucks or large retainers, and scheduling construction operations to avoid dry seasons and high air inversion periods.

Construction activities should be scheduled to avoid noise generation during the early morning and late evening hours, and to minimize noise at all other times. Construction noise mitigation should include reducing the speed of construction vehicles and requiring the maintenance of all vehicles and heavy equipment motors to conform to applicable federal, state, and local noise regulations. In addition, techniques are available for the addition of equipment to the major noise generators that will minimize noise from them.

Certain impacts can be mitigated, and certain impacts cannot be mitigated. It is helpful to the reader of an EIS to have these presented in a summarized tabular form and to have them associated with a particular alternative or with the alternatives being considered.

The advantages and disadvantages of each alternative considered for a proposed action, including the no-action alternative, should be concisely listed with the advantages appearing in one column and the disadvantages in another. Here, again, the reader will profit from summarized and concisely stated material that supports the narrative description.

PREPARING THE SUMMARY

The summary provides the major conclusions, areas of controversy, and the issues to be resolved. The preferred alternative is to be identified if one has been selected at the time of public release of a draft EIS. It is possible to prepare a draft EIS without a preferred alternative if one has not been selected, but the public should have an opportunity to comment on an action of an agency regarding a preferred alternative selection. A summary that is prepared for a final EIS should briefly discuss the issues raised during the public comment period on the draft EIS.

Additional areas that the summary should address include the proposed action, the existing environment for the preferred alternative and the other alternatives considered, including the no-action alternative; environmental impacts related to the alternatives considered, mitigative measures, and the advantages and disadvantages of the alternatives, including the no-action alternative. Liberal use of the summary matrices and tables prepared for the section on environmental consequences may be made in the summarized material.

The summary should be brief and concise, yet contain the essential ingredients of the EIS narrative. Generally, a summary of an EIS, or any report, will have a larger readership than the total EIS or report. It should be prepared with that in mind. Stringent review and editing is recommended to ensure that explanations do not leave reader questions unanswered.

REFERENCES CITED AND SELECTED READING

40 CFR Parts 1500–1508.

Kennedy, W. V. 1988. "Environmental Impact Assessment in North America, Western Europe, What Has Worked, Where, How, and Why." *International Environmental Reporter*, as reproduced by the Bureau of National Affairs, Inc., Washington, D.C.

U.S. EPA. (Revised Annually). "Review of Federal Actions Impacting the Environment. A Manual." U.S. Environmental Protection Agency, Office of Federal Activities, Washington, D.C.

Wathern, P. (Ed.) 1988. *Environmental Impact Assessment, Theory and Practice.* Unwin Hyman Publisher, London.

21 QUALITY ASSURANCE AND QUALITY CONTROL

THE CONCEPT OF QUALITY ASSURANCE

Quality assurance is a managed program designed to achieve product excellence at every opportunity. It entails planning and plans; documentation and records; audits and inspections. Where environmental data are collected, quality assurance provides the means to determine the quality of those data. Quality control is a part of quality assurance that concerns control measures when samples are tested or examined. Data quality is known when there are verifiable and defensible documentation and records associated with sample collection, transportation, sample analyses, and other data management activities. In laboratory sample testing and analyses, quality control procedures require testing of duplicate samples, spiked samples containing a known quantity of a sample constituent, standard samples containing known quantities of known constituents, and performance-evaluation samples containing quantities of constituents revealed to the quality assurance officer but unknown to the sample analyst.

Quality assurance has become a significant emerging program during the past decade. There is justifiable reason for this because of the unknown quality of much early (1960s and 1970s) data entered into STORET, EPA's storage and retrieval system for water quality data, for example. Permit compliance monitoring, enforcement, and litigation is more prevalent now in the environmental arena than a decade ago. These require documented data of known quality that will be sustained in litigation.

In 1983, the EPA promulgated a quality assurance rule (40 CFR Part 30 and 48 FR 45061, September 30, 1983). In this rule, the EPA stated its policy that all environmentally related measurements and data collected and used in EPA assistance programs must be scientifically sound, defensible, and of known, acceptable, documented quality. The rule contained two definitions of importance to this chapter. A quality assurance program plan was defined as a formal document that describes an orderly assembly of management policies, objectives, principles, organizational responsibilities, and procedures by which an agency or laboratory specifies how it intends to

267

produce data of documented quality and provide for the preparation of quality assurance project plans and standard operating procedures. A facility would have one quality assurance program plan. A quality assurance project plan was defined as an organization's written procedures that delineate how it produces quality data for a specific project or measurement method. There would be a quality assurance project plan for each identified action that generates data for the EPA.

On April 3, 1984, the EPA issued Order No. 5360.1 that established policy and program requirements for the conduct of quality assurance for all environmentally related measurements performed by or for the EPA.

DOCUMENT CONTROL

Page indexing in a standardized manner allows for revision and replacement of a section or subsection of a document without disturbing the entire document. A convenient system developed by the EPA is to use a paragraph numbering system for narrative format and to provide the indexing information at the top right of each page. The indexing information should contain the report section number, revision number, date of revision, and page number, along with the total number of pages in the report (Figure 21-1).

The contents page may be arranged so that it shows the report section, the subject of the section, page number, revision number, and date of revision, e.g.,

Section	Subject	Page	Pages in Section	Revision	Date
4.0	Quality Assurance Program	6	2	0	09-15-90
4.1	Statement of Policy	8	6	0	09-15-90

QUALITY ASSURANCE PROGRAM PLAN

Introduction

A Quality Assurance Program Plan is the formal documentation that defines and establishes a quality assurance program. Audits of the plan's implementation and the program's accomplishments provide a means for establishing the quality assurance program's effectiveness. The several attributes of a good Quality Assurance Program Plan include:

1. The quality assurance policy should be clearly articulated.
2. The commitment of management to quality assurance should be clearly stated, and specific management roles and responsibilities should be documented.
3. The activities essential for an effective program should be defined.
4. It should be stipulated how these activities will be carried out.

Section: 4.0
Revision: 0
Date: September 15, 1990
Page: 6   of 22

4.0   QUALITY ASSURANCE PROGRAM

4.1   Statement of Policy

4.2.   Project Organization

4.2.1   Position of Quality Assurance Officer Within Organization

Figure 21-1.   Pagination for a controlled document.

5. The criteria for judging whether an approved quality assurance program is being implemented should be provided.
6. There should be a specific commitment to performing various categories of audits and there should be criteria for scheduling them.
7. The quality assurance officer should have clearly documented authority, responsibilities, qualification, and direct reporting to a senior management official.
8. Responsibilities for preparing, revising, and using standard operating procedures should be clearly defined.
9. There should be a commitment to and specific process for developing data quality objectives for new data collection activities.
10. The training needs of staff should be considered.
11. Criteria and responsibilities for developing and reviewing Quality Assurance Project Plans should be clear.

12.   There should be a commitment for resources needed to develop and implement the quality assurance program.

Program Plan

Concurrences

The Quality Assurance (QA) Program Plan should have concurrences of the QA officer, as well as those of higher organizational management.

Statement of Policy

The organization's QA policy statement should address those factors that comprise an effective QA program plan. Many of them are delineated above. The objective of a QA program should be to provide experienced and qualified personnel suited to assigned tasks to collect and analyze data and other information in a manner commensurate with accepted standard practices, exhibiting high standards of quality, integrity, and professionalism, and to provide data of known quality.

A statement of policy should provide for a program commensurate with the following factors:

1.   The development and implementation of a QA Project Plan for any project involving environmental measurements.
2.   The intended use of the data and the associated accepted criteria for data quality should be determined before the data collection effort begins. Data quality objectives should be established to ensure the utility of collected data for their intended use. The intended data uses, level of quality, specific QA activities, and data acceptance criteria needed to meet the data quality needs of these uses should be described in each data generating activity's QA Project Plan.
3.   Analytical methods and procedures used in measurement and monitoring efforts should be fully documented and should include quality control procedures implicit in good laboratory practices.
4.   A QA program should involve a continuing program of planned evaluation, inspections, and audits, including use of specific products and services in order to initiate corrective measures where necessary.
5.   A QA program plan should be reviewed at least annually by the QA officer, and others as deemed necessary, and updated as required.
6.   Resources allocated for the QA program should be appropriate for implementing the policy statement.

An Organization's Major Mission Elements Requiring Quality Assurance

The QA Program Plan should contain a section describing those major programs within the organization and their respective missions that require quality assurance associated with environmental data generation.

Data Generation

The QA Program Plan should describe the objectives for measurement data. Data quality objectives are statements of the quality of environmental data required to support program decisions or actions. They establish the level of risk or uncertainty that the program is willing to accept in the environmental data it needs in order to make defensible decisions. Developing these objectives is a formally structured process whereby it is determined which environmental data are needed, what data quality is required, and what the appropriate balance between time and resources and data quality is. Data generation, along with data terms such as *precision*, *accuracy*, *representativeness*, *comparability*, and *completeness*, are issues properly addressed in Quality Assurance Project Plans specific to a data collection effort.

The Quality Assurance Officer

The principal authority and responsibilities of a quality assurance officer could include:

1. Review and approve QA Project Plans.
2. Routinely and periodically audit all phases of a project against the QA Project Plan to ensure compliance with the plan and with the objectives of the QA program. As a minimum, such audits will include facilities, equipment, recordkeeping, data validation, operational, maintenance, and calibration procedures.
3. Report in writing to appropriate authority regarding the quality assurance status of a project at 30-day intervals.
4. If a breach in high standards of quality occurs, or a circumvention of the QA Project Plan such as to potentially alter or give cause for concern regarding quality of project output, the QA officer should have authority to alter or stop progress of the project until the breach has been closed or the cause of concern alleviated. On such matters, a report to appropriate authority should be direct and immediate.

5. Coordinate and serve as the focal point for information on the QA program.
6. Ensure that all information used meets the same quality assurance standards as those applied to the parent organization.

The qualifications for the position of quality assurance officer could include

1. Previous experience in application of quality assurance and quality control procedures
2. College degree in chemistry, the sciences, engineering, or an MBA
3. Experience in sponsored research and development as investigator, principal investigator, or project manager
4. Experience in two or more applied fields of science and technology
5. Demonstrated ability to communicate well by written, as well as oral means
6. Ability to function independently or as a team member
7. Commitment to the production of high quality and reliable results from sponsored investigative, research, and development projects

Audits and Reviews

Program audits and reviews, as well as periodic schedules for their completion, should be described. These include management system reviews, audits of data quality, technical system audits, and performance evaluations. Management system reviews investigate the implementation of the approved QA Program Plan, including procedures for developing and approving QA Project Plans and standard operating procedures, procedures and schedules for conducting audits, tracking systems, financial and personnel resources, management support, and responsibilities and authorities of key program officials to implement the QA program. Audits of data quality, as the name implies, examine the management of data and determine whether or not sufficient information exists with a data set to support an assessment of its quality. Technical system audits focus on calibration records, sampling and measurement procedures, equipment and facilities, maintenance and repair, and laboratory operation, sample control, and cleanliness. Performance evaluation examines the analytical techniques of laboratory analysts through the analysis of samples containing concentrations of specific constituents unknown to the analyst.

A quality assurance audit of a facility, such as a chemical and biological analytical laboratory, combines some features of the audits and reviews described above. Documents, records, and procedures to be examined during a laboratory audit would include

1. The Quality Assurance Program Plan and laboratory personnel adherence to it
2. Previous quality assurance audit reports and inspection records
3. Laboratory certification records
4. Equipment calibration records

5. Sample management, storage, and security within the laboratory; recordkeeping; the ease with which a sample may be traced through the laboratory from the time of receipt to its ultimate disposition; the elapsed time between receipt of a sample and the reporting of results; and an examination of the facilities and management of the wet- and dry-chemistry areas
6. Chain-of-custody and responsible-person procedures
7. Experience and training of laboratory personnel. An examination of resumés and personnel interviews should determine the strong and outstanding qualities of the laboratory operation, as well as the weaknesses and needs. Active support and participation in professional and trade organizations should be determined
8. Physical laboratory facilities, including adequacy for current operations, condition, arrangement, and housekeeping practices
9. Laboratory equipment, including an inventory of major analytical equipment, age, condition, care and attention received, and storage when not in service
10. Safety, including fire, explosion, hazardous chemicals storage and use, contingency plans, and ventilation
11. Use of standard test solutions, including a determination of shelf life and labeling of reagents and standards
12. Methods for preparation of laboratory standards and synthetic or artificial waters, including the source of any sea salts used
13. Deviations from standard procedures and how these may be recorded
14. An examination of test results that were rejected for unacceptable QA/QC by a regulatory agency
15. Source, maintenance, and apparent health of test organisms used in bioassay toxicity testing
16. Source and results of the use of reference toxicants and test organism control survival
17. Adequacy of space and equipment for workload
18. New initiatives undertaken in biology, chemistry, data management hardware and software
19. Methods for laboratory waste disposal

An inspection or audit should determine compliance with minimum acceptable criteria for collecting samples, conducting the tests, and analyzing the test results. In addition to examining the equipment and facilities, the acquisition, culture, maintenance, and acclimation of test organisms should be investigated.

Quality Assurance Project Plans

The purpose of a Quality Assurance Project Plan is to ensure that a study complies with the best scientific, recorded procedures to minimize the possibility of error. The plan should ensure that the level of needed data quality will be determined and stated before the data collection begins and that all environmental data generated and processed will reflect the quality and integrity established by the QA Project Plan. The QA Program Plan should detail how and when these plans will be developed, as well as the process for their approval. QA Project Plans will be discussed later in this chapter.

Standard Operating Procedures

Standard operating procedures (SOPs) are documented methods for performing certain routine or repetitive tasks. These tasks include such operations as sampling, sample tracking, analysis, glassware preparation, instrument or method calibrations, preventative and corrective maintenance, and data reduction and analysis. SOPs are written documents that detail an operation, analysis, or action whose mechanisms are thoroughly prescribed and that is commonly accepted as the method of performing certain routine or repetitive tasks. They should be developed by personnel performing the task routinely so that the actual practices may be recorded. They provide a record of performance of those tasks addressed at a specific time. Items that may be addressed in standard operating procedures format include

1. Specific sampling-site selection
2. Sampling and analytical methodology
3. Use of probes, collection devices, storage containers, and sample additives such as preservatives
4. Special precautions, such as holding times and protection from heat
5. Federal reference, equivalent, and alternate test procedures
6. Instrumentation selection and use
7. Calibration and standardization procedures
8. Preventative and remedial maintenance
9. Use of duplicate, spiked, blank, and standard sample analyses
10. Split sample protocols
11. Documentation, sample custody, transportation and handling procedures
12. Data-handling assessment procedures
13. Specific quantitative determinations of precision, accuracy, completeness, representativeness, and comparability

Resources

A discussion of the personnel and other resources assigned to the management of the QA program should be presented.

Annual Planning

The planning process for maintaining and updating the QA Program Plan should be described.

Training

Training needs and efforts and schedules to fulfill those needs of personnel associated with the QA program should be delineated. This may include on-the-job training, as well as formal training, professional symposia, and professional meetings.

QUALITY ASSURANCE PROJECT PLAN

1. **Document control.** All Quality Assurance Project Plans should be prepared using a document control format consisting of the section number, revision number, date of revision, and page of total pages in document placed in the upper right-hand corner of each document page.

2. **Title page.** The title page should state that the document is a Quality Assurance Project Plan for a particular project that was prepared by an individual or group for a specific entity. At the bottom of the title page, provisions should be made for the signatures and date of signature of approving personnel, including the organization's project manager, the organization's QA officer, the funding organization's project officer, and the funding organization's QA officer.

3. **Table of contents.** The contents page should list the section, the title of the section, page number, number of pages in section, revision number for section, and the date of initial issuance or of the most recent revision whichever is more recent. At the end of the table of contents, all individuals receiving official copies of the plan and any subsequent revisions should be indicated.

4. **Frontispage.** A frontispage should be inserted that includes the project name, the authority requesting the project, date of request, date of project initiation, project officer, and quality assurance officer.

5. **Project description.** This section should include (1) a statement of the objectives of the project, (2) scope of the project, (3) description of the intended use of the data generated, and (4) description of the project design. Objectives should be clear, concise, positive definitions of the study's purpose, scope, and boundary limits. Statements should detail how each itemized objective will be met. The general background for the project should be summarized. The scope should detail the range of activities that the project would involve and should describe the sequential course of action that will be pursued.

    This section should clearly describe how the data generated during the project will be used. The project design should include a complete and detailed description of the project and the rationale behind the project design. It should include a description of sampling and analytical procedures to be used, a table or listing of all field samples and measurements to be taken, and a table describing the laboratory analyses to be conducted and the method employed for each analysis.

If analysis of samples within a designated time period is important to the integrity of the samples, holding times should be specified on the laboratory analysis table. If the data are used in any regulatory or other activity where the U.S. Environmental Protection Agency has jurisdiction or oversight, EPA-approved analytical methods are required whenever they are appropriate and available. If methods other than EPA-approved methods are to be used, a justification for their use should be included in the QA Project Plan.

6. **Schedule of tasks and products.** This section should identify milestones and tasks, including deliverable products, with dates for completion or delivery. Key individuals responsible for each task, with appropriate telephone numbers, should be included. The planned progress of the project from conception to implementation should be followed, from the initial request to the final project report.

7. **Project organization and responsibility.** A chart should show the organizational location of the project officer and the quality assurance officer. Both should report to the same supervision authority. Key individuals with appropriate telephone numbers should be identified for sampling operations, sampling quality control, laboratory analysis, laboratory quality control, data processing activities, data processing quality control, data quality review, performance auditing, system auditing or on-site evaluations, overall quality assurance, and overall project coordination.

8. **Data quality requirements and assessments.** It is important in project planning that a cooperative effort be undertaken by the project officer, sampling, and analytical personnel to define the levels of quality required for the data. These data quality requirements should be based on a common understanding of the intended use of the data, the measurement process, and the availability of resources. The objective is to define individual data quality in terms of precision, accuracy, completeness, representativeness, and comparability. As a minimum, requirements should be specified for detection limits, precision, and accuracy for all types of measurements, where these are appropriate. Representativeness is a quality characteristic. For most water monitoring studies, it should be considered a goal to be achieved rather than a characteristic that can be described in quantitative terms. The question to be addressed is how a sample will be collected to ensure its relationship to the media being sampled. Comparability must be assured in the project in terms of sampling plans, analytical methodology, quality control, data reporting, and similar essential factors. Completeness may be evaluated by carefully comparing project objectiveness with proposed data acquisition.

    Precision is an expression of the degree of reproducibility of results, or the degree of mutual agreement among independent, similar, or repeated measurements. Precision is monitored through the use of replicate samples or measurements and is reported as a standard deviation, standard error, or relative standard deviation. Multiple replicate samples normally are taken to assess precision in field sampling. In toxicity testing, the ability of a laboratory to obtain consistent, precise results should be demonstrated with reference toxicants before measuring effluent toxicity. The single laboratory precision of each type of test to be used in a laboratory should be determined by performing five or more tests with a reference toxicant.

Accuracy is the degree of agreement between a measured value and the true value. It may be monitored in a program through the use of blank samples or standard reference materials. For field quality control, samples are routinely spiked with a known reference material.

In an analytical laboratory, accuracy generally is expressed in terms of percent recovery of a standard. Examples of ways to help meet accuracy goals include standard methodology, performance audits, traceability of instrumentation, traceability of standards, traceability of samples, traceability of data, and referenced or spiked samples. In a biological toxicity test, testing protocols are designed with replication sufficient to ensure that organism mortality or other effects will be as close to the true value as practicable when dealing with life sciences.

Completeness is the amount of data collected compared to the amount of data expected or required under ideal conditions. One expression of completeness would be the percentage of collected samples that were completely analyzed or the percentage of data points actually required compared to those planned to be acquired. Completeness may represent the quantity of data that must be acquired in order to meet project needs, as well as the percent recovery required to ensure data adequacy.

Representativeness refers to the degree to which the data collected accurately reflect the universe of data from which they are drawn, or the degree to which samples represent true systems. The acquisition of a representative sample may be based on statistical sampling that dictates the approach, number, conditions, and even location of samples to be collected or analyzed. In conducting biological toxicity testing, there are two areas of representativeness concern. One is in collecting the sample of test solution to which the test organisms are exposed, and the other is the selection of species or organisms used as test organisms in the test. Methods of sample collection and test organism species selection are detailed in EPA testing protocols.

Comparability is the degree to which data from one study can be compared to other, similar studies. Such comparisons are facilitated when internally consistent measures are used throughout the effort. Important examples of data comparability are standardized siting, sampling, and analyses; reporting units consistently; and standardized data format. Strict adherence to standardized methods and protocols when conducting a test, along with use of performance evaluation samples and referenced materials, alleviates many of the comparability concerns that otherwise would occur.

9. **Sampling procedures.** What data are to be collected? Where will data collections be made? When will data collections be made? Who will collect the data and what are the qualifications of the collector? How will data collection be made? How, where, and by whom will samples by analyzed? What post-analytical treatment will the data receive? For each environmental constituent or group of constituents to be measured, a complete description of the sampling procedure should be documented. Included as vital elements in the sampling documentation are flow diagrams or tracking mechanisms to chart sampling operations; descriptions of sampling devices, sampling containers, preservation techniques, sample holding times, and identification forms; and methods and security for sample transport and storage en route to the analytical laboratory.

10. **Sample custody.** Proper chain-of-custody procedures allow the possession and handling of samples to be traced and identified at any moment from the time that sample containers are initially prepared for sampling to the final disposition of the sample. A written record of the laboratory's source and manner of preparation of all sample containers should be referenced. This should include the laboratory's quality control procedures for assuring that a container is clean and ready to accept a sample. The procedure for management of sample containers, both in the field and laboratory, to prevent either inadvertent contamination or potential opportunities for tampering, should be documented.

The field supervisor of sample collection should maintain a bound field logbook in a manner such that field activity can be completely constructed without reliance on the memory of the field crew. All entries should be made in indelible ink, with each signed and dated by the author. Items noted in the logbook should include the following:

1.   Date and time of activity
2.   Names of field supervisor and team members
3.   Purpose of sampling effort
4.   Description of sampling site
5.   Location of sampling site
6.   Sampling equipment used
7.   Any deviations from standard operating procedures and the reason for same
8.   Field observations
9.   Field measurements made
10. Results of any field measurements
11. Sample identification
12. Type and number of samples collected
13. Sample handling, packaging, labeling, and shipping information

The logbook should be kept in a secure place until a unit effort of activity for which a particular logbook is maintained has been completed, whereupon the

CHAIN OF CUSTODY RECORD

PROJECT				SAMPLERS: (Signed)								
LAB #	STATION	DATE	TIME	SAMPLE TYPE						NUMBER CONTAINERS	REMARKS	
				WATER	SEDIMENT	TISSUE	AIR	OIL	OTHER			

RELINQUISHED BY: (Signed)	RECEIVED BY: (Signed)	DATE/TIME
RELINQUISHED BY: (Signed)	RECEIVED BY: (Signed)	DATE/TIME
RELINQUISHED BY: (Signed)	RECEIVED BY: (Signed)	DATE/TIME
RELINQUISHED BY: (Signed)	RECV'D BY MOBILE LAB FOR FIELD ANAL.: (Signed)	DATE/TIME
DISPATCHED BY: (Signed)	DATE/TIME	RECEIVED FOR LAB BY: (Signed)	DATE/TIME

METHOD OF SHIPMENT:

Distribution: Original — Accompany Shipment
One Copy — Survey Coordinator Field Files

Figure 21-2.   Example chain of custody record.

logbook should be kept in a secure project file. Sample labels should be waterproof, marked with indelible ink, and secured to the body of the sample bottle. They should contain the sample number, preservation technique if any, data and time of collection, location of collection, and initials of the collector. A chain-of-custody record (Figure 21-2) should accompany each group of samples from the time of collection to their destination at the receiving laboratory. Each person who has custody of the samples at any time must sign the chain-of-custody form and ensure that the samples are not left unattended unless secured properly. Gummed paper custody seals or custody tape should be used to ensure that the seal must be broken when the container is opened.

Within the laboratory, security and confidentiality of all stored material should be maintained at all times. This may require that an analyst sign for any sample removed from a storage area for purposes of performing analyses and note the time and date of returning a sample to storage. Before releasing analytical results, all information on sample labels, data sheets, tracking logs, and custody records should be cross-checked to ensure that data pertaining to a sample are consistent throughout the record.

11.   **Calibration procedures and preventive maintenance.** This section should list each key piece of equipment or instrumentation used for a project, state how frequently the equipment is calibrated and routine maintenance is performed on it, reference calibration and maintenance procedures, and indicate where calibration and maintenance records are kept in the laboratory or project files.

12.   **Documentation, data reduction, and reporting.** A description should be included in the plan of how the raw data will be recorded and organized, as well as how data will be analyzed and reported. The latter includes a description of calculations and statistical methods. Included also should be description of measures taken to avoid errors during data transcription, reduction, and transmittal.

13.   **Data validation.** Data validation involves all procedures used to accept or reject data after collection and prior to use, including editing, screening, checking, auditing, verification, and review. Validation criteria must be such that data will be accepted or rejected in a uniform and consistent manner. Criteria for data validation should include checks for internal consistency, checks for transmittal errors, and verification of laboratory results. Laboratory results are verified through split-sample analysis, duplicate-sample analysis, spiked-sample addition and recovery, interlaboratory comparison, instrument calibration, and reagent checks.

14.   **Performance and system audits.** When and how often to be conducted? By whom? What will be the audit protocol? Who will receive written audit reports? The objectives of a program audit are to establish the degree of compliance with the Quality Assurance Project Plan and with good laboratory and project-management practices. With these objectives in mind, the conduct of an audit entails:

1.   A solicitation of responses to questions designed to uncover inadequacies in current practices
2.   A survey of facilities, equipment, and records
3.   An evaluation of the results from 1 and 2 above
4.   A written statement of findings of fact and needs for compliance Despite any efforts to the contrary, the conduct of an audit is an adversary exercise

Performance and system audits are an essential part of every quality control program. A performance audit independently collects measurement data using performance evaluation samples. A systems audit consists of a review of the total data production process, which includes on-site reviews of a field and laboratory's operational systems and physical facilities for sampling, calibration, and measurement protocols. To the extent possible, audits should be conducted by individuals who are not directly involved with the project under audit. Performance evaluation samples with constituent concentrations unknown to the analyst can be obtained from U.S. Environmental Protection Agency Environmental Monitoring and Support Laboratories.

15. **Corrective action**. A corrective action program with the capability to detect errors at any point in the project implementation process is an essential management tool. The corrective action scheme should be designed to identify defects, trace defects to their source, plan and implement measures to correct identified defects, maintain documentation of the results of the corrective process, and continue the process until each defect is eliminated. What are the criteria to trigger corrective action? What is the procedure for taking corrective action? Who will implement corrective action? What records of action will be maintained?

16. **Reports.** Formal reports should be issued to inform appropriate management personnel of progress in the execution of the QA Project Plan. The reports should include an assessment of the status of the project in relation to the proposed time table and should address any results of ongoing performance and systems audits, data quality assessments, and significant quality assurance problems with proposed corrective action procedures.

QUALITY ASSURANCE IN BIOLOGICAL TOXICITY TESTING

One example of the application of quality assurance to life sciences projects would be that of effluent biological toxicity testing. As discussed in Chapter 5, there is a continuing and developing program by the EPA to require toxicity testing for compliance with NPDES discharge permits. These tests require the selection of sampling locations, dilution water, and test organisms; the use of test chambers and tubing to transport wastewater and dilution water; care and feeding of test organisms; and recordkeeping. These items and others will be discussed in the paragraphs that follow.

Sampling Locations

For effluent toxicity testing, the effluent sampling point should be the same as specified in the National Pollutant Discharge Elimination System permit. The collector of a sample should be recorded. When chlorination of the effluent is practiced, some regulatory authorities measure the toxicity of the effluent prior to chlorination, after chlorination, and after dechlorination. Receiving water taken upstream from the outfall may be specified as a source of dilution water in effluent toxicity tests. Aeration during collection and transfer of effluents should be minimized to reduce the loss of volatile chemicals. Sample holding time before initiation of the test should not exceed 36 hours. Samples collected for off-site toxicity testing are to be chilled to 4°C when collected, shipped iced to the laboratory, and there transferred to a refrigerator at 4°C until used.

Precautions should be taken to ensure that any materials used in sample collection or throughout the testing process will not affect the integrity of the sample being tested. Any alterations to effluent or dilution water samples should be well documented, even if that adjustment is standard, including the use of sea salts to adjust the salinity of freshwater effluents.

Facilities, Equipment, and Test Chambers

Special requirements are contained in toxicity testing protocols for facilities and equipment. All materials that come in contact with the effluent must be such that there is no leaching or reaction that potentially would alter the integrity of the wastewater being tested. New plastic products of a type not previously used should be tested for toxicity before initial use by exposing the test organisms in the test system where the material is used. Silicone adhesive used to construct glass test chambers absorbs some organochlorine and organophosphorus pesticides. As little of the adhesive as possible should be in contact with the water, and any beads of adhesive inside the containers should be removed.

Dilution Water

Dilution water should be the same as specified in the permit. If required, dilution water may be synthetic water, groundwater, seawater, artificial seawater, or hypersaline brine made from a noncontaminated source of natural seawater appropriate to the objectives of the study. Dilution water is considered acceptable if test organisms have adequate survival, growth, and reproduction in the test chambers during a test. Water temperatures within the test chambers must be monitored continually and maintained within the limits specified for each test. Dissolved oxygen concentrations must also be maintained within the limits specified, and pH should be checked and recorded at the beginning of the test and at least daily throughout the test. If it is necessary to aerate during the test to maintained dissolved oxygen, and the protocol allows aeration, all concentrations and controls must be aerated and the fact noted on the test report.

Recordkeeping

Records should detail all information about a sample and test organisms, including

1. Collection — date; time; locations; pre-, post-, or dechlorinated; weather conditions; methods; and collector
2. Transportation — method, chain of custody, packing to ensure correct temperature maintenance, and security
3. Laboratory — storage, analysis, and security
4. Testing — elapsed time from sample collection, treatment, and type of test
5. Test organisms — species, source, age, health, and feeding
6. Records of diseased or discarded organisms
7. Test results, including replicates and controls
8. All calculations that impact test results and data interpretation
9. Any observations of a nonroutine occurrence that may be important in interpretation of results
10. Equipment and instrument calibrations
11. Any deviation from the protocol

Notebook data and observations should be initiated and dated by the observer at the time of recording.

Reference Toxicants

When organism breeding cultures are maintained, the sensitivity of the offspring should be determined in a toxicity test performed with a reference toxicant at least once a month. Reference toxicants are standard chemicals that can be used to evaluate organism sensitivity, laboratory procedures, and equipment. Their use allows a laboratory to compare the response of test organisms to a reference toxicant under local laboratory conditions. When a toxicity value from a test with a reference toxicant does not fall within the expected range for the test organisms when using standard dilution water, the sensitivity of the organisms and the overall credibility of the test system are suspect, should be examined for defects, and the health of the organisms questioned. Four reference toxicants are available from EPA's Environmental Monitoring and Support Laboratory to establish the precision and validity of toxicity data generated by biomonitoring laboratories. These include copper sulfate, sodium chloride, sodium dodecylsulfate, and cadmium chloride. Failure to use reference toxicants to test the sensitivity of a new group of test organisms has been known to invalidate a series of test results.

AN APPROACH FOR ACCOMPLISHING QA SPECIFICATIONS

Facilities and Equipment

The laboratories, data processing, and other operational areas should be neat and orderly. Laboratory benches should be kept clear of all but necessary tools, glassware, and pertinent equipment. Personal items, such as coats, hats, and lunch boxes, should not be left in the working area; storage should be provided for these items.

If new instruments are purchased for laboratory use, they should be checked carefully after initial setup to determine whether they meet the required specifications. This will include use of reference and calibration materials to establish that detection limits, ease of operation, and automated procedures meet the anticipated performance standards and these standards are adequate to provide the desired quality of data.

Maintenance procedures should be performed as specified by the manufacturer and as required. Operational manuals should be kept in a convenient place to ensure that they are readily available and can easily be consulted when appropriate.

Laboratories should be inspected to determine that lighting, humidity controls, temperature controls, dust levels, and ventilation meet the requirements for good practices and operations. General maintenance activities, including housekeeping services, should maintain cleanliness to preclude contamination of samples being analyzed. Analytical instrumentation must meet requirements for precision, accuracy, and sensitivity.

All field equipment must function properly and be free from contamination. All field equipment should be inspected thoroughly prior to being taken in the field to ensure that established specifications are met and that quality data can be produced. Personnel performing the sampling should be protected by special equipment, such as hard hats, steel-toed shoes, safety glasses, fire extinguishers, ear-protection devices, and other applicable OSHA-mandated safety equipment, as a field site dictates. All inspection and preventative maintenance activities should be thoroughly documented to provide easy accessibility and a clear understanding of action actions performed.

Consumable Materials

Consumable materials are those materials used during a project activity that either are consumed as a result of that activity or are rendered useless for the conduct of further activity. All chemicals and other materials used during the course of laboratory operations should have a quality sufficient to preclude contamination or interference with the resulting conclusions and data. When chemicals are received in the laboratory from the chemical supplier, the date of receipt and the initials of the receiver should be recorded on the container. When a container is opened to remove a portion of the chemical to produce a standard solution, or for other purposes, the initials of the person opening the container, along with the date of opening, should also be recorded on the container before it is returned to the storage shelf. Good laboratory practice requires that a standard or other solution of a chemical used daily or periodically in the laboratory should bear a label identifying the solution, the initials of the person who prepared the solutions, the date the solution was prepared, and the date or shelf-life expiration, or the date beyond which the solution should no longer be used.

For field sampling or monitoring efforts, consumable materials refer to items such as transfer efficiency test foil, weight-percent solids dishes, reagents, and filter systems or other kinds of materials that frequently are used in field efforts. Such materials must not be allowed to contaminate samples during collection efforts. Reagents must not become contaminated. They must not be used in field operations beyond their expected shelf life.

REFERENCES CITED AND SELECTED READING

U.S. EPA. 1979. "Handbook for Analytical Quality Control in Water and Wastewater Laboratories." U.S. Environmental Protection Agency, Cincinnati, OH (EPA-600/4-79-019).

U.S. EPA. 1980. "Interim Guidelines and Specifications for Preparing Quality Assurance Project Plans." U.S. Environmental Protection Agency, Washington, D.C. Office of Monitoring Systems and Quality Assurance (QAMS-005/80).

U.S. EPA. 1983. 40 CFR Part 30. 48 FR 45061, September 30, 1983.

U.S. EPA. 1984. "Policy and Program Requirements to Implement the Mandatory Quality Assurance Program." EPA Order 5360.1, April 3, 1984.

U.S. EPA. 1984. "Guidance for Preparation of Combined Work/Quality Assurance Project Plans for Environmental Monitoring." U.S. Environmental Protection Agency, Washington, D.C., Office of Water Regulations and Standards (OWRS QA-1).

U.S. EPA. 1985. "Guidelines and Specifications for Preparing Quality Assurance Program Plans for National Program Offices, ORD Headquarters, and ORD Laboratories." U.S. Environmental Protection Agency, Washington, D.C., Quality Assurance Management Staff.

U.S. EPA. 1985. "Interim Policy and Guidance for Management Systems Audits of National Program Offices." U.S. Environmental Protection Agency, Washington, D.C., Quality Assurance Management Staff.

U.S. EPA. 1985. "Methods for Measuring the Acute Toxicity of Effluents to Freshwater and Marine Organisms." U.S. Environmental Protection Agency, Cincinnati, OH (EPA-600/4-85/013).

U.S. EPA. 1986. "Development of Data Quality Objectives." U.S. Environmental Protection Agency, Washington, D.C., Quality Assurance Management Staff.

U.S. EPA. 1986. "Interim Policy and Guidance for Management Systems Audits of Regional Offices." U.S. Environmental Protection Agency, Washington, D.C., Quality Assurance Management Staff.

U.S. EPA. 1986. "Quality Assurance Program Plan for the Chesapeake Bay Program." U.S. Environmental Protection Agency, Region III, Chesapeake Bay Liaison Office, Annapolis, MD.

U.S. EPA. 1988. "Implementing the Data Quality Objective Process in Surface Water Monitoring Programs." U.S. Environmental Protection Agency, Washington, D.C., Office of Water Regulations and Standards (OWRS QA-2).

U.S. EPA. 1988. "Incorporating Data Quality Objectives in Quality Assurance Project Plans — Interim Report." U.S. Environmental Protection Agency, Washington, D.C., Office of Water Regulations and Standards (OWRS QA-3).

U.S. EPA. 1988. "Quality Assurance Program Plan for the Office of Water Regulations and Standards." U.S. Environmental Protection Agency, Washington, D.C., Office of Water Regulations and Standards (OWRS QA-4).

U.S. EPA. 1988. "Guide for Preparation of Quality Assurance Project Plans for the National Estuarine Program." U.S. Environmental Protection Agency, Washington, D.C. (EPA-556/2-88-01).

U.S. EPA. 1988. "Short-Term Methods for Estimating the Chronic Toxicity of Effluents and Receiving Waters to Marine and Estuarine Organisms." U.S. Environmental Protection Agency, Cincinnati, OH (EPA-600/4-87/028).

U.S. EPA. 1989. "Short-Term Methods for Estimating the Chronic Toxicity of Effluents and Receiving Waters to Freshwater Organisms." Second Edition. U.S. Environmental Protection Agency, Cincinnati, OH (EPA-600/4-89-001).

INDEX